National Aeronautics and
Space Administration

HUMAN ADAPTATION TO SPACEFLIGHT: THE ROLE OF FOOD AND NUTRITION

Second Edition

Scott M. Smith

Nutritionist;
Manager for Nutritional Biochemistry

Nutritional Biochemistry Laboratory

Biomedical Research and
Environmental Sciences Division

Human Health and Performance
Directorate

NASA Johnson Space Center
Houston, Texas USA

Sara R. Zwart

Senior Scientist;
Deputy Manager for Nutritional
Biochemistry

Nutritional Biochemistry Laboratory

Biomedical Research and
Environmental Sciences Division

Human Health and Performance
Directorate

NASA Johnson Space Center
Houston, Texas USA

&

Preventive Medicine and
Population Health

University of Texas Medical Branch
Galveston, Texas USA

Grace L. Douglas

Advanced Food Technology Lead Scientist;
Manager for Exploration Food Systems

Space Food Systems Laboratory

Human Systems Engineering and
Integration Division

Human Health and Performance
Directorate

NASA Johnson Space Center
Houston, Texas USA

Martina Heer

Nutritionist;
Program Director Nutritional Sciences

IU International University of
Applied Sciences
Bad Reichenhall, Germany

&

Adjunct Professor of Nutrition Physiology

Institute of Nutritional and Food Sciences
University of Bonn, Germany

ПРОГРЕСС
СОЮЗ

Table of Contents

Preface

This book marks our third effort to review available literature regarding the role of nutrition in astronaut health. In 2009, we reviewed the existing knowledge and history of human nutrition for spaceflight, with a key goal of identifying additional data that would be required before NASA could confidently reduce the risk of an inadequate food system or inadequate nutrition to as low as possible in support of human expeditions to the Moon or Mars. We used a nutrient-by-nutrient approach to address this effort, and we included a brief description of the space food systems during historical space programs. This previous review is available for free download, most recently at https://www.nasa.gov/hhp/education.

In 2014, we published a second volume of the book, which was not so much a second edition, but rather a view of space nutrition from a different perspective. Also available at the link mentioned above, this volume updated research that had been published in the intervening 6 years and addressed space nutrition with a more physiological systems-based approach.

The current version is an expanded, updated version of that second book, providing both a systems approach overall, but also including details of nutrients and their roles within each system. As such, this book is divided into chapters based on physiological systems (e.g., bone, muscle, ocular); highlighted in each chapter are the nutrients associated with that particular system. We provide updated information on space food systems and constraints of the same, and provide dietary intake data from International Space Station (ISS) astronauts.

We present data from ground-based analog studies, designed to mimic one or more conditions similar to those produced by spaceflight. Head-down tilt bed rest is a common analog of the general (and specifically musculoskeletal) disuse of spaceflight. Nutrition research from Antarctica relies on the associated confinement and isolation, in addition to the lack of sunlight exposure during the winter months. Undersea habitats help expand our understanding of nutritional changes in a confined space with a hyperbaric atmosphere. We also review spaceflight research, including data from now "historical" flights on the Space Shuttle, data from the Russian space station Mir, and earlier space programs such as Apollo and Skylab. The ISS, now more than 20 years old, has provided (and continues to provide) a wealth of nutrition findings from extended-duration spaceflights of 4 to 12 months. We review findings from this platform as well, providing a comprehensive review of what is known regarding the role of human nutrition in keeping astronauts healthy.

With this book, we hope we have accurately captured the current state of the field of space food and nutrition, and that we have provided some guideposts for work that remains to be done to enable safe and successful human exploration beyond low-Earth orbit.

Scott M. Smith

Sara R. Zwart

Grace L. Douglas

Martina Heer

1 Introduction

The importance of nutrition in exploration has been documented repeatedly throughout history, on voyages across oceans, on expeditions across polar ice, and on treks across unexplored continents (1-5). Scurvy is a prime example of an exploration-induced nutritional discovery. Although most people now understand that scurvy is associated with vitamin C deficiency, and that this was an issue for sailors centuries ago, few realize the magnitude of this problem. Over the roughly 400-year period between Christopher Columbus' voyage in 1492 and the invention of the steam engine, scurvy resulted in the deaths of more sailors than did all other causes of death combined (2). Ships that sailed with a crew of hundreds often returned with tens. It is estimated that more than 2 million sailors perished from scurvy during this time (2). Although in the last 100 years we have gained significant nutritional knowledge that can benefit food system planning, a key difference between past journeys and space exploration is that astronauts are not likely to find food along the way. Thus, understanding the nutritional requirements of space travelers, the role of nutrition in human adaptation to microgravity, and the food system requirements over long durations are as critical to crew safety and mission success as any of the mechanical systems of the spacecraft itself (6).

More basic concerns during spaceflight include loss of body mass and depletion of body nutrient stores because of inadequate food supply, inadequate food intake, increased metabolism, and/or irreversible loss or degradation of nutrients in the food supply. Physiological changes associated with spaceflight (e.g., bone and muscle loss, cardiovascular degradation, ophthalmic pathologies, impaired immune function) may have nutritional underpinnings as well, potentially as cause and/or effect. Environmental issues, including radiation exposure and the cabin environment (e.g., oxygen [O_2], and carbon dioxide [CO_2], temperature, humidity) can have profound effects on nutritional requirements. Nutrients could serve as countermeasures to these stressors. Food and nutrition also have profound effects on behavior and performance.

All these elements become critical in a closed spacecraft that has a limited food system and a limited ability for resupply or return to Earth. Food and nutrition are essential to support astronaut health and performance and therefore mission success.

Stressors of Spaceflight

Microgravity or Partial Gravity

Entry into weightlessness (technically referred to as microgravity) is associated with a shift of fluids from the lower extremities into the thorax and head. Astronauts often experience "puffy" faces in the initial days of flight. This effect lasts much longer in some individuals than in others. This individual variability in response is not well characterized; however, it might involve genetic influence on ophthalmic pathologies.

This headward shift of fluids is associated with a negligible (≈1% of body mass) reduction in total body water observed as soon as within the first hours of flight, and is accompanied by a 10% to 15% reduction in blood volume that takes about 2 weeks to stabilize (7-9). The associated reduction in circulating red blood cells (RBCs) affects iron requirements and iron stores and can have downstream effects on oxidative stress (10).

Scientists often speculate as to whether the partial gravity of the Moon (0.16 g) or of Mars (0.38 g) will affect human physiology. Bone researchers typically assert that gravity levels of more than 0.5 g are required to stimulate enough bone loading to mitigate bone and calcium loss; however, proving this experimentally is difficult in terrestrial analogs. Partial gravity would likely affect fluid redistribution to some degree, with potential implications for cardiovascular health and cerebrovascular fluid dynamics. Regardless, partial gravity on a planetary surface should be less problematic than microgravity conditions in a spacecraft (i.e., providing means to perform loading exercises will be easier on a planetary surface).

Radiation

Long-duration exploration missions beyond low-Earth orbit will be accompanied by high-linear energy transfer (LET) galactic cosmic rays consisting of high-energy protons and high-charge, high-energy nuclei (11, 12). High-LET radiation deposits part of its energy in ion tracks known as cores, and the remaining energy is dispersed randomly outside of the core by energetic electrons. By contrast, low-LET ionizing radiation, including x-rays or gamma rays, deposit energy uniformly (13). In addition to galactic cosmic rays, solar particle events comprised mainly of low- to medium-energy protons periodically bombard the solar system. The timing of these events is difficult to predict; however, they are more prevalent during periods of the solar cycle when the Sun is at maximum activity (14). Galactic cosmic radiation exposures during exploration missions to Mars will be about 10 times higher than exposures on the International Space Station (ISS) (15). These higher radiation doses will increase the astronauts' risk of both short- and long-term health effects.

Isolation

Isolation and confinement during space missions can increase an astronaut's risk of developing symptoms of depression (16, 17), which can lead to nutritional issues (e.g., over or under consumption of food). Available data from early spaceflights indicate that neurological incidents do occur; however, the etiologies are typically unknown. Two psychiatric events were reported among seven NASA astronauts who carried out long-duration increments on Mir between 1995 and 1998 (18); at least one of these events was accompanied by a significant reduction in dietary intake and weight loss. A crewmember who flew on the ISS for 1 year had some cognitive decline during and after flight (19), along with significant weight loss. The risk of depression or cognitive changes will undoubtedly be greater as mission durations extend to several years. While participating in the MARS-500 project, six people who lived in a hermetically sealed habitat for 520 days had measurable effects in the microstructure of their brain's white matter, as determined using diffusion tensor imaging (20). This finding suggested changes in underlying processes of myelin plasticity during the 520 days of isolation and confinement.

Environment

The spacecraft environment can also affect crewmembers' health, performance, dietary intake, and nutritional status. The cabin pressure, gas mixture (i.e., percentages of O_2 and CO_2) in the cabin air, temperature, and humidity can all have profound effects on physiology, behavior and performance, and food and nutrition. Given that the concentrations of CO_2 on the ISS are approximately 10 times greater than those on Earth (21-23), it is possible that this could affect crew behavior and performance (e.g., cognition, sleep, headaches) (22-26), bone and calcium loss (27, 28), metabolism (29), cerebral blood flow (21, 30), and ophthalmic pathologies (31).

As of this writing, studies are planned to further examine how a proposed exploration vehicle atmosphere of 32% oxygen at 8 psi (pounds per square inch, compared to sea level: 21% O_2 at 14.7 psi) affects crew health (32), including how this atmosphere affects nutritional status, immune system function, and oxidative stress and damage.

When crewmembers are outside the spacecraft (i.e., on extravehicular activities [EVAs], also referred to as spacewalks), the spacesuit becomes their spacecraft. Nutritional concerns could arise (high O_2 exposure, limited water availability, inability to eat for up to 8 to 10 hours at a time while in the suit). These limitations have generally been acceptable on missions to date because relatively few (2-6) EVAs occur during a 6-month ISS mission. However, the increased frequency and intensity of spacewalks on the lunar or Martian surface will be much more demanding, requiring the suits to include nutrition, or allowing crewmembers to get in and out of the suit quickly for meal breaks.

Duration

The duration of exposure to spaceflight-associated stressors defines the limits of what can feasibly be accomplished on any given mission. Space Shuttle missions, which lasted from a few days to 2 weeks, were in many ways seen as camping trips. Although nutrition was not a significant factor on these missions, maintaining hydration and dietary intake continue to be important for many aspects of health on short or long missions. Hydration is important for performance and cognitive function, and for minimizing the risk of developing renal stones (which occurred even on short-duration missions), among other concerns.

Dietary intake and nutritional status became more important on what could be considered medium-duration missions—2- to 6-month ISS expeditions. Loss of body mass became problematic, exacerbating muscle and bone loss and cardiovascular decrements. The Earth provides some protection against radiation on vehicles in low-Earth orbit; however, radiation exposure remains a career-limiting factor for astronauts. During 18 months of spaceflight, astronauts are exposed to levels of radiation that are roughly equivalent to the maximum lifetime levels allowed for terrestrial radiation workers. The physiological changes that occur during the span of an ISS mission are typically not associated with chronic disease incidence, although concerns clearly exist with regard to accelerating risks of bone loss and other diseases.

Missions in the coming decade will be the same duration as a mission on the ISS (i.e., up to 1 year); however, they will involve operations in lunar orbit and on the lunar surface. Periodic cargo vehicles that deliver fresh fruits and vegetables will no longer be possible, as they are for ISS missions, and the foods will likely be prepositioned given logistics issues. Prepositioning will not support provisioning of individual-preference foods due to the potential for late crew changes, thus resulting in less variety and choice, and a greater risk of menu fatigue and reduced consumption. The astronauts of these missions will be exposed to higher doses of radiation compared to exposures on the ISS, thereby incurring significantly greater risk despite the similar durations.

Mars-class missions will be altogether more challenging than lunar missions, and will include greater challenges from a food and nutrition perspective. Exposures to radiation, isolation, etc. for the expected nominal 2.5-year prototype missions will be profound. The stability of food for the required shelf life is at this point untenable. This issue represents one of the four "red risks" for Mars missions: Food, Radiation, Psychological Issues, and Ophthalmic Pathologies (currently dubbed SANS, Spaceflight-Associated Neuro-ocular Syndrome) (33). It is possible that missions of this duration could accelerate the incidence of chronic diseases, which will be difficult to discriminate from diseases that astronauts might have developed on Earth anyway. Regardless, nutrition provides the greatest potential for mitigating chronic diseases such as osteoporosis, sarcopenia, cancer, dementia, neuropathy, atherosclerosis, and cardiovascular disease, to name a few. Although nutrition will not be a panacea and is by no means advocated as the end to spaceflight maladies, food and nutrition can improve or optimize health and mitigate disease, or they can worsen health and exacerbate disease, as they do on Earth.

Expedition 34 crew fruit and vegetables within a Cargo Transfer Bag. Photo Credit: NASA.

References for Chapter 1

1. Smith SM, Zwart SR, Kloeris V, Heer M. Nutritional biochemistry of space flight. New York: Nova Science Publishers; 2009.
2. Bown SR. Scurvy. New York: St. Martin's Press; 2003.
3. De Luca LM, Norum KR. Scurvy and cloudberries: a chapter in the history of nutritional sciences. J Nutr. 2011;141:2101-5.
4. Stuster JW. Bold endeavors: behavioral lessons from polar and space exploration. Gravit Space Biol Bull. 2000;13:49-57.
5. McIntosh EN. The Lewis and Clark Expedition: Food, Nutrition, and Health Rock Island, IL: Center for Western Studies, Augustana College; 2003.
6. Douglas GL, Zwart SR, Smith SM. Space food for thought: Challenges and considerations for food and nutrition on exploration missions. J Nutr. 2020;150:2242-4.
7. Leach CS, Alfrey CP, Suki WN, Leonard JI, Rambaut PC, Inners LD, Smith SM, Lane HW, Krauhs JM. Regulation of body fluid compartments during short-term spaceflight. J Appl Physiol (1985). 1996;81:105-16.
8. Alfrey CP, Udden MM, Huntoon CL, Driscoll T. Destruction of newly released red blood cells in space flight. Med Sci Sports Exerc. 1996;28:S42-4.
9. Alfrey CP, Udden MM, Leach-Huntoon C, Driscoll T, Pickett MH. Control of red blood cell mass in spaceflight. J Appl Physiol (1985). 1996;81:98-104.
10. Zwart SR, Morgan JLL, Smith SM. Iron status and its relations with oxidative damage and bone loss during long-duration space flight on the International Space Station. Am J Clin Nutr. 2013;98:217-23.
11. Norbury JW, Slaba TC, Aghara S, Badavi FF, Blattnig SR, Clowdsley MS, Heilbronn LH, Lee K, Maung KM, Mertens CJ, Miller J, Norman RB, Sandridge CA, Singleterry R, Sobolevsky N, Spangler JL, Townsend LW, Werneth CM, Whitman K, Wilson JW, Xu SX, Zeitlin C. Advances in space radiation physics and transport at NASA. Life Sci Space Res (Amst). 2019;22:98-124.
12. Sobel A, Duncan R. Aerospace environmental health: Considerations and countermeasures to sustain crew health through vastly reduced transit time to/from Mars. Front Public Health. 2020;8:327.
13. Cekanaviciute E, Rosi S, Costes SV. Central nervous system responses to simulated galactic cosmic rays. Int J Mol Sci. 2018;19.
14. Kiffer F, Boerma M, Allen A. Behavioral effects of space radiation: A comprehensive review of animal studies. Life Sci Space Res (Amst). 2019;21:1-21.
15. Krukowski K, Feng X, Paladini MS, Chou A, Sacramento K, Grue K, Riparip LK, Jones T, Campbell-Beachler M, Nelson G, Rosi S. Temporary microglia-depletion after cosmic radiation modifies phagocytic activity and prevents cognitive deficits. Sci Rep. 2018;8:7857.
16. Palinkas LA, Johnson JC, Boster JS. Social support and depressed mood in isolated and confined environments. Acta Astronaut. 2004;54:639-47.
17. Gemignani A, Piarulli A, Menicucci D, Laurino M, Rota G, Mastorci F, Gushin V, Shevchenko O, Garbella E, Pingitore A, Sebastiani L, Bergamasco M, L'Abbate A, Allegrini P, Bedini R. How stressful are 105 days of isolation? Sleep EEG patterns and tonic cortisol in healthy volunteers simulating manned flight to Mars. Int J Psychophysiol. 2014;93:211-9.
18. National Academy of Sciences Institute of Medicine. Safe passage: Astronaut care for exploration missions: The National Academies Press: Washington DC2001.
19. Garrett-Bakelman FE, Darshi M, Green SJ, Gur RC, Lin L, Macias BR, McKenna MJ, Meydan C, Mishra T, Nasrini J, Piening BD, Rizzardi LF, Sharma K, Siamwala JH, Taylor L, Vitaterna MH, Afkarian M, Afshinnekoo E, Ahadi S, Ambati A, Arya M, Bezdan D, Callahan CM, Chen S, Choi AMK, Chlipala GE, Contrepois K, Covington M, Crucian BE, De Vivo I, Dinges DF, Ebert DJ, Feinberg JI, Gandara JA, George KA, Goutsias J, Grills GS, Hargens AR, Heer M, Hillary RP, Hoofnagle AN, Hook VYH, Jenkinson G, Jiang P, Keshavarzian A, Laurie SS, Lee-McMullen B, Lumpkins SB, MacKay M, Maienschein-Cline MG, Melnick AM, Moore TM, Nakahira K, Patel HH, Pietrzyk R, Rao V, Saito R, Salins DN, Schilling JM, Sears DD, Sheridan CK, Stenger MB, Tryggvadottir R, Urban AE, Vaisar T, Van Espen B, Zhang J, Ziegler MG, Zwart SR, Charles JB, Kundrot CE, Scott GBI, Bailey SM, Basner M, Feinberg AP, Lee SMC, Mason CE, Mignot E, Rana BK, Smith SM, Snyder MP, Turek FW. The NASA Twins Study: A multidimensional analysis of a year-long human spaceflight. Science. 2019;364.

20. Brem C, Lutz J, Vollmar C, Feuerecker M, Strewe C, Nichiporuk I, Vassilieva G, Schelling G, Choukér A. Changes of brain DTI in healthy human subjects after 520 days isolation and confinement on a simulated mission to Mars. Life Sci Space Res (Amst). 2020;24:83-90.

21. Frey MA, Sulzman FM, Oser H, Ruyters G. The effects of moderately elevated ambient carbon dioxide levels on human physiology and performance: a joint NASA-ESA-DARA study--overview. Aviat Space Environ Med. 1998;69:282-4.

22. Law J, Watkins S, Alexander D. In-flight carbon dioxide exposures and related symptoms: Association, susceptibility, and operational implications. Houston, TX: National Aeronautics and Space Administration Lyndon B. Johnson Space Center. 2010. Report No.: NASA/TP-2010-21626.

23. Law J, Young M, Alexander D, Mason SS, Wear ML, Mendez CM, Stanley D, Ryder VM, Van Baalen M. Carbon dioxide physiological training at NASA. Aerosp Med Hum Perform. 2017;88:897-902.

24. Manzey D, Lorenz B. Joint NASA-ESA-DARA Study. Part three: effects of chronically elevated CO_2 on mental performance during 26 days of confinement. Aviat Space Environ Med. 1998;69:506-14.

25. Law J, Van Baalen M, Foy M, Mason SS, Mendez C, Wear ML, Meyers VE, Alexander D. Relationship between carbon dioxide levels and reported headaches on the international space station. J Occup Environ Med. 2014;56:477-83.

26. Gundel A, Parisi RA, Strobel R, Weihrauch MR. Joint NASA-ESA-DARA Study. Part three: characterization of sleep under ambient CO_2-levels of 0.7% and 1.2%. Aviat Space Environ Med. 1998;69:491-5.

27. Davies DM, Morris JE. Carbon dioxide and vitamin D effects on calcium metabolism in nuclear submariners: a review. Undersea Biomed Res. 1979;6 Suppl:S71-80.

28. Drummer C, Friedel V, Borger A, Stormer I, Wolter S, Zittermann A, Wolfram G, Heer M. Effects of elevated carbon dioxide environment on calcium metabolism in humans. Aviat Space Environ Med. 1998;69:291-8.

29. Bishop PA, Lee SM, Conza NE, Clapp LL, Moore AD, Jr., Williams WJ, Guilliams ME, Greenisen MC. Carbon dioxide accumulation, walking performance, and metabolic cost in the NASA launch and entry suit. Aviat Space Environ Med. 1999;70:656-65.

30. Sliwka U, Krasney JA, Simon SG, Schmidt P, Noth J. Effects of sustained low-level elevations of carbon dioxide on cerebral blood flow and autoregulation of the intracerebral arteries in humans. Aviat Space Environ Med. 1998;69:299-306.

31. Stenger MB, Tarver WJ, Brunstetter T, Gibson CR, Laurie SS, Macias BR, Mader TH, Otto C, Smith SM, Zwart SR. Evidence Report: Risk of spaceflight associated neuro-ocular syndrome (SANS) [online]. National Aeronautics and Space Administration. https://humanresearchroadmap.nasa.gov/evidence/reports/SANS.pdf. 2017.

32. Norcross J, Norsk P, Law J, Arias D, Conkin J, Perchonok M, Menon A, Huff J, Fogarty J, Wessel JH, Whitmire S. Effects of the 8 psia / 32% O_2 atmosphere on the human in the spaceflight environment. Hanover, MD: National Aeronautics and Space Administration Center for AeroSpace Information. 2013.

33. Patel ZS, Brunstetter TJ, Tarver WJ, Whitmire AM, Zwart SR, Smith SM, Huff JL. Red risks for a journey to the red planet: The highest priority human health risks for a mission to Mars. NPJ Microgravity. 2020;6.

The obvious, primary role of any space food system is to deliver requisite nutrients to the astronauts. Defining and meeting astronaut nutritional requirements has been an ongoing challenge since the dawn of human spaceflight. The foods provided to astronauts for short-duration missions (i.e., days to weeks) generally follow terrestrial nutritional requirements. These missions are often considered analogous to camping trips, where the duration is assumed to be short enough to negate any effects of inadequate nutritional intakes during the mission.

Requirements Definition and Evolution

The first concerted effort to define nutritional requirements for astronauts came in 1991, as NASA prepared to send crews on 90- to 180-day missions to the planned Space Station Freedom (34), which would eventually evolve to be the ISS. For these flights, the panel of the 1991 conference recommended terrestrial nutritional requirements with specific modifications and suggestions based on known losses of bone and muscle tissue and assumed increased stress levels in astronauts. The panel noted "nutritional status should absolutely be assessed before and after flight, and if at all possible during flight." (34). The panel recommended nutrients be provided in the form of foods, as opposed to supplements, and specifically advocated against iron supplementation given "that serum ferritin levels increase with age…". The 1991 panel report was codified into a NASA requirements documents in 1993 (35) aimed at Freedom missions and planned 30- to 90-day Space Shuttle missions, which never came to fruition.

The next set of nutritional requirements came during the joint U.S.-Russian Shuttle-Mir and NASA-Mir Programs of the early and mid-1990s. NASA defined a bilateral set of nutritional requirements in 1996 (36) (Table 1) that were based largely on the previously defined requirements but were targeted for missions of up to 360 days on the ISS (Figure 1). A multilateral group with representation from all the ISS partner agencies—Canada, Europe, Japan, Russia, and the United States—reevaluated these requirements in 1999; however, no formal documentation of these discussions were ever published.

In 2005, NASA defined a set of nutritional requirements for future exploration missions (37) (Table 1). These were not intended to affect the ISS requirements. However, they offered a first look at potential missions outside of low-Earth orbit; i.e., the Moon, Mars, or an asteroid in between.

In 2016, a panel of nutrition experts was invited to the Johnson Space Center to evaluate the current data regarding nutrition and space, and to define an updated set of nutritional requirements for exploration missions up to 1 year. These nutritional requirements, documented in 2020 (38) (Table 1), were intended to cover planned missions outside low-Earth orbit, namely Orion, Lunar Gateway, and Artemis/Human Landing System missions to the Moon. The panel suggested that requirements be based on terrestrial nutritional requirements, with a few exceptions.

Table 1. Nutritional Requirements Defined for ISS and Exploration Missions. Adapted from (36-38).

Nutrient	ISS Requirements (1996)	Exploration Requirements (2005)	Exploration Requirements (2020)
Energy	Based on World Health Organization equations (40)	Based on Dietary Reference Intake (DRI) equations (41)	Based on DRI equations (41)
Protein	12% – 15% of total daily energy intake, and the ratio of animal:vegetable protein no higher than 60:40	0.8 g/kg body weight, < 35% of total daily energy intake, and the ratio of animal:vegetable protein is about (2/3):(1/3)	1.2 – 1.8 g/kg body weight, and the ratio of animal:vegetable protein no higher than 60:40
Carbohydrate	50% – 55% of the total daily energy intake < 10% of energy from added sugars	50% – 55% of the total daily energy intake	45% – 65% of the total daily energy intake <10% of energy from added sugars
Fat	30%– 35% of the total daily energy intake	25% – 35% of the total daily energy intake	20% – 35% of the total daily energy intake
Omega-6 Fatty Acids	N/A	14 g	Women: 12 g Men: 17g
Omega-3 Fatty Acids	N/A	1.1 – 1.6 g	Women: 1.1 g Men: 1.6g
Saturated Fat	Polyunsaturated: monounsaturated: saturated = 1:1.5 – 2:1	as low as possible	ALARA, <10% of total calories
Trans Fatty Acids	N/A	as low as possible	ALARA, < 1% of total calories
Cholesterol	N/A	as low as possible	< 300 mg
Fiber	N/A	10 – 14 g/1000 kcal	Women: 25 g Men: 38 g
Fluid	1 – 1.5 ml/kcal	1 – 1.5 ml/kcal	32 mL/kg body weight
	>2000 ml	> 2000 ml	Women: > 2100 ml Men: > 2500 ml
Vitamin A	1000 µg RE	700 – 900 µg RE	Women: 700 µg RE Men: 900 µg RE
Vitamin D	10 µg	25 µg	1000 IU (25 µg)
Vitamin K	80 µg	Women: 90 µg Men: 120 µg	Women: 90 µg Men: 120 µg
Vitamin E	20 mg Tocopherol Equivalents	15 mg Tocopherol Equivalents	15 mg Tocopherol Equivalents
Vitamin C	100 mg	90 mg	Women: 110 mg Men: 125 mg
Vitamin B_{12}	2.0 µg	2.4 µg	2.4 µg
Vitamin B_6	2.0 mg	1.7 mg	1.3 mg
Thiamin	1.5 mg	Women: 1.1 mg Men: 1.2 mg	Women: 1.1 mg Men: 1.2 mg
Riboflavin	2.0 mg	1.3 mg	Women: 1.1 mg Men: 1.3 mg
Folate	400 µg	400 µg	400 µg
Niacin	20 mg NE	16 mg NE	Women: 14 mg NE Men: 16 mg NE
Biotin	100 µg	30 µg	30 µg
Pantothenic Acid	5 mg	30 mg	5 mg

Choline	N/A	N/A	Women: 425 mg Men: 550 mg
Calcium	1,200 – 2,000 mg	1,200 – 2,000 mg	1,000 – 1,200 mg
Phosphorus	≤ 1.5 x calcium intake	700 mg, and ≤ 1.5 x calcium intake	700 mg, and ≤ 1.5 x calcium intake
Magnesium	350 mg	Women: 320 mg Men: 420 mg	Women: 320 mg Men: 420 mg
		< 350 mg from supple-ments per day	< 350 mg from supple-ments per day
Sodium	1,500 – 3,500 mg	1,500 – 2,300 mg	1,500 – 2,300 mg
Potassium	3,500 mg	4.7 g	Women: 2600 mg Men: 3400 mg
Iron	< 10 mg	8 – 10 mg	8 mg/d for men and women, 18 mg/d for women under 50 who do not pharmacologically suppress menstruation
Copper	1.5 – 3.0 mg	0.5 – 9 mg	900 μg
Manganese	2 – 5 mg	Women: 1.8 mg Men: 2.3 mg	Women: 1.8 mg Men: 2.3 mg
Fluoride	4.0 mg	Women: 3 mg Men: 4 mg	Women: 3 mg Men: 4 mg
Zinc	15 mg	11 mg	Women: 8 mg Men: 11 mg
Selenium	70 μg	55 – 400 μg	55 μg
Iodine	150 μg	150 μg	150 μg
Chromium	100 – 200 μg	35 μg	Women: 25 μg Men: 35 μg
Chloride	N/A	N/A	2300 mg
Molybdenum	N/A	N/A	45 μg

Terrestrial nutritional requirements are typically used as the starting point for spaceflight requirements, with exceptions in cases where evidence leads to a different requirement. The Food and Nutrition Board of the National Academies of Science, Engineering, and Medicine recommend requirements that are designed to mitigate nutrient deficiency in the vast majority of the population. That is, the nutritional requirements are not designed to prevent chronic diseases, even though many of these diseases (e.g., cancer, osteoporosis, sarcopenia, dementia) have nutritional underpinnings. Although there has been much discussion and initial attempts to expand recent nutritional requirements to address disease (39), much more needs to be known before this can be fully implemented on Earth. For space travel, especially on longer missions beyond low-Earth orbit, it will be critical that nutrition not only prevent nutrient deficiency, but also serve as a countermeasure against the many negative effects on human physiology. This represents a major gap in our understanding of the role of nutrition in spaceflight.

Food Provisioning and Standard Menu

Food provision during early ISS missions followed the same plan as was initiated during the NASA-Mir missions: the Russian Space Agency provided approximately half of the space food, and NASA provided the other half. This covered ISS missions from 2000 (Expedition 1) until approximately 2007 (Expedition 16), when the ISS crew complement expanded to six, and it was easier logistically for each agency to provide food for their respective crews (although, mathematically, both agencies were still providing half of the food). During this period, NASA also opted for a "standard menu" for food provision, as opposed to individual-preference menus. This came about because the vagaries of launch schedules and slippages made it complicated to ensure each crewmember's specific food was on board at the same time they were. The phrase "standard menu" is in quotes because there is no menu defined for crewmembers; rather, they receive a standard set of food containers from which to eat over a specified number of days, typically 7 to 9 days. The "standard menu" is one way to select from those containers to make a menu; however, that information is not provided to crewmembers (unless they specifically ask for it), and astronauts are not required to follow that menu. In other words, it is an idealized menu created from the standard food containers to assess to what degree crewmembers could meet nutritional requirements from the food system.

Throughout this book, reported intakes are shown alongside the content of this idealized "standard menu." Key points in considering this is that the "standard menu" is expected to provide, on average, approximately 2300 to 2400 kcals/d, and crews are expected to consume only 80% to 90% of their daily intake from the standard food containers, with the rest coming from preference containers. These estimates are just that, in part because the allowed rate of food usage is increased or decreased depending on the estimated requirements for the crew on board at any given time. Individual astronaut requirements will affect the percent contribution of the standard food system to their intake.

Figure 1. The ISS as seen from the last Space Shuttle mission. Photo Credit: NASA.

In addition to the standard food set, crewmembers were provided with a set of "preference containers." A 6-month mission included nine preference containers (not counting coffee/tea preference containers) that augmented the nominal food system with the astronauts' selections of their choice. It should be noted that, although nutritional requirements were defined and documented, the ISS food system was largely the same as the Space Shuttle food system, with some exclusions of food with shorter shelf life because food was often pre-positioned. As a result, the ISS food system was very high in sodium and iron.

References for Chapter 2

34. National Aeronautics and Space Administration Johnson Space Center. Nutritional requirements for Space Station Freedom crews. NASA Conference Publication #3146 Houston, TX, 1991.

35. National Aeronautics and Space Administration Johnson Space Center. Nutritional requirements for Extended Duration Orbiter missions (30-90 d) and Space Station Freedom (30-120 d). Report No.: JSC-32283. Houston, TX: National Aeronautics and Space Administration Lyndon B. Johnson Space Center, 1993.

36. National Aeronautics and Space Administration Johnson Space Center. Nutritional requirements for International Space Station (ISS) missions up to 360 days. Report No.: JSC-28038. Houston, TX: National Aeronautics and Space Administration Lyndon B. Johnson Space Center, 1996.

37. National Aeronautics and Space Administration Johnson Space Center. Nutrition requirements, standards, and operating bands for exploration missions. Report No.: JSC-63555. Houston, TX: Lyndon B. Johnson Space Center; 2005.

38. National Aeronautics and Space Administration Johnson Space Center. Nutrition requirements for exploration missions up to 365 days. Report No.: JSC-67378. Houston, TX: Lyndon B. Johnson Space Center; 2020.

39. National Academies of Sciences, Engineering, and Medicine. Dietary Reference Intakes for sodium and potassium. Washington, DC: The National Academies Press. 2019.

40. World Health Organization. Energy and protein requirements. Report of a joint FAO/WHO/UNU expert consultation. Geneva, Switzerland: World Health Organization; 1985.

41. Institute of Medicine. Dietary reference intakes for energy, carbohydrate, fiber, fat, fatty acids, cholesterol, protein, and amino acids (macronutrients). Washington, DC: National Academy Press; 2002.

Astronauts Julie Payette, Koichi Wakata, Frank De Winne, and Michael Barratt enjoy a meal in the ISS Node 1 during Expedition 20. Photo Credit: NASA.

3 Space Food Systems

A space food system, developed and provisioned to deliver all the defined nutritional requirements, should be available on every human mission as an essential countermeasure to health and performance decrements. However, resources are limited on every mission. The adequacy of the food system may be impacted by how resources are distributed and prioritized across life support and vehicle systems. The first edition of this book included a review of food systems from the Apollo Program through the beginning of the ISS Program (1). This edition focuses on the factors essential to providing an adequate food system for spaceflight, upcoming challenges, and the known and unknown risks that future exploration missions may introduce as resources are prioritized for missions to the Moon and Mars. Nutrition is only one facet of the food system. Acceptability, safety, shelf life, and resource requirements are equally important, and require integrated solutions for spaceflight. As missions become longer, and alternative food systems (such as growing foods) are considered, many other factors must also be considered in trades between food systems and other resources such as hardware, crew time, and system acceptability.

NASA maintains a set of human-system standards (42, 43) as a starting point for all mission scenarios. Standards for a basic food system framework include nutritional content (e.g., as defined in Chapter 1, Table 1), acceptability, hot and cold water, food-warming capability, time for meals, and microbiological testing requirements. Although these standards provide a baseline for an adequate food system, they do not guarantee an optimal solution. As mentioned in Chapter 2, nutritional requirements have been established to mitigate deficiency, not to prevent disease or promote performance (44). Some standards may not become requirements on every spacecraft or during every mission scenario due to resource restrictions. For instance, although Apollo astronauts rated hot water as non-negotiable (45), neither hot water nor the ability to heat food may be available on every segment of every future mission due to resource constraints. Foods are considered more acceptable at their expected serving temperature, and the ability to quickly and easily heat foods is associated with increased food intake (46, 47). Heating also improves rehydration of some freeze-dried foods. The impact that the inability to heat foods and beverages will have on intake over multiple days of high-tempo missions is currently unknown. In fact, despite the central link between food and nutrition and every aspect of physiology (44), many of the physiological and behavioral outcomes that have been reported in spaceflight, such as immune dysregulation, increased incidence of rashes and headaches, and increased stress, have yet to be formally investigated in relation to food intake during spaceflight (48, 49). Given the central role that food and nutrition have on astronaut health and performance, and therefore mission success, it is imperative to assess the risks of implementing variations of the food system standards to effectively inform mission risk and resource trades before exploration missions commence.

Although past spaceflight food systems will not be reviewed in detail here, specific points need to be highlighted. NASA met food system challenges at the beginning of the space food program more than 60 years ago by focusing more on resources and safety than on nutrition and acceptability. Even on short missions during the Mercury,

Gemini, and Apollo Programs, foods were underconsumed and astronauts lost weight (1, 50). Although the food system has advanced with every NASA program, as previously described, astronauts in general still do not consume enough food to maintain body weight (1, 50). Multiple factors besides food acceptability have the potential to contribute to underconsumption, and research is needed to further investigate these factors. Based on anecdotal reports, potential contributors to underconsumption during flight could include factors such as physiological changes, time allotted for meals, and menu fatigue. The degree of underconsumption may vary by individual and with mission length (50-52). This chapter describes considerations for product development, acceptability of food and mealtime factors, and menu fatigue. Physiological factors that may be associated with underconsumption are discussed in detail in Chapter 4.

International Space Station Food System

Astronauts in the United States Operating Segment (USOS; includes International Partners from the European Space Agency [ESA], Canadian Space Agency [CSA], and the Japan Aerospace Exploration Agency [JAXA]) on the ISS share a standard food set of shelf-stable foods, described previously (1, 50). These standard foods provide a commonly accepted set of foods to the crew regardless of resupply delays or late crew changes, which preference menus cannot accommodate. Meal items include retort thermostabilized, irradiated, or freeze-dried products, low- and intermediate-moisture fruits and snacks, and powdered beverages. Products are developed and produced by NASA when a food item is not available commercially (based on required nutrition, shelf life, and food type), or an item is procured commercially and repackaged for spaceflight use, as necessary. All items are packaged as individual servings in lightweight flexible laminates, from which foods are directly consumed. The only preparation capability on the ISS is the addition of hot or ambient temperature water through a septum adapter assembly attached to freeze-dried packages and beverage bags, or heating via a conduction oven (Figure 2). A small chiller is available for condiments and for cooling a limited number of foods, if preferred,

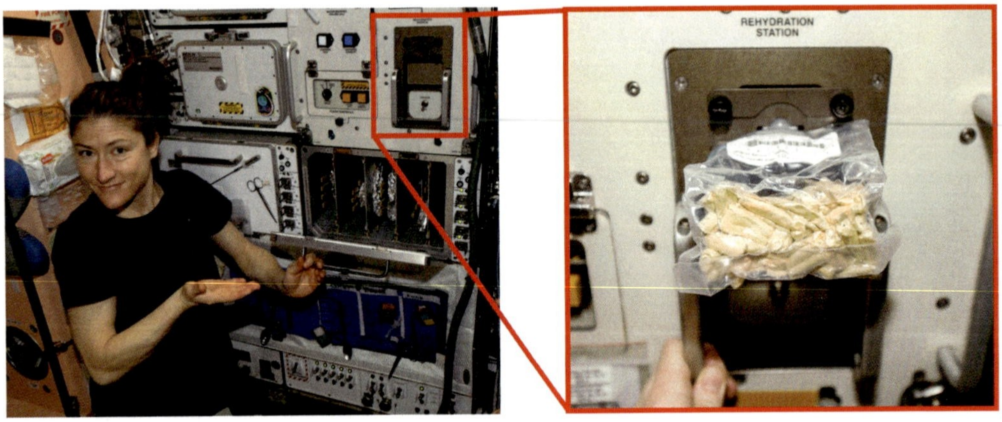

Figure 2. The ISS Galley in the USOS includes a conduction food warmer and a Potable Water Dispenser with metered hot or ambient temperature water. NASA astronaut Christina Koch is heating pizzas, part of the limited shelf life foods that may be included in some resupply provisions to the ISS. Inset: Example of a food package during rehydration. Photo Credits: NASA.

prior to consumption. The bulk supply of foods is stored under ambient conditions.

Astronauts select their own meals from standard containers, stowed pantry-style, which rotate based on the number of crewmembers sharing the set (e.g., 7- to 9-day rotation cycle for three astronauts). Currently, more than 200 standard foods and beverages are available for consumption on the ISS, and products continue to be developed to increase availability of acceptable, healthy, shelf-stable options and to replace items that are less popular. The current system provides a lot of variety in each container but few replicates of each item (1 to 3 servings of a particular item in a rotation cycle). Astronaut preferences vary from crew to crew, which changes the items that are in high demand and those that are less preferred in each increment. The dynamic of changing preferences is alleviated on the ISS by regular crew changes and resupply vehicles; however, the supply chain requires food to be ready for launch several months in advance. In addition, a multi-month supply of food must always be maintained on the ISS. Therefore, the food system on the ISS is, by necessity, a mostly closed system, meaning astronauts are restricted to the foods that are available, and logistically the oldest food must be consumed first.

Preference containers, known as Crew Specific Menu (CSM) containers, are delivered to the ISS, typically on cargo vehicles. These containers provide astronauts with around 10% to 20% of their foods, depending on individual astronaut requirements. Although Russian crewmembers are provisioned separately (i.e., by the Russian Space Agency) from USOS crew, NASA, CSA, ESA, and JAXA crews can choose some Russian and some international partner foods, as available, as part of their CSM food supply. Astronauts can also share food with their crewmates at their own discretion. Astronauts on the ISS also receive a small supply of fresh foods (e.g., apples, oranges, carrots) and limited shelf life foods (e.g., pizza kits) on resupply vehicles, which have increased in occurrence with the regularity of commercial vehicles in recent years. Although limited, these fresh produce, crew-specific foods, international partner foods, foods in crew care packages, and even occasional cold supply foods (e.g., ice cream and cheese) have greatly increased the variety and quality of the food system on the ISS. The actual quantity of non-standard foods consumed may be 20% to 25% for some astronauts. During debriefs, astronauts comment regularly on the importance of CSM foods, and the variety of foods in general during 6-month ISS missions. Despite the increased variety of foods, astronauts still comment that they would like more crew-specific food and more fresh food than is available (50). Although the wide variety of preference foods helps to support caloric intake, many of these foods might not be available on future missions that are longer and farther from Earth because resupply will be unlikely during these missions. Currently, no food system exists to meet the nutrition, acceptability, safety, and resource challenges of extended-exploration missions, such as a mission to Mars.

Food System Requirements

Food has both a nutritional role and a social role in supporting physical and behavioral health and performance. Many requirements must be met to support both of these roles, described in detail here, reviewed in (6), and depicted in Figure 3.

Nutrition

A good approach to supporting adequate nutritional intake is to provide a variety of high-quality whole foods for the length of the mission. A balanced diet of whole foods provides all essential nutrients and thousands of bioactive compounds. Many previous studies have shown that

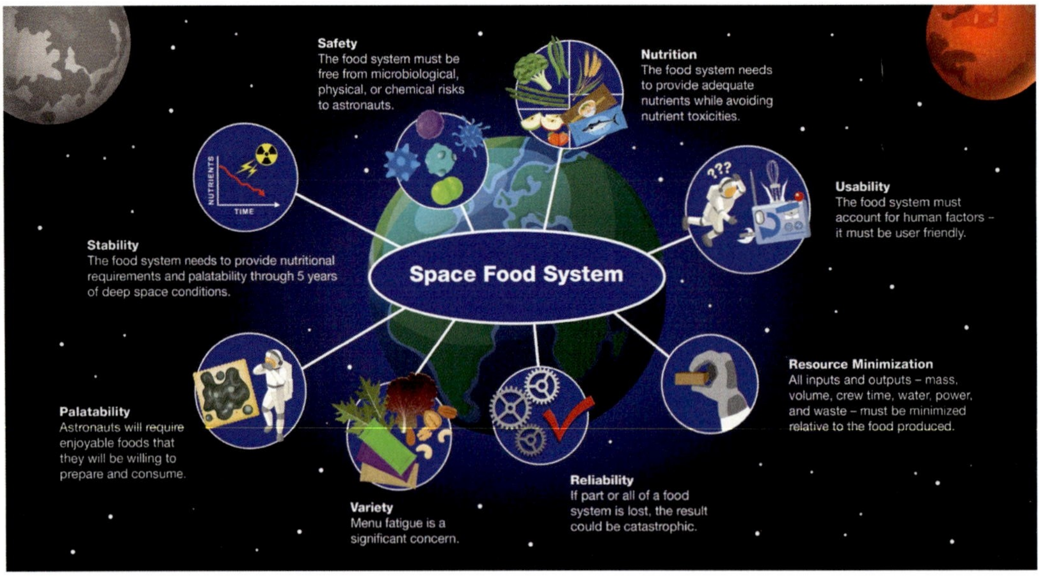

Figure 3. Space food system requirements. Adapted from (6).

the complex synergistic benefits provided by whole foods cannot be replicated by supplements (53-57). Nutrients provided by foods have a direct impact at the biochemical level, and also an influence on the composition and metabolism of the microbiome, which converts metabolites that human digestion cannot break down (58). The metabolites produced from human digestion and from the microbiome are used throughout the body, providing the required substrates to maintain all physiological systems (44, 59). Nutrients and metabolites can be essential or beneficial to factors such as immunity, sleep, performance, mood, and cognition (60-65). Metabolites can also affect the brain and behavioral health through interaction via the gut-brain axis (66). An adequate diet can stave off deficiency, an exceptional diet can promote health and performance, and a deficient diet can result in health and performance decrements that, if extended long enough, could end with loss of life and the mission (44, 67).

In addition to the complex synergistic benefits of whole foods, they have several other advantages over supplements. First, over-supplementation of some nutrients can result in toxicity or even death (68, 69). Second, supplements cannot effectively support adequate caloric and macro-nutritional intake over time. These points are discussed further in Chapter 13.

Acceptability and Variety

Caloric intake may be affected by the acceptability of the food system, and acceptability may be affected by variety and choice (70), quality after storage (71), and menu fatigue over time (72). Food acceptability is critical to support consistent consumption throughout the mission. Astronauts receive no benefit from nutritious foods that they are unwilling to consume. It is commonly assumed that high-performing groups of people, such as astronauts, will “eat anything” to successfully complete a mission. On the contrary, military, spaceflight, and test data show that if the food is not considered acceptable for the length of the mission, then body mass and nutritional intake will not be maintained (50, 73, 74). In the military, the risk to health and performance from consuming meals-ready-to-eat for extended periods has resulted in a policy to limit their continuous use to 21 days (73, 75). However, limiting the use of shelf-stable food is not an option for spaceflight because no alternative is currently available, and continued work is warranted to understand and ensure that an acceptable food system is provisioned for all missions.

Standard spaceflight foods are developed based on several factors, including crew feedback, safety and shelf life requirements, allocation of spacecraft mass and volume, capabilities for preparing food, and the variety and nutrition of the menu complement. Because foods are provided as a standard set and crewmembers change regularly, foods are developed to provide nutritional variety that most consumers will find acceptable. A greater variety of meal options can prevent menu fatigue that may occur from consuming the same foods repeatedly, which may impact consumption (72).

Providing all nutritional needs and promoting adequate consumption within a processed, shelf-stable system is a challenge. On Earth, fruits and vegetables are generally refrigerated or stored in a freezer before being consumed; current and planned spacecraft are not able to accommodate these storage methods. Additionally, many Earth-based processed foods are high in sugar or sodium, which promotes acceptability with the flavor and texture changes that occur during processing. Given the concern regarding the high concentrations of sodium in space food (as reviewed in other chapters of this book), the sodium content of the space food system was reduced by about a third during the last decade by reformulating many of the foods (76). Reformulations focused on high-quality ingredients, flavor combinations, and spices, while maintaining or even increasing acceptability of individual items.

It is important to note that the sodium reformulation was the only opportunity, to date, for significant nutritional change to the food system. Prior to this, the majority of foods were acquired commercially and further processed or repackaged as necessary for compatibility with spaceflight. Although the sodium reformulation provided an opportunity to develop healthier choices, many commercially available foods are still used, and many are fortified. The standard food set, and suggested standard menu, were developed to meet nutritional requirements within these limitations, which is an important consideration throughout this book. When possible, healthier choices are developed and evaluated for potential addition to the standard food set.

After the foods are developed, they are evaluated for sensory acceptability. All foods selected for spaceflight must receive an acceptability score of a 6.0 or higher on a 9-pt hedonic scale, as evaluated by a panel of Johnson Space Center (JSC) volunteers that includes astronauts (50). These requirements and evaluations mean that the food provisioned to the ISS has acceptable sensory attributes; however, several factors besides appearance, aroma, flavor, and texture of individual foods can affect consumption. The behavioral factors that affect food consumption can be more challenging to solve in a resource-limited environment that contains a closed food system.

Preference and Behavior

Food familiarity, choice, and the social aspects surrounding food (time and space to gather and consume meals together [Figures 4 and 5]) become more important with extended isolation, confinement, and distance from Earth (51). Beyond the effects on health and performance, the adequacy of the food system may become a factor in crewmembers' moods, and the dynamics and cohesion of the team (77). Food was one of the top 10 items discussed by the astronauts who participated in the Journals experiment, which entailed crewmembers recording general feelings about their daily activities and their fellow crewmembers during long-duration space missions on the ISS (4, 78, 79). To quote from Dr. Stuster's final report of the Journals experiment:

> "Food assumes added importance when access to friends, family, leisure pursuits and other normal sources of gratification are denied. The importance of food during isolation and confinement is well-known to the managers of oil rigs, commercial ships, Antarctic research stations and nuclear submarines, all of whom serve large quantities and varieties of high-quality food daily." (79)

The quality, variety, and availability of food, the stability of nutrients, the ease of preparation, the timing of meals, and the ability to warm or chill food have the potential to affect both nutrient intake and behavioral health, as have been observed previously during spaceflight, Antarctic and sea explorations, and military deployments (4, 73, 79). However, resources, and the ability to support variety, choice, and even cold storage, are more limited in space exploration than they are in most remote Earth-based deployments, as discussed below, which adds an additional challenge to supporting these psychosocial factors.

Self-selection or avoidance of food items in a closed food system has the potential to unintentionally affect nutrient intake. If a crewmember over- or under-consumes certain items (e.g., dairy, meat,

Figure 4. The Expedition 50 crewmembers share a meal during the Christmas holidays. Back row (left to right): Cosmonauts Sergei Ryzhikov, Andrei Borisenko, Oleg Novitskiy. Front row (left to right): ESA astronaut Thomas Pesquet (wearing Santa cap), NASA astronauts Shane Kimbrough, Peggy Whitson. Food, and gatherings around the table, are important to celebrations and holidays in spaceflight, just as they are on Earth. Photo Credit: NASA.

or even vegetables) this also restricts the remaining food selections for their crewmates. This could impact nutritional intake for the whole crew, or even negatively affect team dynamics. Another concern may be dishonorable food practices, such as eating a crewmate's food, which can lead to feelings of resentment (78).

These scenarios were evident in ground-based chamber studies with closed or semi-closed food systems, where crewmembers did not get enough nutrients despite the food system containing enough of each nutrient. For example, during the ESA Experimental Campaign for the European Manned Space Infrastructure (EXEMSI) study, a 60-day closed food system provided all nutrient requirements; however, crewmembers' actual vitamin intake (vitamins B_1 and B_6 in particular) was below the dietary requirements, indicating that they were not selecting completely nutritionally balanced meals (80). In yet another example, during a 105-day chamber study in Russia, subjects that intentionally excluded specific food items became protein deficient and lost body mass (81). During the Mars 500 mission, it was reported that "food became probably the greatest problem in isolation," likely impacted by a lack of variety in general, and a lack of culturally familiar foods for all crew (82).

Several of these factors become more concerning as distance from Earth and mission duration increases and the ability to resupply food is not possible. It is likely that food will be prepositioned ahead of missions, before the crewmembers have been assigned, thus eliminating the opportunity for crewmembers to select their preference. Therefore, preference foods may not be available for these missions. A food system without preference diets will not support individuals with food allergies or restrictions, even on near-term missions. In addition, crew timelines, and therefore

Figure 5. NASA astronaut Sandra Magnus, Expedition 18 flight engineer, experiments with mixing food in weightlessness while preparing a Christmas meal at the Galley in the Zvezda Service Module. Photo Credit: NASA.

mealtimes, may be constrained during some mission scenarios. If crew time-lines are constricted and food must be consumed quickly, then food must be packaged so that it can be prepared quickly and still be acceptable to support adequate consumption. This can be essential to morale (51).

Further work will be warranted to determine acceptable food factors (e.g., variety, choice, social requirements) that support adequate intake as mission duration increases. More on this topic is discussed in Chapter 14.

Safety

Safety is another critical factor that includes physical, chemical, and microbiological risks. Because limited medical capability is available on a spacecraft, an incidence of foodborne illness could result in loss of a mission, and even loss of life as distance from Earth increases. NASA, U.S. Army Natick Soldier Research, Development & Engineering Center, and Pillsbury collaborated to develop The Hazard Analysis Critical Control Point for the spaceflight food system. Because this system was so successful in improving the safety of spaceflight food, it was implemented throughout the food industry (83). The safety of the current, shelf-stable food system is managed on Earth (50) through processing, packaging, and microbiological testing. Flight orbital debris, which can become a hazard to spacecraft systems and to humans in microgravity, is mitigated by food selection or by preparing foods to minimize or eliminate crumbs. These processing, packaging, and testing capabilities require substantial resources that are not available in current or planned spacecraft.

Stability

Some nutritional and quality factors in spaceflight foods degrade during storage, and many foods and some critical nutrients reach unacceptable levels within 1 to 3 years (71, 84) (Figure 6). Recently, three NASA space foods—brown rice, split pea soup, and barbeque beef—were tested at three different storage temperatures to determine whether degradation of thiamin depends on the matrix (85). Levels of thiamin rapidly decreased in the barbeque beef, suggesting that food matrix is very important. Packaging and preservation method, and the compatibility of these factors, are also central to shelf stability (86). A processing technology that produces high-quality products may not maintain the quality through the required shelf life if the compatible packaging does not provide an adequate oxygen and moisture barrier, as is the case to date with Microwave Assisted Thermal Sterilization (50).

The nutritional status of astronauts and the nutritional content of space food should continue to be monitored as we begin to embark on longer missions, including the 1-year missions on the ISS planned for 2021 onward. Supplements would not solve the issue of nutritional degradation because nutrients also degrade in supplement form (87). Supplement inadequacy is discussed further in Chapter 13.

The current shelf life of space food is sufficient for ISS missions because food is regularly resupplied. For some upcoming missions, food will be launched with the crew or could be prepositioned for no more than a year. However, preventing nutritional and quality degradation will be a greater challenge for missions lasting more than a year. It is important to note that shelf-stable processed foods will remain safe to eat well after the quality and nutritional value have degraded if the foods are stored in a dry, controlled room temperature environment and the packaging remains intact.

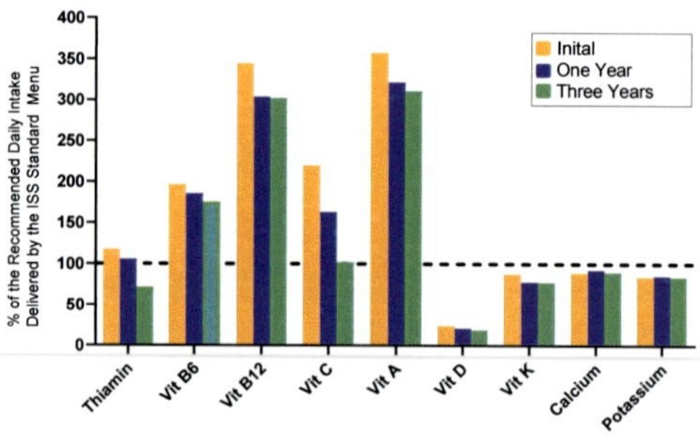

Figure 6. Nutrient stability over 3 years of study. Data are presented based on the content (after processing) of each nutrient as included in the standard menu. Although there is an expectation that crews will consume at least 10% (and often 20% to 25%) of their food from CSM containers, the content of vitamin D, vitamin K, calcium, and potassium start below nominal recommendations. Thiamin and vitamin C degrade to inadequate amounts over the 3-year study period. Other nutrients (vitamins A, B_6, and B_{12}) degrade, but remain above required minimums. Adapted from Cooper et al. (84).

Resource Minimization

The limited resources available on a spacecraft often conflict with the goals of providing a nutritious, acceptable variety of safe foods. Resources include mass, volume, power, water, crew time, and waste management that must have a dedicated system, as well as resources that impact other systems (e.g., heat load or volatile management). Mass, volume, and power limitations have eliminated refrigerators, freezers, and microwaves from all spaceflight programs to date, except during the Skylab Program when cold storage was provided. Mass and volume limitations have also necessitated a shift from cans and rigid packaging to lightweight, flexible laminates, which further limit the commercially available products that are compatible with spaceflight. As missions get longer and farther from Earth, and greater propulsion is needed to provide the same quantity of supplies, it will be important to minimize resources for every system. As such, providing an adequate food system will become a greater challenge.

Food System Considerations for Future Exploration Missions

The Moon: Artemis (Orion/Gateway/Lunar)

Although the ideal scenario for near-term Orion, Gateway, and lunar missions is to launch food with the crew to accommodate preference food and shorten the storage durations, some food may need to be prepositioned due to mass and volume constraints. This will limit those prepositioned foods to a standard set. In addition, astronauts will be performing high-tempo EVAs that will require an increase in caloric intake during these missions, and these increased calories must be provided within the resource limitations.

The use of meal replacement bars could reduce the mass and volume of the food system, but it will also reduce choice, which may affect caloric intake and behavior even over short durations (74). Weight loss, even on short missions, can impact crew status; weight loss has been associated previously with cardiovascular

Figure 7. Depiction of Orion, Gateway, and Artemis mission profile. Image Credit: NASA.

changes that could affect crew health and performance (88).

Increasing the fat content of food could potentially reduce the mass and volume of the food system by increasing energy density of the food. Calories could also be consumed quicker in an energy-dense food system, which may be useful during short meal timelines. However, a high-fat diet could also introduce unacceptable physiological outcomes, such as gastrointestinal (GI) complaints (89, 90) that may impact high-tempo EVA schedules. Alternatively, if astronauts try to avoid GI issues, this could result in inadequate energy intake. High-fat diets may also induce some cognitive effects, even over short durations (91-93). The type of fat consumed will influence any associated health effects; however, healthier unsaturated fats are more unstable and not as compatible with shelf life requirements for spaceflight food systems (94). Although multiple factors may influence the onset of performance decrements, such as the initial nutritional status of an individual (89), the issues described above highlight the need to evaluate and understand the risks of imposing each potential food system solution in the intended mission scenarios. Once quantified, risks to human health and performance from the proposed food system could be appropriately evaluated and prioritized with other vehicle and mission risks.

Mars and other Deep Space Exploration

Currently, no food system exists that meets the nutrition, acceptability, safety, and resource challenges of extended-exploration missions, such as a Mars mission (95). Logistics may require a processed food system to be prepositioned in space or on the Martian surface before the crew departs from Earth, resulting in a food system that is 5 to 7 years old by the end of the mission. Several critical nutrients and quality factors in the shelf-stable spaceflight food system will degrade to unacceptable levels well before 5 years of storage under current ambient temperatures, and solutions to ensure a nutritious and adequate food system for extended durations are needed (71, 84).

Shelf-stable foods still have many advantages; they are safe, familiar, and easy to prepare. Evaluation of novel processing and packaging, or alternative storage temperatures, may identify solutions to extend the shelf life of these foods; however, all cold storage solutions, whether the passive cold of space or active refrigeration, require resources and infrastructure. Shelf-stable foods also require significant mass and volume when launched from Earth.

Alternative food systems, or combinations of food systems, may provide options. However, additional challenges will be introduced if current methods to produce or process foods on Earth are used during spaceflight or on an extraterrestrial surface (6). Much is still unknown regarding even more-advanced systems, such as food crop production in space (96).

The first challenge is resources. Although it is commonly believed that producing food during spaceflight will require less resources than supplying a readily available food source, this has yet to be confirmed. The requirements of an alternative food system in a closed-loop environment is still unknown, including the required equipment, crew time, cleaning and sanitizing, substrates and ingredients, storage conditions of ingredients, power, volume, water, and waste processing. For example, even if water is recycled, more water may be required for processing, cleaning, and sanitizing food, which would increase the resources required for the mission.

A second challenge is reliability, or the risk of food scarcity. If astronauts rely on a system that produces a portion of their nutrition, then loss of that system could result in loss of the mission and loss of life. The effects of radiation add an additional unknown to risk of food scarcity. All ingredients and equipment for producing food may need to be prepositioned, requiring a 5- to 7-year shelf life. Although the data available to date indicate that deep space radiation may have no significant effect on shelf-stable foods (87), the effects of radiation on food growth are currently unknown. Opportunities to understand radiation effects are limited to space missions and to Earth-based facilities that simulate deep space radiation conditions (97).

A third challenge is acceptability of food production and human factors. If a system requires extensive crew time or is difficult to use, then it may be less likely to be used, thereby generating a risk of inadequate food availability and underconsumption. Food growth and processing may be more suited to longer planetary residences than to exploration-class missions. On near-term exploration missions, astronauts will not have the time or the skills to produce food. Similar to food production on Earth, food production in space must be something that a person will want to come home and do after a long day of work, an enjoyable activity that efficiently produces a meal. If the end-to-end process of preparing food is generally unacceptable to most people, then it is unlikely to be a successful candidate for exploration missions; however, the fourth challenge, which is food production and preparation equipment, may also be a factor. The food preparation equipment currently available for spaceflight adds only water or heat. New, efficient, and acceptable equipment that produces a variety of nutritious and acceptable food options, while keeping the entire food system within resource requirements, could revolutionize both a Mars exploration food system and food sustainability on Earth. However, additional equipment will factor into resource trades for mass, volume, power, crew time, cleaning and sanitizing, and maintenance resources.

The fifth challenge is safety. Unlike prepackaged foods where safety is confirmed on Earth, producing food in space will introduce new food safety challenges. For example, cleaning and sanitizing the equipment could produce volatile compounds that will need to be removed from the air, supplies for microbiological testing will introduce mass and waste, and mechanical safety (touch temperatures) will need to be addressed, while fitting everything within the resource limitations of the mission.

The sixth challenge is cost and schedule feasibility. These are not clear for many alternative food systems. Finally, even if a food system is successfully developed with acceptable resource trades, the risks to crew health and performance of any planned food system must be evaluated in realistic mission scenarios—either on Earth or on a lunar base—before being implemented on a mission to Mars, where there will be no opportunity for early crew return and no possibility for resupply.

References for Chapter 3

1. Smith SM, Zwart SR, Kloeris V, Heer M. Nutritional biochemistry of space flight. New York: Nova Science Publishers; 2009.

4. Stuster JW. Bold endeavors: behavioral lessons from polar and space exploration. Gravit Space Biol Bull. 2000;13:49-57.

6. Douglas GL, Zwart SR, Smith SM. Space food for thought: Challenges and considerations for food and nutrition on exploration missions. J Nutr. 2020;150:2242-4.

42. National Aeronautics and Space Administration. NASA-STD-3001. NASA Space Flight Human-System Standard, Volume 1, Revision A: Crew Health. Washington, DC. 2014.

43. National Aeronautics and Space Administration. NASA-STD-3001. NASA Space Flight Human-System Standard, Volume 2, Revision B: Human Factors, Habitability, and Environmental Health. Washington, DC. 2019.

44. Wallace TC, Bailey RL, Blumberg JB, Burton-Freeman B, Chen CO, Crowe-White KM, Drewnowski A, Hooshmand S, Johnson E, Lewis R, Murray R, Shapses SA, Wang DD. Fruits, vegetables, and health: A comprehensive narrative, umbrella review of the science and recommendations for enhanced public policy to improve intake. Crit Rev Food Sci Nutr. 2019:1-38.

45. Scheuring RA, Jones JA, Novak JD, Polk JD, Gillis DB, Schmid J, Duncan JM, Davis JR. The Apollo Medical Operations Project: Recommendations to improve crew health and performance for future exploration missions and lunar surface operations. Acta Astronaut. 2008;63:980-7.

46. Lester LS, Matthew Kramer F. The effects of heating on food acceptability and consumption. Food Res Int. 1991;6:69-87.

47. Cardello AV, Maller O. Acceptability of water, selected beverages and foods as a function of serving temperature. J Food Sci. 1982;47:1549-52.

48. Crucian B, Babiak-Vazquez A, Johnston S, Pierson DL, Ott CM, Sams C. Incidence of clinical symptoms during long-duration orbital spaceflight. Int J Gen Med. 2016;9:383-91.

49. Crucian BE, Makedonas G, Sams CF, Pierson DL, Simpson R, Stowe RP, Smith SM, Zwart SR, Krieger SS, Rooney B, Douglas G, Downs M, Nelman-Gonzalez M, Williams TJ, Mehta S. Countermeasures-based improvements in stress, immune system dysregulation and latent herpesvirus reactivation onboard the International Space Station - relevance for deep space missions and terrestrial medicine. Neurosci Biobehav Rev. 2020;115:68-76.

50. Douglas GL, Cooper M, Bermudez-Aguirre D, Sirmons T. Evidence Report: Risk of performance decrement and crew illness due to an inadequate food system [online]. National Aeronautics and Space Administration. https://humanresearchroadmap.nasa.gov/evidence/reports/AFT.pdf. 2016.

51. Stuster JW. Bold endeavors: behavioral lessons from polar and space exploration. Annapolis, MD: Naval Institute Press; 1996.

52. Olabi AA, Lawless HT, Hunter JB, Levitsky DA, Halpern BP. The effect of microgravity and space flight on the chemical senses. J Food Sci. 2002;67:468-78.

53. American Dietetic Association. Position of the American Dietetic Association: fortification and nutritional supplements. J Am Diet Assoc. 2005;105:1300-11.

54. Clarke JD, Hsu A, Riedl K, Bella D, Schwartz SJ, Stevens JF, Ho E. Bioavailability and inter-conversion of sulforaphane and erucin in human subjects consuming broccoli sprouts or broccoli supplement in a cross-over study design. Pharmacol Res. 2011;64:456-63.

55. Burton-Freeman B, Sesso HD. Whole food versus supplement: comparing the clinical evidence of tomato intake and lycopene supplementation on cardiovascular risk factors. Adv Nutr. 2014;5:457-85.

56. Liu RH. Health benefits of fruit and vegetables are from additive and synergistic combinations of phytochemicals. Am J Clin Nutr. 2003;78:517S-20S.

57. Liu RH. Health-promoting components of fruits and vegetables in the diet. Adv Nutr. 2013;4:384S-92S.

58. Heiman ML, Greenway FL. A healthy gastrointestinal microbiome is dependent on dietary diversity. Mol Metab. 2016;5:317-20.

59. Kawabata K, Yoshioka Y, Terao J. Role of intestinal microbiota in the bioavailability and physiological functions of dietary polyphenols. Molecules. 2019;24.

60. Levy M, Blacher E, Elinav E. Microbiome, metabolites and host immunity. Curr Opin Microbiol. 2017;35:8-15.

61. Lieberman HR. Nutrition, brain function and cognitive performance. Appetite. 2003;40:245-54.

62. Godos J, Currenti W, Angelino D, Mena P, Castellano S, Caraci F, Galvano F, Del Rio D, Ferri R, Grosso G. Diet and mental health: review of the recent updates on molecular mechanisms. Antioxidants (Basel). 2020;9.

63. Lieberman HR, Bukhari AS, Caldwell JA, Wilson MA, Mahoney CR, Pasiakos SM, McClung JP, Smith TJ. Two days of calorie deprivation induced by underfeeding and aerobic exercise degrades mood and lowers interstitial glucose but does not impair cognitive function in young adults. J Nutr. 2017;147:110-6.

64. Day DS, Young A, Askew EW. Nutrition and military performance. In: KE Friedl WS, editor. Military quantitative physiology: Problems and concepts in military operational medicine. Ft Detrick, MD: Office of the Surgeon General; 2012. p. 157-79.

65. Peuhkuri K, Sihvola N, Korpela R. Diet promotes sleep duration and quality. Nutr Res. 2012;32:309-19.

66. Cryan JF, O'Riordan KJ, Cowan CSM, Sandhu KV, Bastiaanssen TFS, Boehme M, Codagnone MG, Cussotto S, Fulling C, Golubeva AV, Guzzetta KE, Jaggar M, Long-Smith CM, Lyte JM, Martin JA, Molinero-Perez A, Moloney G, Morelli E, Morillas E, O'Connor R, Cruz-Pereira JS, Peterson VL, Rea K, Ritz NL, Sherwin E, Spichak S, Teichman EM, van de Wouw M, Ventura-Silva AP, Wallace-Fitzsimons SE, Hyland N, Clarke G, Dinan TG. The microbiota-gut-brain axis. Physiol Rev. 2019;99:1877-2013.

67. Feeney R. Polar journeys: the role of food and nutrition in early exploration. Washington DC: University of Alaska Press; 1997.

68. Penniston KL, Tanumihardjo SA. The acute and chronic toxic effects of vitamin A. Am J Clin Nutr. 2006;83:191-201.

69. De Sanctis V, Soliman N, Soliman AT, Elsedfy H, Di Maio S, El Kholy M, Fiscina B. Caffeinated energy drink consumption among adolescents and potential health consequences associated with their use: a significant public health hazard. Acta bio-medica : Atenei Parmensis. 2017;88:222-31.

70. Sorensen LB, Moller P, Flint A, Martens M, Raben A. Effect of sensory perception of foods on appetite and food intake: a review of studies on humans. Int J Obes Relat Metab Disord. 2003;27:1152-66.

71. Catauro PM, Perchonok MH. Assessment of the long-term stability of retort pouch foods to support extended duration spaceflight. J Food Sci. 2012;77:S29-39.

72. Meiselman HL, deGraaf C, Lesher LL. The effects of variety and monotony on food acceptance and intake at a midday meal. Physiol Behav. 2000;70:119-25.

73. Marriott BM. Not eating enough: Overcoming underconsumption of military operational rations. Washington, D.C.: National Academies Press; 1995.

74. Sirmons TA, Roma PG, Whitmire AM, Smith SM, Zwart SR, Young M, Douglas GL. Meal replacement in isolated and confined mission environments: Consumption, acceptability, and implications for physical and behavioral health. Physiol Behav. 2020;219:112829.

75. Friedl KE, Hoyt RW. Development and biomedical testing of military operational rations. Annu Rev Nutr. 1997;17:51-75.

76. Lane HW, Bourland C, Barrett A, Heer M, Smith SM. The role of nutritional research in the success of human space flight. Adv Nutr. 2013;4:521-3.

77. Landon LB, Douglas GL, Downs ME, Greene MR, Whitmire AM, Zwart SR, Roma PG. The behavioral biology of teams: Multidisciplinary contributions to social dynamics in isolated, confined, and extreme environments. Front Psychol. 2019;10:2571.

78. Stuster J. Behavioral issues associated with long-duration space expeditions: Review and analysis of astronaut journals. Experiment 01-E104 (Journals): Final Report (NASA/TM-2010-216130). Houston, TX: National Aeronautics and Space Administration Johnson Space Center. 2010.

79. Stuster J. Behavioral issues associated with long duration space expeditions: Review and analysis of astronaut journals Experiment 01-E104 (Journals) Phase 2 Final Report (NASA/TM-2016-218603). Houston, TX: National Aeronautics and Space Administration Johnson Space Center. 2016.

80. Milon H, Decarli B, Adine AM, Kihm E. Food intake and nutritional status during EXEMSI. Experimental Campaign for the European Manned Space Infrastructure. Adv Space Biol Med. 1996;5:79-91.

81. Agureev AN, Afonin BV, Sedova EA, Solovieva AA, Valuev VA, Sidorenko LA. Nutritional status in the experiment with 105-day isolation as the first phase of the Mars-500 project. Hum Physiol. 2018;43:793-801.

82. Poláčková Šolcová I, Šolcová I, Stuchlíková I, Mazehóová Y. The story of 520 days on a simulated flight to Mars. Acta Astronaut. 2016;126:178-89.

83. Heidelbaugh ND. Space flight feeding concepts: Characteristics, concepts for improvement, and public health implications. J Am Vet Med Assoc. 1966;149:1662-71.

84. Cooper M, Perchonok M, Douglas GL. Initial assessment of the nutritional quality of the space food system over three years of ambient storage. NPJ Microgravity. 2017;3:17.

85. Goulette TR, Zhou J, Dixon WR, Normand MD, Peleg M, McClements DJ, Decker E, Xiao H. Kinetic parameters of thiamine degradation in NASA spaceflight foods determined by the endpoints method for long-term storage. Food Chem. 2020;302:125365.

86. Perchonok M, Douglas G. The spaceflight food system: A case study in long duration preservation. In: Melton L, Shahidi, F., Varelis, P., editor. Encyclopedia of Food Chemistry: Elsevier; 2018. p. 183-7.

87. Zwart SR, Kloeris VL, Perchonok MH, Braby L, Smith SM. Assessment of nutrient stability in foods from the space food system after long-duration spaceflight on the ISS. J Food Sci. 2009;74:H209-17.

88. Carpentier WR, Charles JB, Shelhamer M, Hackler AS, Johnson TL, Domingo CMM, Sutton JP, Scott GBI, Wotring VE. Biomedical findings from NASA's Project Mercury: a case series. NPJ Microgravity. 2018;4:6.

89. Friedl KE. When does energy deficit affect soldier physical performance? In: Marriott BM, editor. Not Eating Enough: Overcoming Underconsumption of Military Operational Rations. Washington, D.C.: National Academies Press; 1995. p. 253-83.

90. Rehrer NJ, van Kemenade M, Meester W, Brouns F, Saris WH. Gastrointestinal complaints in relation to dietary intake in triathletes. Int J Sport Nutr. 1992;2:48-59.

91. Holloway CJ, Cochlin LE, Emmanuel Y, Murray A, Codreanu I, Edwards LM, Szmigielski C, Tyler DJ, Knight NS, Saxby BK, Lambert B, Thompson C, Neubauer S, Clarke K. A high-fat diet impairs cardiac high-energy phosphate metabolism and cognitive function in healthy human subjects. Am J Clin Nutr. 2011;93:748-55.

92. Madison AA, Belury MA, Andridge R, Shrout MR, Renna ME, Malarkey WB, Bailey MT, Kiecolt-Glaser JK. Afternoon distraction: a high-saturated-fat meal and endotoxemia impact postmeal attention in a randomized crossover trial. Am J Clin Nutr. 2020;111:1150-8.

93. Burke LM, Ross ML, Garvican-Lewis LA, Welvaert M, Heikura IA, Forbes SG, Mirtschin JG, Cato LE, Strobel N, Sharma AP, Hawley JA. Low carbohydrate, high fat diet impairs exercise economy and negates the performance benefit from intensified training in elite race walkers. J Physiol. 2017;595:2785-807.

94. Martín-Polvillo M, Márquez-Ruiz G, Dobarganes MC. Oxidative stability of sunflower oils differing in unsaturation degree during long-term storage at room temperature. J Am Oil Chemists' Soc. 2004;81:577-83.

95. Baisden DL, Beven GE, Campbell MR, Charles JB, Dervay JP, Foster E, Gray GW, Hamilton DR, Holland DA, Jennings RT, Johnston SL, Jones JA, Kerwin JP, Locke J, Polk JD, Scarpa PJ, Sipes W, Stepanek J, Webb JT, Ad Hoc Committee of Members of the Space Medicine A, Society of NFS. Human health and performance for long-duration spaceflight. Aviat Space Environ Med. 2008;79:629-35.

96. Anderson MS, Barta D, Douglas G, Fritsche R, Massa GD, Wheeler R, Quincy C, Romeyn M, Motil B, Hanford A, editors. Key gaps for enabling plant growth in future missions. AIAA Space and Astronautics Forum and Exposition; 2017; Orlando, FL: AIAA.

97. La Tessa C, Sivertz M, Chiang IH, Lowenstein D, Rusek A. Overview of the NASA space radiation laboratory. Life Sci Space Res (Amst). 2016;11:18-23.

4 Energy

Adequate energy intake is perhaps the single most important aspect of astronaut nutrition, not only because energy in and of itself is more important than other nutritional factors, but because if enough food is consumed to meet energy needs, then generally other nutrients (i.e., vitamins and minerals) will also be consumed in reasonable amounts. This assumes that the food system provides a balanced set of food choices, because plenty of diets provide adequate caloric intake but are associated with undernutrition.

Many facets are involved in maintaining eucaloric intake during spaceflight, including: energy requirements; potential physiological changes in taste and satiety; scheduling issues of allotting time for meal preparation, consumption, and cleanup; food quality; and preference for the available food. Little research has been done on differences in fuel components (i.e., protein, carbohydrate, fat) during spaceflight, or on cofactors (e.g., vitamins) of energy use. We review these here, highlighting what has been done as well as potential areas of future research.

Total energy expenditure (TEE) is the sum of the energy needed to maintain the body's function and physiological homeostasis at rest plus the energy needed for any physical activity. Energy expenditure has long been hypothesized to be lower during flight than on the ground because of the presumed relative hypokinesia during spaceflight (98). An early example that supports this is that lower energy expenditure was observed during EVA on the lunar surface than during similar activities at 1g (99). This was determined through indirect calorimetry in the space suit. However, Space Shuttle crewmembers' energy expenditure during EVA was no different than their energy expenditure before flight (100).

Studies have documented that Space Shuttle astronauts' energy expenditure during flight was unchanged from their preflight levels (101). In cases where the crewmember performed intensive exercise during the mission, their energy expenditure during flight was higher than before flight (102). For these studies, the doubly labeled water (i.e., water enriched with deuterium and 18O) technique was used to determine oxygen consumption (103). The benefits of this technique are that it is noninvasive, and it accounts for the energy cost of all activities over a period of several days. The drawback of the method is that it cannot be used to determine individual variation of TEE during specific activities, such as rest, sleep, and exercise, which would be important to assess given the inter-individual differences in intake and body mass loss. Although it is assumed that moving the body mass around the cabin requires less expenditure of energy during weightlessness than at 1g, other metabolic activities, such as maintaining resting metabolic rate and responding to stress, may require increased energy expenditure during weightlessness.

In ground-based bed rest studies, an analog of microgravity, resting energy expenditure did not change; however, TEE was less during bed rest than before bed rest (104). Because TEE during flight is unchanged (101) or increased (102) from preflight levels, the lower TEE during bed rest may indicate that bed rest is not an appropriate model for studies of energy metabolism during flight. One possible explanation for this difference between bed rest and spaceflight is the lack of a metabolic response to stress during bed rest (105). Attempts have been made to improve the utility of bed rest studies by administering a metabolic stressor (such as triiodothyronine or cortisol) to provide a better ground-based model than bed rest alone for the metabolic effects of spaceflight on energy and fuel metabolism (106). Another explanation for the difference between bed rest and spaceflight could be that physical activity is the main driver for changes of TEE in spaceflight, because the level of physical activity is very different for space travelers during missions and for bed rest subjects.

Energy requirements for early ISS missions were typically estimated using standard equations, including the World Health Organization (WHO) (40) equation and the Dietary Reference Intake (DRI) equation (41), and using a “moderately active” or “active” adjustment for activity level for these two equations, respectively. The DRI equation includes the effects of age, sex, weight, and height in estimating energy requirements. More recently, a direct method—namely, indirect calorimetry—has been used to determine individual astronaut’s actual resting energy expenditure before flight. These data can then be used to more accurately estimate the individual’s energy expenditure levels. However, the actual energy expenditure of individual physical activity, which might cause large variations in TEE (107), is not measured and this might be the next step to more accurately determine TEE.

In a recent study on the ISS, core body temperature was shown to increase by about 1°C during rest in microgravity (108). Changes in core body temperature have a significant effect on TEE. A reduction of 0.25°C in postmenopausal women induces a 3.25% reduction in energy expenditure (109). Presuming that temperature induced changes in energy expenditure are linear, the 1°C increase in core body temperature in space travelers would increase TEE by 13%, resulting in the need for about 350 kcal more per day for a space traveler with a TEE of 2700 kcal/d. However, this change of TEE during space travel needs to be confirmed by directly measuring TEE during flight. An ESA-sponsored experiment, initiated in 2012, aims to do this by determining energy expenditure during 6-month missions on the ISS. These data will help us understand whether any adaptation effect occurs on these longer missions, and thus may be important in estimating energy requirements for exploration missions (i.e., missions beyond low-Earth orbit).

Energy Intake

Historically, inadequate energy intake and subsequent loss of body mass have been considered hallmarks of spaceflight, and they have occurred on many missions and programs (1, 7, 101, 110-120). From Apollo through the Space Shuttle Program, dietary intakes during flight averaged about 70% of predicted requirements (111) (Figure 8), and intakes on the ISS have averaged about 80% of requirements. There are exceptions to this finding, including the Skylab missions during the early 1970s (121, 122), European flights to the Mir (123) and, more recently, some of the ISS missions (124). In the Skylab and Mir examples, crew participation in metabolic experiments required that they consume balanced, controlled, eucaloric diets. As a result, crewmembers met their recommended energy intake requirements. It is difficult to determine whether the intakes on Skylab were related more to the requirement to consume the food or to the fact that the food was more palatable because of the additional variety available with frozen foods; however, increased palatability is obviously beneficial.

The ISS has accommodated 4- to 6-month missions dating back to 2000. Many aspects of these missions have evolved during this time, and new

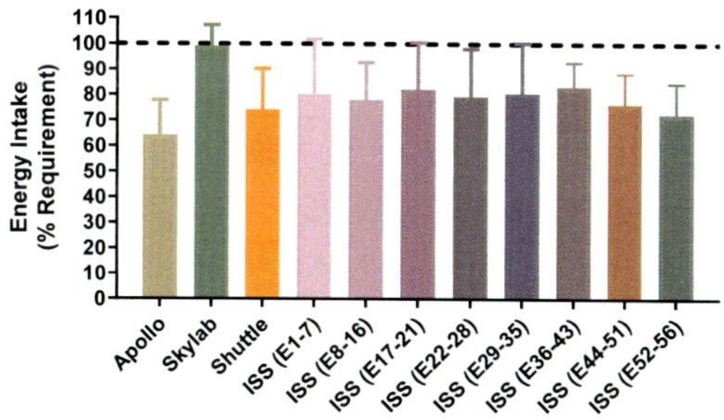

Figure 8. In-flight energy intake of crewmembers in different space programs. Data are expressed as percentage of energy requirements predicted by the World Health Organization equation (40) and are mean ± SD. Apollo and Skylab data are from Bourland et al. (125). Figure is adapted from earlier publications (1, 126), with additional published data included (111, 124, 127).

exercise equipment, reformulations of many space food items, and international foods from all partner agencies have debuted. These factors, coupled with the passage of lessons learned from one crew to the next, may have been responsible for our observation that many of the ISS crewmembers now consume recommended dietary intakes of energy, and also maintain body mass (111, 124).

Many potential explanations have been proposed in cases where energy intakes do not meet requirements, absent definitive causes (98, 114, 128). Appetite may vary significantly, as indicated in a Russian study in which 40% of Mir crewmembers reported decreased appetite, 40% reported no change, and 20% reported increased appetite (129).

Anecdotal reports exist of changes in the taste of food during flight (52, 130, 131). One hypothesis is that fluid shifts and congestion associated with the first days of introduction into microgravity can alter perception of taste and smell. The lack of convection in microgravity, along with competing odors from living in a relatively small, confined, and closed volume may affect food aromas. There has been speculation about other potential impacts on olfaction during flight, including higher concentrations of CO_2, or compounds in the recycled water on board, which might alter taste perception after rehydrating food (132, 133). Other possibilities exist as well, including effects of other atmospheric contaminants, stress, radiation, and psychological factors (52). To date, research has not been able to clearly document changes in taste or olfaction during spaceflight or during head-down-tilt bed rest (52, 134, 135).

When taste perception was measured before, during, and after 30 days of –6° head-down bed rest, subjects reported decreased appetite and lack of taste early in the bed rest phase (135, 136). By day 13 of the bed rest phase, the sensitivity threshold for almost all tastes (i.e., sweet, salt, acidic, bitter) had increased. In contrast, a bed rest study in the 1990s found no changes in odor or taste perception after 14 days of head-down bed rest (137).

Current food strategies focus on providing astronauts with as much variety and choice as possible, and with condiments to tailor foods during flight. In low-Earth orbit, these approaches can be implemented in the resource-restricted spaceflight environment, and they receive positive feedback in debriefs. If ground-based or in-flight research is pursued to assess contributions of factors, such as potential changes in taste and smell, to inadequate energy consumption, then carefully designed and executed studies would be required. A large number of subjects would likely be required to determine whether perception of taste and odor are altered for any, or many, individuals, and to delineate the physiological or environmental factors that contribute to these changes.

Flight-related changes in GI function may also occur. Fluid shifts, in combination with reduced fluid intake, would tend to decrease GI motility. GI transit time has not been systematically studied during spaceflight; however, during 10 days of –6° head-down bed rest, mouth-to-cecum transit time was significantly longer than it was during ambulatory control periods (138). In a 520-day isolation study (MARS-500), the 13C-octanoic breath test was successfully used to determine that confinement had no effect on GI motility (139). However, because the Skylab astronauts and others were able to maintain a eucaloric diet in space, hypotheses about inability to consume the requisite amount of food because of stomach fullness or other factors are not likely to fully explain decreased dietary intake during flight. Russian studies of GI function in humans and in animal models during actual and simulated spaceflight have been reviewed (140). A common cause of reduced dietary intake during the first days of a mission (141) is space motion sickness (131, 141-144). The effects of space motion sickness typically pass after the first several days of flight; however, the decreased dietary intake can extend well beyond the first week (128). Hypoxia was investigated in a recent series of bed rest studies and was not found to affect body mass or fat mass loss, nor did it affect resting energy expenditure (145). Levels of oxidative stress were increased, which could be countered by exercise (146).

Implications for Inadequate Energy Intake

The obvious and immediate reason for concern about reduced dietary intake is the risk of losing body mass and, more specifically, loss of lean mass and bone tissue. Body mass losses of 1% to 5% of preflight body mass have been typical in the history of spaceflight, although some crewmembers have been able to maintain body mass (111, 124, 147). In-flight body mass data from ISS crews are shown in Figure 9. Documented weight losses have occurred on short- and long-duration flights in both the U.S. and Russian space programs (114, 148-150). Indeed, all crewmembers on Gemini, Apollo, Skylab, and Apollo-Soyuz Test Project missions lost body mass (151); thus, ingestion of the prescribed energy intake on the U.S. Skylab missions did not ensure maintenance of body mass (121). In one study of 13 male Space Shuttle crewmembers, body mass losses ranged from 0 to 3.9 kg (101). Body mass losses of more than 10% of preflight body mass were recorded on Mir (152). Crewmembers on the ISS have similar patterns of mass loss during flight (153). An extrapolation of all the data of body weight changes in spaceflight up to now gives an average loss of 2.4% of body weight per 100 days (107). Data from Apollo missions clearly

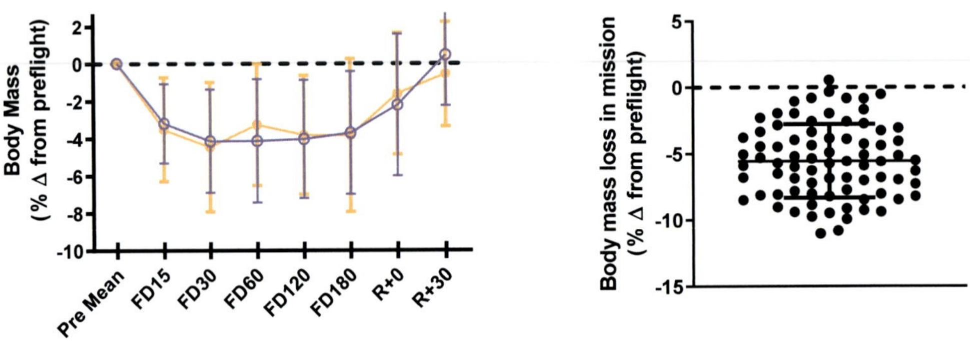

Figure 9. Body mass during flight. The left panel shows body mass in 49 male (blue line, open symbols) and 12 female (gold line, solid symbols) ISS astronauts during and after flight as a percent of preflight. In the right panel, each point represents the lowest point for each crewmember as compared to preflight. Three percent of astronauts (2 of 79) lost >10% body mass, whereas 57% (45 of 79) lost 5% to 10% of preflight mass.

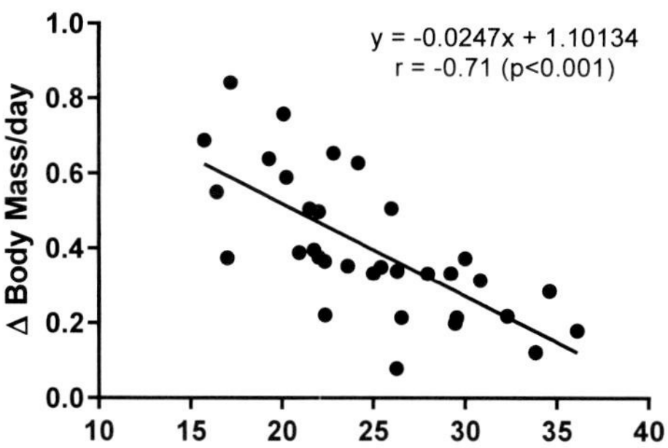

Figure 10. Relationship between energy intake (kcal/kg body mass/d) and weight loss (change in body mass/d, kg) during Apollo missions. N=33. Data are courtesy of William Carpentier, as previously published. (154).

document the relationship between energy intake and weight loss (Figure 10).

Data that relate reduced dietary intake during semi-starvation to loss of body mass were collected in two ground-based studies not related to spaceflight. In the first study (155), subjects who consumed 580 kcal/d lost 7% of their body mass in 12 days, and subjects who consumed 1010 kcal/d lost 11% of their body mass in 24 days. In the second study, starved subjects lost 9% of their body mass after 11 days, 15% by day 18, and 18% by day 43 (156).

Only about 1% of the loss of body mass can be explained by loss of body water (7); most of the observed loss of body mass is accounted for by loss of muscle and fat tissue (100, 157). The water loss may be confounded by lean tissue loss, because metabolic water loss is associated with depletion of glycogen stores and protein catabolism, both of which occur with inadequate energy intake. Inadequate energy intake is associated not only with loss of fat tissue, but also with decreased protein synthesis (158) (during spaceflight), increased protein catabolism (159) (during bed rest), and subsequent loss of lean tissue mass.

Besides the obvious concerns about loss of body mass and dehydration (160), existing data suggest that many systems are affected by inadequate nutrient intake, including the muscle, bone, cardiovascular, and immune systems. The German Institute of Aerospace Medicine at the German Aerospace Center conducted a study jointly with the ESA to evaluate the impact of hypocaloric nutrition on multiple systems. They used a crossover design, with hypocaloric and eucaloric phases, and bed rest and ambulatory phases. Data from this study document that undernutrition exacerbates the negative effects of bed rest on musculoskeletal and cardiovascular systems, and on energy metabolism (159, 161, 162).

Undernutrition can also impair cardio-vascular performance (orthostatic tolerance) in controlled bed rest settings (161) and after spaceflight (88) (see additional information in Chapter 8). The mechanism for this energy-cardiovascular connection has been hypothesized to involve multiple functions of many endocrine factors, including insulin, leptin, and growth hormone (163).

Anecdotal reports from crewmembers on long-duration missions indicate that crewmembers who had lost a significant amount of body mass on orbit had an excess amount of rebound weight gain after landing. In general, however, the data do not support these reports (1).

Deficiency of dietary energy intake leads to wasting and ultimately tissue breakdown, or even death. The loss of lean body mass during spaceflight is significant and is associated with increased proteolysis and catabolism related to metabolic stress (164). Inadequate energy intake can also have negative effects on bone, and is exacerbated by exercise-induced energy expenditure (165, 166). This highlights the interaction between systems, and the fact that exercise regimens must be coordinated with energy provision.

It is difficult to predict the effects of suboptimal (or lack of) energy intake on otherwise healthy individuals.

One issue is that the energy equivalent of the lost mass changes with time because different body fuels are used at different times during semi-starvation (155, 167). It is reasonable to expect that a person could survive for more than 4 to 6 months on partial rations (e.g., 1000 kcal/d), and potentially longer if the metabolic rate were to decrease because of decreased intake. If energy availability were restricted further, survivability would range from 4 to 6 months; without food, survivability from 1 to 2 months would be possible. These projections obviously include many assumptions, unknowns, and extrapolations. Data from 10 Irish Republican Army hunger strikers, who consumed water ad libitum but no energy, vitamins, or minerals, indicate that an average 25-year-old male could survive no longer than 60 days without energy (168, 169). Although a crew may survive a short period under these conditions, the associated physical and cognitive performance capability might be severely degraded. A high-stress contingency situation during transit or on a planetary surface, and any need to perform, would likely exacerbate the basic effects of limited rations and may shorten projections of survivability estimated from ground-based studies. Other possible effects, such as decreased motor and cognitive function, could impair an astronaut's ability to perform work-related tasks necessary for landing. According to military survival studies, astronauts on limited rations would be expected to experience early decreases in endurance, and a later decrease in strength that would parallel the decrease in lean body mass (170). During total fasting, degradation of coordination, speed, and cognitive function would be evident within the first 2 weeks (170).

The metabolic condition of ketosis, which would be expected to result from starvation, would not only have metabolic effects (including decreased appetite) but might also affect other aspects of the mission (e.g., the life-support systems might be unable to remove the ketones from the air). Ketoacidosis can have negative effects on acid-base balance, which in turn can affect bone, muscle, and other systems.

Insufficient dietary intake and subsequent loss of body mass are significant not only for crew health; medical operations and research studies will also be affected because clear interpretation of essentially all physiological data is impossible in malnourished subjects. As such, virtually all human research data collected on the Space Shuttle, Mir, and many ISS missions are confounded by inadequate dietary intake. Investigators who have studied bone and muscle, cardiovascular function, immune response, and other systems during spaceflight cannot say to what degree undernutrition affected and confounded their findings.

A key question is: What level of negative energy balance—i.e., energy expenditure exceeding energy intake—can be tolerated while preserving physical performance? In a systematic review, the military tried to find the threshold of energy deficit that impairs performance, i.e., declines in lower-body power and strength (171). The authors showed that the combination of the degree and the duration of negative energy balance correlated with the decline in lower-body performance. Their regression model determined that the negative energy balance for an entire operation should be limited to -5,686 to -19,109 kcal, corresponding to a total body mass loss of < 3.3% of baseline, to prevent or limit decline in physical performance. They determined that moderate to large declines in physical performance would occur with a negative energy balance of -39,243 to -59,377 kcal, corresponding to a body weight loss of >7.7 % (171). When projecting the average body weight loss of 2.4% per 100 days for spaceflight crewmembers (107), moderate to large loss of physical performance could occur within 1 year of space travel; however, this estimate does not consider the additional effect of microgravity.

Although research may be warranted to better understand why astronauts typically do not consume 100% of their recommended intakes, recent data from ISS crewmembers clearly document that intakes can be met during spaceflight (124). In addition to maintaining energy intake and vitamin D status, in conjunction with exercise, these crewmembers maintained body mass, came home leaner, with less fat, and maintained bone mineral density (BMD) at preflight levels (124). Additional details are provided in Chapter 6.

A key decision when designing bed rest studies is whether to provide subjects with ad libitum calories or whether to regulate caloric intake to maintain body mass or to maintain body composition. At least two approaches can be used to control body mass and composition while studying human adaptation to bed rest: maintaining body mass, or allowing subjects to lose total mass while keeping fat mass constant (and thus losing lean tissue). Although this latter approach sounds intriguing, implementing it has proven very challenging given the difficulties in measuring fat mass and adapting intake in a timely manner. Nonetheless, Biolo and colleagues have reported data suggesting that the more the fat mass increases during bed rest, the more lean tissue is lost, and that this loss is confounded by increases in oxidative and inflammatory damage markers (172). Altered fuel homeostasis has been documented in other bed rest studies (173-175) and in animal studies (176, 177), but remains to be fully elucidated in bed rest or spaceflight (177, 178).

Fuel Sources

Carbohydrate (and Fiber)

Carbohydrates play an important role in the body because they supply the primary, readily available source of energy. This energy is oxidized and used by various organs and cells in the body, particularly the brain and RBCs, which depend solely on carbohydrate for energy. The human body stores about 150 to 500 g of carbohydrates as glycogen in the liver and skeletal muscle (179). Most of the body's glycogen is in skeletal muscle. Stores of muscle glycogen are used mainly by muscle, whereas the smaller glycogen stores in the liver are used to maintain, store, and export blood glucose. Glycogen stores, especially those in the liver, fluctuate greatly during the day in response to food intake, and these fluctuations may be involved in the regulation of food intake (180). Stores of glycogen in the liver are depleted after 12 to 18 hours of fasting (179). In skeletal muscle, glycogen synthesis is triggered by a rise in insulin after the consumption of carbohydrates. De novo synthesis of glucose from non-carbohydrate precursors occurs in the body, if needed, allowing the liver to maintain adequate blood glucose concentrations. Insulin is required for the uptake of glucose into cells, and various transporter systems are found in different types of tissues that use glucose.

Requirements for carbohydrates during spaceflight are thought to be similar to those on Earth. However, to date, few investigations have been conducted to assess how microgravity affects the metabolism of dietary carbohydrate, and those studies have had conflicting results.

Studies that German investigators conducted on the Space Shuttle showed no effect of 7 days of flight on glucose tolerance tests (181). A Russian study documented a reduction in fasting plasma glucose after 60 or 88 days of flight on a Salyut-Soyuz spacecraft complex, and a reduced peak of blood glucose in glucose tolerance tests (182, 183). Insulin resistance (i.e., lack of sensitivity to insulin) can result in humans who are exposed to simulated weightlessness (i.e., during bed rest) (173, 184-188), and in animals that are flown in space (189). Using C-peptide excretion as a proxy for insulin secretion, Stein, et al. found evidence of insulin resistance during actual and simulated spaceflight (190). After 3 weeks of bed rest, glucose tolerance was altered for more than 4 days after re-ambulation (191). In another bed rest study, subjects took whey protein supplements to improve their reduced insulin sensitivity; however, the higher protein intake was unable to prevent impaired insulin sensitivity during bed rest. (188).

A first study of insulin resistance on the ISS demonstrated that insulin resistance increased—with a more pronounced increase in men than women—after about 3 to 5 months in microgravity (192). Data from bed rest studies indicate that a decrease in mitochondrial respiration may contribute to the increase in insulin resistance (187). Efforts continue to maintain muscle mass during spaceflight (and presumably correct the insulin resistance); however, little research has been done to understand the implications of insulin resistance, or methods to counteract it.

Suboptimal carbohydrate intake before and during spaceflight may affect the crewmember's productivity and impede their ability to respond in emergency situations (193). Deficiency of carbohydrate leads to ketosis. A ketotic state would likely impair performance of crewmembers, as seen in studies conducted by the military (170), and could increase renal stone risk secondary to reduced urinary pH (194-196). In a review by Cai et al. on safety and tolerability of ketogenic diets, the authors found more than 40 categories of adverse events in 45 studies. The adverse events included constipation, GI disturbances, vomiting, hyperlipidemia and hyperuricemia, acidosis, weight loss, and hypoglycemia (197). Although hypoglycemia resulting from a ketogenic diet might counteract the onset of insulin resistance in microgravity, other adverse effects of a ketogenic diet could occur, including exacerbating loss of body mass and musculoskeletal losses. A ketogenic diet could also put other aspects of the mission at risk (e.g., the life-support systems may be unable to remove exhaled ketones from the air). At the other extreme, impacts of very high carbohydrate have not been well studied, although it would likely be an issue only because it would displace other nutrients (i.e., protein and fat) from the diet.

Although few data are currently available to assess the impact of spaceflight on carbohydrate metabolism, the subtle changes observed in insulin secretion, insulin resistance, and glucose intolerance during spaceflight and ground-based bed rest studies make it critically important to consider its likelihood, nature, and consequences during exploration missions (185, 186, 198, 199) (187, 188, 192).

Dietary fiber is important for GI health and microbiome maintenance (described in detail in Chapter 11). An analysis of dietary intake from ISS astronauts revealed that the standard menu did not provide, nor did crewmembers select, foods to meet recommended daily intakes of fiber (Figure 11).

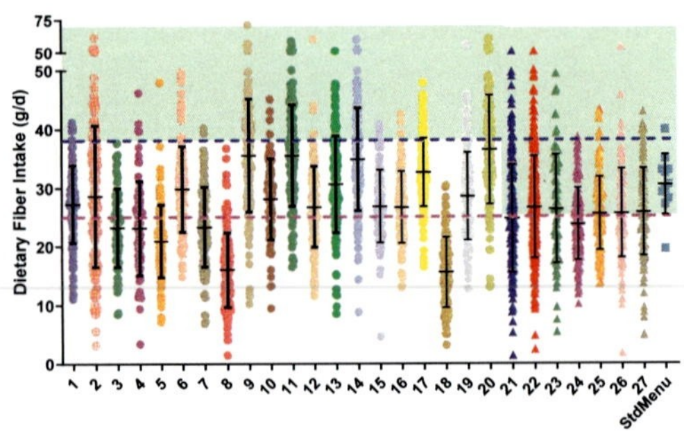

Figure 11. Dietary fiber intake in 27 astronauts and the ISS "standard menu." Green shaded area represents intakes meeting the daily requirement. Each symbol represents a day's intake during flight. Circles are male astronauts, and triangles are females. These represent crewmembers who recorded dietary intake with the ISS FIT App or kept a detailed food log. The black lines represent mean ± SD for each crewmember.

Fat (and Fatty Acids)

Fat is the most energy-dense of all the nutrients, and therefore is a major energy source for the body. Chemically, dietary fat is mainly in the form of triacylglycerols, which contain a glycerol backbone with as many as three fatty acids attached. Many types of fatty acids exist, including saturated, monounsaturated, polyunsaturated, and trans. Dietary fat assists in the absorption of fat-soluble vitamins and supplies the body with the two essential fatty acids—linoleic acid and linolenic acid. These essential fatty acids are necessary for growth and development as well as many other biochemical processes, including production of eicosanoids (physiologically active substances derived from arachidonic acid). Lipids, in the form of phospholipids, make up a large proportion of the structural components of the cellular membrane bilayer. Energy stored as fat is released in the process of fatty acid oxidation, and fat supplies more energy than any other macronutrient because of its higher content of carbon-to-hydrogen bonds. According to case studies, people following fat-free diets can exhibit symptoms of essential fatty acid deficiencies after only 1 month (200, 201).

Future missions outside of low-Earth orbit will include constraints of volume and mass that will impinge on the food system (6). A more energy-dense food system would be one solution to reduce the mass of the food system; however, higher fat diets are a concern for many reasons, as discussed in Chapter 3.

The ISS "standard menu" and crew-selected diets are generally higher in cholesterol and saturated fat than recommendations (Figure 12). These intakes were associated with higher circulating lipids during flight.

Voluminous data from routine medical examinations conducted before and after spaceflight, along with annual medical exams, were reviewed previously (1). Contrary to the typical lipoprotein response to weight loss, low-density lipoprotein concentrations tended to increase in crewmembers who lost weight during long-duration flights. This relationship seemed to return to normal by the subsequent nominal medical exam (1).

Alterations in fuel homeostasis and regulatory hormones have been noted during spaceflight and in ground-based studies. Bed rest studies have documented alterations in fuel homeostasis (202), including gender differences (173). Specifically, lipogenesis increased during bed rest, more so in women than in men. Additionally, men had increased carbohydrate oxidation (173).

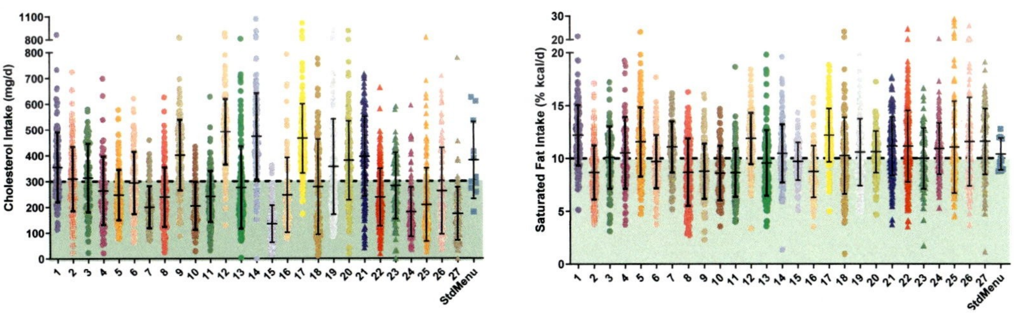

Figure 12. Dietary cholesterol (left panel) and saturated fat (right panel) intake in 27 astronauts and the ISS "standard menu." Green shaded area represents intakes meeting the recommended intakes. Each symbol represents a day's intake during flight. Circles are male astronauts, and triangles are females. These represent crewmembers who recorded dietary intake with the ISS FIT App or kept a detailed food log. The black lines represent mean ± SD for each crewmember.

The capacity of an organism to adapt fuel oxidation to fuel availability was originally defined by Kelley and Mandarino as 'metabolic flexibility' (203). However, Rynders et al. contend that a broader definition that includes physical activity and inactivity be considered in the definition of metabolic flexibility (204). Physical inactivity, such as during bed rest, decreases the switch from fat oxidation to carbohydrate oxidation in the fed state—i.e., physical inactivity causes metabolic inflexibility, even in neutral energy balance. Physical inactivity is also accompanied by fatty acid infiltration into the muscle, which, together with the metabolic inflexibility, might support the development of insulin resistance (188, 205). Reduction in glucose oxidation in an insulin-stimulated state is often accompanied by a triglyceride accumulation in myocytes, which is also seen in insulin resistance. Other studies have reported inflammatory changes in sedentary bed rest subjects, along with insulin resistance, leading to increased body fat and altered fatty acid metabolism (206). Given these data, and the changes in insulin, leptin, and other endocrines noted during bed rest and spaceflight (105, 207-210), changes in fuel homeostasis and metabolic inflexibility in bed rest clearly warrant additional investigation.

Omega-3 fatty acids have multiple roles in physiology and biochemistry, with generally accepted positive health benefits. The role of omega-3 fatty acids in preventing radiation-induced cancer has been investigated in animal models (211, 212). Not only do omega-3 fatty acids (in combination with pectin) show promise in alleviating cancer risk (211-215), these fatty acids also have well-documented cardiovascular benefits (216). Abundant data show that eicosapentaenoic acid can successfully prevent muscle atrophy in other muscle-wasting circumstances, such as cancer or sepsis (217-225), as well as in muscle wasting induced by a single leg immobilization (226). During a 14-day single leg immobilization study, omega-3 fatty acid supplements prevented changes in mitochondrial content, function, and lipid metabolism, which might have helped maintain muscle mass and strength in the immobilized leg (226). These observations indicate a high likelihood that eicosapentaenoic acid has similar beneficial effects on muscle atrophy during spaceflight or in ground-based analogs of spaceflight including bed rest.

Increased dietary intake of omega-3 fatty acid protects bone in the general population (227-230) and in spaceflight analog studies, including bed rest and cell cultures (231). Although omega-3 fatty acids have not been studied in a controlled fashion during actual spaceflight, a positive correlation was found between fish intake and bone maintenance in astronauts (231). That is, those who ate more fish lost less bone (Figure 13). These data provide additional evidence of the potential importance of fish oils as a countermeasure for loss of muscle and bone, and for the health risks of radiation exposure during spaceflight. Studies showing positive effects of omega-3 fatty acids typically look at intake of fish or other food sources of these nutrients (232-234). Studies of fish oil supplements that are added to typical diets often fail to document any benefit (235-237), thus highlighting the need for

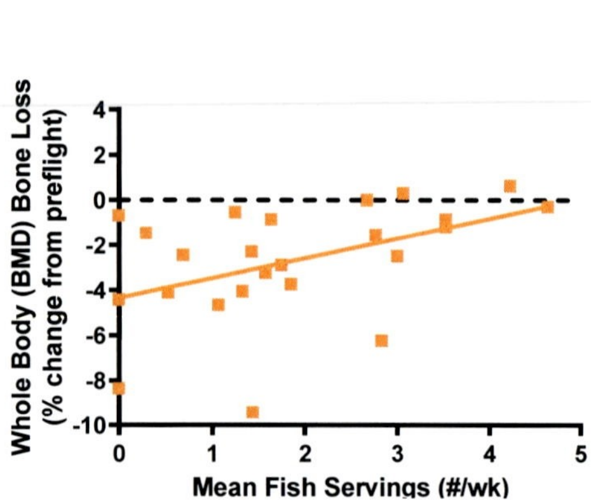

Figure 13. Relationship between fish intake during long-duration flight and loss of whole-body BMD after flights on the ISS. Figure adapted from (231).

dietary modification, and not simply supplementation.

Protein

As the major structural component of all cells in the body, protein includes molecules that perform many essential physiological functions, serving as enzymes, hormones, transporters, and other important molecules. The total energy contribution of protein to the average diet is about 15%. The nitrogen core of amino acids contributes to protein structure, along with nucleic acids, one of the major nitrogen-containing macromolecules.

Protein is one of the most important limiting factors when the body is deprived of energy, because essential amino acids are neither stored in the body nor can they be synthesized by the body. A complete depletion of energy and protein reserves is said to be the cause of death from starvation. It is estimated that when 33% to 50% of total body protein is lost, death results (238). Loss of more than 40% to 50% of initial body mass is not compatible with life (170, 239). In one case report, individuals on a hunger strike lost 30% of their total body mass and 19% of total body protein before they died (168, 169).

Maintaining a proper protein intake is vital because both low-protein and high-protein diets can cause harm (and, at the extreme, death). A low-protein diet (i.e., below the recommended dietary allowance) for up to 4 weeks can decrease calcium absorption and cause increased secretion of parathyroid hormone in otherwise healthy subjects (240, 241). Low-protein diets are associated with loss of bone density (242, 243) and as reviewed in (244).

Provision of protein and intake during spaceflight typically exceed the recommendations (1), Chapter 2, Table 1, and Figure 14. European studies have shown that on long-duration missions, reaching (or exceeding) nominal protein intakes is common; however, on short flights (e.g., Space Shuttle missions), protein intake is less than the recommended amount because of insufficient food intake (113). On ISS missions, protein intake, on average, is more than adequate (Figure 14, Figure 15).

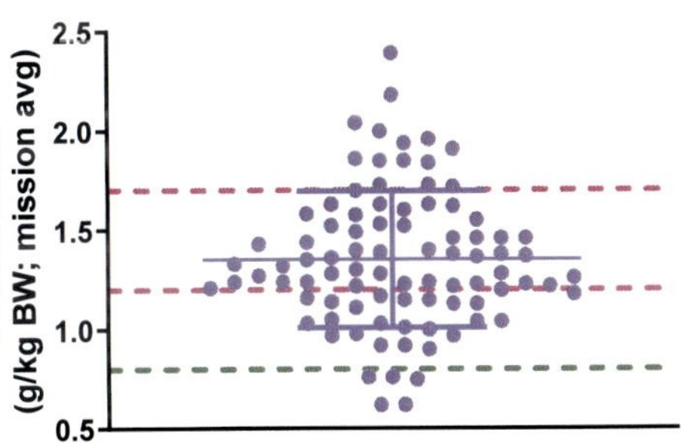

Figure 14. Protein intake during spaceflight on ISS missions. Each point represents the reported average intake for an individual crewmember over the course of their mission. Green dashed line represents the US Recommended Dietary Allowance (41), and the range of protein intakes (1.2.-1.7 g/kg) recommended by the American Dietetic Association, Dietitians of Canada, and American College of Sports Medicine for high-intensity athletes (245).

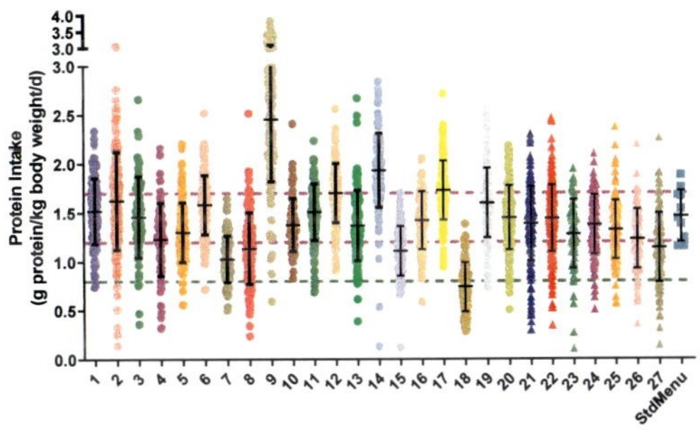

Figure 15. Protein intake for 27 ISS astronauts and the "standard menu." Each symbol represents a day's intake during flight. Circles are male astronauts, and triangles are females. These represent crewmembers who recorded dietary intake with the ISS FIT App or kept a detailed food log. Standard menu data are calculated for an 83 kg individual—i.e., the average male astronaut's body mass. The black lines represent mean ± SD for each crewmember. Dashed lines are as described in Figure 14.

Too much dietary protein and too high dietary acid loads may lead to a transient low-grade metabolic acidosis, which consequently may increase osteoclasts activity and lead to lower BMD over time (246). If protein intake reaches levels of 1.6-1.8 g/kg body weight/d during physical inactivity (bed rest or spaceflight) when osteoclasts are already activated, this may exaggerate the bone resorbing effect (247-249).

Some data suggest that during the recovery period after short-duration Space Shuttle flights, protein was a limiting nutrient, and that competition for substrate to replenish plasma proteins and muscle mass strains the system (250). This has not been tested experimentally; however, obviously, good nutrition is required for rapid return to optimal health.

Nutrients Associated with Energy Metabolism

Many micronutrients—vitamins and minerals—are involved in energy homeostasis, including thiamin, riboflavin, niacin, pantothenic acid, iodine, manganese, and even chromium. We previously reviewed sources of these nutrients, their functions, deficiency symptoms, and concerns for spaceflight for these nutrients (1). In general, few data are available on these nutrients with respect to effects of spaceflight, or on the availability and stability of these nutrients in the space food system. No specific concerns have been raised at this point; however, we must ensure that astronauts consume adequate amounts of these nutrients and understand their metabolism during spaceflight, and the nutrients must remain stable in the food system during exploration missions (see additional discussion in Chapter 3).

Although B vitamins are associated with energy metabolism, they are also linked to the development of optic disc edema—a disorder associated with spaceflight. Changes in vitamin B status in space travelers are reviewed in detail in Chapter 10.

Vitamin B_6

Vitamin B_6 comprises a group of three compounds and their 5-phosphates (P): pyridoxal (PL) and PLP; pyridoxine (PN) and PNP; and pyridoxamine (PM) and PMP (251). We previously reviewed the basics of vitamin B_6 function, sources, and deficiency symptoms (1). Weightlessness has been shown to reduce the cross-sectional area of muscle fibers and is associated with a change from type I to type II muscle fibers (252). Because vitamin B_6 is stored mainly in muscle tissue (253), a decrease in muscle cross-sectional area could reduce the amount of the vitamin that is stored. Increased excretion of 4-pyridoxic acid (4-PA) during bed rest, a finding observed in short- (254) and long-duration bed rest studies (255), likely reflects this loss of muscle stores of vitamin B_6.

Given the changes observed in vitamin B_6 metabolism during bed rest, vitamin B_6 status during and after long-duration spaceflight warrants further attention. Deficiency of vitamin B_6 causes a decrease in the synthesis of serotonin and catecholamines, which has been shown to be associated with depression (256). Excess vitamin B_6 can lead to neuropathy (257-259), which can be of concern given the very high content of this vitamin in many supplements and energy drinks.

Thiamin

Thiamin functions as a coenzyme in the metabolism of carbohydrates and branched-chain amino acids. This process is mediated by enhancing the activity of pyruvate dehydrogenase and thereby reducing generation of the cofactors nicotinamide-adenine dinucleotide

(NADH2) and flavin-adenine dinucleotide (FADH2), which leads to the synthesis of adenosine triphosphate (ATP) in the respiratory chain. We previously reviewed the basics of thiamin function (1). Thiamin is a therapeutic option for mitochondrial diseases because it supports the availability of mitochondrial electron transport chain substrate and the activity of pyruvate dehydrogenase, leading to increased catabolism of pyruvate to acetyl-CoA, (260).

In a study of 17 astronauts on ISS missions, estimated thiamin intake during flight was 1.87 ± 0.60 mg/d (249), approximately 50% higher than the recommended intake of 1.2 mg/d for men, and 1.1 mg/d for women. Thiamin has been shown to be one of the more unstable nutrients in food during storage (84) (Figure 6), as discussed earlier, and it will be essential to establish stability for exploration missions.

No change in the activity of erythrocyte transketolase, an index of thiamin status (261), was detected before and after spaceflight (Figure 16). Similarly, no changes were observed in erythrocyte transketolase activation after a 30-day bed rest study (262).

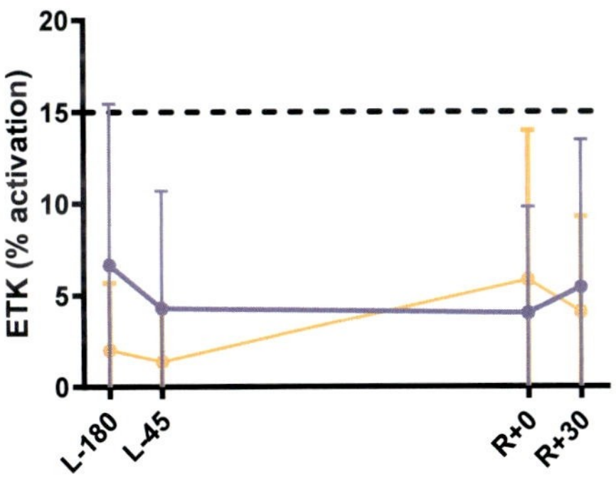

Figure 16. Erythrocyte transketolase activation before and after flight in ISS astronauts. Data are mean ± SD of 49 male astronauts (blue line) and 12 female astronauts (gold line). The black dashed line represents the normal range (i.e., <15% is considered adequate thiamine status).

Riboflavin

Riboflavin is a water-soluble B vitamin (vitamin B_2). In its role in the mitochondrial electron transport chain, riboflavin acts as a cofactor (flavin mononucleotide and flavin adenine dinucleotide) to metabolize fat, protein, and carbohydrate into energy. The basics of riboflavin function have been reviewed previously (1). Because riboflavin is required to synthesize flavoproteins, and flavoproteins are involved in lipid metabolism, deficiency of riboflavin primarily affects lipid metabolism and consequently ATP synthesis. Hence, symptoms such as skin dyscrasias, which are associated with deficiencies in essential fatty acids, are also seen with marginal riboflavin deficiencies (263). Riboflavin is also required to maintain reduced glutathione, an endogenous antioxidant; therefore, the antioxidant defense mechanism is also affected by riboflavin deficiency (263). Riboflavin status is analyzed by measuring the activation of erythrocyte glutathione reductase.

Deficiencies of riboflavin are rare but can be present in individuals who consume a poor diet, have malabsorption issues, or have reached an advanced age (264). Veganism, alcoholism, and certain medications (e.g., birth control pills, chemotherapeutic agents, antibiotics) can also lower riboflavin status (265).

To date, no studies have reported changes in the activation of erythrocytes glutathione reductase during spaceflight (Figure 17). In a study of 17 astronauts on the ISS, riboflavin intake was estimated at 2.16 ± 0.69 mg/d (249), well above the 1.1 and 1.3 mg/d recommended for women and men, respectively (38, 266). In 3-week (254) and 30-day (262) bed rest studies, no change occurred in erythrocytes glutathione reductase activation. Nonetheless, riboflavin levels could degrade in food that is stored during future longer-duration exploration missions, and it will be important to establish the supply needs for these missions.

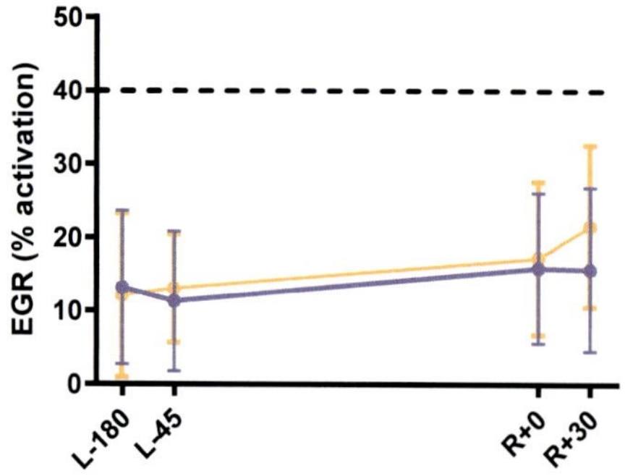

Figure 17. Erythrocyte glutathione reductase activation before and after flight in ISS astronauts. Data are mean ± SD of 49 male astronauts (blue line) and 12 female astronauts (gold line). The black dashed line represents the normal range (i.e., <40% is consider adequate riboflavin status).

Niacin

Niacin is a precursor of nicotinamide adenine dinucleotide (NAD), which functions in most energy-producing reactions that metabolize carbohydrates, fats, proteins, and alcohol. Unlike other water-soluble vitamins, niacin can be synthesized in limited amounts from the indispensable amino acid tryptophan. In its reduced form, NADH is used as substrate to generate ATP in the respiration chain in mitochondria. The basics of niacin function have been reviewed previously (1). Although niacin could degrade in foods stored long-term in a microgravity and space radiation environment, niacin does not appear to be of concern (84). One study demonstrated that niacin concentration was preserved in freeze-dried black tomato powder, a fruit rich in water-soluble vitamins, for up to 274 days during spaceflight (267).

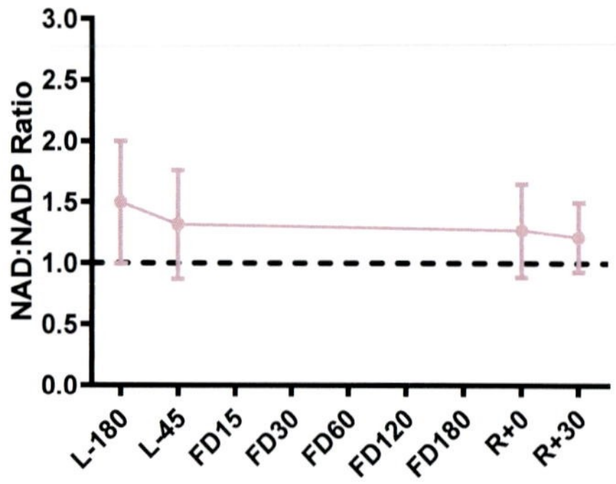

Figure 18. NAD:NADP in 23 ISS astronauts before and after flight. An NAD:NADP ratio >1.0 is considered to reflect adequate niacin status.

Niacin status in astronauts is assessed with the ratio of erythrocyte NAD:NADP (268), and, in general, crews are in good status (Figure 18). Given the processing required for this test, the niacin status may only be evaluated before and after flight.

Niacin intake in a study of 17 astronauts was estimated at 25.6 ± 9.3 mg niacin equivalents/d (249), more than the requirement of 14 and 16 mg/d for women and men, respectively. The ISS "standard menu" often exceeds this estimate, as do astronauts, depending on their food (and, in some cases, supplement) selections (Figure 19). Although there is no upper limit for natural sources of niacin, consumption of niacin from supplements and fortification should not exceed

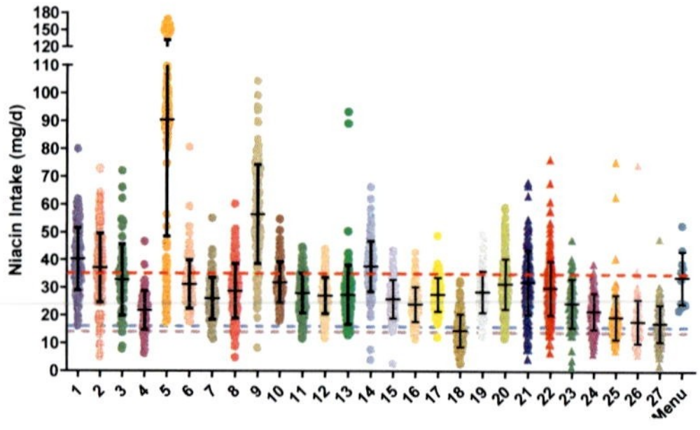

Figure 19. Niacin intake in 27 astronauts and the ISS "standard menu." Each symbol represents a day's intake during flight. Circles are male astronauts, and triangles are females. These represent crewmembers who recorded dietary intake with the ISS FIT App or kept a detailed food log. The black lines represent mean ± SD for each crewmember. Dashed lines represent required intakes for men (blue line) and women (purple line), red line represents the upper limit for niacin intake from supplements or fortification (266).

35 mg/d, given risks of vasodilatory effects, i.e., flushing as a critical adverse effect, along with risk of headaches, which are likely secondary to increased intracranial blood flow (266).

Pantothenic acid

Pantothenic acid is required for the synthesis of coenzyme A, which is essential—with regard to energy metabolism—for metabolizing and synthesizing fatty acids (269). Hence, pantothenic acid is mandatory for synthesis of acetyl-CoA, the substrate that enters the citric acid cycle to convert the reduced cofactors NADH and FADH2 to energy rich substances. The basics of pantothenic acid function have been reviewed previously (1, 270). Deficiency of pantothenic acid is very rare and is only observed in rare cases of severe malnutrition.

Pantothenic acid intake in a study of 17 astronauts was estimated at 6.63 ± 2.93 mg/d (249), more than the requirement of 5 mg/d for both women and men. Space food, however, is rather balanced with regard to supply of pantothenic acid, and thus further research on this topic is not considered a high priority at this time.

Iodine

The mineral iodine is essential for synthesizing thyroid hormones (triiodothyronine [T3] and thyroxin [T4]), which are required to regulate basal energy metabolism and control metabolic processes such as energy production, lipolysis and glycolysis. Iodine excretion in 24-hour urine collections is a valid method to judge iodine intake because most dietary intake is excreted in urine. In general, when the range of urinary iodine excretion lies between 0.8 and 1.6 µmol/L the iodine intake is considered sufficient.

Iodine excretion was determined in two ISS experiments—the Nutrition Supplemental Medical Objective (SMO) and Biochemical Profile—and, with the exception of a few outliers, generally are within normal range (Figure 20). Data from the 1-year twin study demonstrate that iodine intake was sufficient during spaceflight, at least for that astronaut, being on average 2.6 µmol/day (19). Iodine deficiency can lead to insufficient synthesis of T3 and T4. Within the thyroid gland, associated increases in cell development can cause enlargement of the gland. Additionally, iodine deficiency decreases basal metabolic rate leading to lower TEE.

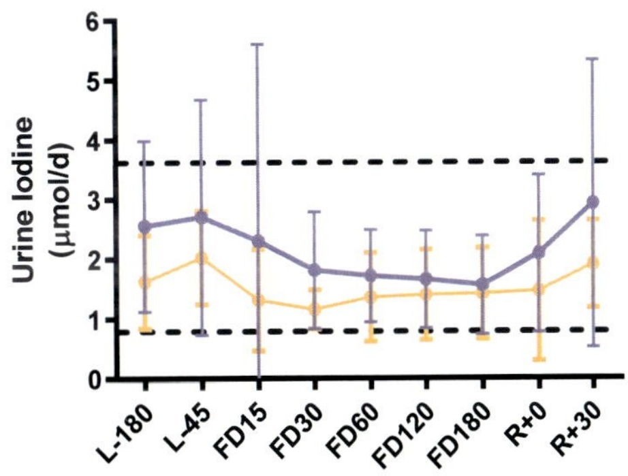

Figure 20. Urine iodine excretion in male (blue line) and female (gold line) ISS astronauts. Black dashed line represents normal limits.

Manganese

Manganese is a micronutrient that functions as a cofactor for enzymes involved in energy production in the human body, mainly in the metabolism of carbohydrates and amino acids (271, 272). For instance, pyruvate carboxylase and phosphoenolpyruvate carboxykinase are enzymes involved in gluconeogenesis from non-carbohydrate sources such as amino acids. Through these enzymes, manganese plays a role in regulating blood glucose levels

(271). The basics of manganese function have been reviewed previously (1, 271). Dietary manganese should be provided in adequate amounts, considering the likelihood of developing glucose intolerance during exploration missions.

In a study of 17 ISS astronauts, manganese intake was 5.17 ± 1.67 mg/d, compared to the recommended intake of 1.8 and 2.3 mg/d for women and men, respectively (273, 274). Manganese status is difficult to assess, and has not been attempted in astronauts, to our knowledge.

Chromium

Chromium is a trace element that is involved in energy metabolism by improving the efficiency of insulin. Scientists do not have a clear understanding of how chromium might affect glucose metabolism, but a widely accepted hypothesis is that this is achieved through the involvement of an oligopeptide named chromodulin, which binds chromium (275). Chromodulin is thought to cause an insulin-sensitive stimulation of the insulin receptor, thereby amplifying the insulin signaling (276).

Because no symptoms of chromium deficiency have been established, in 2014, the European Food and Safety Authority concluded that there was insufficient evidence demonstrating a beneficial effect of chromium, and that defining an adequate intake of chromium therefore was not appropriate (277). Animal studies, however, have demonstrated beneficial effects on glucose tolerance and insulin resistance (278). Future research is necessary to investigate whether chromium could play a role in mitigating this effect, considering that insulin resistance could develop in exploration missions.

References for Chapter 4

1. Smith SM, Zwart SR, Kloeris V, Heer M. Nutritional biochemistry of space flight. New York: Nova Science Publishers; 2009.

6. Douglas GL, Zwart SR, Smith SM. Space food for thought: Challenges and considerations for food and nutrition on exploration missions. J Nutr. 2020;150:2242-4.

7. Leach CS, Alfrey CP, Suki WN, Leonard JI, Rambaut PC, Inners LD, Smith SM, Lane HW, Krauhs JM. Regulation of body fluid compartments during short-term spaceflight. J Appl Physiol (1985). 1996;81:105-16.

19. Garrett-Bakelman FE, Darshi M, Green SJ, Gur RC, Lin L, Macias BR, McKenna MJ, Meydan C, Mishra T, Nasrini J, Piening BD, Rizzardi LF, Sharma K, Siamwala JH, Taylor L, Vitaterna MH, Afkarian M, Afshinnekoo E, Ahadi S, Ambati A, Arya M, Bezdan D, Callahan CM, Chen S, Choi AMK, Chlipala GE, Contrepois K, Covington M, Crucian BE, De Vivo I, Dinges DF, Ebert DJ, Feinberg JI, Gandara JA, George KA, Goutsias J, Grills GS, Hargens AR, Heer M, Hillary RP, Hoofnagle AN, Hook VYH, Jenkinson G, Jiang P, Keshavarzian A, Laurie SS, Lee-McMullen B, Lumpkins SB, MacKay M, Maienschein-Cline MG, Melnick AM, Moore TM, Nakahira K, Patel HH, Pietrzyk R, Rao V, Saito R, Salins DN, Schilling JM, Sears DD, Sheridan CK, Stenger MB, Tryggvadottir R, Urban AE, Vaisar T, Van Espen B, Zhang J, Ziegler MG, Zwart SR, Charles JB, Kundrot CE, Scott GBI, Bailey SM, Basner M, Feinberg AP, Lee SMC, Mason CE, Mignot E, Rana BK, Smith SM, Snyder MP, Turek FW. The NASA Twins Study: A multidimensional analysis of a year-long human spaceflight. Science. 2019;364.

38. National Aeronautics and Space Administration Johnson Space Center. Nutrition requirements for exploration missions up to 365 days. Report No.: JSC-67378. Houston, TX: Lyndon B. Johnson Space Center; 2020.

40. World Health Organization. Energy and protein requirements. Report of a joint FAO/WHO/UNU expert consultation. Geneva, Switzerland: World Health Organization; 1985.

41. Institute of Medicine. Dietary reference intakes for energy, carbohydrate, fiber, fat, fatty acids, cholesterol, protein, and amino acids (macronutrients). Washington, DC: National Academy Press; 2002.

52. Olabi AA, Lawless HT, Hunter JB, Levitsky DA, Halpern BP. The effect of microgravity and space flight on the chemical senses. J Food Sci. 2002;67:468-78.

84. Cooper M, Perchonok M, Douglas GL. Initial assessment of the nutritional quality of the space food system over three years of ambient storage. NPJ Microgravity. 2017;3:17.

88. Carpentier WR, Charles JB, Shelhamer M, Hackler AS, Johnson TL, Domingo CMM, Sutton JP, Scott GBI, Wotring VE. Biomedical findings from NASA's Project Mercury: a case series. NPJ Microgravity. 2018;4:6.

98. Smith MC, Berry CA. Dinner on the moon. Nutr Today. 1969;4:37-42.

99. Waligora JM, Horrigan DJ. Metabolism and heat dissipation during Apollo EVA periods. In: Johnston RS, Dietlein LF, Berry CA, editors. Biomedical results of Apollo (NASA SP-368). Washington, DC: National Aeronautics and Space Administration; 1975. p. 115-28.

100. Lane HW, Gretebeck RJ, Smith SM. Nutrition, endocrinology, and body composition during space flight. Nutr Res. 1998;18:1923-34.

101. Lane HW, Gretebeck RJ, Schoeller DA, Davis-Street J, Socki RA, Gibson EK. Comparison of ground-based and space flight energy expenditure and water turnover in middle-aged healthy male US astronauts. Am J Clin Nutr. 1997;65:4-12.

102. Stein TP, Leskiw MJ, Schluter MD, Hoyt RW, Lane HW, Gretebeck RE, LeBlanc AD. Energy expenditure and balance during spaceflight on the space shuttle. Am J Physiol. 1999;276:R1739-48.

103. Schoeller DA, Ravussin E, Schutz Y, Acheson KJ, Baertschi P, Jequier E. Energy expenditure by doubly labeled water: validation in humans and proposed calculation. Am J Physiol. 1986;250:R823-30.

104. Gretebeck RJ, Schoeller DA, Gibson EK, Lane HW. Energy expenditure during antiorthostatic bed rest (simulated microgravity). J Appl Physiol (1985). 1995;78:2207-11.

105. Stein TP, Schluter MD, Leskiw MJ. Cortisol, insulin and leptin during space flight and bed rest. J Gravit Physiol. 1999;6:P85-6.

106. Lovejoy JC, Smith SR, Zachwieja JJ, Bray GA, Windhauser MM, Wickersham PJ, Veldhuis JD, Tulley R, de la Bretonne JA. Low-dose T(3) improves the bed rest model of simulated weightlessness in men and women. Am J Physiol. 1999;277:E370-9.

107. Laurens C, Simon C, Vernikos J, Gauquelin-Koch G, Blanc S, Bergouignan A. Revisiting the role of exercise countermeasure on the regulation of energy balance during space flight. Front Physiol. 2019;10:321.

108. Stahn AC, Werner A, Opatz O, Maggioni MA, Steinach M, von Ahlefeld VW, Moore A, Crucian BE, Smith SM, Zwart SR, Schlabs T, Mendt S, Trippel T, Koralewski E, Koch J, Choukér A, Reitz G, Shang P, Rocker L, Kirsch KA, Gunga HC. Increased core body temperature in astronauts during long-duration space missions. Sci Rep. 2017;7:16180.

109. Neff LM, Hoffmann ME, Zeiss DM, Lowry K, Edwards M, Rodriguez SM, Wachsberg KN, Kushner R, Landsberg L. Core body temperature is lower in postmenopausal women than premenopausal women: potential implications for energy metabolism and midlife weight gain. Cardiovasc Endocrinol. 2016;5:151-4.

110. Smith SM, Davis-Street JE, Rice BL, Nillen JL, Gillman PL, Block G. Nutritional status assessment in semiclosed environments: ground-based and space flight studies in humans. J Nutr. 2001;131:2053-61.

111. Smith SM, Zwart SR, Block G, Rice BL, Davis-Street JE. The nutritional status of astronauts is altered after long-term space flight aboard the International Space Station. J Nutr. 2005;135:437-43.

112. Smith SM, Wastney ME, O'Brien KO, Morukov BV, Larina IM, Abrams SA, Davis-Street JE, Oganov V, Shackelford LC. Bone markers, calcium metabolism, and calcium kinetics during extended-duration space flight on the Mir space station. J Bone Miner Res. 2005;20:208-18.

113. Heer M, Boerger A, Kamps N, Mika C, Korr C, Drummer C. Nutrient supply during recent European missions. Pflugers Arch. 2000;441:R8-14.

114. Johnson PC, Leach CS, Rambaut PC. Estimates of fluid and energy balances of Apollo 17. Aerosp Med. 1973;44:1227-30.

115. Altman PL, Talbot JM. Nutrition and metabolism in spaceflight. J Nutr. 1987;117:421-7.

116. Rambaut PC, Smith MC, Jr, Wheeler HO. Nutritional studies. In: Johnston RS, Dietlein LF, Berry CA, editors. Biomedical results of Apollo (NASA SP-368). Washington, DC: National Aeronautics and Space Administration; 1975. p. 277-302.

117. Rambaut PC, Leach CS, Johnson PC. Calcium and phosphorus change of the Apollo 17 crew members. Nutr Metab. 1975;18:62-9.

118. Stein TP, Schluter MD. Excretion of amino acids by humans during space flight. Acta Astronaut. 1998;42:205-14.

119. Heer M. Nutritional interventions related to bone turnover in European space missions and simulation models. Nutrition. 2002;18:853-6.

120. Vorobyov EI, Gazenko OG, Genin AM, Egorov AD. Medical results of Salyut-6 manned space flights. Aviat Space Environ Med. 1983;54:S31-40.

121. Rambaut PC, Leach CS, Leonard JI. Observations in energy balance in man during spaceflight. Am J Physiol. 1977;233:R208-12.

122. Leach CS, Rambaut PC. Biochemical responses of the Skylab crewmen: an overview. In: Johnston RS, Dietlein LF, editors. Biomedical results from Skylab (NASA SP-377). Washington, DC: National Aeronautics and Space Administration; 1977. p. 204-16.

123. Drummer C, Hesse C, Baisch F, Norsk P, Elmann-Larsen B, Gerzer R, Heer M. Water and sodium balances and their relation to body mass changes in microgravity. Eur J Clin Invest. 2000;30:1066-75.

124. Smith SM, Heer MA, Shackelford LC, Sibonga JD, Ploutz-Snyder L, Zwart SR. Benefits for bone from resistance exercise and nutrition in long-duration spaceflight: evidence from biochemistry and densitometry. J Bone Miner Res. 2012;27:1896-906.

125. Bourland C, Kloeris V, Rice B, Vodovotz Y. Food systems for space and planetary flights. In: Lane HW, Schoeller DA, editors. Nutrition in spaceflight and weightlessness models. Boca Raton, FL: CRC Press; 2000. p. 19-40.

126. Smith SM, Lane HW, Zwart SR. Spaceflight metabolism and nutritional support. In: Barratt MR, Baker ES, Pool SL, editors. Principles of clinical medicine for space flight, 2nd edition. New York: Springer; 2019. p. 413-39.

127. Smith SM, Zwart SR. Nutritional biochemistry of spaceflight. Adv Clin Chem. 2008;46:87-130.

128. Lane HW, Smith SM. Nutrition in space. In: Shils ME, Olson JA, Shike M, Ross AC, editors. Modern nutrition in health and disease. 9th ed. Baltimore, MD: Lippincott Williams & Wilkins; 1999. p. 783-8.

129. Agureev AN, Kalandarov S, Segal DE. [Optimization of cosmonauts' nutrition during the period of acute adaptation and at the closing stage of the mission]. Aviakosm Ekolog Med. 1997;31:47-51.

130. Baranski S, Kubiczkowa J, Piorko A, Skibniewski F, Bryanov, II, Milova EP, Nefedova MV, Yakovleva IJ. Electrogustometric investigations during manned space flight. Aviat Space Environ Med. 1983;54:1-5.

131. Seddon MR, Fettman MJ, Phillips RW. Practical and clinical nutritional concerns during spaceflight. Am J Clin Nutr. 1994;60:825S-30S.

132. Taylor AJ, Beauchamp J, Briand L, Demaria Pesce V, Heer M, Hummel T, McGrane S, Margot C, Pieters S, Pittia P, Spence C. A taste for space. Food Sci Technol. 2019;33:36-41.

133. Taylor AJ, Beauchamp JD, Briand L, Heer M, Hummel T, Margot C, McGrane S, Pieters S, Pittia P, Spence C. Factors affecting flavor perception in space: Does the spacecraft environment influence food intake by astronauts? Compr Rev Food Sci Food Saf. 2020;19:3439-75.

134. Watt DG, Money KE, Bondar RL, Thirsk RB, Garneau M, Scully-Power P. Canadian medical experiments on Shuttle flight 41-G. Can Aeronaut Space J. 1985;31:215-26.

135. Budylina SM, Khvatova VA, Volozhin AI. Effect of orthostatic and antiorthostatic hypokinesia on taste sensitivity in men. Kosm Biol Aviakosm Med. 1976;10:27-30.

136. Kurliandskii V, Khvatova VA, Budylina SM. [Functional mobility of taste receptors of the tongue under conditions of prolonged hypodynamia]. Stomatologiia (Mosk). 1974;53:13-5.

137. Vickers ZM, Rice BL, Rose MS, Lane HW. Simulated microgravity [bed rest] has little influence on taste, odor or trigeminal sensitivity. J Sens Stud. 2001;16:23-32.

138. Lane HW, LeBlanc AD, Putcha L, Whitson PA. Nutrition and human physiological adaptations to space flight. Am J Clin Nutr. 1993;58:583-8.

139. Roda A, Mirasoli M, Guardigli M, Simoni P, Festi D, Afonin B, Vasilyeva G. Non-invasive panel tests for gastrointestinal motility monitoring within the MARS-500 Project. World J Gastroenterol. 2013;19:2208-16.

140. Smirnov KV, Ugolev AM. Digestion and absorption. In: Leach Huntoon CS, Antipov VV, Grigoriev AI, editors. Space biology and medicine Volume III, Book 1, Humans in spaceflight. Reston, VA: American Institute for Aeronautics and Astronautics; 1996. p. 211-30.

141. Heer M, Paloski WH. Space motion sickness: incidence, etiology, and countermeasures. Auton Neurosci. 2006;129:77-9.

142. Reschke MF, Bloomberg JJ, Harm DL, Paloski WH. Space flight and neurovestibular adaptation. J Clin Pharmacol. 1994;34:609-17.

143. Lackner JR, Dizio P. Space motion sickness. Exp Brain Res. 2006;175:377-99.

144. Nicogossian A. Medicine and space exploration. Lancet. 2003;362 Suppl:s8-9.

145. Debevec T, Bali TC, Simpson EJ, Macdonald IA, Eiken O, Mekjavic IB. Separate and combined effects of 21-day bed rest and hypoxic confinement on body composition. Eur J Appl Physiol. 2014;114:2411-25.

146. Debevec T, Pialoux V, Ehrstrom S, Ribon A, Eiken O, Mekjavic IB, Millet GP. FemHab: The effects of bed rest and hypoxia on oxidative stress in healthy women. J Appl Physiol (1985). 2016;120:930-8.

147. Smith SM, Zwart SR, Heer M, Hudson EK, Shackelford L, Morgan JLL. Men and women in space: bone loss and kidney stone risk after long-duration spaceflight. J Bone Miner Res. 2014;29:1639-45.

148. Lane HW, Schulz LO. Nutritional questions relevant to space flight. Annu Rev Nutr. 1992;12:257-78.

149. Leonard JI, Leach CS, Rambaut PC. Quantitation of tissue loss during prolonged space flight. Am J Clin Nutr. 1983;38:667-79.

150. LaChance PA, Berry CA. Luncheon in space. Nutr Today. 1967:2-11.

151. Leach CS. Medical results from STS 1-4: analysis of body fluids. Aviat Space Environ Med. 1983;54 (12 Suppl):S50-4.

152. Smith SM, Wastney ME, Morukov BV, Larina IM, Nyquist LE, Abrams SA, Taran EN, Shih CY, Nillen JL, Davis-Street JE, Rice BL, Lane HW. Calcium metabolism before, during, and after a 3-mo spaceflight: kinetic and biochemical changes. Am J Physiol. 1999;277:R1-10.

153. Zwart SR, Launius RD, Coen GK, Morgan JLL, Charles JB, Smith SM. Body mass changes during long-duration spaceflight. Aviat Space Environ Med. 2014;85:897-904.

154. Smith SM, Zwart SR, Heer M. Human adaptation to spaceflight: The role of nutrition (NP-2014-10-018-JSC). Houston, TX: National Aeronautics and Space Administration Lyndon B. Johnson Space Center; 2014.

155. Brozek J, Grande F, Taylor HL, Anderson JT, Buskirk ER, Keys A. Changes in body weight and body dimensions in men performing work on a low calorie carbohydrate diet. J Appl Physiol. 1957;10:412-20.

156. Faintuch J, Soriano FG, Ladeira JP, Janiszewski M, Velasco IT, Gamma-Rodrigues JJ. Changes in body fluid and energy compartments during prolonged hunger strike. Rev Hosp Clin Fac Med Sao Paulo. 2000;55:47-54.

157. Johnson PC, Driscoll TB, Alexander WC, Lambertsen CJ. Body fluid volume changes during a 14-day continuous exposure to 5.2% O2 in N2 at pressure equivalent to 100 FSW (4 ata). Aerosp Med. 1973;44:860-3.

158. Stein TP, Leskiw MJ, Schluter MD, Donaldson MR, Larina I. Protein kinetics during and after long-duration spaceflight on MIR. Am J Physiol. 1999;276:E1014-21.

159. Biolo G, Ciocchi B, Stulle M, Bosutti A, Barazzoni R, Zanetti M, Antonione R, Lebenstedt M, Platen P, Heer M, Guarnieri G. Calorie restriction accelerates the catabolism of lean body mass during 2 wk of bed rest. Am J Clin Nutr. 2007;86:366-72.

160. Wade CE, Miller MM, Baer LA, Moran MM, Steele MK, Stein TP. Body mass, energy intake, and water consumption of rats and humans during space flight. Nutrition. 2002;18:829-36.

161. Florian JP, Baisch FJ, Heer M, Pawelczyk JA. Caloric restriction decreases orthostatic tolerance independently from 6 degrees head-down bedrest. PLoS One. 2015;10:e0118812.

162. Florian JP, Baisch FJ, Heer M, Pawelczyk JA. Caloric restriction diminishes the pressor response to static exercise. Extrem Physiol Med. 2016;5:2.

163. Blanc S, Somody L, Gharib C. Are energy metabolism alterations involved in cardiovascular deconditioning after weightlessness? An hypothesis. Pflugers Arch. 2000;441:R39-47.

164. Ferrando AA, Paddon-Jones D, Wolfe RR. Alterations in protein metabolism during space flight and inactivity. Nutrition. 2002;18:837-41.

165. Ihle R, Loucks AB. Dose-response relationships between energy availability and bone turnover in young exercising women. J Bone Miner Res. 2004;19:1231-40.

166. Baek K, Barlow AA, Allen MR, Bloomfield SA. Food restriction and simulated microgravity: effects on bone and serum leptin. J Appl Physiol (1985). 2008;104:1086-93.

167. Oritsland NA. Starvation survival and body composition in mammals with particular reference to Homo sapiens. Bull Math Biol. 1990;52:643-55.

168. Korcok M. Hunger strikers may have died of fat, not protein, loss. JAMA. 1981;246:1878-9.

169. Leiter LA, Marliss EB. Survival during fasting may depend on fat as well as protein stores. JAMA. 1982;248:2306-7.

170. Phillips WJ. Starvation and survival: some military considerations. Mil Med. 1994;159:513-6.

171. Murphy NE, Carrigan CT, Philip Karl J, Pasiakos SM, Margolis LM. Threshold of energy deficit and lower-body performance declines in military personnel: A meta-regression. Sports Med. 2018;48:2169-78.

172. Biolo G, Agostini F, Simunic B, Sturma M, Torelli L, Preiser JC, Deby-Dupont G, Magni P, Strollo F, di Prampero P, Guarnieri G, Mekjavic IB, Pisot R, Narici MV. Positive energy balance is associated with accelerated muscle atrophy and increased erythrocyte glutathione turnover during 5 wk of bed rest. Am J Clin Nutr. 2008;88:950-8.

173. Blanc S, Normand S, Pachiaudi C, Fortrat JO, Laville M, Gharib C. Fuel homeostasis during physical inactivity induced by bed rest. J Clin Endocrinol Metab. 2000;85:2223-33.

174. Bergouignan A, Momken I, Schoeller DA, Normand S, Zahariev A, Lescure B, Simon C, Blanc S. Regulation of energy balance during long-term physical inactivity induced by bed rest with and without exercise training. J Clin Endocrinol Metab. 2010;95:1045-53.

175. Bergouignan A, Rudwill F, Simon C, Blanc S. Physical inactivity as the culprit of metabolic inflexibility: evidence from bed-rest studies. J Appl Physiol (1985). 2011;111:1201-10.

176. Stein TP, Schluter MD, Galante AT, Soteropoulos P, Ramirez M, Bigbee A, Grindeland RE, Wade CE. Effect of hind limb muscle unloading on liver metabolism of rats. J Nutr Biochem. 2005;16:9-16.

177. Stein TP, Wade CE. Metabolic consequences of muscle disuse atrophy. J Nutr. 2005;135:1824S-8S.

178. Zahariev A, Bergouignan A, Caloin M, Normand S, Gauquelin-Koch G, Gharib C, Blanc S. Skinfold thickness versus isotope dilution for body fat assessment during simulated microgravity: results from three bed-rest campaigns in men and women with and without countermeasures. Eur J Appl Physiol. 2005;95:344-50.

179. Levine DS, Greenleaf JE. Immunosuppression during spaceflight deconditioning. Aviat Space Environ Med. 1998;69:172-7.

180. Stubbs RJ, Harbron CG, Murgatroyd PR, Prentice AM. Covert manipulation of dietary fat and energy density: effect on substrate flux and food intake in men eating ad libitum. Am J Clin Nutr. 1995;62:316-29.

181. Maaß H, Raabe W, Wegmann HM. Effects of microgravity on glucose tolerance. In: Sahm PR, Keller MH, Schiewe B, editors. Proceedings of the Norderney Symposium on Scientific Results of the German Spacelab Mission D-2. Norderney, Germany: Wissenschaftliche Projectführung D-2; 1995. p. 732-5.

182. Smirnov KV, Rubinova LG, Afonin BV, Noskov VB, Kravchenko VV. [Functional carbohydrate test during 237-day space flight]. Kosm Biol Aviakosm Med. 1991;25:61-2.

183. Alexandrov A, Gharib C, Grigoriev AI, Güell A, Kojarinov Y, Ruvinova L, Smirnov KV. [Oral glucose tolerance tests in man during a space flight of 150 days (Salyut 7-Soyuz T9)]. C R Seances Soc Biol Fil. 1985;179:192-5.

184. Biolo G, Ciocchi B, Stulle M, Piccoli A, Lorenzon S, Dal Mas V, Barazzoni R, Zanetti M, Guarnieri G. Metabolic consequences of physical inactivity. J Ren Nutr. 2005;15:49-53.

185. Vernikos-Danellis J, Leach CS, Winget CM, Goodwin AL, Rambaut PC. Changes in glucose, insulin, and growth hormone levels associated with bedrest. Aviat Space Environ Med. 1976;47:583-7.

186. Stuart CA, Shangraw RE, Prince MJ, Peters EJ, Wolfe RR. Bed-rest-induced insulin resistance occurs primarily in muscle. Metabolism. 1988;37:802-6.

187. Kenny HC, Rudwill F, Breen L, Salanova M, Blottner D, Heise T, Heer M, Blanc S, O'Gorman DJ. Bed rest and resistive vibration exercise unveil novel links between skeletal muscle mitochondrial function and insulin resistance. Diabetologia. 2017;60:1491-501.

188. Rudwill F, O'Gorman D, Lefai E, Chery I, Zahariev A, Normand S, Pagano AF, Chopard A, Damiot A, Laurens C, Hodson L, Canet-Soulas E, Heer M, Meuthen PF, Buehlmeier J, Baecker N, Meiller L, Gauquelin-Koch G, Blanc S, Simon C, Bergouignan A. Metabolic inflexibility is an early marker of bed-rest-induced glucose intolerance even when fat mass is stable. J Clin Endocrinol Metab. 2018;103:1910-20.

189. Macho L, Kvetnansky R, Vigas M, Nemeth S, Popova I, Tigranian RA, Noskov VB, Serova L, Grigoriev IA. Effect of space flights on plasma hormone levels in man and in experimental animal. Acta Astronaut. 1991;23:117-21.

190. Stein TP, Schulter MD, Boden G. Development of insulin resistance by astronauts during spaceflight. Aviat Space Environ Med. 1994;65:1091-6.

191. Heer M, Baecker N, Wnendt S, Fischer A, Biolo G, Frings-Meuthen P. How fast is recovery of impaired glucose tolerance after 21-day bed rest (NUC study) in healthy adults? Sci World J. 2014;2014:803083.

192. Hughson RL, Robertson AD, Arbeille P, Shoemaker JK, Rush JW, Fraser KS, Greaves DK. Increased postflight carotid artery stiffness and inflight insulin resistance resulting from 6-mo spaceflight in male and female astronauts. Am J Physiol Heart Circ Physiol. 2016;310:H628-38.

193. Lane HW, Rambaut PC. Nutrition. In: Nicogossian AE, Huntoon CL, Pool SL, editors. Space physiology and medicine. 3rd ed. Philadelphia: Lea & Febiger; 1994. p. 305-16.

194. Pietrzyk RA, Feiveson AH, Whitson PA. Mathematical model to estimate risk of calcium-containing renal stones. Miner Electrolyte Metab. 1999;25:199-203.

195. Pietrzyk RA, Jones JA, Sams CF, Whitson PA. Renal stone formation among astronauts. Aviat Space Environ Med. 2007;78:A9-13.

196. Zerwekh JE, Odvina CV, Wuermser LA, Pak CY. Reduction of renal stone risk by potassium-magnesium citrate during 5 weeks of bed rest. J Urol. 2007;177:2179-84.

197. Cai QY, Zhou ZJ, Luo R, Gan J, Li SP, Mu DZ, Wan CM. Safety and tolerability of the ketogenic diet used for the treatment of refractory childhood epilepsy: a systematic review of published prospective studies. World J Pediatr. 2017;13:528-36.

198. Lipman RL, Ulvedal F, Schnure JJ, Bradley EM, Lecocq FR. Gluco-regulatory hormone response to 2-deoxy-d-glucose infusion in normal subjects at bedrest. Metabolism. 1970;19:980-7.

199. Dolkas CB, Greenleaf JE. Insulin and glucose responses during bed rest with isotonic and isometric exercise. J Appl Physiol Respir Environ Exerc Physiol. 1977;43:1033-8.

200. Paulsrud JR, Pensler L, Whitten CF, Stewart S, Holman RT. Essential fatty acid deficiency in infants induced by fat-free intravenous feeding. Am J Clin Nutr. 1972;25:897-904.

201. Holman RT. Polyunsaturated fatty acid profiles in human disease. In: Bazan NG, Paoletti R, Iacono JM, editors. New trends in nutrition, lipid research and cardiovascular diseases. New York: Alan R. Liss; 1981. p. 25-42.

202. Ritz P, Acheson KJ, Gachon P, Vico L, Bernard JJ, Alexandre C, Beaufrere B. Energy and substrate metabolism during a 42-day bed-rest in a head-down tilt position in humans. Eur J Appl Physiol Occup Physiol. 1998;78:308-14.

203. Kelley DE, Mandarino LJ. Fuel selection in human skeletal muscle in insulin resistance: a reexamination. Diabetes. 2000;49:677-83.

204. Rynders CA, Blanc S, DeJong N, Bessesen DH, Bergouignan A. Sedentary behaviour is a key determinant of metabolic inflexibility. J Physiol. 2018;596:1319-30.

205. Pagano AF, Brioche T, Arc-Chagnaud C, Demangel R, Chopard A, Py G. Short-term disuse promotes fatty acid infiltration into skeletal muscle. J Cachexia Sarcopenia Muscle. 2018;9:335-47.

206. Mazzucco S, Agostini F, Biolo G. Inactivity-mediated insulin resistance is associated with upregulated pro-inflammatory fatty acids in human cell membranes. Clin Nutr. 2010;29:386-90.

207. Macho L, Koska J, Ksinantova L, Pacak K, Hoff T, Noskov VB, Grigoriev AI, Vigas M, Kvetnansky R. The response of endocrine system to stress loads during space flight in human subject. Adv Space Res. 2003;31:1605-10.

208. Stein TP, Schluter MD, Moldawer LL. Endocrine relationships during human spaceflight. Am J Physiol. 1999;276:E155-62.

209. Smith SM, Heer M, Wang Z, Huntoon CL, Zwart SR. Long-duration space flight and bed rest effects on testosterone and other steroids. J Clin Endocrinol Metab. 2012;97:270-8.

210. Smith SM, Heer M, Shackelford LC, Sibonga JD, Spatz J, Pietrzyk RA, Hudson EK, Zwart SR. Bone metabolism and renal stone risk during International Space Station missions. Bone. 2015;81:712-20.

211. Davidson LA, Nguyen DV, Hokanson RM, Callaway ES, Isett RB, Turner ND, Dougherty ER, Wang N, Lupton JR, Carroll RJ, Chapkin RS. Chemopreventive n-3 polyunsaturated fatty acids reprogram genetic signatures during colon cancer initiation and progression in the rat. Cancer Res. 2004;64:6797-804.

212. Turner ND, Braby LA, Ford J, Lupton JR. Opportunities for nutritional amelioration of radiation-induced cellular damage. Nutrition. 2002;18:904-12.

213. Chapkin RS, Davidson LA, Ly L, Weeks BR, Lupton JR, McMurray DN. Immunomodulatory effects of (n-3) fatty acids: putative link to inflammation and colon cancer. J Nutr. 2007;137:200S-4S.

214. Hong MY, Bancroft LK, Turner ND, Davidson LA, Murphy ME, Carroll RJ, Chapkin RS, Lupton JR. Fish oil decreases oxidative DNA damage by enhancing apoptosis in rat colon. Nutr Cancer. 2005;52:166-75.

215. Sanders LM, Henderson CE, Hong MY, Barhoumi R, Burghardt RC, Wang N, Spinka CM, Carroll RJ, Turner ND, Chapkin RS, Lupton JR. An increase in reactive oxygen species by dietary fish oil coupled with the attenuation of antioxidant defenses by dietary pectin enhances rat colonocyte apoptosis. J Nutr. 2004;134:3233-8.

216. Jayedi A, Shab-Bidar S. Fish consumption and the risk of chronic disease: an umbrella review of meta-analyses of prospective cohort studies. Adv Nutr. 2020;11:1123-33.

217. Tisdale MJ. Molecular pathways leading to cancer cachexia. Physiology. 2005;20:340-8.

218. Whitehouse AS, Smith HJ, Drake JL, Tisdale MJ. Mechanism of attenuation of skeletal muscle protein catabolism in cancer cachexia by eicosapentaenoic acid. Cancer Res. 2001;61:3604-9.

219. Whitehouse AS, Tisdale MJ. Downregulation of ubiquitin-dependent proteolysis by eicosapentaenoic acid in acute starvation. Biochem Biophys Res Commun. 2001;285:598-602.

220. Tisdale MJ. Loss of skeletal muscle in cancer: biochemical mechanisms. Front Biosci. 2001;6:D164-74.

221. Tisdale MJ. Cancer anorexia and cachexia. Nutrition. 2001;17:438-42.

222. Wigmore SJ, Ross JA, Falconer JS, Plester CE, Tisdale MJ, Carter DC, Fearon KC. The effect of polyunsaturated fatty acids on the progress of cachexia in patients with pancreatic cancer. Nutrition. 1996;12(1 Suppl):S27-30.

223. Bayram I, Erbey F, Celik N, Nelson JL, Tanyeli A. The use of a protein and energy dense eicosapentaenoic acid containing supplement for malignancy-related weight loss in children. Pediatr Blood Cancer. 2009;52:571-4.

224. Tisdale MJ. Mechanisms of cancer cachexia. Physiol Rev. 2009;89:381-410.

225. Pappalardo G, Almeida A, Ravasco P. Eicosapentaenoic acid in cancer improves body composition and modulates metabolism. Nutrition. 2015;31:549-55.

226. Miotto PM, McGlory C, Bahniwal R, Kamal M, Phillips SM, Holloway GP. Supplementation with dietary omega-3 mitigates immobilization-induced reductions in skeletal muscle mitochondrial respiration in young women. FASEB J. 2019;33:8232-40.

227. Abdelhamid A, Hooper L, Sivakaran R, Hayhoe RPG, Welch A, Group P. The relationship between omega-3, omega-6 and total polyunsaturated fat and musculoskeletal health and functional status in adults: A systematic review and meta-analysis of RCTs. Calcif Tissue Int. 2019;105:353-72.

228. Griel AE, Kris-Etherton PM, Hilpert KF, Zhao G, West SG, Corwin RL. An increase in dietary n-3 fatty acids decreases a marker of bone resorption in humans. Nutr J. 2007;6:2-10.

229. Orchard TS, Ing SW, Lu B, Belury MA, Johnson K, Wactawski-Wende J, Jackson RD. The association of red blood cell n-3 and n-6 fatty acids with bone mineral density and hip fracture risk in the women's health initiative. J Bone Miner Res. 2013;28:505-15.

230. Mangano K, Kerstetter J, Kenny A, Insogna K, Walsh SJ. An investigation of the association between omega 3 FA and bone mineral density among older adults: results from the National Health and Nutrition Examination Survey years 2005-2008. Osteoporos Int. 2014;25:1033-41.

231. Zwart SR, Pierson D, Mehta S, Gonda S, Smith SM. Capacity of omega-3 fatty acids or eicosapentaenoic acid to counteract weightlessness-induced bone loss by inhibiting NF-kappaB activation: from cells to bed rest to astronauts. J Bone Miner Res. 2010;25:1049-57.

232. Orchard TS, Cauley JA, Frank GC, Neuhouser ML, Robinson JG, Snetselaar L, Tylavsky F, Wactawski-Wende J, Young AM, Lu B, Jackson RD. Fatty acid consumption and risk of fracture in the Women's Health Initiative. Am J Clin Nutr. 2010;92:1452-60.

233. Terano T. Effect of omega 3 polyunsaturated fatty acid ingestion on bone metabolism and osteoporosis. World Rev Nutr Diet. 2001;88:141-7.

234. Rousseau JH, Kleppinger A, Kenny AM. Self-reported dietary intake of omega-3 fatty acids and association with bone and lower extremity function. J Am Geriatric Soc. 2009;57:1781-8.

235. Rizos EC, Ntzani EE, Bika E, Kostapanos MS, Elisaf MS. Association between omega-3 fatty acid supplementation and risk of major cardiovascular disease events: a systematic review and meta-analysis. JAMA. 2012;308:1024-33.

236. Andreeva VA, Touvier M, Kesse-Guyot E, Julia C, Galan P, Hercberg S. B vitamin and/or omega-3 fatty acid supplementation and cancer: ancillary findings from the supplementation with folate, vitamins B_6 and B_{12}, and/or omega-3 fatty acids (SU.FOL.OM3) randomized trial. Arch Intern Med. 2012;172:540-7.

237. Bassey EJ, Littlewood JJ, Rothwell MC, Pye DW. Lack of effect of supplementation with essential fatty acids on bone mineral density in healthy pre- and postmenopausal women: two randomized controlled trials of Efacal v. calcium alone. Br J Nutr. 2000;83:629-35.

238. Silber T. Anorexia nervosa: morbidity and mortality. Pediatr Ann. 1984;13:851, 5-9.

239. Garrow JS, Fletcher K, Halliday D. Body composition in severe infantile malnutrition. J Clin Invest. 1965;44:417-25.

240. Kerstetter JE, Caseria DM, Mitnick ME, Ellison AF, Gay LF, Liskov TA, Carpenter TO, Insogna KL. Increased circulating concentrations of parathyroid hormone in healthy, young women consuming a protein-restricted diet. Am J Clin Nutr. 1997;66:1188-96.

241. Kerstetter JE, O'Brien KO, Insogna KL. Dietary protein affects intestinal calcium absorption. Am J Clin Nutr. 1998;68:859-65.

242. Freudenheim JL, Johnson NE, Smith EL. Relationships between usual nutrient intake and bone-mineral content of women 35-65 years of age: longitudinal and cross-sectional analysis. Am J Clin Nutr. 1986;44:863-76.

243. Promislow JH, Goodman-Gruen D, Slymen DJ, Barrett-Connor E. Protein consumption and bone mineral density in the elderly : the Rancho Bernardo Study. Am J Epidemiol. 2002;155:636-44.

244. Shams-White MM, Chung M, Du M, Fu Z, Insogna KL, Karlsen MC, LeBoff MS, Shapses SA, Sackey J, Wallace TC, Weaver CM. Dietary protein and bone health: a systematic review and meta-analysis from the National Osteoporosis Foundation. Am J Clin Nutr. 2017;105:1528-43.

245. Rodriguez NR, DiMarco NM, Langley S, American Dietetic A, Dietitians of C, American College of Sports Medicine N, Athletic P. Position of the American Dietetic Association, Dietitians of Canada, and the American College of Sports Medicine: Nutrition and athletic performance. J Am Diet Assoc. 2009;109:509-27.

246. Remer T, Krupp D, Shi L. Dietary protein's and dietary acid load's influence on bone health. Crit Rev Food Sci Nutr. 2014;54:1140-50.

247. Zwart SR, Hargens AR, Smith SM. The ratio of animal protein intake to potassium intake is a predictor of bone resorption in space flight analogues and in ambulatory subjects. Am J Clin Nutr. 2004;80:1058-65.

248. Heer M, Baecker N, Frings-Meuthen P, Graf S, Zwart SR, Biolo G, Smith SM. Effects of high-protein intake on bone turnover in long-term bed rest in women. Appl Physiol Nutr Metab. 2017;42:537-46.

249. Zwart SR, Rice BL, Dlouhy H, Shackelford LC, Heer M, Koslovsky MD, Smith SM. Dietary acid load and bone turnover during long-duration spaceflight and bed rest. Am J Clin Nutr. 2018;107:834-44.

250. Stein TP, Schluter MD. Plasma protein synthesis after spaceflight. Aviat Space Environ Med. 2006;77:745-8.

251. Ueland PM, Ulvik A, Rios-Avila L, Midttun O, Gregory JF. Direct and functional biomarkers of vitamin B_6 status. Annu Rev Nutr. 2015;35:33-70.

252. Kraemer WJ, Staron RS, Gordon SE, Volek JS, Koziris LP, Duncan ND, Nindl BC, Gomez AL, Marx JO, Fry AC, Murray JD. The effects of 10 days of spaceflight on the shuttle Endeavor on predominantly fast-twitch muscles in the rat. Histochem Cell Biol. 2000;114:349-55.

253. Coburn SP, Lewis DL, Fink WJ, Mahuren JD, Schaltenbrand WE, Costill DL. Human vitamin B-6 pools estimated through muscle biopsies. Am J Clin Nutr. 1988;48:291-4.

254. Zwart SR, Crawford GE, Gillman PL, Kala G, Rodgers AS, Rogers A, Inniss AM, Rice BL, Ericson K, Coburn S, Bourbeau Y, Hudson E, Mathew G, Dekerlegand DE, Sams CF, Heer MA, Paloski WH, Smith SM. Effects of 21 days of bed rest, with or without artificial gravity, on nutritional status of humans. J Appl Physiol (1985). 2009;107:54-62.

255. Coburn SP, Thampy KG, Lane HW, Conn PS, Ziegler PJ, Costill DL, Mahuren JD, Fink WJ, Pearson DR, Schaltenbrand WE, et al. Pyridoxic acid excretion during low vitamin B-6 intake, total fasting, and bed rest. Am J Clin Nutr. 1995;62:979-83.

256. Hvas AM, Juul S, Bech P, Nexo E. Vitamin B_6 level is associated with symptoms of depression. Psychother Psychosom. 2004;73:340-3.

257. Bassler KH. Use and abuse of high dosages of vitamin B_6. Int J Vitam Nutr Res Suppl. 1989;30:120-6.

258. Gdynia HJ, Muller T, Sperfeld AD, Kuhnlein P, Otto M, Kassubek J, Ludolph AC. Severe sensorimotor neuropathy after intake of highest dosages of vitamin B_6. Neuromuscul Disord. 2008;18:156-8.

259. Katan MB. [How much vitamin B_6 is toxic?]. Ned Tijdschr Geneeskd. 2005;149:2545-6.

260. El-Hattab AW, Zarante AM, Almannai M, Scaglia F. Therapies for mitochondrial diseases and current clinical trials. Mol Genet Metab. 2017;122:1-9.

261. Polivka D, von Arnim CA. [Vitamins and nutritional supplements in older persons: How to diagnose and when to substitute?]. Internist (Berl). 2015;56:1318-24.

262. Morgan JLL, Zwart SR, Heer M, Ploutz-Snyder R, Ericson K, Smith SM. Bone metabolism and nutritional status during 30-day head-down-tilt bed rest. J Appl Physiol (1985). 2012;113:1519-29.

263. Pinto JT, Zempleni J. Riboflavin. Adv Nutr. 2016;7:973-5.

264. Flynn A, Moreiras O, Stehle P, Fletcher RJ, Muller DJ, Rolland V. Vitamins and minerals: a model for safe addition to foods. Eur J Nutr. 2003;42:118-30.

265. Thakur K, Tomar SK, Singh AK, Mandal S, Arora S. Riboflavin and health: A review of recent human research. Crit Rev Food Sci Nutr. 2017;57:3650-60.

266. Institute of Medicine. Dietary reference intakes for thiamin, riboflavin, niacin, vitamin B_6, folate, vitamin B_{12}, pantothenic acid, biotin, and choline. Washington, DC: National Academy Press; 2000.

267. Dong HS, Chen P, Lin JM. Research on the variations in the volatile compound and vitamin content in space foods after storage on the TG-1 spacecraft. CyTA - J Food. 2018;16:1-6.

268. Fu CS, Swendseid ME, Jacob RA, McKee RW. Biochemical markers for assessment of niacin status in young men: levels of erythrocyte niacin coenzymes and plasma tryptophan. J Nutr. 1989;119:1949-55.

269. Litwak G. Vitamins and nutrition. Human Biochemistry: Academic Press; 2018. p. 645-80.

270. Tahiliani AG, Beinlich CJ. Pantothenic acid in health and disease. Vitam Horm. 1991;46:165-228.

271. Aschner M, Erikson K. Manganese. Adv Nutr. 2017;8:520-1.

272. Chen P, Bornhorst J, Aschner M. Manganese metabolism in humans. Front Biosci (Landmark Ed). 2018;23:1655-79.

273. Institute of Medicine. Dietary reference intakes for vitamin A, vitamin K, arsenic, boron, chromium, copper, iodine, iron, manganese, molybdenum, nickel, silicon, vanadium, and zinc. Washington, DC: National Academy Press; 2001.

274. Institute of Medicine. Dietary Reference Intakes: The essential guide to nutrient requirements. Washington DC: National Academies Press; 2006.

275. Lewicki S, Zdanowski R, Krzyzowska M, Lewicka A, Debski B, Niemcewicz M, Goniewicz M. The role of Chromium III in the organism and its possible use in diabetes and obesity treatment. Ann Agric Environ Med. 2014;21:331-5.

276. Vincent JB. The biochemistry of chromium. J Nutr. 2000;130:715-8.

277. Vincent JB, Lukaski HC. Chromium. Adv Nutr. 2018;9:505-6.

278. Feng W, Ding Y, Zhang W, Chen Y, Li Q, Wang W, Chen H, Feng Y, Zhao T, Mao G, Yang L, Wu X. Chromium malate alleviates high-glucose and insulin resistance in L6 skeletal muscle cells by regulating glucose uptake and insulin sensitivity signaling pathways. Biometals. 2018;31:891-908.

SpaceX Crew-1 Pilot and Expedition 64 Flight Engineer Victor Glover of NASA sips on a water bag during his first week aboard the ISS. Photo Credit: NASA.

5 Fluid

Fluid intake and fluid homeostasis are important elements for health. Given the physiological changes that occur in microgravity, these two elements take on an even greater importance. Adequate fluid intake must be assured to maintain hydration and reduce renal stone risk. Fluid shifts during spaceflight can also have implications.

Fluid Intake

Adequate fluid intake is necessary to maintain the body's normal hemodynamic state and normal fluid osmolality, which are important for cardiovascular health and for maintenance of fluid and electrolyte homeostasis. Water is a structural component of the body and the solvent for transportation of nutrients and waste. Fluid and electrolytes can be lost from the body by a variety of routes and for a variety of reasons. They are excreted in sweat, urine, and feces. In abnormal situations, excessive amounts can be lost by these routes and others. Significant losses may occur through the GI tract as a result of diarrhea, vomiting, or gastric drainage. Loss through the skin increases with fever, increased metabolism, sweating, and burns (279).

Fluid Homeostasis

Total body water makes up about 50% to 70% of body mass (280). Fluid requirements increase with metabolic rate and heat stress. Death from dehydration can occur within days to weeks of depriving the body of all water (281). Fluid and electrolyte homeostasis are significantly altered during spaceflight, and this has been extensively reviewed (7, 123, 282-290). The originally proposed hypothesis to explain this suggested that when entering weightlessness, the human body would experience a headward shift of fluids, with subsequent diuresis and dehydration.

A series of flight experiments were conducted to assess fluid and electrolyte homeostasis during spaceflight; the most comprehensive of these took place on the 2 Spacelab Life Sciences missions in the early 1990s. Despite much research, the hypothesis of diuresis and subsequent dehydration secondary to the headward fluid shifts has never been confirmed during actual spaceflight (7, 287, 289, 291-293).

A reduction in volume of both plasma and extracellular fluid occurs within hours of the onset of weightlessness (the earliest available data point), accompanied by the "puffy" faces typically observed early during spaceflight (7, 294). Initially, the decrement in plasma volume (~17%) is larger than the decrement in extracellular fluid volume (~10%), suggesting that interstitial fluid volume (the other four-fifths of extracellular fluid) is conserved proportionally more than plasma volume (7). Indication that interstitial fluid volume is conserved is supported by rapid decreases in total circulating protein, specifically albumin (7), suggesting that protein, and associated oncotic pressure, shifts from the intravascular to the extravascular space. This would facilitate the initial changes in plasma volume (7).

After the initial adaptation, extracellular fluid volume further decreases between the first days of flight and 8 to 12 days after launch, from the initial ~10% below preflight levels to ~15% below preflight levels (7). Plasma volume is partially restored during this period, from the initial ~17% below preflight levels to ~11% below preflight levels (7), and it remains 10% to 15% below preflight levels even for extended-duration flights (295).

Leach et al. (7) and Norsk et al. (292) have hypothesized that the shift of protein and fluid to the extravascular space represents an adaptation to weightlessness, and that after several days, some of the extravascular albumin has been metabolized, resulting in a loss of oncotic force and a subsequent decrease in extracellular fluid volume and increase in plasma volume. This loss of extracellular protein (intra- and extravascular) and the associated decrease in oncotic potential probably play a role in postflight orthostatic intolerance, which may partly result from reduced plasma volume at landing (296). Furthermore, the loss of protein may in part explain why fluid loading alone does not restore circulatory volume (297, 298), because additional solute load cannot maintain the fluid volume. Another (or perhaps partial) explanation for the failure of fluid loading could be due to the high levels of sodium in the astronauts' diets; additional salt cannot further increase plasma or extracellular fluid volumes. This explanation has been documented in metabolic ward studies (299).

The effect of spaceflight on total body water has been evaluated to assess hydration. Space Shuttle and Skylab astronauts experienced decreases of about 1% in total body water during flight (7, 300, 301), and the percentage of body mass represented by water did not change. Thus, the often-proposed weightlessness-induced dehydration does not exist. European investigations during Space Shuttle and Mir missions have also shown this (287, 292, 293, 302, 303).

Diuresis and Dehydration

Diuresis is also typically not observed during flight (157, 282, 289, 292, 293, 302, 304-306), for several possible reasons. Operational constraints have made it difficult to document urine volume accurately on the first day of spaceflight; however, on the Spacelab Life Sciences missions, urine volume on the first 3 days of flight was significantly less than preflight volume, and urine volume tended to be less than preflight volume throughout the flight (7). Urine volumes on a week-long flight on Mir were also less than preflight volumes (305). During the first week of the 59- and 84-day Skylab flights (122), urine volume was less than it was before flight, and it remained at preflight levels for the remainder of the flight. Decreased fluid intake likely accounted for the decreased urine volume, which was accompanied by little or no change in total body water. Adequate urine volume during flight is important for reducing the risk of renal stone formation (307-310).

As mentioned above, the percentage of body mass represented by total body water is relatively unchanged during flight (7). However, on a volume basis, the change in extracellular fluid volume was greater than the change (or lack of change) in total body water (7). Thus, intracellular fluid volume increased during spaceflight. This had been previously hypothesized from ground-based studies and observed in postflight studies of Apollo crewmembers (114). The mechanism for a spaceflight-induced increase in intracellular fluid volume is unknown. One possible explanation is that a shift in fuel use results in increased glycogen storage—a condition known to increase cellular water content.

Diuresis has been observed in bed rest studies (311-313). Urinary albumin, a marker of kidney function, is reduced both in spaceflight (relative to before flight) and in bed rest (relative to the ambulatory state) (314-316). However, spaceflight, but not bed rest, results in reduced urine flow rates (293). Taken together, these data suggest that differences in fluid metabolism exist between analog studies and actual spaceflight (287, 291-293, 303, 306, 313). Such differences do not seem to be a simple effect of abnormal renal function, and thus require further investigation (317).

Although no spaceflight-induced dehydration occurs, care must be taken to ensure adequate fluid intake and hydration status. Inadequate fluid intake increases the risk of dehydration and renal stone formation. Fluid intake during flight is typically less than preflight intake, and often below the recommended quantity, as evidenced in Figure 21. Water is often a limiting resource in closed flight vehicles; however, rationing of water should be avoided.

Deficiency of fluid leads to dehydration and can ultimately lead to death. However, chronic mild hypohydration can lead to cardiovascular disease risk, along with altered performance, cognition, thermoregulation, and endocrine function (318). Despite variability among studies, dehydration impairs cognitive performance, particularly for tasks involving attention, executive function, and motor coordination when water deficits exceed 2% body mass loss (319, 320). Likewise, an excess of fluid intake leads to water intoxication and ultimately death. Obviously, the risk of water intoxication occurring during spaceflight, where water is a limited commodity, is extremely low.

Decreased fluid intake during spaceflight may be a consequence of reduced thirst during flight (193); however, the reason for reduced thirst is unknown. Because studies have documented that total body water is unchanged during flight (7), this has led to the hypothesis that there is a shift of fluid from the extracellular to the intracellular compartment. If this does indeed occur, it would be important to assess cell size and cell function (such as how change in the density of receptors on cell membranes affects cell function), because this may contribute to some of the microgravity-induced changes that have been noted in other systems (e.g., endocrine, cardiovascular, immune systems).

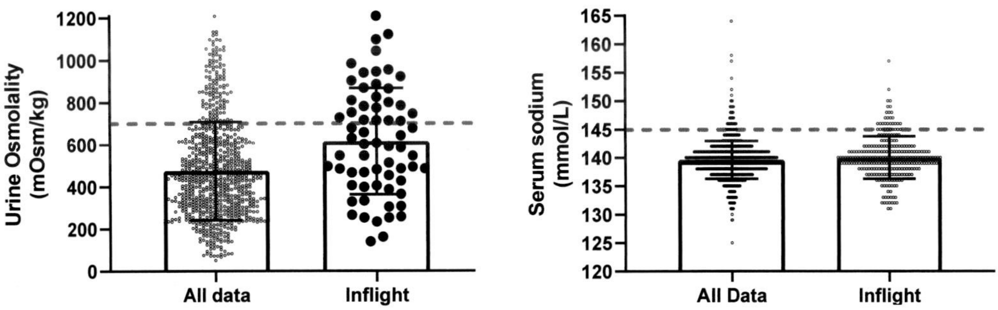

Figure 21. Hydration status of astronauts by two measures: urine osmolality (left panel) and serum sodium concentration (right panel). Forty percent of ISS astronauts met the sports medicine definition of dehydration with urine osmolality above 700 mOsm/kg (above the red dashed line, left panel). 8.7% of astronauts met the clinical definition of dehydration (serum Na >145 mmol/L, above the red dashed line, right panel).

References for Chapter 5

7. Leach CS, Alfrey CP, Suki WN, Leonard JI, Rambaut PC, Inners LD, Smith SM, Lane HW, Krauhs JM. Regulation of body fluid compartments during short-term spaceflight. J Appl Physiol (1985). 1996;81:105-16.

122. Leach CS, Rambaut PC. Biochemical responses of the Skylab crewmen: an overview. In: Johnston RS, Dietlein LF, editors. Biomedical results from Skylab (NASA SP-377). Washington, DC: National Aeronautics and Space Administration; 1977. p. 204-16.

123. Drummer C, Hesse C, Baisch F, Norsk P, Elmann-Larsen B, Gerzer R, Heer M. Water and sodium balances and their relation to body mass changes in microgravity. Eur J Clin Invest. 2000;30:1066-75.

157. Johnson PC, Driscoll TB, Alexander WC, Lambertsen CJ. Body fluid volume changes during a 14-day continuous exposure to 5.2% O2 in N2 at pressure equivalent to 100 FSW (4 ata). Aerosp Med. 1973;44:860-3.

193. Lane HW, Rambaut PC. Nutrition. In: Nicogossian AE, Huntoon CL, Pool SL, editors. Space physiology and medicine. 3rd ed. Philadelphia: Lea & Febiger; 1994. p. 305-16.

279. Oh MS, Uribarri J. Electrolytes, water, and acid-base balance. In: Shils ME, Olson JA, Shike M, Ross AC, editors. Modern nutrition in health and disease. 9th ed. Baltimore, MD: Lippincott Williams & Wilkins; 1999. p. 105-40.

280. Sawka MN, Coyle EF. Influence of body water and blood volume on thermoregulation and exercise performance in the heat. Exerc Sport Sci Rev. 1999;27:167-218.

281. Sullivan RJ, Jr. Accepting death without artificial nutrition or hydration. J Gen Intern Med. 1993;8:220-4.

282. Leach Huntoon CS, Grigoriev AI, Natochin YV. Fluid and electrolyte regulation in spaceflight. San Diego: Univelt, Inc.; 1998.

283. Leach CS. A review of the consequences of fluid and electrolyte shifts in weightlessness. Acta Astronaut. 1979;6:1123-35.

284. Leach CS. An overview of the endocrine and metabolic changes in manned space flight. Acta Astronaut. 1981;8:977-86.

285. Leach CS. Fluid control mechanisms in weightlessness. Aviat Space Environ Med. 1987;58:A74-9.

286. Leach CS, Johnson PC, Jr. Fluid and electrolyte control in simulated and actual spaceflight. Physiologist. 1985;28(6 Suppl):S-34-7.

287. Drummer C, Gerzer R, Baisch F, Heer M. Body fluid regulation in micro-gravity differs from that on Earth: an overview. Pflugers Arch. 2000;441:R66-72.

288. De Santo NG, Christensen NJ, Drummer C, Kramer HJ, Regnard J, Heer M, Cirillo M, Norsk P. Fluid balance and kidney function in space: introduction. Am J Kidney Dis. 2001;38:664-7.

289. Smith SM, Krauhs JM, Leach CS. Regulation of body fluid volume and electrolyte concentrations in spaceflight. Adv Space Biol Med. 1997;6:123-65.

290. Leach CS, Cintron NM, Krauhs JM. Metabolic changes observed in astronauts. J Clin Pharmacol. 1991; 31:921-7.

291. Gerzer R, Heer M. Regulation of body fluid and salt homeostasis--from observations in space to new concepts on Earth. Curr Pharm Biotechnol. 2005;6:299-304.

292. Norsk P, Drummer C, Christensen NJ, Cirillo M, Heer M, Kramer HJ, Regnard J, De Santo NG. Revised hypothesis and future perspectives. Am J Kidney Dis. 2001;38:696-8.

293. Norsk P, Christensen NJ, Bie P, Gabrielsen A, Heer M, Drummer C. Unexpected renal responses in space. Lancet. 2000;356:1577-8.

294. Nicogossian AE, Sawin CF, Huntoon CL. Overall physiologic response to space flight. In: Nicogossian AE, Huntoon CL, Pool SL, editors. Space physiology and medicine. 3rd ed. Philadelphia, PA: Lea & Febiger; 1994. p. 213-27.

295. Johnson PC, Driscoll TB, LeBlanc AD. Blood volume changes. In: Johnston RS, Dietlein LF, editors. Biomedical results from Skylab (NASA SP-377). Washington, DC: National Aeronautics and Space Administration; 1977. p. 235-41.

296. Bungo MW, Johnson PC, Jr. Cardiovascular examinations and observations of deconditioning during the space shuttle orbital flight test program. Aviat Space Environ Med. 1983;54:1001-4.

297. Vernikos J, Convertino VA. Advantages and disadvantages of fludrocortisone or saline load in preventing post-spaceflight orthostatic hypotension. Acta Astronaut. 1994;33:259-66.

298. Hyatt KH, West DA. Reversal of bedrest-induced orthostatic intolerance by lower body negative pressure and saline. Aviat Space Environ Med. 1977;48:120-4.

299. Heer M, Frings-Meuthen P, Titze J, Boschmann M, Frisch S, Baecker N, Beck L. Increasing sodium intake from a previous low or high intake affects water, electrolyte and acid-base balance differently. Br J Nutr. 2009;101:1286-94.

300. Thornton W, Ord J. Physiological mass measurements on Skylab 1/2 and 1/3. Acta Astronaut. 1975;2:103-13.

301. Leach CS, Inners LD, Charles JB. Changes in total body water during spaceflight. J Clin Pharmacol. 1991;31:1001-6.

302. Drummer C, Heer M, Dressendorfer RA, Strasburger CJ, Gerzer R. Reduced natriuresis during weightlessness. Clin Investig. 1993;71:678-86.

303. Norsk P. Cardiovascular and fluid volume control in humans in space. Curr Pharm Biotechnol. 2005;6:325-30.

304. Balakhovskiy I, Natochin Y. [Metabolism under the extreme conditions of spaceflight and during its simulation]. Moscow: Nauka Press; 1973.

305. Gerzer R, Drummer C, Heer M. Antinatriuretic kidney response to weightlessness. Acta Astronaut. 1994;33:97-100.

306. Gerzer R, Heer M, Drummer C. Body fluid metabolism at actual and simulated microgravity. Med Sci Sports Exerc. 1996;28:S32-S5.

307. Whitson PA, Pietrzyk RA, Morukov BV, Sams CF. The risk of renal stone formation during and after long duration space flight. Nephron. 2001;89:264-70.

308. Harm DL, Jennings RT, Meck JV, Powell MR, Putcha L, Sams CP, Schneider SM, Shackelford LC, Smith SM, Whitson PA. Invited review: gender issues related to spaceflight: a NASA perspective. J Appl Physiol (1985). 2001;91:2374-83.

309. Whitson PA, Pietrzyk RA, Pak CY, Cintron NM. Alterations in renal stone risk factors after space flight. J Urol. 1993;150:803-7.

310. Whitson PA, Pietrzyk RA, Pak CY. Renal stone risk assessment during Space Shuttle flights. J Urol. 1997;158:2305-10.

311. Vernikos J. Metabolic and endocrine changes. In: Sandler H, Vernikos J, editors. Inactivity: physiological effects. Orlando, FL: Academic Press, Inc.; 1986. p. 99-121.

312. Norsk P. Renal adjustments to microgravity. Pflugers Arch. 2000;441:R62-5.

313. Norsk P, Christensen NJ, Vorobiev D, Suzuki Y, Drummer C, Heer M. Effects of head-down bed rest & microgravity on renal fluid excretion. J Gravit Physiol. 1998;5:P81-4.

314. Cirillo M, De Santo NG, Heer M, Norsk P, Elmann-Larsen B, Bellini L, Stellato D, Drummer C. Urinary albumin in space missions. J Gravit Physiol. 2002;9:P193-4.

315. Cirillo M, De Santo NG, Heer M, Norsk P, Elmann-Larsen B, Bellini L, Stellato D, Drummer C. Low urinary albumin excretion in astronauts during space missions. Nephron Physiol. 2003;93:102-5.

316. Cirillo M, Stellato D, Heer M, Drummer C, Bellini L, De Santo NG. Urinary albumin in head-down bed rest. J Gravit Physiol. 2002;9:P195-6.

317. Regnard J, Heer M, Drummer C, Norsk P. Validity of microgravity simulation models on earth. Am J Kidney Dis. 2001;38:668-74.

318. Watso JC, Farquhar WB. Hydration status and cardiovascular function. Nutrients. 2019;11.

319. Wittbrodt MT, Millard-Stafford M. Dehydration impairs cognitive performance: A meta-analysis. Med Sci Sports Exerc. 2018;50:2360-8.

320. Bethancourt HJ, Kenney WL, Almeida DM, Rosinger AY. Cognitive performance in relation to hydration status and water intake among older adults, NHANES 2011-2014. Eur J Nutr. 2020;59:3133-48.

Tim Kopra of NASA is carried to a medical tent after he and Tim Peake of the European Space Agency and Yuri Malenchenko of Roscosmos landed in their Soyuz TMA-19M spacecraft after six months onboard the ISS. Photo Credit: NASA.

6

Bone health and bone loss during spaceflight has been a leading concern dating back to before humans had even left the planet (321, 322). Multiple risks are associated with spaceflight-induced bone loss, including the risk of developing renal stones during the mission, and the concern that astronauts will have an increased risk of bone fracture after flight (323). This topic has been reviewed many times with respect to both spaceflight (324-348) and ground-based analogs of spaceflight that include musculoskeletal disuse in humans and animal models (324, 326, 336, 337, 343, 349-351).

Bone is lost during spaceflight, primarily from the weight-bearing bones (333). This was first documented in astronauts after they returned from Skylab missions (352, 353), and later after Mir (354-358) and ISS missions. On average, about 1% to 1.5% of total bone is lost per month of spaceflight (330, 335, 339, 356, 357, 359), roughly similar to the rate of postmenopausal bone loss over a year. Losses of BMD at landing after 6-month ISS missions are estimated to range between 2% and 9% for different bone sites (330, 360-362), with significant site-to-site and individual-to-individual variability (327, 335, 356). The subject-to-subject variability seems a characteristic of spaceflight-induced bone loss (330, 335, 336, 359), and may provide insight into a means to mitigate this loss; that is, astronauts can be evaluated to determine what they did differently that caused them to lose more (or less) bone than did other astronauts (e.g., exercise, diet).

Long-term follow-up data on bone recovery are far from complete (361, 363, 364). Assessments using calcium tracer kinetic data (112, 152) estimate that after flights of up to about 6 months, it would take 2 to 3 times the mission duration to recover the lost bone (327, 329). Analysis of bone recovery using dual-energy x-ray absorptiometry (DXA) suggests that although regional differences in recovery exist, the half-life of bone recovery after 6 months of spaceflight is on the order of 5 to 9 months (330, 361). Quantitative computerized tomography (QCT) assessments performed long after flight show that overall bone density can recover by 2 to 4.5 years after 5- to 6-month ISS missions, although trabecular bone takes even longer to recover (364). For longer exploration missions, however, the usefulness of these assumptions comes into question because very little spaceflight data are available for durations greater than 6 months. The 1-year Twins study evaluated bone and biochemistry; however, the astronaut changed exercise habits mid-mission, which confounded the results (19). Beyond BMD, changes to bone architecture and bone strength, and the recovery of these losses, also remain unknown. Additionally, concern has been expressed that DXA assessments of bone density do not provide an accurate picture, and that 3-dimensional analysis using QCT is required to better understand bone responses to spaceflight (330, 362, 365).

Negative calcium balance was observed in astronauts after they returned from the Skylab (122, 352, 366-370) and Mir (112, 152) missions. During the 84-day Skylab 4 mission, calcium balance averaged negative 200 mg/d (366, 370, 371); increased excretion of calcium in urine and feces accounted for most of the deficit (112, 122, 152, 310, 352, 366, 367, 369). Multiple studies using various techniques suggest that about 250 mg of bone calcium is lost per day during spaceflight (112, 152, 366, 372). When this rate of loss may slow down is not yet known; however, it does not appear to be within the first 6 months of flight. For comparison, bone loss after spinal cord injury is profound, yet seems to stabilize after about 6 to 12 months (342, 373-375), which is around the duration of many ISS missions.

Bone Biochemistry

Bone is a metabolically active tissue, constantly undergoing turnover through breakdown (resorption) and formation processes. When these two processes are in balance, no net loss (or gain) of bone occurs. Alterations in either, or both, of these processes can be problematic. Biochemical markers of these processes, and their associated regulatory factors, can provide tremendous insight into bone physiology.

Historically, bone resorption has been difficult to quantify. Hydroxyproline excretion is often used as a marker of bone resorption. However, data are confounded by dietary intake of the many foods that contain collagen (e.g., meat). Nonetheless, studies have shown that plasma concentrations of hydroxyproline were elevated during Skylab flights (122, 352, 366, 376), and even during short-duration Space Shuttle flights (377).

In the late 1980s, collagen crosslinks were identified as markers of bone resorption (378-383). Collagen crosslinks—post-translational chemical linkages that give mature collagen its strength—are released during the bone resorption process and are not metabolized before renal excretion, thus they present a valuable urine test that can reflect changing trends in bone resorption. Many commercially available variants of this assay are based on immunoassay techniques that bind to different portions of the crosslink. This analytical tool clearly shows increased excretion of collagen cross-links, and thus bone resorption, during spaceflight (112, 152, 210, 358, 377, 384-386). Calcium tracer kinetic studies, which involve more complex detection techniques than those required to assess collagen crosslinks, also provided data indicating that bone resorption increased about 50% during flight relative to preflight (112, 152) levels.

Without countermeasures, levels of bone formation either remain unchanged or decrease during spaceflight (112, 152, 358). Serum concentrations of bone-specific alkaline phosphatase (BSAP) and osteocalcin indicate that the level of bone formation was unchanged during Mir flights, but increased 2 to 3 months after landing (112, 152). Trends toward decreased levels of bone formation markers were noted in two subjects who each participated in a Mir mission (358, 386). Calcium tracer techniques examining bone formation in three Mir crewmembers (112, 152) were equivocal (i.e., formation was unchanged or decreased).

Together, increased levels of bone resorption and decreased or unchanged levels of bone formation during spaceflight yield an overall negative calcium balance and result in bone loss. The exact triggering mechanism for these changes in bone metabolism during spaceflight has yet to be identified; however, physiological and endocrine responses to these changes are as expected, and meet longstanding theories of bone loading (and unloading) responses (387). The release of calcium from bone suppresses parathyroid hormone (PTH) (358, 388, 389) and results in lower levels of activated vitamin D (1,25-dihydroxyvitamin D) (384), which then leads to a reduction in calcium absorption from the GI tract (112, 152, 384). Although it remains important to maintain calcium intake during spaceflight, the lower amount of calcium absorption during flight suggests that increasing calcium intake is not a viable countermeasure for weightlessness-induced bone loss, a fact that was proven in bed rest studies (390, 391).

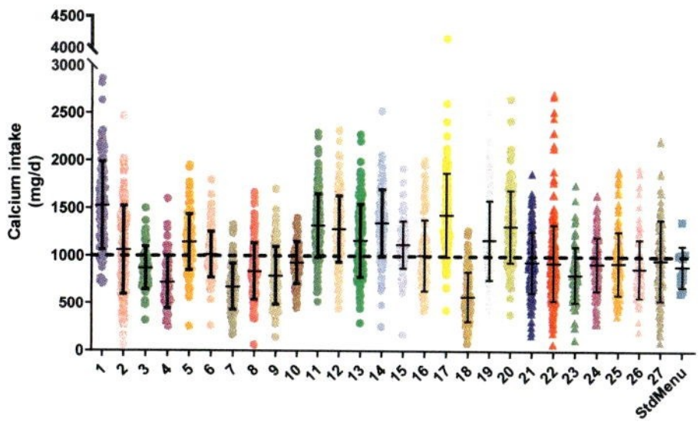

Figure 22. Calcium intake in 27 crewmembers and the ISS "standard menu." Each symbol represents a day's intake during flight. Circles are male astronauts, and triangles are females. These represent crewmembers who recorded dietary intake with the ISS FIT App or kept a detailed food log. The black lines represent mean ± SD for each crewmember. Dashed lines represent the DRI and exploration mission requirement of 1000 mg calcium/d.

The increased level of bone resorption in microgravity is associated with the release of calcium (and other minerals) into the circulation. Calcium is filtered by the kidneys as the body regulates blood calcium concentration, and this results in increased urinary calcium (and mineral) excretion—a process that increases the risk of developing kidney stones (147, 194, 195, 210, 307, 309, 310, 392) (see Renal Stone section below).

Ground Analogs and Animal Models of Spaceflight-Induced Bone Loss

Bed rest is the most common way to simulate spaceflight-induced bone loss in humans (336, 393-396), and to evaluate countermeasures (described in a separate section below). Studies have shown that bed rest induces effects on bone and calcium homeostasis similar to those induced during spaceflight, whereas quantitative effects were generally less. Although biologically relevant changes in bone density (i.e., greater than measurement error) are more evident after 2 months of bed rest, and for only some skeletal sites, many studies substantiate that biochemical markers may serve as harbingers of changes in bone mass (397-400). Bone loss has been assessed during horizontal bed rest as opposed to head-down tilt, which induces more cardiovascular effects (401). As with any research, it is important to understand the details of study design and the controls because these vary widely from study to study.

Bed rest induces loss of bone mass and bone density (402-411), and this is associated with negative calcium balance (412), decreased calcium absorption (413), and increased urinary excretion of calcium (321, 367, 399, 408, 410, 412, 414, 415).

Bone resorption, the result of osteoclast activity, increases during bed rest. This has been documented using histomorphometry (404, 416), and has been detected extensively using bone biochemical markers. Excretion of hydroxyproline, an imperfect marker of bone resorption, is increased during bed rest (412, 413, 415, 417, 418). Collagen crosslinks, including N-telopeptide (NTX) and/or C-telopeptide (CTX), are also excreted in higher amounts during bed rest (262, 385, 398, 399, 405, 406, 408, 413, 419-424); levels are elevated about 50% from pre-bed rest levels in untreated controls. For comparison, crosslink excretion during actual spaceflight typically increases more than 100% compared to preflight levels (112, 152, 385).

Biochemical markers indicate that bone formation is unresponsive during bed rest. BSAP is perhaps the most commonly studied formation marker (262, 399, 403, 408, 413, 419, 420, 422-424), although amino-terminal propeptide of type I collagen is another formation marker reflecting little systemic change in bone formation during bed rest (399, 406, 408). Sclerostin is a factor produced in the osteocyte, which is considered the "gravity sensing" cell, and serves to inhibit osteoblast activity. Circulating concentrations of sclerostin are increased during bed rest (406). Conversely, histomorphometry data from bone biopsies show that bone formation decreases during bed rest (404, 414, 416). This seeming discrepancy between BSAP (no change) and histomorphometry (decrease) likely reflects the difference between site-specific (biopsy) and systemic (biochemical markers) indices of bone formation. Once ambulation begins after bed rest, bone formation generally increases (403, 413). Recent evidence indicates that during longer periods of bed rest (e.g., 90 days), bone formation markers tend to increase (405, 419). Likewise, in the initial ISS reports (124), serum concentrations of the bone formation marker BSAP did not change significantly over time; however, later studies of a larger number of astronauts did document statistically significant increases in BSAP (210).

Endocrine adaptations to bed rest include decreased serum concentrations of parathyroid hormone (262, 408, 414, 419, 420, 423-425), and a subsequent decrease in 1,25 dihydroxyvitamin D (262, 413, 414, 423, 426).

Only a few studies have evaluated how demographic factors relate to bone metabolism during bed rest. Sex differences in baseline bone mass and metabolism exist; however, men and woman had the same response to bed rest (427). Similar findings have been documented in ground-based animal studies (428). One study found that although younger (23 years old, n=8) and older (60 years old, n=16) men had similar responses to bed rest, bone turnover was lower in the older subjects (425).

Dry immersion is another model used to mimic the effects of spaceflight on human physiology (429-431). This has most commonly been implemented in Russia, and involves the subject lying on top of a plastic sheet over water. The few dry immersion studies that have assessed bone markers have been relatively short (3-7 days), but have found similar effects as those induced during bed rest (432).

Animal models have been studied extensively to evaluate changes to bone during real and simulated (e.g., tail suspension) spaceflight (351, 428, 433-438). Early animal studies, which used growing rats, suggested that the primary change in bone metabolism was related to decreased bone formation with no change in resorption during spaceflight (439-446). When additional studies were conducted using adult animals, results were similar to the findings in humans; that is, bone resorption increases and bone formation decreases or does not change significantly during actual or simulated spaceflight (428, 447-449). These findings substantiate that spaceflight disrupts the balance between bone resorption and formation, which can lead to a net loss in bone mass.

Renal Stone Risk

Bone demineralization and calcium loss is associated with an increased risk of developing kidney stones. Renal stone risk is elevated during and after spaceflight (195, 210, 307, 309, 310, 392, 450-454) as part of routine Medical Operations Clinical Nutritional Assessment testing (455) and has been evaluated during and after bed rest (427, 456-459). A renal stone risk profile is generated based on urine volume and chemistry, including determinations of urinary oxalate, uric acid, citrate, calcium, sodium, magnesium, sulfate, potassium, pH, and phosphorus. These data are used to determine the risk of supersaturation, which could lead to one or more of several types of kidney stones (e.g., calcium oxalate, brushite [calcium phosphate], sodium urate, uric acid, and struvite [magnesium ammonium phosphate]) (460). Calcium oxalate risk in ISS crewmembers between 2006 and 2018 are shown in Figure 23. Collection of urine samples for analysis of renal stone risk during flight ceased in 2018 with the end of the Biochemical Profile project.

Astronauts have significant variability for different elements of the renal stone profile (154). For example, some crewmembers had a very high risk of developing brushite or calcium oxalate supersaturation during spaceflight, whereas others did not. Environmental and dietary factors can greatly affect the risk of developing renal stones, and fluid intake and related urine volume are critical elements (450, 454). Exposure to microgravity with concomitant bone loss and hypercalciuria increases urinary sodium and decreases urinary output, thus further increasing the risk of a renal stone forming during spaceflight.

As provided by the Lifetime Surveillance of Astronaut Health team, 29 astronauts and payload specialists have reported renal stone events as of 2020, and the majority of these events occurred after their mission (Table 2).

Table 2. Incidents of Urinary Tract Stones in Astronauts (as of December-2020)

Time	Total # Events (Post LD # Events)	Comments
Before flight	5	No previous flight experience
0–90 days after spaceflight	1 (1)	
90–180 days after space-flight *	3 (1)	
180–270 days after space-flight *	1	
270 –360 days after space-flight *	2	
Between Flights	4 (1)	>360 days, and flew again
Post Flight Career	26 (1)	>360 days, did not fly again
Total	43 (4)	

*Data from U.S. astronauts and payload specialists (n=371). Total number of astronauts and payload specialist reporting events = 29. Post LD- After Long Duration Spaceflight Post flight career - includes both active and retired crewmembers. * None of these crewmembers had any record of preflight events. Data provided by the Lifetime Surveillance of Astronaut Health program.*

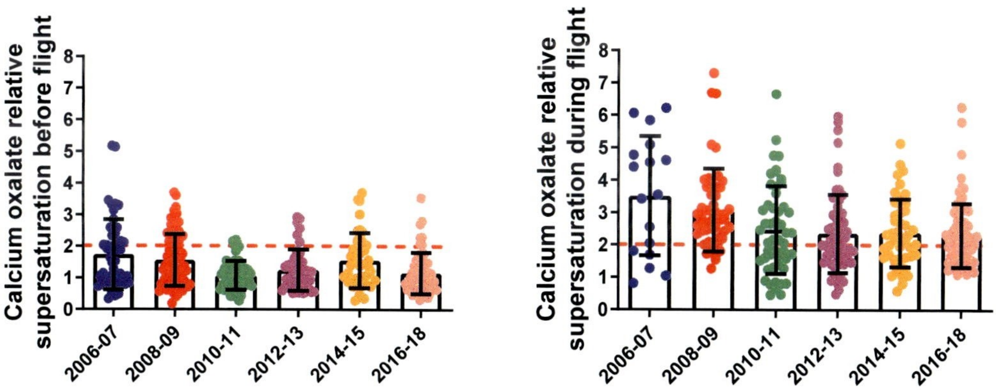

Figure 23. Calcium oxalate relative supersaturation risk before (left panel) and during (right panel) flight. Each symbol represents a 24-hour urine pool. The box/error bars reflect the group mean and SD. Data are shown over the course of Nutrition SMO and Biochemical Profile projects on ISS (2006-2018), n=61. The red dashed line is the point above which the risk is greater than in the non-stone-forming population. Data adapted and expanded from (210).

Potassium citrate (KCit) and potassium magnesium citrate supplements have successfully reduced the number of incidents of renal stones during bed rest (196) and on the ISS (453). This countermeasure strategy has been "transitioned to operations," meaning that KCit is now available on the ISS for use at the flight surgeon's discretion, if clinically indicated. KCit increases the pH of urine, increasing the solubility of calcium and thereby decreasing the risk that a calcium oxalate stone will form. The dosage of KCit must be carefully prescribed to avoid increasing the risk of developing brushite stones due to elevated urinary pH. However, given that maintaining hydration by fluid intake is an easy, non-pharmacologic countermeasure (210, 454), and some concerns exist regarding the side effects of potassium supplementation, NASA decided not to routinely provide KCit to crewmembers. Magnesium and citrate can both mitigate the risk of developing calcium-containing renal stones; however, they do not mitigate the risk of developing sodium urate kidney stones (154). Thus, taking KCit or KMgCit should not be perceived as a panacea to remove kidney stone risk.

Urine Processing and Water Reclamation

The ability to reclaim water from urine will be an absolute requirement for exploration-class missions. Installation of the Urine Processor Assembly (UPA) on the ISS in 2009 was a significant first step toward this goal. Unfortunately, after just a few months of use, the device clogged with what was later found to be calcium sulfate precipitate. Twenty-four-hour urine volume is about 17% lower and urinary calcium concentration is 50% greater during flight than before flight (461). This increased urinary calcium concentration during flight was identified as the primary reason for the UPA failure. New recommendations for water recovery and fluid intakes were made because of those findings. Specifically, fluid intakes above 32 ml/kg were associated with urinary calcium concentrations below the threshold concentration for precipitation (Figure 25).

Based on analysis conducted in 2012 and the recommended higher fluid intakes, a decision was made to increase the amount of water recovered from urine, saving the ISS Program from launching

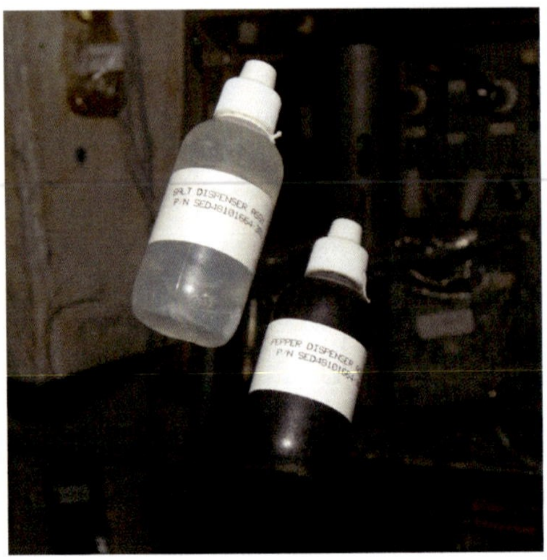

Figure 24. Liquid salt and pepper dispensers float on the Space Shuttle Columbia's middeck during STS-94. Photo Credit: NASA.

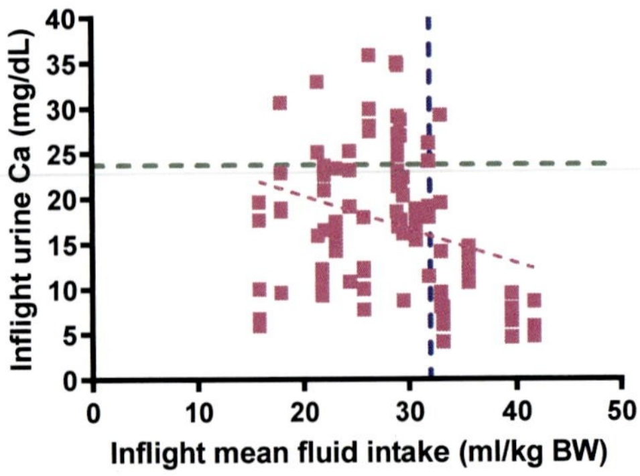

Figure 25. Fluid intake in relation to the concentration of calcium in the urine. The green dashed line represents the concentration above which precipitation would be expected. The vertical line at 32 ml/kg represents the level of fluid intake recommended to mitigate this risk.

an estimated >80 L of water per year. These findings have been employed as an educational tool for astronauts because the chemistry that caused the UPA to clog and fail is the same chemistry that causes kidney stones. The fact that both can be alleviated by increased fluid intake is important to remember.

During the UPA troubleshooting, many suggestions were made for ways to mitigate high calcium concentrations in the system. One of these suggestions was to exclude the first morning void from the system, based on the assumption that this is typically more concentrated than other voids throughout the day. Another suggestion was to administer bisphosphonates to all crewmembers to reduce calcium excretion. Data from the in-flight single-void analyses showed that neither of these suggestions are likely to mitigate high calcium concentrations in the UPA (154, 461).

Bone Loss Countermeasures

Exercise

Exercise is typically the first countermeasure considered to counteract spaceflight-induced deconditioning, and to counter bone loss in particular (334, 345, 360, 462-468). Bungee cords were used on Gemini and Apollo missions, more to relieve muscle stiffness in the cramped capsule than for conditioning (469). In-flight exercise to mitigate deconditioning during spaceflight was first implemented on Skylab missions, largely because this was the first vehicle with enough room for exercise; however, these exercises were not effective for protecting bone (352, 366). Similarly, exercises using the treadmill and cycle devices available on Mir (462) did not prevent loss of bone and calcium (112, 152, 334, 357, 470). The general assumption was that resistance exercise that loads bones

Figure 26. NASA astronauts Michael Finke and Chris Ferguson hold beverages with notes written on them: TODAY'S COFFEE and YESTERDAY'S COFFEE. Eric Boe and Donald Pettit are in the background. Photo Credit: NASA.

would be required to mitigate bone loss (465, 471). For treadmill exercise, the inability to generate sufficient ground-reaction force in weightlessness negated its effectiveness as a bone countermeasure (472, 473).

Astronauts used the interim resistance exercise device (iRED) (Figure 27) to perform resistance exercise on early ISS missions (474). This initial—and aptly named—interim device was deployed on the inaugural ISS expedition, when time and other constraints did not permit development of all desired hardware requirements before this expedition was launched. Thus, the intent was to use the iRED until a more-advanced device capable of allowing heavier loads could be developed, tested, and launched to the ISS. Unfortunately, the iRED provided no additional benefit over the Mir equipment (i.e., bungee cords) (124, 475).

In late 2008, the Advanced Resistance Exercise Device (ARED) was launched to the ISS (476) (Figure 27). This device accommodated additional exercise protocols and had almost twice the loading capability of the iRED (124, 466, 477). Comparing crewmembers exercising with the iRED vs the ARED was initially somewhat confounded, given that early crews using the ARED maintained their energy intake and body mass and had better vitamin D status than earlier crews who used the iRED. These better-nourished crewmembers exercising with the ARED maintained body mass during flight (and came back leaner, with less body fat) (Figure 28), and, as assessed by DXA whole-body scans (124, 329), maintained mineral density in most bone regions (124) (Figure 29). A follow-on evaluation of 42 astronauts (33 male, 9 female) documented that the flight-induced BMD response was the same for men and women (147) (Figure 30).

Figure 27. Left: NASA astronaut Sunita Williams uses the iRED. The iRED was launched in 2000 with the first ISS crew. The Advanced Resistive Exercise Device (ARED) replaced it in late 2008. Right: Canadian Space Agency astronaut Robert Thirsk using the ARED in the Node 1 module. Photo Credits: NASA.

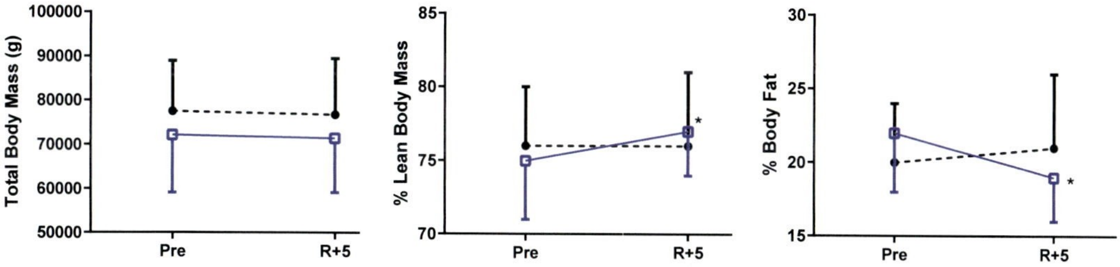

*Figure 28. Body mass and composition changes (left panel, total body mass; middle panel, % lean body mass; right panel, % body fat) in astronauts exercising with iRED (dashed red line) or ARED (solid blue line). Data are from pre- and postflight DXA, and are mean ± SD. * denotes significant group x time interaction (P<0.01). Figure adapted from (124).*

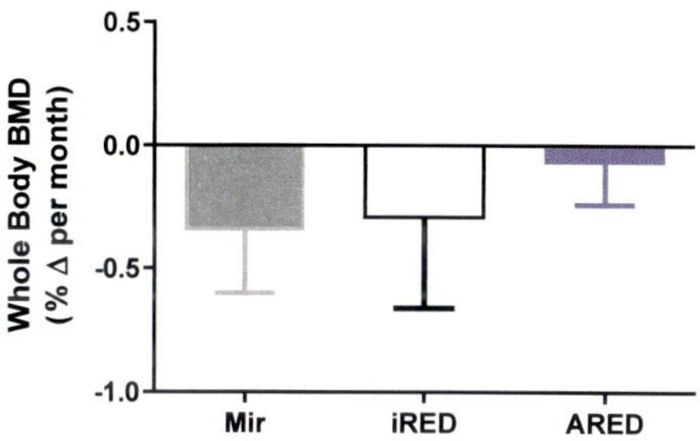

Figure 29. BMD loss in astronauts on Mir (n=17) and ISS missions. The ISS crews had access to either the iRED (n=7) or the ARED (n=40) exercise device. Data are expressed as percent change per month of flight. Figure updated and adapted from (124), with Mir data from (357, 360).

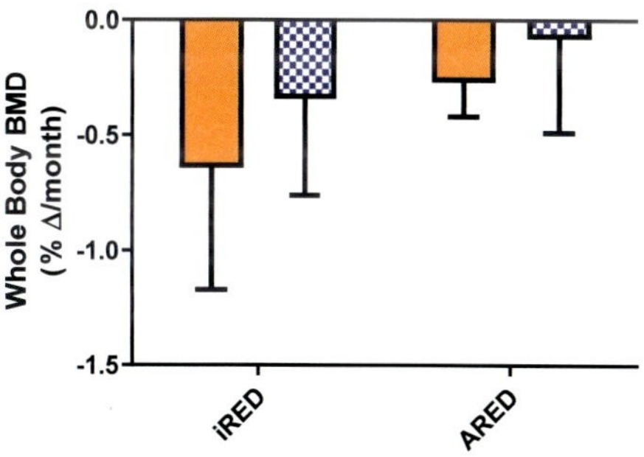

Figure 30. Whole-body BMD loss after flight in men (blue checked bars) and women (gold solid bars) who used either the iRED or the ARED exercise device. Data are expressed as percent change per month of flight and are mean ± SD. Figure adapted from (147).

Three-dimensional bone densitometry assessments using QCT showed that some astronauts who exercised using the ARED maintained (volumetric) BMD, whereas others did not (478). In fact, some of these crewmembers maintained higher BMD than some others who took bisphosphonates and also used the ARED (discussed in more detail later).

Although exercise on the ARED protected BMD, albeit better in some astronauts than others, this exercise protocol did not mitigate the typical spaceflight-induced increase in bone breakdown. Rather, resistance exercise was associated with increased bone formation (124, 210, 478). ARED exercise also did not have a significant effect on the levels of serum total calcium or urinary calcium. The slow increase in bone formation over time during flight is likely related to the fact that the astronauts' conditioning and strength trainers were initially reluctant to have crewmembers exercise too hard with the ARED, to minimize the risk of injury. This slow and steady increase in bone formation over time (124, 210) is different from results of the bed rest study, where formation markers plateaued at 6 weeks of bed rest, the first blood collection during the bed rest study (479).

Although this exercise-induced bone remodeling, with increases in both bone resorption and bone formation, maintained BMD, concerns remained that it may impact bone architecture and strength, which are not currently routinely evaluated (365). Studies to assess bone architecture and strength identified a variability in response among astronauts; however, yet again, exercise helped attenuate the declines in bone mineral and bone density (478).

Extensive ground-based research has been conducted to evaluate the effectiveness of different types of exercise as a countermeasure for musculoskeletal deconditioning. Assessments have included resistive exercise using weights (479), pneumatic devices (406, 480, 481), or a flywheel device (458, 482, 483); aerobic and resistance exercise (484); resistance exercise coupled with vibration (406, 410, 485-487); resistance exercise with pulleys or bone compression (488); aerobic exercise using treadmill and cycle (489); treadmill exercise while in a lower-body negative pressure (LBNP) chamber (423, 490); treadmill exercise while in a LBNP chamber coupled with flywheel exercise (420); and treadmill exercise with addition cycle ergometry (491). LBNP is used as a means to draw blood from the head and torso into the lower extremities (492, 493), presenting a means to counteract the headward shift of fluids (494-496).

Heavy resistance exercise during bed rest protected BMD (479)—not by suppressing the bed rest-induced bone resorption, but rather by increasing bone formation (Figure 31), as was observed in actual spaceflight (124, 210). Heavy resistance exercise 6 days a week during bed rest led to dramatic increases in markers of bone formation (479). During the bed rest study dubbed WISE (WISE-2005, Women International Space Simulation for Exploration), resistance exercise was achieved using a flywheel device, but it was used only every other day (with a treadmill/LBNP protocol on alternating days). Subjects had roughly half the bone formation response (420) of subjects in the first study who performed heavy resistance exercises 6 days a week (479). Similar findings (i.e., increased formation, unchanged resorption) were seen when subjects performed resistance exercise with a flywheel device (458).

Male bed rest subjects who exercised on a treadmill while wearing a LBNP device had reduced bone resorptive response (423). Similar trends were observed in female bed rest subjects who performed these exercises (490), although these changes did not reach statistical significance in women. Treadmill exercise in real or simulated weightlessness is typically not thought

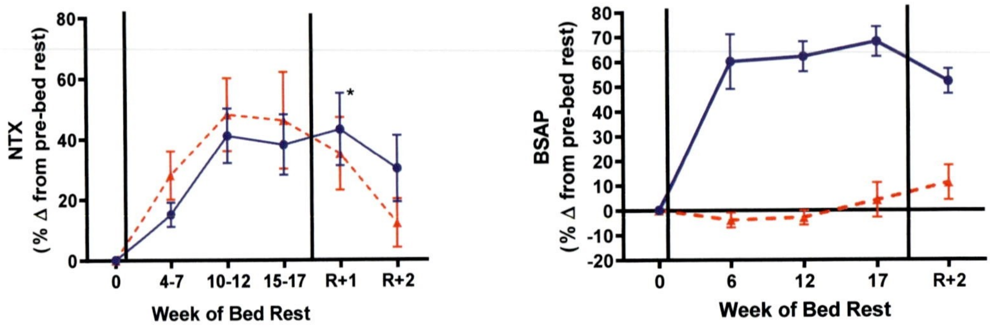

Figure 31. Bone resorption (as indicated by urinary NTX, left panel) and bone formation (as evaluated by serum BSAP, right panel) during 17 weeks of bed rest with (solid blue line) or without (dashed red line) heavy resistance exercise. Data are expressed as percentage of pre-bed rest values, and are mean ± SD. The vertical lines represent the beginning and end of the bed rest phase. Data adapted from (479).

to affect bone, given the difficulty in attaining significant ground reaction force; however, the ground reaction force (approximately 1.2 x body mass) attained during this novel exercise using the LBNP device was apparently enough to trigger bone loading. Earlier studies of LBNP alone had no effect on loss of bone calcium during bed rest (488).

In the subsequent WISE-2005 60-d bed rest study, the exercise treatment group performed a combination of flywheel resistance and LBNP/treadmill exercises on alternating days. These subjects had approximately half the bone formation response than did bed rest subjects who performed only resistance exercise every day during the same bed rest period (420). This is intriguing given that the amount of resistance exercise performed in the WISE-2005 study was essentially half that performed in the resistance exercise only study. However, treadmill/LBNP exercise had no effect on bone resorption in the WISE-2005 study.

Although testing continues on potential exercise regimens (484), the exact advanced exercise concepts for exploration missions are currently unknown. These protocols must protect crew fitness while likely being required to fit in a much smaller footprint than exercise hardware on ISS.

Gravity

Because it is assumed that lack of gravity stimulates spaceflight-induced bone loss, gravity induced by centrifugation ("artificial gravity") has been suggested as a countermeasure to protect multiple body systems (497-504), particularly bone, during spaceflight. In early bed rest studies, 2-, 3-, or 4-hour intervals of standing or walking mitigated the increase in urinary calcium excretion associated with bed rest (497, 505, 506). Sitting for 8 hours followed by 16-hour bed rest did not mitigate the increased urinary calcium (506).

Some studies have used short-radius centrifuges to induce artificial gravity (507), whereas others have used rotating exercise devices (508, 509) intended to provide gravitational impact as well as physical exercise. Artificial gravity during space simulations and during hypergravity (above unit gravity) has been shown to positively affect bone in human and some animal studies (510-512).

An extensive pilot study used centrifugation to create artificial gravity transients during a 21-day bed rest study (513). One hour per day of centrifugation resulting in 1 Gz exposure at the heart and 2.5 Gz at the feet was beneficial for some systems (e.g., cardiovascular, muscle) (513-515); however, this regimen did not have any effect on bone or calcium metabolism (424, 481). Similarly, during a 5-day bed rest study, 30 minutes per day of centrifugation resulting in 1 Gz at the center of mass, applied continuously or in 5-minute increments, did not affect bone metabolism (516). Although greater durations of centrifugation, intermittent application, increased g forces, or centrifugations combined with exercise protocols have all been proposed (497, 508, 513, 516, 517), these have not yet been extensively tested. The optimal artificial gravity prescription for protecting bone during spaceflight (or bed rest for that matter), including the g level, duration, and frequency of centrifugation, remains to be clarified (501), as do the potential effects of this treatment on nutritional needs and related systems (518).

Vibration

Protocols for exposure to vibration of high or low frequency have also been proposed and tested in spaceflight analogs, as reviewed by Rittweger (487). Although low-frequency vibration protocols showed promise for protecting bone in both animal and ambulatory human studies (519-529), the beneficial findings were more limited when testing occurred during head-down tilt bed rest (530).

Higher-frequency vibration coupled with resistive exercise, often referred to as resistance vibration exercise (531), has generally shown positive effects on bone and muscle during bed rest (408, 410, 486, 487, 532), but not in all cases (399). Generally, resistance exercise yielded similar effects on bone metabolism as did resistance vibration exercise (406). Debate continues over the usefulness of resistance vibration exercise as a potential countermeasure protocol and the safety concerns regarding potential neuromuscular issues that could occur with repeated exposure to vibration.

Pharmacological Agents

Pharmacological agents, the most common being the bisphosphonate class of compounds, have long been proposed as a potential method to mitigate weightlessness-induced bone loss. Interest in bisphosphonates arose when it was discovered that they suppress hydroxyapatite dissolution (i.e., bone resorption) in vitro and in vivo (533-535), and because they could be used to successfully treat patients with bone diseases (536) and individuals immobilized because of spinal cord injury or other reasons (537, 538). As with most pharmaceuticals, they work as expected. In this case, through cytotoxicity of the osteoclast (539, 540).

In the early 1970s, etidronate (ethane-1-hydroxy-1,1-diphosphonate, aka EHDP) (541) was administered to four individuals during 20 weeks of bed rest; two individuals received a high dose (20 mg/kg/d) and two received a low dose (5 mg/kg/d). The high dose had significant effects on calcium balance and on the bone markers available at the time (e.g., hydroxyproline) compared to calcium balance and bone markers in untreated bed rest subjects. However, both groups of subjects had the same amount of bone loss; the lower dose of etidronate was determined to be ineffective (488, 542, 543). During a 120-day bed rest study conducted in Moscow, etidronate (900 mg/d, approximately 11.25 mg/kg/d as determined from reported body weights of the test subjects) mitigated negative effects of bed rest on bone biochemistry and cellular activities as determined from iliac crest biopsies (491, 540). However, bone loss was not detected in these studies, attributed at the time to the short duration of the bed rest (404). During a 360-day bed rest study, etidronate (900 mg/d, approximately 11.25 mg/kg/d as determined from reported body weights of test subjects) coupled with exercise (treadmill and bicycle) was effective at mitigating losses of bone and calcium (489) and changes to the bones as detected by bone biopsy (491). Parathyroid hormone concentrations were increased in these bisphosphonate-treated subjects (489), likely because their bodies were attempting to maintain circulating calcium concentrations when the bone was unable to release calcium.

Clodronate (dichloromethylene diphosphonate) was the next bisphosphonate to be considered to inhibit bone resorption (536). Clodronate administration during a 17-wk bed rest study significantly affected calcium and bone metabolism, and phosphorus and fluoride balance (418, 544).

In a 90-day bed rest study, pamidronate (60 mg, administered intravenously 14 days before bed rest) protected against bone loss (458, 483). It also reduced urinary calcium and reduced the number of renal stones identified by abdominal radiograph after bed rest, although this was not statistically significant given the small number of subjects (457). Nonetheless, this result was used to advocate for the use of bisphosphonates to mitigate renal stone risk during flight (456).

A 17-week bed rest study was used to test alendronate (10 mg/d), the next-generation bisphosphonate.

Findings documented that alendronate protected bone: alendronate-treated subjects had biochemical changes reflecting reduced activity of osteoclasts and osteoblasts (545). Urine calcium excretion was reduced and calcium balance improved in the treated subjects as compared to levels in control subjects (545). Alendronate-treated subjects also had significantly higher circulating PTH concentrations, and a significant reduction in serum concentration of total and ionized calcium than did the non-treated subjects (545).

Alendronate (70 mg administered once per week) was tested in a spaceflight experiment on the ISS (478, 546) when seven astronauts took the bisphosphonate throughout their mission. Three other astronauts had signed up for the study but discontinued participation—two of those due to gastric issues (478, 546). This study was complicated by the change in resistive exercise devices on the ISS (546). The control group exercised using the iRED, whereas the bisphosphonate group exercised using the ARED. Additional controls were recruited later and were included in the results published in 2019 (478). In general, the bisphosphonate treatment protected bone. Yet, intriguingly, at every bone region measured, the subjects who responded best to the ARED exercise protocol alone lost less bone than did the subjects who responded least to bisphosphonate plus ARED exercise protocol. The nature of this individual variability is unknown but warrants investigation.

Bisphosphonates are often advocated not only for their bone-protective effects, but also for reducing urinary calcium and mitigating renal stone risk. Although bisphosphonate-treated bed rest subjects have documented reductions in urinary calcium, spaceflight studies have not documented a clear effect of bisphosphonates on urine calcium. Specifically, when urinary calcium excretion during flight was compared to preflight levels (i.e., expressed as percent change), the subjects who took bisphosphonate did indeed have lower urinary calcium excretion (546). However, examination of the raw data revealed that the subjects who took bisphosphonate had higher baseline calcium excretion (329) (Figure 32), which influenced the percent change from preflight. When comparing urine calcium excretion in subjects who exercised on the ARED with those who exercised on the ARED and took bisphosphonate, the bisphosphonate-treated subjects' calcium excretion was lower at flight day (FD)15 and FD30. However, by FD60, both groups of crewmembers were excreting the same amount of calcium per day (329). Whether this is an escape from the effect of the drug is not known; however, data from animal studies suggest that the disuse-induced or the spaceflight-induced increase in bone resorption cannot fully, or chronically, be mitigated by bisphosphonates (547, 548).

Discussion and debate have always surrounded the use of bisphosphonate in otherwise healthy individuals (astronauts), as opposed to the target population for whom the drugs were

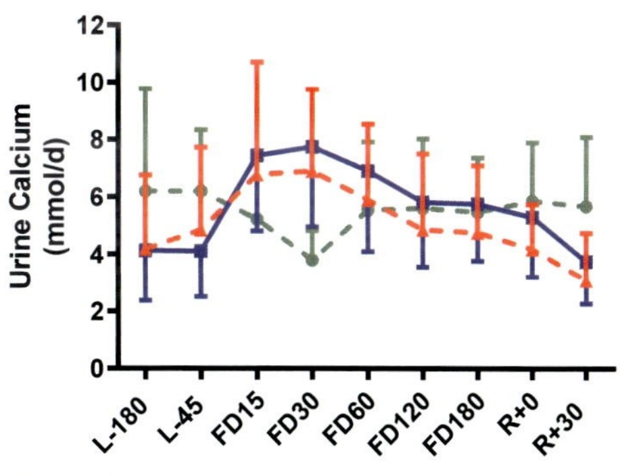

Figure 32. Urine calcium excretion before, during, and after spaceflight in astronauts who had access to iRED (dashed line, red triangles), ARED (solid line, blue squares), or bisphosphonate+ARED (dashed line, green circles). Data adapted from (329).

developed (patients with bone diseases, such as osteoporosis). Although there are some concerns regarding use in the general clinical population (e.g., related to incidence of diseases such as osteonecrosis of the jaw), those concerns will not be addressed here.

One concern of bisphosphonate use is hypocalcemia secondary to the pharmacologic blocking of the body's ability to get calcium from bone. Data from astronauts show that, indeed, serum calcium concentrations were lower in the bisphosphonate-treated astronauts (Figure 33), and, in some cases, levels are outside of normal range (329).

Bisphosphonates have an approximate 10-year half-life in the bone, which is one of the concerns of administering them to generally healthy 40- to 50-year-old astronauts. Given the long transient in bone, potential exists for long-term influence on bone health; i.e., after the return to Earth. An evaluation of BMD and estimates of hip strength in astronauts soon after landing showed a protective effect of bisphosphonate treatment in combination with ARED exercise protocols. However, when measured a year later, these individuals had significant losses in BMD and bone strength (478).

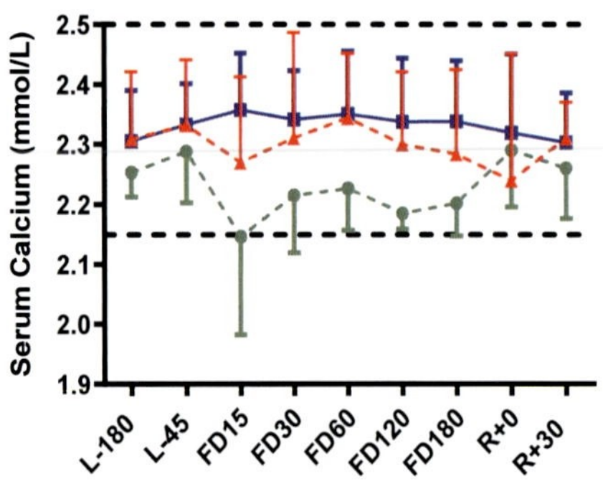

Figure 33. Serum calcium before, during, and after spaceflight in astronauts who had access to iRED (dashed line, red triangles), ARED (solid line, blue squares), or bisphosphonate+ARED (dashed line, green circles). Data adapted from (329).

Although this study involved a small number of subjects, and the individual variability was significant, these findings should give pause to the use of these potent pharmaceuticals until more extensive testing is conducted.

Endocrine therapies, including administration of exogenous calcitonin (415, 488), have also been tested for their ability to reduce bone loss, albeit unsuccessfully. In animal models, testosterone has also been suggested as a countermeasure for bone loss (549, 550) on the basis of limited data showing a reduction in testosterone concentrations during flight in human, animal, and cellular models (551-556). However, recently it has been shown that reduction of testosterone is likely not a concern during spaceflight. See Chapter 7 for a more detailed discussion of these data.

Nutritional Countermeasures

It has been noted that "Nutrition is critical for maintenance of bone mass, yet adequate nutrition alone is unlikely to prevent bone loss in all crewmembers." (351). This statement was validated in a more recent systematic review that came to the same conclusion (557). The converse is no doubt also true—that inadequate nutrition will likely exacerbate bone loss in all crewmembers. As detailed below, inadequate intake of energy, protein, vitamin D, or calcium will all lead to loss of bone and calcium. The key to successful exploration missions is to find the optimal diet, and to ensure it is safe, stable, nutritious, palatable, and resistant to menu fatigue.

One of the most obvious nutritional countermeasures—providing calcium—does not protect against spaceflight-induced bone loss (558, 559), probably because of decreased calcium absorption that occurs during bed rest (413, 481) and spaceflight (112, 152, 384). This is likely related to reduced circulating parathyroid hormone and 1,25-dihydroxyvitamin D.

Phosphate supplementation, used in an attempt to reduce calcium excretion, was also ineffective at mitigating bone loss and hypercalciuria (560), as was combination therapy with calcium and phosphorus (415).

Supplementing potassium bicarbonate to an already alkaline diet was able to reduce calcium excretion but failed to prevent immobilization-induced bone resorption in a 21-day bed rest study (561). Whether this effect could be obtained when applying an alkaline salt together with an acidic diet during immobilization is not known yet.

Omega-3 fatty acids have been shown to protect bone in the general population (228-230) and in animal studies (562), as well as in spaceflight analog studies, including bed rest and cell culture (231). Although omega-3 fatty acids have not been studied in a controlled fashion during actual spaceflight, a positive correlation was found between fish intake and bone loss in astronauts (231). See Chapter 4 and Figure 13 for additional details.

Other nutrients, specifically sodium, protein, potassium, and vitamin K, have been documented to have effects on bone, and/or have been proposed or tested as countermeasures to bone loss (341). These are discussed in detail below and in other sections of this book.

Although it is easier to evaluate specific nutrients and their effect on bone health, dietary patterns are also important. One key example is vegetarian or vegan diets and implications for bone health. The literature are somewhat mixed in this regard. Some studies suggest vegetarianism is beneficial (or, at a minimum, not detrimental) for acid/base balance and bone (563-568), and others suggest that vegetarians are at greater risk for low BMD and increased fractures (569-571). However, vegetarian (572) and Mediterranean (573) diets have been associated with reduced incidence of renal stone formation.

Nutrients Associated with Bone Health

The role of nutrition and bone health is complex. Many nutrients are required to maintain bone tissue. Whereas some nutrients have been evaluated and identified as potential countermeasures for spaceflight-induced bone loss, others can be detrimental to bone in insufficient quantities (e.g., energy, calcium, vitamin D) or when provided in excess (e.g., iron).

Energy

Adequate energy intake is required for bone health or, conversely, energy restriction leads to altered bone metabolism and bone loss. A critical element of the success of the ARED exercise protocol in mitigating BMD loss was likely due to the astronauts maintaining energy intake and body mass (124). The effect of energy restriction on bone has been demonstrated in humans (165, 574) and in animal models (166, 575-578). Conversely, providing additional energy aided bone formation during military operations (579).

Weight loss in obese individuals is known to lead to bone loss and increased fracture risk (580-582). Although this may not be the best comparison group for astronauts, it raises the intriguing concept that bone loss in these two groups is actually similar in that the effective body mass and mechanical loading of bone is reduced, either by loss of weight through dieting, exercise, etc. or by reducing the gravitational pull of the Earth.

Calcium

Calcium metabolism is of critical importance for bone health, and for health in general (583, 584). Effects of spaceflight (and space analogs) on calcium balance and metabolism are described above. As mentioned in other sections of this book, excess dietary calcium will not mitigate bone loss during spaceflight (391, 585).

Intriguingly, calcium can potentially be used to analytically assess bone metabolism. Densitometry techniques (such as DXA and quantitative computerized tomography) provide valuable assessment of specific bones, although these techniques detect only relatively large changes in bone, which could take months to occur, while the initiation of biochemical changes likely commence within hours of exposure to spaceflight. Studying calcium metabolism requires either intensive balance studies or tracer kinetic studies because calcium excretion alone is confounded by too many factors to be useful in non-controlled studies. Markers of bone formation and resorption provide the ability to assess changes in bone biochemistry. However, assessing the relative association of these two factors has not been possible to date, and thus it is difficult (or impossible) to assess net changes in bone mineral from these markers.

A technique to rapidly detect and predict changes in whole-body bone mineral balance has been studied (586, 587) and has been validated in bed rest (588). This technique is based on biologically induced variations in the presence of the naturally occurring stable (nonradioactive) calcium isotopes (^{40}Ca, ^{42}Ca, ^{43}Ca, ^{44}Ca, ^{46}Ca, and ^{48}Ca), which react at different rates depending on their mass (589). These variations exist because bone formation favors the lighter isotopes, and thus the blood and urine (and other "soft tissue") tends to have the "heavier" calcium isotopes. Bone resorption, however, releases whatever calcium is in bone, and that tends to be the lighter isotopes. Thus, when bone is being resorbed (as it is during bed rest), the urine contains greater amounts of the lighter calcium isotopes than it did before resorption levels increased.

When the isotope ratio technique was applied to a bed rest study, it showed that the calcium isotope ratio shifted in a direction consistent with bone loss after just 7 days of bed rest—long before changes in bone density were detected. Consistent with this interpretation, the calcium isotope variation accompanied changes in n-telopeptide, whereas BSAP—a bone-formation biomarker—was unchanged (588).

Because the relationship between calcium isotopes and whole-body bone mineral balance is well established (586, 587, 590), this relationship can be used to quantitatively translate the changes in the calcium isotope ratio in urine to changes in BMD using a simple model. Using this model, it was estimated that subjects lost 0.25 ± 0.07% (1 SD) of their bone mass from day 7 to day 30 of bed rest (588). This rate of loss extrapolates to a loss of 1.36 ± 0.38% of skeletal mass over 119 days, which is equivalent, within error, to bone loss rates determined by DXA scans in long-term (119-d) bed rest studies (405).

Given that calcium isotope measurements can detect changes in bone long before densitometry, and their potential for use in assessing bone loss, this technique is ideally suited for spaceflight studies in which changes in bone formation and resorption are not only being altered by spaceflight itself but are being manipulated by various countermeasures. Although work has been initiated, results have not been published as of this writing.

Vitamin D

The best-understood role of vitamin D is its involvement in calcium metabolism. One of the major functions of this vitamin is to maintain normal blood levels of calcium and phosphorus. The liver converts vitamin D to 25-hydroxyvitamin D, which to date is the gold-standard measurement for assessing vitamin D status. 25-hydroxyvitamin D is converted to 1,25-dihydroxyvitamin D in the kidney, a conversion that is regulated by parathyroid hormone. After release into the circulation, it is transported systemically to target organs. Classic target organs include bone, intestine, and kidney.

In 2011, the Institute of Medicine (IOM, now the Health and Medicine Division of the National Academies of Sciences, Engineering, and Medicine) conducted an extensive review of the literature and raised the recommended dietary allowance (RDA) for vitamin D to 600 IU/d (from 400 IU/d) for healthy males and females 9 to 70 years old, and to 800 IU/d (from 600 IU/d) for those older than 70 years (584). The main factors that were taken into account included changes in bone density and fracture risk. The IOM Committee felt there was not a strong enough evidence base to make dietary recommendations based on the role of vitamin D in extraskeletal health outcomes (584), and the committee maintains that additional evidence is required (591-594).

People who are exposed to sunlight make vitamin D in their skin. Ultraviolet B light, a component of sunlight, converts 7-dehydrocholesterol to 25-hydroxyvitamin D3 in the skin (595). Although sunlight has a positive effect on health through its role in making vitamin D, caution must still be exercised to avoid too much sun exposure (596-598).

Examination of vitamin D on short (7-d) Space Shuttle missions found essentially no differences in 25(OH)vitamin D or 1,25(OH)2-vitamin D during flight (599), although significant preflight variability existed. Rodent studies showed no effect of unloading on 25(OH)vitamin D, and reductions in 1,25(OH)2-vitamin D during unloading (600, 601) were likely secondary to transient hypercalcemia (602).

Starting with ISS Expedition 1 in 2000, ISS crews were provided 400 IU vitamin D/d, based on evidence that vitamin D status (i.e., serum 25-hydroxyvitamin D) decreased after long-duration spaceflight (110-112, 122, 152). The absence of ultraviolet light during spaceflight diminishes vitamin D stores in the body, as observed during the 84-day Skylab mission (122), Mir missions (112, 152), and early ISS expeditions (111). Despite the reported use of vitamin D supplements by some of the astronauts on early ISS expeditions (average supplement use was 3.0 ± 2.8 per week of a 400-IU vitamin D supplement), the mean serum concentration of 25-hydroxyvitamin D for the ISS crewmembers was about 25% less after landing compared to concentration before launch.

In 2006, vitamin D supplement recommendations for ISS crews increased from 400 IU vitamin D/d to 800 IU vitamin D/d. Coincidentally, that same year, a project (the Nutritional Status Assessment SMO) was initiated to collect blood and urine samples during flight. 25-hydroxyvitamin D analysis of samples collected during flight provide evidence that 800 IU vitamin D/d is enough to maintain vitamin D status during long-duration spaceflight (Figure 34) (124, 210). Adequate vitamin D status is believed to have been a contributing factor in the ability of the ARED exercise to maintain BMD in astronauts (124), as described above.

An ideal ground-based analog for individuals lacking ultraviolet light exposure is the Antarctic, where winter levels of ultraviolet B radiation are essentially zero. Research conducted at McMurdo Station in Antarctica helped determine the dose of supplemental vitamin D required to sustain serum levels of 25-hydroxyvitamin D, without increasing risks of hypercalcemia, during a 5- to 6-month period when there is little to no ultraviolet B exposure (603, 604). These and other ground-based studies (performed in Antarctica and at the Johnson Space Center) provide evidence that a vitamin D supplement dose in the range of 800-2000 IU/d is tolerable and safe, and can maintain vitamin D status for 3 to 6 months even in environments with no ultraviolet light exposure

(603-605). This dietary recommendation is for at-risk populations (584).

One study conducted at McMurdo Station showed an interactive effect of stress (i.e., serum cortisol) and vitamin D status on immune function (604): higher serum cortisol and lower vitamin D status was associated with higher incidence of latent virus reactivation. This may be relevant to other viruses (606). Thus, vitamin D appears to affect other systems besides bone. However, further research is required before evidence-based recommendations can be made for the other systems.

Vitamin D deficiency is linked to calcium metabolism and can lead to osteomalacia and osteoporosis in adults (and rickets in children). Supplementation of vitamin D to ISS crews is intended

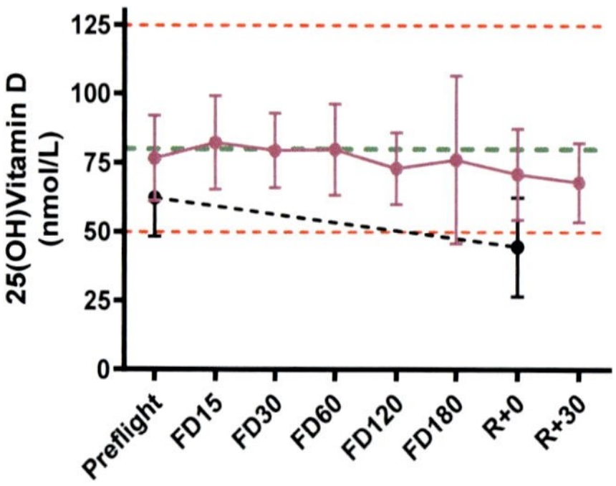

Figure 34. Pre- and postflight data from early ISS missions show that vitamin D status decreased after long-duration spaceflight, despite provision of 400 IU vitamin D3/d supplement (black dashed line, N=16). In-flight data (purple line) show that 800 IU vitamin D3/d is enough to maintain status during flight (N=26). Red dashed lines depict IOM-defined upper and lower acceptable limits (with respect to bone health) (584). The green dashed line at 80 nmol/L reflects what many perceive as an optimal level with respect to parathyroid hormone suppression and non-bone health outcomes. Data are mean ± SD. Figure adapted, and data updated, from (111, 327).

to prevent deficiency and to ensure optimal vitamin D status. It should not be misinterpreted that this is intended as a countermeasure for spaceflight-induced bone loss. Activation of vitamin D from 25-hydroxyvitamin D to 1,25-dihydroxyvitamin D requires parathyroid hormone action, which is typically decreased during flight (112, 152). As described above, this is likely the result of the increased release of calcium from resorbed bone, and results in decreased intestinal absorption of calcium. Adequate stores of 25-hydroxyvitamin D will not affect this process. Any attempt to directly provide the 1,25-dihydroxyvitamin D—or, as in some cases on Earth, excess 25-hydroxyvitamin D levels—may lead to hypercalcemia, renal stones, soft-tissue calcification, and even death. Controlled trials in bedridden subjects have also proven that several months of supplementation fail to affect bone metabolism. In one trial, bedridden elderly people took supplemental vitamin D (400 or 1200 IU/d, or placebo) for 6 months. Little effect was found on parathyroid hormone, and no effect on bone markers (607). In a similar 40-week trial, neither 1000 IU of vitamin D2 (plant-based vitamin D) nor vitamin D3 (two groups), had an effect on bone markers (390). The problem of weightlessness-induced bone loss must be solved; however, vitamin D is not the answer. Nevertheless, even if bone loss is not stemmed, ensuring an adequate amount of vitamin D will remain important. The ISS space food system includes few dietary sources of vitamin D, and vitamin D cannot be synthesized endogenously due to lack of ultraviolet light. Therefore, decreased vitamin D status is a serious concern for exploration missions that could last 1000 days.

The DRI report includes a recommended upper limit of vitamin D intake of 4000 IU/d (584), which was also the upper limit defined in Europe (608). The IOM also defined upper limits for circulating 25-hydroxyvitamin D (125 nmol/L) and levels associated with toxicity (>200 nmol/L) (584). Additional studies have indicated that high doses of supplementation are detrimental (609-611). Toxicity of vitamin D is typically less likely to occur than a deficiency (612-615). However, use of supplements, especially very large dose supplements, increase the likelihood of toxicity. Excessive levels of vitamin D in the blood can lead to hypercalcemia, nephrocalcinosis, arteriosclerosis, and soft tissue calcification. In one study conducted in Houston in healthy individuals, a 50,000 IU dose of vitamin D administered weekly for 4 weeks and then monthly for 3 months increased mean urinary calcium excretion to levels outside the normal range (605). In that study, a daily dose of 2000 IU or a single weekly dose of 10,000 IU did not increase the incidence of hypercalciuria. Most studies evaluating the safety of high doses of vitamin D rarely collect 24-hour urine samples. If they collect urine at all, they only collect a spot urine sample, which does not provide sufficient evidence to declare these doses safe, especially for individuals in a remote spacecraft.

Vitamin K

The function of vitamin K was originally assumed to be limited to involvement in blood coagulation. However, an increasing amount of evidence indicates that this vitamin affects multiple physiological systems (616). Vitamin K is a cofactor in the posttranslational synthesis of gamma-carboxyglutamic acid (GLA). γ-Carboxyglutamic acid is a constituent of all vitamin K-dependent proteins, and its role is related to increasing the affinity of the proteins for calcium (617, 618). Vitamin K-dependent proteins include blood coagulation proteins and bone proteins (e.g., osteocalcin, matrix GLA protein) (618, 619). Given the association with bone proteins, the relationships between vitamin K and bone health have begun to be elucidated (618-622). It seems that perhaps analogous to vitamin D, vitamin K deficiency is associated with fracture risk and other bone issues. However, supplemental vitamin K above nominal requirements has not proven effective as a countermeasure to bone loss (618, 623).

Studies on Mir (624) determined that undercarboxylated osteocalcin was elevated (a sign of vitamin K insufficiency) as early as day 8 of spaceflight, and remained high during 21- and 180-day missions (625). Markers of vitamin K status were decreased after 12.5 weeks of spaceflight during the EuroMir 95 mission. Vitamin K supplementation (10 mg/d for 6 wk) reversed these effects (626). Vitamin K supplementation elevated GLA and decreased undercarboxylated osteocalcin (625, 626). Based on these limited findings, vitamin K had been proposed as a countermeasure for spaceflight-induced bone loss (345).

Data from 11 U.S. astronauts who participated in early ISS missions (Expeditions 1 to 8, mission durations of 128 to 195 days during 2000-2004) revealed that on landing day, their serum phylloquinone (vitamin K1) was 42% lower than it was before flight, whereas urinary GLA did not change (111). Despite the changes on landing day, monitoring of vitamin K status during flight has documented no evidence that vitamin K status is decreased during spaceflight.

Fifteen astronauts on Expeditions 14 to 22 had no major changes in phylloquinone, urinary GLA, or undercarboxylated osteocalcin during their flights (627). Phylloquinone data from those 15 crewmembers (627) plus an additional 10 are shown in Figure 35. The additional data confirm that vitamin K status does not significantly decrease during flight.

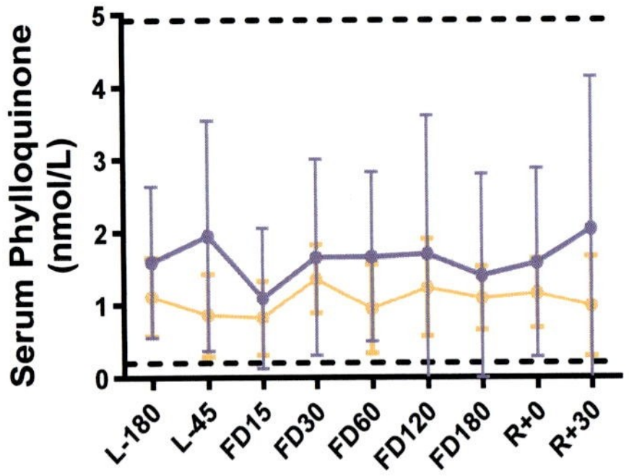

Figure 35. Serum phylloquinone before, during, and after flight in 25 male (blue line) and 8 female (gold line) ISS astronauts. The dashed lines indicate the normal range for phylloquinone. Data are mean ± SD. Data and N are expanded from the original publication of these findings (627).

Vitamin C

Vitamin C is discussed in greater detail in Chapter 12, but as a cofactor in collagen synthesis, vitamin C has been investigated for potential effects on bone health. Although, in the Framingham Study, higher vitamin C intake was found to be associated with lower bone mass (628), the significance of this association was marginal when data were adjusted for potassium intake. This suggests that vitamin C may be a secondary factor in bone loss, related to fruit and vegetable reduction (629-632), as described elsewhere in this text. Other studies have found that vitamin C intake or supplement use is related to improved bone health and bone mass. This relationship, however, depends on adequate calcium intake (633-636). Vitamin C has been related to cataract and cancer incidence (637-639), both of concern for space travelers.

Sodium and Chloride

Sodium is the major cation of extracellular fluid (279). Together with chloride, sodium is used by the body to maintain normal water distribution, osmotic pressure, and anion cation balance in the extracellular fluid compartment (640). Electrolytes in the body are essential for proper cardiovascular function, and concentrations are under renal and hormonal control (39). Increases in blood sodium levels can be caused by diabetes, renal polyuria, diarrhea, insufficient water intake, excessive sweating, or increased dietary sodium intake. Sodium levels decrease with edema, excessive water intake, vomiting, diarrhea, diuretic therapy, renal tubular damage, hyperaldosteronism, or lower dietary intake. For the normal adult, total body sodium averages about 60 mmol/kg body weight. Forty to 45% of total sodium resides in bone, and the balance is in extracellular and intracellular fluid. These sodium stores are classified as either exchangeable (42 mmol/kg body weight) or nonexchangeable, the exchangeable stores being composed of all cellular sodium and less than half of bone sodium (641). Exchangeable sodium becomes available by diffusion when plasma sodium levels become low. In states of edema, the exchangeable sodium stores absorb sodium.

Animal studies show that symptoms of sodium deficiency occur after 3 to 4 weeks of dietary sodium restriction (642). During acute starvation, excretion of urinary sodium decreases to less than 0.2 g within 10 days (643) and can be affected by the amount of sweat (644). Plasma sodium levels are maintained fairly well during acute starvation: an initial decrease is followed by a return toward normal values (645). Blood sodium is also maintained during semi-starvation. During the Minnesota Experiment, plasma sodium levels in samples taken after the 6-month semi-starvation period were 0.6% ± 7.3% higher than baseline levels (N = 4) (644). Six days of undernutrition resulted in large negative balances of sodium chloride (–12.8 ± 3.6 g/d), likely related to changes in water balance (644).

Concentrations of sodium and chloride in plasma were measured in astronauts before, during, and after Apollo, Skylab, and Space Shuttle missions, and results have been reviewed extensively (1, 113, 289, 291, 292, 646). Daily sodium intakes during Skylab and Space Shuttle flights averaged 4 to 5 g, which was similar to the astronauts' preflight intakes (125). Sodium homeostasis and blood sodium levels are generally maintained during real and simulated spaceflight (647).

The ISS food system was initially very high in sodium content. Typical intakes on the ISS were in excess of 4.5 g, even with suboptimal food intake (111). Intakes as high as 7 to 10 g of sodium per day have occurred, corresponding to 17.5 to 25 g of salt (NaCl) per day. Serum and urine sodium in ISS crews did not change significantly during flight (Figure 36).

An effort was made to reformulate the ISS food system to reduce sodium content in response to astronaut ocular issues (see Chapter 10), along with other health concerns. This resulted in an approximate 40% reduction in sodium content of the food system, which is reflected in dietary intake and urine excretion (Figure 37, Figure 38). ISS astronauts are briefed on nutrition prior to flight, and are reminded of concerns about sodium and the fact that despite reformulating the food system, care must be taken to avoid excesses in specific foods and/or condiments. Sodium is one of the nutrients that the ISS FIT App displays, thus allowing crews to monitor consumption in real time. Sodium intake has improved (Figure 39); however, like most terrestrial humans, needs more effort to lower sodium consumption to <2300 mg/d.

European studies of Mir crewmembers documented that positive sodium balance occurred in a non-osmotic fashion during spaceflight (i.e., without a concomitant increase in fluid compartments) (113, 123, 291, 292, 299, 302). These data were confirmed in a series of ground-based studies that documented an increase in messenger RNA expression of some of the enzymes required for

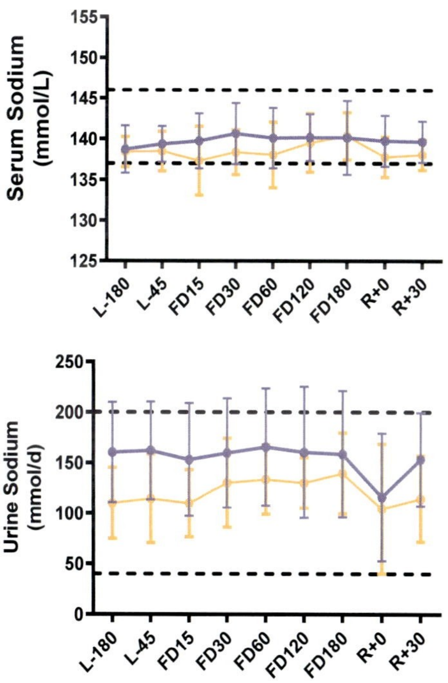

Figure 36. Serum and urine sodium in 47 male (blue line/symbols) and 11 female (gold line/symbols) ISS astronauts. Black dashed lines represent normal ranges.

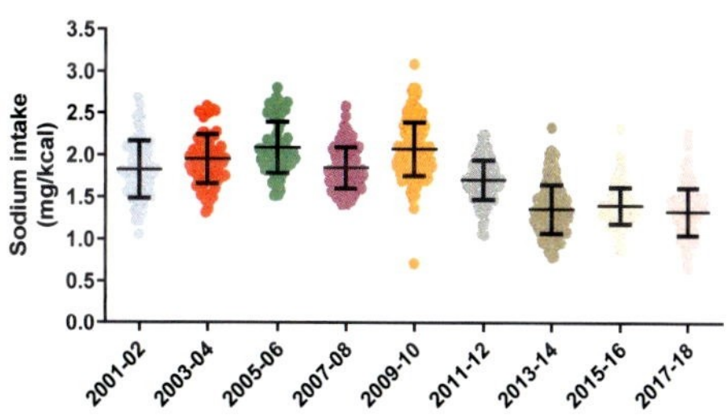

Figure 37. Sodium intake of ISS crewmembers between 2006 and 2018, reflecting the reformulation in the early 2010s. NOTE: these data are not exact, as there was little insight into when specific items transitioned from high to low sodium. Each point represents reported sodium intake expressed as mg/kcal. Mean ± SD are shown for each grouping.

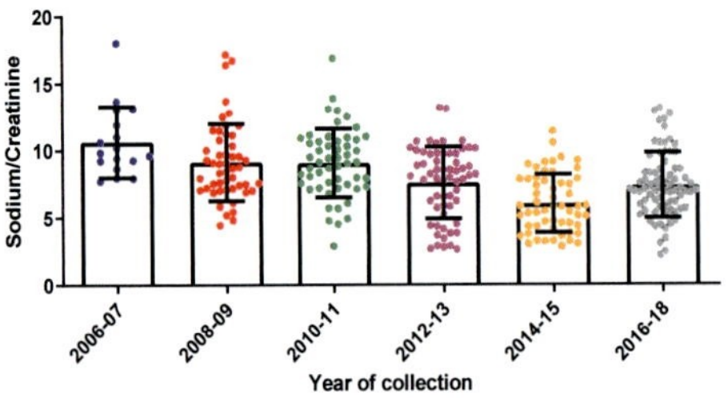

Figure 38. Urine sodium to creatinine ratio in ISS crewmembers between 2006 and 2018. The decrease reflects the reformulation of the food system to lower sodium content. Boxes and error bars reflect mean ± SD.

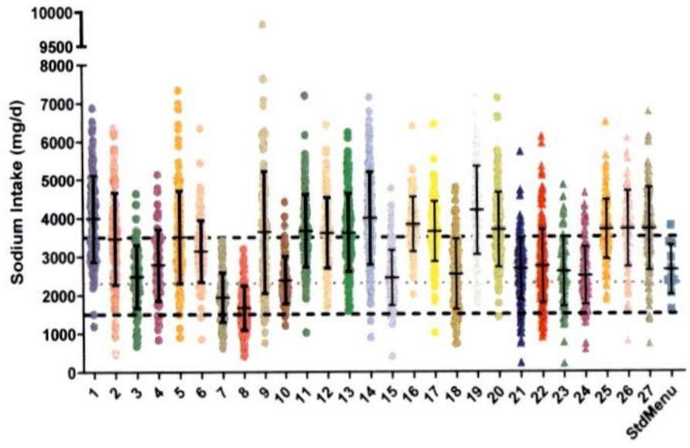

Figure 39. Sodium intake in 27 crewmembers and the ISS "standard menu." Each symbol represents a day's intake during flight. Circles are male astronauts, and triangles are females. These represent crewmembers who recorded dietary intake with the ISS FIT App or kept a detailed food log. The black lines represent mean ± SD for each crewmember. Dashed lines represent the lower intake limit of 1500 mg/d and the ISS recommended <3500 mg/d. The DRI and exploration mission requirement is 2300 mg sodium/d (green dotted line).

glycosaminoglycan syntheses in the skin, the displacement of sodium by hydrogen in the glycosaminoglycans, and a subsequent acidosis (299, 648-653). Increased sodium and proteoglycan binding has been observed in animal studies conducted by Ivanova and colleagues in the 1970s (654). The skin functions as a reservoir that stores sodium in cases of overconsumption, and releases sodium when it is insufficiently supplied. Titze and colleagues (648, 649, 651) demonstrated that the lymph capillary system is involved in clearing sodium and chloride from the skin through a process that increases the density of lymph capillaries in the skin. When hyperplasia of the cutaneous lymph capillary system was inhibited, retention of skin sodium and chloride was augmented, thereby leading to increased blood pressure (655).

Although sodium is also stored in bone, this sodium store does not seem to be exchangeable and therefore does not take part in day-to-day sodium regulation. However, on Earth, excessive intake of sodium has been associated with increased bone turnover (656-658). Dietary sodium is known to affect calcium homeostasis (659-664). A predictable relationship exists between urinary sodium and calcium; that is, for each 100 mmol of sodium excreted in urine, 1 mmol of calcium is excreted (665)—a phenomenon that occurs with high intakes of sodium. More than 90% of dietary sodium is absorbed even when intake is high (666). Sodium is excreted mostly in the urine; however, about two-thirds of the sodium filtered by the kidney is reabsorbed by mechanisms thought to involve solvent drag, electrochemical gradients, and urea-dependent water conservation mechanisms to preserve total body water content (655). The sodium-dependent calcium transport system uses the energy stored in the electrochemical gradient of sodium to drive calcium into the lumen of the proximal renal tubule. Ultimately, the presence of calcium in this location leads to increased calcium loss secondary to increased sodium excretion. In the distal tubule, calcium is preferentially reabsorbed—an event stimulated by PTH and cyclic adenosine monophosphate (cyclic AMP) (667). Cyclic AMP also influences reabsorption of sodium (668).

A small amount of sodium is excreted in feces. When 550 mmol sodium was ingested each day for 7 days, an average of 1.8 ± 0.4% of the total dose was excreted in feces. When smaller amounts of sodium were ingested (50 mmol/d), an average of 6.0 ± 1.0% was excreted in the feces (1).

Salt loading alone increases intestinal calcium absorption. In hypoparathyroid patients, dietary salt increased intestinal calcium absorption in one study conducted by Meyer (669) but not in another study conducted by Breslau (670). In Breslau's study, calcium absorption correlated with serum concentration of 1,25-dihydroxyvitamin D. Thus, conclusions about the role that PTH plays in increasing intestinal calcium absorption after a sodium load are speculative.

Studies in premenopausal women suggest that increased intestinal calcium absorption, rather than increased resorption of bone, compensates for sodium-induced hypercalciuria in subjects with intact adaptive processes related to bone metabolism (671, 672).

Ginty et al. (671) examined how 7 days of high or low intake of dietary sodium affected bone markers in young women. Although high intakes (180 mmol/d) of sodium resulted in increased levels of urinary calcium, low levels (80 mmol/d) or high levels of sodium intake had no effect on markers of bone resorption (671). Lietz et al. (672) also found that intakes of 170 mmol/d or 60 mmol/d of sodium for 8 days had no effect on bone resorption markers in postmenopausal women. However, Evans et al. (658) reported that postmenopausal women who ingested 300 mmol sodium per day for 7 days had greater excretion of bone resorption markers than those ingesting 50 mmol sodium per day—an effect not observed in a premenopausal group (658). Similar results were obtained in ambulatory metabolic ward studies of healthy male test subjects (673). Bone resorption markers significantly increased only when sodium intake was increased from 2.8 mmol/kg body weight/day (approximately 220 mml/d) to 7.7 mmol/kg body weight/day (approximately 550 mmol/d), and not when sodium was increased from 0.7 mmol/kg body weight/day (approximately 50 mmol/d) to 2.8 mmol/kg body weight/day. This is in line with results of a study of pre- and postmenopausal Korean women (n=9526, >18 years of age with a sodium intake of >2000 mg/d): woman who had lower bone mass had a higher odds ratio for osteoporosis after adjusting for confounding variables (674). These results suggest that bone resorption is increased in situations where the adaptive responses of bone are limited or altered, as they are after menopause or during inactivity, and might also suggest that above a certain level of sodium intake per day, the regulatory processes are different.

Data from human and animal studies suggest that high intake of dietary sodium chloride leads to bone loss from increased bone resorption (675-681), thereby increasing the risk of osteoporosis (682). These studies even suggest that restriction of dietary sodium will reduce bone resorption (683). In a review of the interactions between dietary salt, calcium, and bone, Massey and Whiting (679) suggested that habitual excessive intake of salt contributes to bone loss. Other reviewers have concluded that increased intake of sodium chloride negatively affects acid-base balance, with subsequent loss of calcium (684, 685).

Massey and Whiting (679) found that specific subpopulations modulate the bone loss induced by excessive intake of salt. For example, people who tend to form renal calcium stones are more responsive to changes in dietary salt than are non-stone formers. Although stone formers and non-stone formers typically consume similar amounts of sodium (686, 687), the detrimental effects of high intakes of sodium intake on renal stone risk have been well documented (675, 681, 685). Increasing sodium intake from 50 mmol/d to 300 mmol/d increased renal stone risk by elevating urinary saturation of calcium phosphate and monosodium urate, and reducing inhibition of calcium oxalate crystallization (688).

Work by Goulding (656, 657) and Matkovic et al. (689) has generated interest in how dietary sodium affects bone mass. High levels of dietary sodium are not only major predictors of urinary calcium and hydroxyproline excretion, but are also associated with greater loss of bone with age, unless dietary calcium is supplemented (690). There is a significant bone resorption response to high levels of dietary sodium, and acid-base balance plays a role in this process (673). Dietary sodium also seems to exacerbate the calciuric responses to musculoskeletal unloading in weightlessness (Figure 40). Bed rest subjects consuming a low-sodium diet (100 mmol/d) had no change in urinary calcium, whereas those on a high-sodium diet (190 mmol/d) had hypercalciuria (417). Another bed rest study documented that the increased levels of bone resorption induced by a high-sodium diet exceeded the levels of bone resorption induced by bed rest, and that excess sodium induces bone resorption through a mechanism mediated by acid-base balance (673, 691) that could involve metabolic acidosis-induced increases in urinary corticosterone (692). Increased consumption of sodium and consequent low-grade metabolic acidosis increased bioactive glucocorticoids (650, 693, 694). Increased levels of glucocorticoid cause muscle wasting because the muscle must provide sufficient urea osmolytes to excrete surplus sodium (655). Even moderate increases in glucocorticoid concentrations, within the normal range, are associated with lower BMD and bone strength in healthy children (695) and can cause rapid bone loss (696-699). Consuming alkaline salt together with high levels of sodium (693) reduced excretion of calcium, bone resorption markers, and bioactive glucocorticoids during bed rest, thus supporting the idea that acid-base balance plays a role in the effects on bone metabolism by consuming excess levels of sodium (700-703).

Consuming high levels of sodium both on Earth and during spaceflight can exacerbate bone loss and lead to an increased risk of developing renal stones. In and of itself, excess sodium can lead to hypernatremia, hypertension, and even death. Although it has not been a concern to date during spaceflight, too little dietary sodium or a deficiency of this electrolyte could lead to hyponatremia, hypotension, and even death.

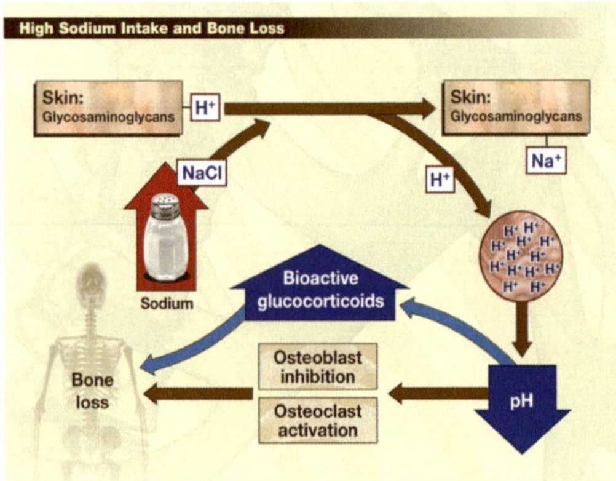

Figure 40. Proposed mechanism of the effects of high dietary sodium on bone loss. Image Credit: NASA.

Although the role of other factors (e.g., other dietary factors, exercise, cabin atmosphere) are not well understood in relation to the effects of excess sodium intake on bone, calcium, and pH, the hypothesis remains that adjustments in sodium intake may serve as a viable countermeasure to bone loss. Furthermore, the role of a high-sodium diet in potassium homeostasis is not well understood. It is possible that nutrition and cardiovascular effects of spaceflight may interact, and dietary countermeasures may mitigate these effects (See Chapter 8).

Protein

Protein is a critical dietary element that provides amino acids to support protein synthesis as well as a source of fuel. Deficiency of protein leads to muscle loss, weakness, wasting, tissue breakdown, inability to perform the job (including getting out of the spacecraft), and ultimately death. The relationship between protein and bone health is complex, and often seemingly contradictory. In certain populations (such as growing children), protein is essential for bone growth. Diets low in protein can have negative consequences for bone (241, 674-676). However, in some cases, consuming too much protein can be detrimental to bone (704). This fact is confounded by the type of protein (and amino acids) consumed and by relations to other factors, including diet and physical activity (705-708). Excess protein can exacerbate the increased excretion of calcium during spaceflight, and increase the risk of bone fracture and renal stone formation (705, 709).

In one 5-year study of 120 men, subjects who consumed a diet with restricted protein (52 g/d) and salt (50 mEq/d) had a 50% lower risk of developing a renal stone than did subjects who consumed a calcium-restricted diet (400 mg/d) (710). The reason for this decreased risk of developing renal stones while consuming a low-protein diet is not well understood; however, it is well accepted that diets with high levels of protein can induce hypercalciuria, and this can contribute to formation of calcium oxalate or calcium phosphate stones. One hypothesis that can explain protein-induced hypercalciuria could be related to the "acid-ash" hypothesis: excessive intake of animal protein provides excess sulfur-containing amino acids that are metabolized to sulfuric acid (711, 712) and, because bone is a large reservoir of base, it can be broken down to provide carbonate or phosphate to neutralize this acid load. Increased uric acid excretion can decrease the pH of urine and reduce urinary excretion of citrate, thereby increasing the risk of stone formation (451). Net acid excretion, as determined by the composition of acid and base components in the diet, has also been associated with calcium loss (713) and a subsequent increase in intestinal absorption of calcium (714). Animal protein is rich in purines that may raise uric acid excretion (451). Although vegetable protein and animal protein have the same sulfur content per gram of protein, a larger mass of vegetables than meat would have to be consumed to ingest the same amount of protein. Subjects who consumed animal protein diets had higher levels of urinary calcium excretion and lower urinary pH than subjects who consumed similar diets consisting mainly of vegetable protein (715). When subjects consumed diets containing either meat or soy protein, with and without additional supplementation of sulfur amino acids, the meat diet elicited higher levels of urinary calcium, sulfur, ammonia, and titratable acids than the soy diet elicited (716). When the soy diet was supplemented with sulfur amino acids, urinary calcium and acid excretion increased. Conversely, the addition of dietary potassium (in the form of fruit or K+ supplement) to both diets decreased excretion of urinary calcium and acid (716). Other studies have shown that consuming greater amounts of protein or higher ratios of animal protein to potassium are more detrimental when bone health is already compromised (such as during bed rest, and potentially during spaceflight) (247, 717).

Although increased dietary protein is associated with increased urinary calcium, debate continues as to whether increased urinary calcium is associated with negative effects on bone (718). Some studies show that high-protein diets increase intestinal absorption of calcium (714); however, this has not been widely accepted. Studies of the relationship between protein consumption and bone are complex.

The many nutrients and environmental factors involved in these studies should be considered when drawing conclusions (244, 567, 632, 707, 719, 720).

Excess consumption of protein, especially specific types of protein, and patterns of acid and base precursors have been associated with increased concentrations of urinary markers of bone resorption during bed rest (247, 341, 490). In one study of male identical twins, the relationship between acid and base precursors in the diet and markers of bone and calcium metabolism during bed rest were investigated (423), and a strong positive correlation was found between markers of bone resorption and the ratio of animal protein to potassium intake. A positive correlation existed between urinary NTX excretion and the ratio of animal protein to potassium consumed during the fourth week of bed rest (247). This study also documented that the dietary animal protein:potassium ratio was less related to markers of bone metabolism in the group of subjects who exercised and more related to bone markers at the end of bed rest, when calcium excretion was highest. These results support the hypothesis that calcium status could have an important role in determining the effect of protein on bone. If calcium is being resorbed from bone, then acid load can be more detrimental to bone, as has been observed in other studies assessing the effects of high-protein intake on bone (704, 705).

A dietary supplement containing essential amino acids and carbohydrate (45 g/d essential amino acids and 90 g/d sucrose) has been assessed to determine whether it can mitigate muscle loss (717). The supplement contained 1.5 g of methionine; i.e., about 1.13 times the recommended daily intake for this amino acid. The sulfur in methionine is converted in the body to sulfuric acid, and thus methionine is an acid precursor. It was evident that more methionine was broken down than was used by the body because urine pH decreased in the amino acid-supplemented group (717). It was hypothesized that this low-grade metabolic acidosis (700) contributed to the higher urinary concentrations of bone resorption markers and calcium excretion in the supplemented group, thereby supporting the hypothesis that levels of acid and base precursors in the diet can affect bone and calcium metabolism.

Studies have been conducted to evaluate supplementing with base, typically potassium bicarbonate ($KHCO_3$), as an external means of counteracting dietary acid load. These studies have documented mitigation of the increased calcium loss and bone turnover (721-723), with questions remaining of long-term efficacy. European studies have combined $KHCO_3$ with whey protein supplements. These are discussed in Chapter 7.

A recent study, dubbed Pro K, has evaluated (249) the relationship between protein:potassium ratio and bone effects during spaceflight. For 4 days, subjects

Figure 41. NASA astronaut T.J. Creamer shown here with his FD15 Pro K food container, with a few items floating loose. Photo Credit: NASA.

consumed diets that contained either high or low ratios of animal protein:potassium, and blood and urine were collected at the end of the 4 days. During one in-flight session, the net endogenous acid production (NEAP) was evaluated in astronauts who consumed the typical spaceflight diet. The controlled diet did not induce changes in biomarkers of bone turnover as hypothesized, and it was suspected that exercise protocols, the high CO_2 cabin environment, and/or some other factor(s), obscured an acute effect of the diet (249). The NEAP of the subjects who consumed the typical spaceflight diet ad libitum, however, was associated with regional bone loss as detected with postflight DXA determinations (Figure 42) (249). Thus, despite the complexity, this is another case where diet provides potential to mitigate bone loss associated with spaceflight (724).

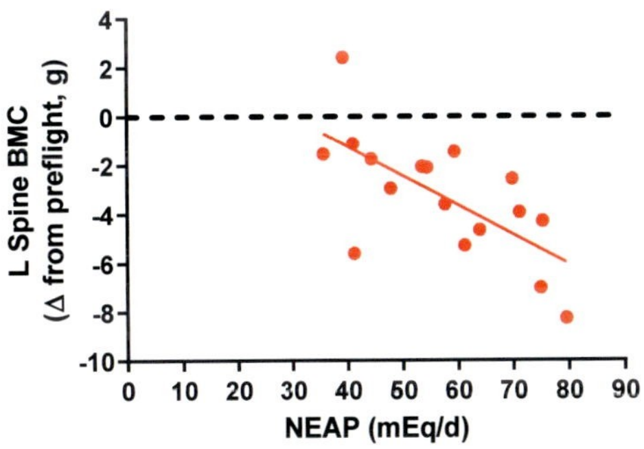

Figure 42. Relationship between NEAP and loss of lumbar spine BMC after flight. Figure adapted from Zwart et al. (249).

Iron

Iron is an essential element involved in oxygen transport, oxidative phosphorylation during metabolism of carbohydrates and lipids, and electron transport by cytochromes and cytochrome oxidase (725-727). Intake of adequate levels of iron is crucial for meeting the needs of many organs and tissues, but excess iron is detrimental to cells and can cause oxidative damage (728), especially in the spaceflight environment, as reviewed by Yang et al. (729). The body achieves iron balance through hepcidin-controlled regulation of iron absorption by enterocytes in the intestine and export of iron from cells (730). Once iron is absorbed into the enterocyte, it can be bound to ferritin and stored. Serum ferritin is a sensitive indicator of iron stores (731, 732).

Iron deficiency is the most common nutritional deficiency worldwide; however, iron toxicity is also worthy of concern. Deficiency of iron leads to anemia, fatigue, reduced work capacity, impaired behavior and impaired intellectual performance, cognitive deficits and memory loss, heart palpitations, impaired thermoregulation, and altered immune function (725-727, 733).

High iron status, as reflected by high serum ferritin concentrations, has been linked to tissue damage, disease incidence, and mortality (734). Excessive intake of iron has also been related to GI distress, and moderately increased iron stores exacerbate bone loss, oxidative stress, cardiovascular disease, and cataracts or other ophthalmic issues. The toxic potential of iron derives from its ability to exist in two oxidative states (ferrous and ferric forms). Iron serves as a catalyst in redox reactions; however, when these reactions are not properly modulated by antioxidants or iron-binding proteins, cellular damage can occur (735). Iron metabolism adapts to maintain normal concentrations of iron in the body despite disparate physiological requirements and dietary supply (735). Levels of iron in the body, about 4 g in the adult human, are determined by physiological demands for iron, dietary supply, and adaptation (735, 736). The amount of iron consumed is a function of both the content and the bioavailability of iron in food; bioavailability is lower in non-heme than in heme iron sources. Dietary sources that inhibit absorption of iron include tea, coffee, bran, calcium, phosphate, egg yolk, polyphenols, and certain forms of dietary fiber (735). Conversely, meat, fish, poultry, and ascorbic acid will enhance the bioavailability of non-heme iron.

When RBC mass decreases, such as during spaceflight, iron subsequently transfers from newly synthesized RBCs into storage proteins, including serum ferritin, an index of iron storage (111, 737, 738). In addition to these physiologic changes that can increase astronauts' iron stores, astronauts typically consume high levels of iron during spaceflight (Figure 43). The iron content of the ISS food system is very high, largely because many of the commercial food items in the ISS menu are fortified with iron (1). The mean iron content of the standard ISS menu is 20 ± 6 mg/d; however, some crew-members have consumed more than 47 mg/d during some weeks on the ISS. For reference, the defined iron requirement for exploration missions is 8 mg/d for both men and women (1, 37), and the current U.S. DRI for individuals 31 to 50 years of age is 8 mg/d for men and 18 mg/d for women. The DRI for both men and women over 51 years of age is 8 mg/d (273). The tolerable upper intake limit for iron as defined by the Institute of Medicine is 45 mg/d (273). Although the nominal spaceflight requirements for iron are the same for men and women, given the assumptions about changes in iron metabolism during flight, individual assessment is required with regard to menstrual cycle status (including possible pharmacological suppression during flight), and preflight iron status. Thus, iron requirements may be higher for some individuals, and intake recommendations and/or supplementation should be considered to prevent iron deficiency and anemia in these individuals. The recommended iron intake for female astronauts not suppressing their menstrual cycle is 18 mg/d.

Indices of iron metabolism and erythropoiesis return toward normal relatively quickly (days) after landing, although the replenishment of RBC mass may take several weeks. The repletion of RBCs usually occurs after the disproportionate return of plasma volume after spaceflight that often induces a dilutional “anemia” effect (739). For example, a 3% to 5% decrease in hematocrit between landing (R+0 d) and R+3 days is common after both short- and long-duration flights (739).

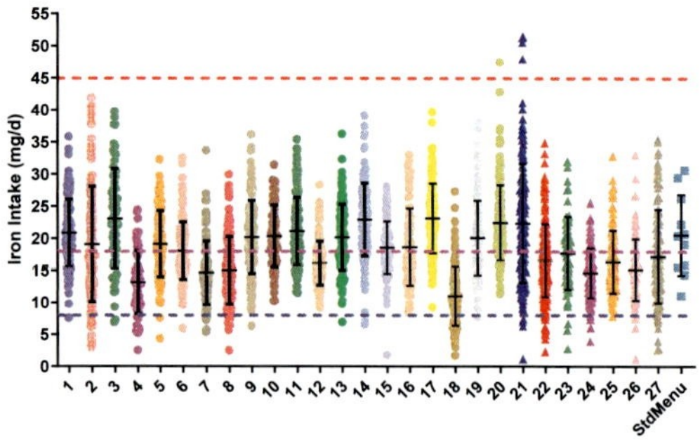

Figure 43. Iron intake in 27 crewmembers and the ISS "standard menu." Each symbol represents a day's intake during flight. Circles are male astronauts, and triangles are females. These represent crewmembers who recorded dietary intake with the ISS FIT App or kept a detailed food log. The black lines represent mean ± SD for each crewmember. Dashed lines represent the upper limit of 45 mg/d (red line), the RDA for women of 18 mg/d (purple line), and the RDA for men of 8 mg/d (blue line). See text for details on spaceflight requirements.

Serum ferritin concentrations often decrease in the weeks after flight because iron is mobilized to replete RBCs and other tissues after flight. This repletion can also result in anemia if iron reserves are not adequate. Anemia and tissue iron depletion have been observed after flight (740).

Although the spaceflight-induced decrease in RBC mass is substantial, the efficient recovery after flight suggests that this change represents an adaptation to weightlessness. After the first weeks of flight, RBC mass and body fluid volumes reach new plateaus (lower than volumes on Earth), as shown by data obtained during long-duration flights (128, 741-743). The triggering mechanism for these changes is unknown. One hypothesis is that the body senses a decreased requirement for blood volume and adapts in response to changes in fluid (circulatory) dynamics. That is, reduced gravitational strain on the circulatory system during flight may result in more-efficient delivery of oxygen to tissues, or may cause the decreased plasma volume and increased concentration of RBCs in the first few days of spaceflight. The decrease in RBC mass has no documented functional consequence.

Iron stores increase early during a mission (within 15 days) and then return to preflight concentrations by the end of a 6-month mission (10). In a recent study of 23 crewmembers who flew for 50 to 247 days, serum ferritin increased about 220% in women and 70% in men by FD15 (10). In the same study, the transferrin index often exceeded 1 μmol iron/μmol transferrin, which provides evidence that iron overload occurred (744). Levels of other acute-phase proteins (C-reactive protein and ceruloplasmin) were not changed during flight, indicating that the ferritin response was likely not just an inflammatory response. The increased iron storage response (i.e., the area under the serum ferritin curve) correlated with the spaceflight-induced change in BMD, and an association was also found between increases in the levels of ferritin and other markers of iron status and increased levels of bone resorption markers. The greater the increase in ferritin during flight (or the longer it was elevated; either case would result in a greater area under the curve), the greater the decrease in BMD in the hip, trochanter, hip neck, and pelvis after long-duration spaceflight (10). The change in ferritin levels over the course of a 6-month mission (Figure 44) is nearly identical to the change in urinary 8-hydroxy-2'-deoxyguanosine (8OHdG, a marker for oxidative damage) during spaceflight. These findings indicate that ferritin concentrations during flight, concentrations that were not outside the normal clinical range, were associated with evidence of oxidative damage and bone resorption, as has been demonstrated in other studies in healthy ground-based populations (745-747). For example, increased body iron stores were related to the rate of change in regional bone loss over a 3-year period in healthy individuals (748). Further evidence exists that radiation, oxidative stress, and bone health are also related (749), as reviewed by Yang et al. (729).

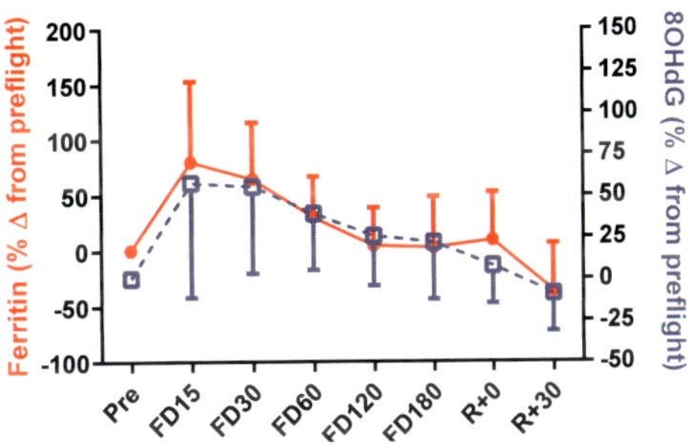

Figure 44. Iron stores, reflected by serum ferritin (red circles, solid line) and oxidative damage to DNA, reflected by urinary 8OHdG (blue squares, dashed line) before, during, and after long-duration spaceflight. Data are mean ± SD for 23 ISS astronauts. Data are expressed as percent change from preflight. Figure adapted from (10).

Bed rest studies have not proven to be consistently reliable models for the hematological changes induced by spaceflight. A decrease in RBC mass was recorded during early bed rest studies, whereas erythropoietin was unchanged and hematocrit increased in these studies (750), suggesting that the mechanisms that bring about hematological changes during bed rest are different from those that act during spaceflight. If the reduced RBC mass during flight is caused by the reduced gravitational load on the circulatory system, it is reasonable to assume that bed rest alone would not alleviate these forces. Bed rest would only change the direction relative to the body. Small changes in iron status have been recorded during bed rest, the most consistent change being a drop in hematocrit and hemoglobin levels after re-ambulation (254, 419), suggesting an effect of plasma volume replacement and a smaller role of hematopoiesis.

An intriguing study of iron metabolism during 5 days of dry immersion showed a shift in iron metabolism (751). Some of these findings may be related to fluid shifts, which resulted in an increased hemoglobin and hematocrit after only 5 days. The changes observed are evidence of a need for future studies concerning the role of iron in adaptation to microgravity, and in astronaut health.

Changes in altitude can induce hematological changes; descent from high to low altitude induces changes similar to those observed during spaceflight (decreased RBC mass, increased iron storage) (752). Exogenous erythropoietin prevented the changes (752), suggesting that erythropoietin is involved as a regulating mechanism, and may also be involved in regulating the initial blood volume changes during spaceflight.

The NASA Extreme Environment Mission Operations (NEEMO) undersea habitat provides an excellent analog for spaceflight-induced changes in iron status (753), as detailed in Chapter 14. Because of the increased air pressure in the habitat, NEEMO crewmembers are exposed to higher oxygen pressures, which increase their risk for oxidative damage to DNA, proteins, and lipids (754-757). Probably because of the increased pressure and greater oxygen availability, body iron stores are elevated during the saturation dive (111, 737). Levels of ferritin in the serum increase during the NEEMO saturation dives (10-14 d), and evidence of oxidative damage and stress is also observed during these dives (753). On a recent NEEMO mission, levels of RBC folate decreased during the dive, and plasma concentration of folate was inversely correlated with serum concentration of ferritin (758). Decreased activity of superoxide dismutase and peripheral blood mononuclear cell poly(adenosine diphosphate [ADP]-ribose) were also evident during the dive, indicating a DNA repair response was activated (758).

Iron overload is also associated with retinal degeneration and cataract risk (759). Increased oxidative damage occurred in the retina and the liver of irradiated rats that consumed excess levels of iron (760). Furthermore, the formation of free radicals subsequent to elevation of iron stores has been linked on Earth to increased risk of cardiovascular disease and cancer. Although some studies provide contradictory evidence (761, 762), a correlation between coronary heart disease and iron status has been described in a number of recent studies (763-765), and an association between increased incidence of myocardial infarction and increased iron stores has been observed (765, 766). In a prospective Finnish study, increased risk of all cancer types combined, and colorectal cancer in particular, was associated with high iron stores (767). The relationship between iron and lipid levels and cancer incidents has also been documented in the Framingham study (768). Excessive iron stores have also been linked to deficiency of ascorbic acid; when reductions in ascorbic acid occur, vitamin A and selenium tend to exacerbate iron-induced peroxidation processes (769). These data suggest that the alterations in erythropoiesis and iron metabolism that occur in microgravity could cause significant changes to crew health.

Better characterization of iron metabolism during spaceflight with respect to other systems is warranted because of the high levels of dietary iron in space food, the increase in iron stores early during flight, and the potential for iron to act as an oxidizing agent during spaceflight, which could be exacerbated by increased radiation exposure during exploration missions. Specific bacteria under some growth conditions can be more virulent in microgravity (770). Ground studies show that elevated iron status can increase risk for infection (771). Investigating the increase in iron status during flight with respect to changes in immune function will be an important next step in understanding the implications of elevated iron status during spaceflight. Furthermore, iron absorption, and any effect on iron status, has yet to be determined during flight.

Phosphorus

Phosphorus is an important component of cell membranes and bone mineral, and it also contributes to cellular energy (772, 773). Phosphate accounts for about 60% of bone mineral (772), and most (85%) of the body's extracellular phosphorus is in bone (772). Phosphorus homeostasis is somewhat analogous to calcium, with controlled circulating concentrations, renal excretion balancing intestinal absorption, and regulatory factors that include PTH and other compounds (772, 774). High levels of phosphorus intake, relative to calcium intake in particular, can have detrimental effects on many systems, including skeletal, renal, and cardiovascular systems (772, 775-780).

The recommended dietary intake of phosphorus for men and women is 700 mg P/d (772, 781). Ideally, the calcium:phosphorus ratio in the diet should be around 1.0 or higher (780), based on evidence that consumption of high levels phosphorus relative to levels of calcium can decrease calcium absorption, increase bone turnover, and ultimately can affect skeletal integrity (780). Phosphorus is found in multiple forms in the diet; a large source being salts added in processed foods (772).

The ISS and exploration mission requirements match the RDA for phosphorus, with a notation that the phosphorus intake should not exceed 1.5 times the calcium intake (1, 36-38). To date, phosphorus intakes have been higher than desired (Figure 45). The ISS "standard menu" has a Ca:P ratio of 0.48 (1) (Figure 43); actual intakes have been slightly lower than that (Figure 46). During bed rest studies, subjects have tended to consume Ca:P ratios closer to 1.0 (782).

After ISS missions, urinary excretion of phosphorus was about 45% lower than levels before flight (111). Excretion of

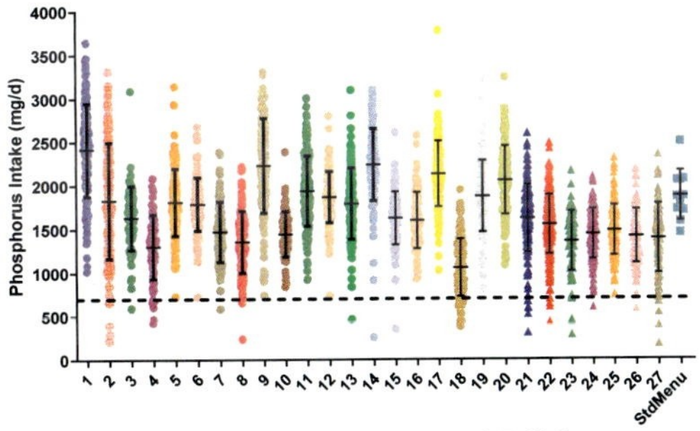

Figure 45. Phosphorus intake in 27 ISS astronauts and in the "standard menu." The dashed line represents the requirement of 700 mg/d.

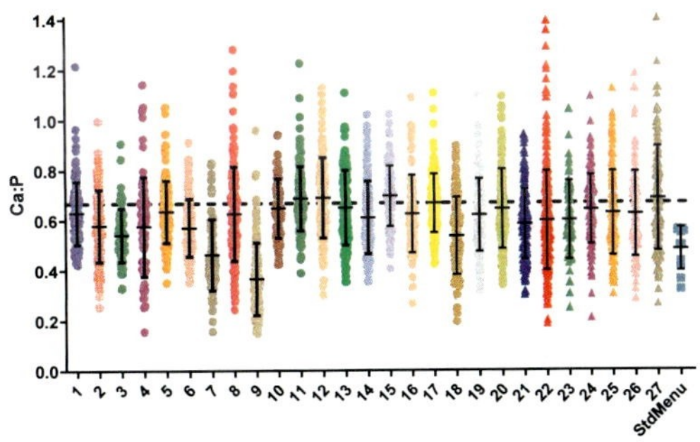

Figure 46. Dietary calcium (Ca):phosphorus (P) ratio in 27 ISS crewmembers and the "standard menu." Ideally, the Ca:P ratio would be no less than 0.67 (i.e., P:Ca <1.5), as shown by the black dashed line.

phosphorus during bed rest was not changed (419) from ambulatory conditions. An earlier study of three bed rest subjects revealed increased urinary phosphorus and negative phosphorus balance (412). Investigators have attempted to use a combination of calcium and phosphorus to mitigate bone loss and hypercalciuria during bed rest, which have induced trends in the right direction but no significant changes (415).

Magnesium

Magnesium is the fourth most abundant cation in the body, and more than half of the body's magnesium is in bone (783). Good-quality diets that are rich in magnesium and potassium have been associated with improved bone health (784, 785). Magnesium is also critical for neuromuscular function, serving as a cofactor in a multitude of cellular functions, and is a keystone of cardiovascular health (786, 787). Excessive magnesium intake from supplements can impair calcium absorption (788), whereas magnesium deficiency leads to bone loss and other health implications (789).

Magnesium status is not easily assessed. Although serum and urinary magnesium are relatively easy to determine, serum contains only 1% of the body pool of magnesium, and changes (or lack of changes) do not necessarily reflect magnesium status (783, 790, 791). The concentration of magnesium in tissue provides a more direct, if not the best, assessment of magnesium status, and can be estimated through analysis of sublingual cells (791, 792). However, these analytical tests are challenging and expensive.

The recommended intake of magnesium for adults (age 31-70 y), is 420 mg/d for men, and 320 mg/d for women (781). These recommendations were proposed for exploration missions (38), whereas the recommendation for ISS crewmembers is only 350 mg/d (36). Additionally, the recommended upper limit for magnesium supplements on exploration missions is defined as 350 mg/d (38).

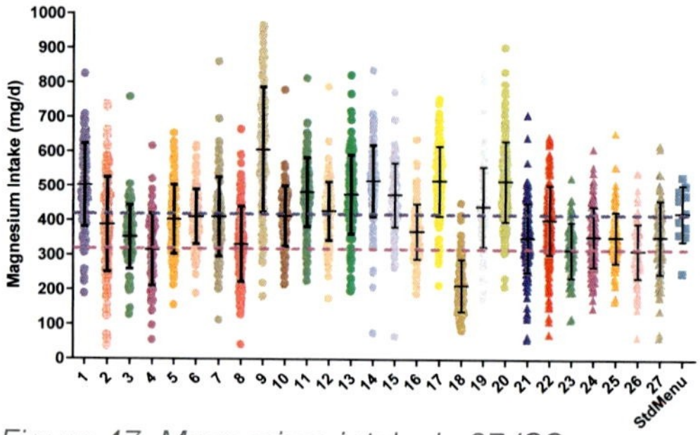

Figure 47. Magnesium intake in 27 ISS astronauts and in the "standard menu." Each symbol represents one 24-hour intake. Female crewmembers are represented as triangles, males as circles. The blue dashed line represents the requirement for men (420 mg/d), and the purple dashed line represents the RDA for women (320 mg/d).

On Earth, a clear relationship exists between energy intake and magnesium intake, and the same holds in flight (Figure 48). As a result, astronauts may not consume enough magnesium due to the overarching concern of

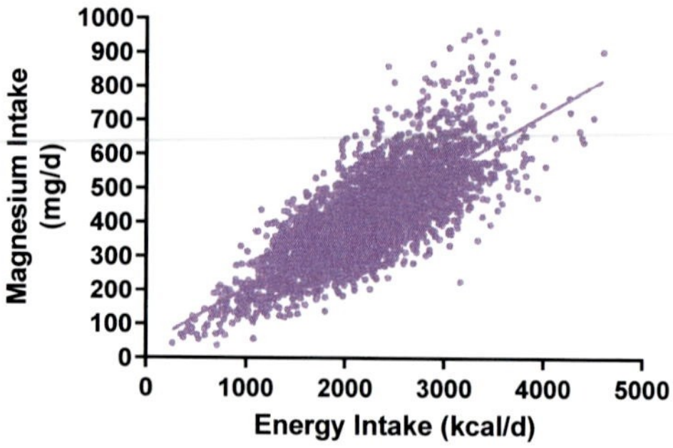

Figure 48. The relationship between magnesium intake and energy intake in astronauts during flight. Each point represents a day's record; however, even partial days were included when available. Data are from 27 astronauts who kept detailed dietary records, and represent 3458 days of collection.

adequate dietary energy intake (1, 111). Athletes who restrict energy intake (e.g., dancers, wrestlers, gymnasts) can also be deficient in magnesium (793).

Magnesium assessments before and after Apollo (794) and 4- to 6-month ISS missions (111) have documented a consistent decrease in urinary magnesium. Small decreases in the concentration of magnesium in serum or plasma were detected after Apollo and Skylab missions (122), and slight increases in the concentration of magnesium were detected after early ISS missions (1). In addition to the limitations of determining magnesium status from assessments of magnesium in serum and urine, postflight assessments need to be interpreted cautiously given the fluid shifts that occur during flight and the fluid loading and recovery that occurs after flight. In-flight analyses during some short-duration (≤ 30 d) space missions and some missions of up to 3 months (1, 795) have shown that the concentration of magnesium in serum is slightly lower than preflight values. The decrease was likely not statistically significant (statistics were not performed due to the small n [2-6]), and the magnitude of change was also small (an average of 2.3-8.3% below preflight values) (1, 795). During Skylab missions, the concentration of urinary magnesium increased during the first 2 months of flight, did not change during the third month, and decreased after flight (122).

Autopsy results after the tragic end of the 24-day Salyut-1 mission documented that, relative to control subjects, the Salyut-1 cosmonauts had 12% to 32% lower concentrations of magnesium in the compact layer of the femoral epiphysis and diaphysis, vertebral body, and sternum (796). These changes were reported "with a high degree of certainty." Magnesium balance was slightly negative during extended-duration bed rest studies conducted in Russia (489), and exercise or bisphosphonate supplements had little effect on this change. Magnesium excretion was lower during both short- and long-duration bed rest (254, 419).

A comprehensive evaluation of magnesium and spaceflight was published in 2015 (797). This publication includes data from short- and long-duration space missions and long-duration bed rest studies, and included not only serum and urine data, but a unique assessment of tissue magnesium status using a sublingual scraping and cellular magnesium analysis (797) (Figure 49).

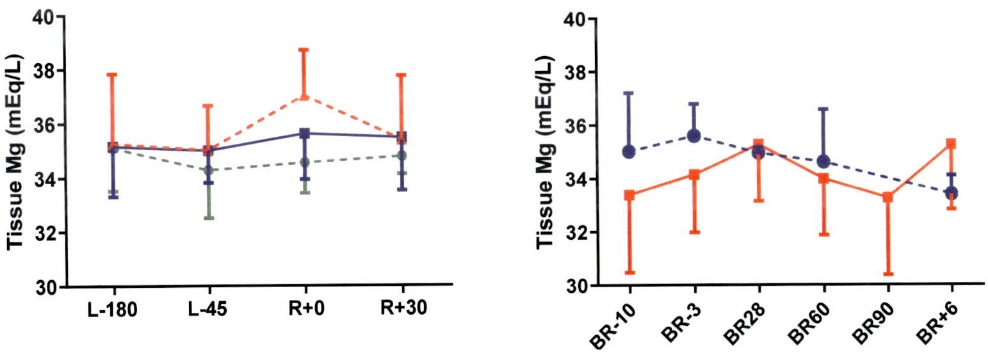

Figure 49. Tissue magnesium concentration, assessed through analysis of sublingual cells, before and after flight (left panel) and bed rest (right panel). In the flight data, solid blue line/squares denotes crewmembers who had access to ARED, dashed red triangles iRED, and dashed green/ circles ARED+ bisphosphonate. In the bed rest data, blue dashed represents 60-day bed rest subjects, and red solid line the 90-day bed rest subjects. Figure adapted from (797).

Magnesium is a critical nutrient that has many important functions. Although magnesium homeostasis can be altered on Earth by disease states and medication use, the available data document that despite consistent and significant alterations in the concentration of urinary magnesium after spaceflight, tissue stores of the mineral are maintained. In addition, in-flight data reveal increased concentrations of magnesium in serum and urine. Thus, there is no general cause for concern that astronauts have magnesium deficiency. Additional studies are warranted to better understand the role of magnesium in astronaut health and to better define astronauts' requirements for magnesium (797).

Copper

Copper is an essential cofactor for enzymes involved in energy production and neuroendocrine signaling, in metabolism of oxygen and iron, and in maturation of extracellular matrix and neuropeptides (798, 799). Deficiencies in copper have implications for bone, nervous system, and cardiovascular health, and for immune function and lipid metabolism (800).

Copper is one of many nutrients that can be toxic at high levels (801-805). When divalent copper is consumed in high amounts, it can accumulate in the brain and enhance the aggregation of amyloid-β into amyloid plaques that become neurotoxic and release oxygen free radicals (806). High concentrations of copper have been implicated in cardiovascular disease (807, 808), and in neurodegenerative conditions such as Alzheimer's disease (801). Divalent copper is found in supplements and in drinking water that is transported in copper pipes.

The involvement of copper in bone health is specifically related to lysyl oxidase function and collagen synthesis (800, 809). Copper is not usually stored in tissues per se; however, liver, brain, and kidney typically contain the largest amounts per unit tissue mass (800). Total amount of copper in the human body ranges from about 50 to 120 mg (0.79-1.9 mmol) (810). Transport and regulation of copper involves the blood protein ceruloplasmin (811).

Copper deficiency leads to normocytic, hypochromic anemia; decreased production of leukocytes and neutrophils; and defects in connective tissue (specifically in collagen synthesis) that can lead to vascular and skeletal problems and central nervous system dysfunction, or even death (812). Heartbeat irregularities have also been reported in cases of copper deficiency (813). Deficiency symptoms, including macrocytic anemia, bone abnormalities, and decreased neutrophil production, have been reported in subjects with serum copper concentrations ranging from 0.9 to 7.2 µmol/L (814). Toxic concentrations of copper can lead to oxidative damage, GI distress, liver damage, or even death (800).

One Russian report (796) documented "non-uniform changes" in copper content of bone from different regions after spaceflight relative to levels in non-flight controls. Copper content of the femoral epiphysis was 81% to 159% greater after flight than before flight, whereas the amounts of copper in the vertebral body and sternum were 36% and 58% less, respectively, after flight. (This study reported autopsy results after the tragic end of the 24-day Salyut-1 mission, relative to controls.)

Serum concentrations of copper and ceruloplasmin (the major copper-carrying protein in blood) were measured before and after early (2000-2005) ISS missions as part of the medical requirement to assess nutritional status in crewmembers, and no significant changes were observed after flight (111). Additional testing was implemented with the Nutrition SMO and Biochemical Profile projects. Results indicated that serum

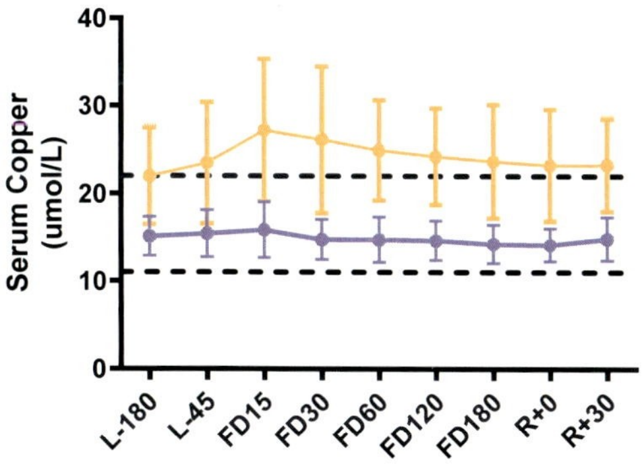

Figure 50. Serum copper in ISS crewmembers before, during, and after flight. Males are represented by blue line, and females the gold. Adapted from (815).

concentration of copper and urinary copper excretion were unchanged during flight (815) (Figure 50).

During a 17-week bed rest study, copper balance was unchanged; however, it increased after re-ambulation (816). During and after 3 weeks of bed rest, concentrations of copper and ceruloplasmin in serum were unchanged (254). After 90 days of bed rest, the concentration of serum copper was only slightly elevated, but the increase was statistically significant (419). During 60 and 90 days of bed rest, ceruloplasmin concentrations were unchanged (419). Copper balance was lower during 21-day bed rest, and seemed to be even lower in subjects who were exposed to 1 hour per day of artificial gravity to counter the effects of bed rest (815). The causes and implications of this are unknown and warrant further investigation.

Zinc (and Lead)

Zinc is an important mineral with a broad range of functions, including a role as a structural and functional enzyme cofactor in a myriad of reactions, and has effects on many systems, including brain function and cognition, immune system function, and bone health (817-820). Studies have identified preliminary associations between zinc deficiency and incidence of diseases such as diabetes and cancer (819). However, as with many nutrition components of disease, the relationships are not always clear (821).

Assessment of zinc status has been a topic of debate. Some claim that zinc content of plasma, urine, and even hair are reliable indicators of zinc status in healthy individuals (822); however, the general consensus remains that circulating zinc levels are an imperfect tool to evaluate zinc status because other physiological factors may affect levels of zinc in the blood (817). Leukocyte metallothionine content has been advocated as a biomarker of zinc exposure, but additional work remains to confirm these findings (823). The recommended dietary intakes of zinc for adult men and women are 11mg/d and 8 mg/d, respectively (273), matching the recommendations for space travelers (38).

Because zinc is stored in bone along with other minerals, the release of zinc and other heavy metals from bones (as a result of demineralization) during spaceflight (or bed rest) raises concerns about potential toxicity. Release of zinc from bone has been noted in bed rest studies (816, 824), and a similar increase in excretion of zinc was noted in Wistar rats flown during COSMOS 1129 (a 20-day spaceflight) (442).

As was seen with copper, zinc levels were lower during 21 days of bed rest than levels before bed rest, and levels seemed to be even lower in subjects who were exposed to 1 hour of artificial gravity per day (815). The mechanism or significance of these finding are unknown but could be related to transient artificial gravity-induced fluid shifts and/or gravitational forces affecting mineral transport and metabolism, or even that the artificial gravity could have decreased GI transit time and thus affected mineral absorption.

On early ISS missions, concentrations of zinc in serum and urine excretion did not change after flight (111). The Nutrition SMO and Biochemical Profile projects allowed for the determination of zinc in serum and urine before, during, and after flight. Serum zinc concentration was unchanged for preflight values during flight, but was significantly lower when tested soon after landing, and again 30 days later (815) (Figure 51). Concentrations of urinary zinc were higher in the first weeks of spaceflight; however, at other time points during the mission, no statistically significant change from preflight was detected (815). Although these changes likely reflect the release of zinc during bone mobilization early inflight, and recovery of musculoskeletal tissue after flight, they require further evaluation.

Concern exists that other metals, including lead, could also be released secondary to weightlessness-induced bone resorption (825, 826). A computational model developed by Garcia et al. predicted that lead levels in the blood would actually decrease during microgravity exposure. The model predicted that for the majority of astronauts, any increase in circulating lead would be more than offset by decreases in ingested or inhaled lead during the mission (827). Postflight data supported this model (827).

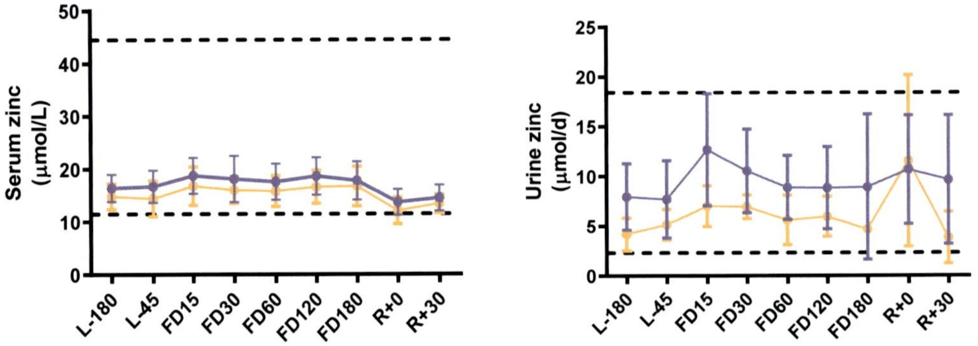

Figure 51. Serum (left) and urine (right) zinc in ISS crewmembers before, during, and after flight. Males (n=48) are represented by the blue line, and females (n=12) the gold. Black dashed lines represent normal ranges. Adapted from (815).

References for Chapter 6

1. Smith SM, Zwart SR, Kloeris V, Heer M. Nutritional biochemistry of space flight. New York: Nova Science Publishers; 2009.

10. Zwart SR, Morgan JLL, Smith SM. Iron status and its relations with oxidative damage and bone loss during long-duration space flight on the International Space Station. Am J Clin Nutr. 2013;98:217-23.

19. Garrett-Bakelman FE, Darshi M, Green SJ, Gur RC, Lin L, Macias BR, McKenna MJ, Meydan C, Mishra T, Nasrini J, Piening BD, Rizzardi LF, Sharma K, Siamwala JH, Taylor L, Vitaterna MH, Afkarian M, Afshinnekoo E, Ahadi S, Ambati A, Arya M, Bezdan D, Callahan CM, Chen S, Choi AMK, Chlipala GE, Contrepois K, Covington M, Crucian BE, De Vivo I, Dinges DF, Ebert DJ, Feinberg JI, Gandara JA, George KA, Goutsias J, Grills GS, Hargens AR, Heer M, Hillary RP, Hoofnagle AN, Hook VYH, Jenkinson G, Jiang P, Keshavarzian A, Laurie SS, Lee-McMullen B, Lumpkins SB, MacKay M, Maienschein-Cline MG, Melnick AM, Moore TM, Nakahira K, Patel HH, Pietrzyk R, Rao V, Saito R, Salins DN, Schilling JM, Sears DD, Sheridan CK, Stenger MB, Tryggvadottir R, Urban AE, Vaisar T, Van Espen B, Zhang J, Ziegler MG, Zwart SR, Charles JB, Kundrot CE, Scott GBI, Bailey SM, Basner M, Feinberg AP, Lee SMC, Mason CE, Mignot E, Rana BK, Smith SM, Snyder MP, Turek FW. The NASA Twins Study: A multidimensional analysis of a year-long human spaceflight. Science. 2019;364.

36. National Aeronautics and Space Administration Johnson Space Center. Nutritional requirements for International Space Station (ISS) missions up to 360 days. Report No.: JSC-28038. Houston, TX: National Aeronautics and Space Administration Lyndon B. Johnson Space Center, 1996.

37. National Aeronautics and Space Administration Johnson Space Center. Nutrition requirements, standards, and operating bands for exploration missions. Report No.: JSC-63555. Houston, TX: Lyndon B. Johnson Space Center; 2005.

38. National Aeronautics and Space Administration Johnson Space Center. Nutrition requirements for exploration missions up to 365 days. Report No.: JSC-67378. Houston, TX: Lyndon B. Johnson Space Center; 2020.

39. National Academies of Sciences, Engineering, and Medicine. Dietary Reference Intakes for sodium and potassium. Washington, DC: The National Academies Press. 2019.

110. Smith SM, Davis-Street JE, Rice BL, Nillen JL, Gillman PL, Block G. Nutritional status assessment in semiclosed environments: ground-based and space flight studies in humans. J Nutr. 2001;131:2053-61.

111. Smith SM, Zwart SR, Block G, Rice BL, Davis-Street JE. The nutritional status of astronauts is altered after long-term space flight aboard the International Space Station. J Nutr. 2005;135:437-43.

112. Smith SM, Wastney ME, O'Brien KO, Morukov BV, Larina IM, Abrams SA, Davis-Street JE, Oganov V, Shackelford LC. Bone markers, calcium metabolism, and calcium kinetics during extended-duration space flight on the Mir space station. J Bone Miner Res. 2005;20:208-18.

113. Heer M, Boerger A, Kamps N, Mika C, Korr C, Drummer C. Nutrient supply during recent European missions. Pflugers Arch. 2000;441:R8-14.

122. Leach CS, Rambaut PC. Biochemical responses of the Skylab crewmen: an overview. In: Johnston RS, Dietlein LF, editors. Biomedical results from Skylab (NASA SP-377). Washington, DC: National Aeronautics and Space Administration; 1977. p. 204-16.

123. Drummer C, Hesse C, Baisch F, Norsk P, Elmann-Larsen B, Gerzer R, Heer M. Water and sodium balances and their relation to body mass changes in microgravity. Eur J Clin Invest. 2000;30:1066-75.

124. Smith SM, Heer MA, Shackelford LC, Sibonga JD, Ploutz-Snyder L, Zwart SR. Benefits for bone from resistance exercise and nutrition in long-duration spaceflight: evidence from biochemistry and densitometry. J Bone Miner Res. 2012;27:1896-906.

125. Bourland C, Kloeris V, Rice B, Vodovotz Y. Food systems for space and planetary flights. In: Lane HW, Schoeller DA, editors. Nutrition in spaceflight and weightlessness models. Boca Raton, FL: CRC Press; 2000. p. 19-40.

128. Lane HW, Smith SM. Nutrition in space. In: Shils ME, Olson JA, Shike M, Ross AC, editors. Modern nutrition in health and disease. 9th ed. Baltimore, MD: Lippincott Williams & Wilkins; 1999. p. 783-8.

147. Smith SM, Zwart SR, Heer M, Hudson EK, Shackelford L, Morgan JLL. Men and women in space: bone loss and kidney stone risk after long-duration spaceflight. J Bone Miner Res. 2014;29:1639-45.

152. Smith SM, Wastney ME, Morukov BV, Larina IM, Nyquist LE, Abrams SA, Taran EN, Shih CY, Nillen JL, Davis-Street JE, Rice BL, Lane HW. Calcium metabolism before, during, and after a 3-mo spaceflight: kinetic and biochemical changes. Am J Physiol. 1999;277:R1-10.

154. Smith SM, Zwart SR, Heer M. Human adaptation to spaceflight: The role of nutrition (NP-2014-10-018-JSC). Houston, TX: National Aeronautics and Space Administration Lyndon B. Johnson Space Center; 2014.

165. Ihle R, Loucks AB. Dose-response relationships between energy availability and bone turnover in young exercising women. J Bone Miner Res. 2004;19:1231-40.

166. Baek K, Barlow AA, Allen MR, Bloomfield SA. Food restriction and simulated microgravity: effects on bone and serum leptin. J Appl Physiol (1985). 2008;104:1086-93.

194. Pietrzyk RA, Feiveson AH, Whitson PA. Mathematical model to estimate risk of calcium-containing renal stones. Miner Electrolyte Metab. 1999;25:199-203.

195. Pietrzyk RA, Jones JA, Sams CF, Whitson PA. Renal stone formation among astronauts. Aviat Space Environ Med. 2007;78:A9-13.

196. Zerwekh JE, Odvina CV, Wuermser LA, Pak CY. Reduction of renal stone risk by potassium-magnesium citrate during 5 weeks of bed rest. J Urol. 2007;177:2179-84.

210. Smith SM, Heer M, Shackelford LC, Sibonga JD, Spatz J, Pietrzyk RA, Hudson EK, Zwart SR. Bone metabolism and renal stone risk during International Space Station missions. Bone. 2015;81:712-20.

228. Griel AE, Kris-Etherton PM, Hilpert KF, Zhao G, West SG, Corwin RL. An increase in dietary n-3 fatty acids decreases a marker of bone resorption in humans. Nutr J. 2007;6:2-10.

229. Orchard TS, Ing SW, Lu B, Belury MA, Johnson K, Wactawski-Wende J, Jackson RD. The association of red blood cell n-3 and n-6 fatty acids with bone mineral density and hip fracture risk in the women's health initiative. J Bone Miner Res. 2013;28:505-15.

230. Mangano K, Kerstetter J, Kenny A, Insogna K, Walsh SJ. An investigation of the association between omega 3 FA and bone mineral density among older adults: results from the National Health and Nutrition Examination Survey years 2005-2008. Osteoporos Int. 2014;25:1033-41.

231. Zwart SR, Pierson D, Mehta S, Gonda S, Smith SM. Capacity of omega-3 fatty acids or eicosapentaenoic acid to counteract weightlessness-induced bone loss by inhibiting NF-kappaB activation: from cells to bed rest to astronauts. J Bone Miner Res. 2010;25:1049-57.

244. Shams-White MM, Chung M, Du M, Fu Z, Insogna KL, Karlsen MC, LeBoff MS, Shapses SA, Sackey J, Wallace TC, Weaver CM. Dietary protein and bone health: a systematic review and meta-analysis from the National Osteoporosis Foundation. Am J Clin Nutr. 2017;105:1528-43.

247. Zwart SR, Hargens AR, Smith SM. The ratio of animal protein intake to potassium intake is a predictor of bone resorption in space flight analogues and in ambulatory subjects. Am J Clin Nutr. 2004;80:1058-65.

249. Zwart SR, Rice BL, Dlouhy H, Shackelford LC, Heer M, Koslovsky MD, Smith SM. Dietary acid load and bone turnover during long-duration spaceflight and bed rest. Am J Clin Nutr. 2018;107:834-44.

254. Zwart SR, Crawford GE, Gillman PL, Kala G, Rodgers AS, Rogers A, Inniss AM, Rice BL, Ericson K, Coburn S, Bourbeau Y, Hudson E, Mathew G, Dekerlegand DE, Sams CF, Heer MA, Paloski WH, Smith SM. Effects of 21 days of bed rest, with or without artificial gravity, on nutritional status of humans. J Appl Physiol (1985). 2009;107:54-62.

262. Morgan JLL, Zwart SR, Heer M, Ploutz-Snyder R, Ericson K, Smith SM. Bone metabolism and nutritional status during 30-day head-down-tilt bed rest. J Appl Physiol (1985). 2012;113:1519-29.

273. Institute of Medicine. Dietary reference intakes for vitamin A, vitamin K, arsenic, boron, chromium, copper, iodine, iron, manganese, molybdenum, nickel, silicon, vanadium, and zinc. Washington, DC: National Academy Press; 2001.

279. Oh MS, Uribarri J. Electrolytes, water, and acid-base balance. In: Shils ME, Olson JA, Shike M, Ross AC, editors. Modern nutrition in health and disease. 9th ed. Baltimore, MD: Lippincott Williams & Wilkins; 1999. p. 105-40.

289. Smith SM, Krauhs JM, Leach CS. Regulation of body fluid volume and electrolyte concentrations in spaceflight. Adv Space Biol Med. 1997;6:123-65.

291. Gerzer R, Heer M. Regulation of body fluid and salt homeostasis--from observations in space to new concepts on Earth. Curr Pharm Biotechnol. 2005;6:299-304.

292. Norsk P, Drummer C, Christensen NJ, Cirillo M, Heer M, Kramer HJ, Regnard J, De Santo NG. Revised hypothesis and future perspectives. Am J Kidney Dis. 2001;38:696-8.

299. Heer M, Frings-Meuthen P, Titze J, Boschmann M, Frisch S, Baecker N, Beck L. Increasing sodium intake from a previous low or high intake affects water, electrolyte and acid-base balance differently. Br J Nutr. 2009;101:1286-94.

302. Drummer C, Heer M, Dressendorfer RA, Strasburger CJ, Gerzer R. Reduced natriuresis during weightlessness. Clin Investig. 1993;71:678-86.

307. Whitson PA, Pietrzyk RA, Morukov BV, Sams CF. The risk of renal stone formation during and after long duration space flight. Nephron. 2001;89:264-70.

309. Whitson PA, Pietrzyk RA, Pak CY, Cintron NM. Alterations in renal stone risk factors after space flight. J Urol. 1993;150:803-7.

310. Whitson PA, Pietrzyk RA, Pak CY. Renal stone risk assessment during Space Shuttle flights. J Urol. 1997;158:2305-10.

321. Deitrick JE, Whedon GD, Shorr E. Effects of immobilization upon various metabolic and physiologic functions of normal men. Am J Med. 1948;4:3-36.

322. Whedon GD, Deitrick JE, Shorr E. Modification of the effects of immobilization upon metabolic and physiologic functions of normal men by the use of an oscillating bed. Am J Med. 1949;6:684-711.

323. Keyak JH, Koyama AK, LeBlanc A, Lu Y, Lang TF. Reduction in proximal femoral strength due to long-duration spaceflight. Bone. 2009;44:449-53.

324. Bloomfield SA, Martinez DA, Boudreaux RD, Mantri AV. Microgravity stress: Bone and connective tissue. Compr Physiol. 2016;6:645-86.

325. Vico L, Hargens A. Skeletal changes during and after spaceflight. Nat Rev Rheumatol. 2018;14:229-45.

326. Demontis GC, Germani MM, Caiani EG, Barravecchia I, Passino C, Angeloni D. Human pathophysiological adaptations to the space environment. Front Physiol. 2017;8:547.

327. Smith SM, Heer M, Zwart SR. Nutrition and bone health in space. In: Holick M, Nieves J, editors. Nutrition and bone health, 2nd ed. New York: Springer; 2015. p. 687-705.

328. Vernikos J, Schneider VS. Space, gravity and the physiology of aging: parallel or convergent disciplines? A mini-review. Gerontology. 2010;56:157-66.

329. Smith SM, Abrams SA, Davis-Street JE, Heer M, O'Brien KO, Wastney ME, Zwart SR. Fifty years of human space travel: implications for bone and calcium research. Annu Rev Nutr. 2014;34:377-400.

330. Orwoll ES, Adler RA, Amin S, Binkley N, Lewiecki EM, Petak SM, Shapses SA, Sinaki M, Watts NB, Sibonga JD. Skeletal health in long-duration astronauts: nature, assessment and management recommendations from the NASA bone summit. J Bone Miner Res. 2013;28:1243-55.

331. Smith SM, Heer M. Calcium and bone metabolism during space flight. Nutrition. 2002;18:849-52.

332. Grimm D, Grosse J, Wehland M, Mann V, Reseland JE, Sundaresan A, Corydon TJ. The impact of microgravity on bone in humans. Bone. 2016;87:44-56.

333. Lang TF. What do we know about fracture risk in long-duration spaceflight? J Musculoskelet Neuronal Interact. 2006;6:319-21.

334. Cavanagh PR, Licata AA, Rice AJ. Exercise and pharmacological countermeasures for bone loss during long-duration space flight. Gravit Space Biol Bull. 2005;18:39-58.

335. Sibonga JD. Spaceflight-induced bone loss: is there an osteoporosis risk? Curr Osteoporos Rep. 2013;11:92-8.

336. LeBlanc AD, Spector ER, Evans HJ, Sibonga JD. Skeletal responses to space flight and the bed rest analog: a review. J Musculoskelet Neuronal Interact. 2007;7:33-47.

337. Carmeliet G, Vico L, Bouillon R. Space flight: a challenge for normal bone homeostasis. Crit Rev Eukaryot Gene Expr. 2001;11:131-44.

338. Cena H, Sculati M, Roggi C. Nutritional concerns and possible countermeasures to nutritional issues related to space flight. Eur J Nutr. 2003;42:99-110.

339. Weaver CM, LeBlanc A, Smith SM. Calcium and related nutrients in bone metabolism. In: Lane HW, Schoeller DA, editors. Nutrition in spaceflight and weightlessness models. Boca Raton, FL: CRC Press; 2000. p. 179-201.

340. Bikle DD, Halloran BP, Morey-Holton E. Spaceflight and the skeleton: lessons for the earthbound. Gravit Space Biol Bull. 1997;10:119-35.

341. Zwart SR, Smith SM. The impact of space flight on the human skeletal system and potential nutritional countermeasures. Intl SportMed J. 2005;6:199-214.

342. Arnaud SB, Schneider VS, Morey-Holton E. Effects of inactivity on bone and calcium metabolism. In: Sandler H, Vernikos J, editors. Inactivity: physiological effects. Orlando, FL: Academic Press, Inc.; 1986. p. 49-76.

343. Zerath E. Effects of microgravity on bone and calcium homeostasis. Adv Space Res. 1998;21:1049-58.

344. Whedon GD, Rambaut PC. Effects of long-duration space flight on calcium metabolism: Review of human studies from Skylab to the present. Acta Astronaut. 2006;58:59-81.

345. Iwamoto J, Takeda T, Sato Y. Interventions to prevent bone loss in astronauts during space flight. Keio J Med. 2005;54:55-9.

346. Smith JK. Microgravity, bone homeostasis, and insulin-like growth factor-1. Appl Sci-Basel. 2020;10.

347. Smith JK. Osteoclasts and microgravity. Life (Basel). 2020;10.

348. Gordienko KV, Novikov VE, Servuli EA, Nosovsky AM, Vasilieva GY. Detailed analysis of the central osteodensitometry data from cosmonauts participating in the Mir and ISS programs. Human Physiol. 2020;45:764-7.

349. Bloomfield SA. Disuse osteopenia. Curr Osteoporos Rep. 2010;8:91-7.

350. Androjna C, McCabe NP, Cavanagh PR, Midura RJ. Effects of spaceflight and skeletal unloading on bone fracture healing. Clin Rev Bone Min Metab. 2011;10:61-70.

351. Globus RK, Morey-Holton E. Advances in understanding the skeletal biology of spaceflight. J Gravit Physiol. 2009;22:3-12.

352. Smith MC, Jr, Rambaut PC, Vogel JM, Whittle MW. Bone mineral measurement—experiment M078. In: Johnston RS, Dietlein LF, editors. Biomedical results from Skylab (NASA SP-377). Washington, DC: National Aeronautics and Space Administration; 1977. p. 183-90.

353. Vogel JM, Whittle MW. Proceedings: Bone mineral content changes in the Skylab astronauts. Am J Roentgenol Radium Ther Nucl Med. 1976;126:1296-7.

354. Stupakov GP, Kazeykin VS, Kozlovskiy AP, Korolev VV. [Evaluation of changes in human axial skeletal bone structures during long-term spaceflights]. Kosm Biol Aviakosm Med. 1984;18(2):33-7.

355. Oganov VS, Grigor'ev AI, Voronin LI, Rakhmanov AS, Bakulin AV, Schneider VS, LeBlanc AD. [Bone mineral density in cosmonauts after flights lasting 4.5-6 months on the Mir orbital station]. Aviakosm Ekolog Med. 1992;26:20-4.

356. Vico L, Collet P, Guignandon A, Lafage-Proust MH, Thomas T, Rehaillia M, Alexandre C. Effects of long-term microgravity exposure on cancellous and cortical weight-bearing bones of cosmonauts. Lancet. 2000;355:607-11.

357. LeBlanc A, Schneider V, Shackelford L, West S, Oganov V, Bakulin A, Voronin L. Bone mineral and lean tissue loss after long duration space flight. J Musculoskelet Neuronal Interact. 2000;1:157-60.

358. Collet P, Uebelhart D, Vico L, Moro L, Hartmann D, Roth M, Alexandre C. Effects of 1- and 6-month spaceflight on bone mass and biochemistry in two humans. Bone. 1997;20:547-51.

359. Sibonga JD, Evans HJ, Smith SA, Spector ER, Yardley G. Evidence Report: Risk of bone fracture due to spaceflight-induced changes to bone. NASA. 2017. p. 1-34.

360. Sibonga JD, Cavanagh PR, Lang TF, LeBlanc AD, Schneider VS, Shackelford LC, Smith SM, Vico L. Adaptation of the skeletal system during long-duration spaceflight. Clin Rev Bone Miner Metab. 2008;5:249-61.

361. Sibonga JD, Evans HJ, Sung HG, Spector ER, Lang TF, Oganov VS, Bakulin AV, Shackelford LC, LeBlanc AD. Recovery of spaceflight-induced bone loss: bone mineral density after long-duration missions as fitted with an exponential function. Bone. 2007;41:973-8.

362. Sibonga JD, Spector ER, Johnston SL, Tarver WJ. Evaluating bone loss in ISS astronauts. Aerosp Med Hum Perform. 2015;86:A38-A44.

363. Tilton FE, Degioanni JJ, Schneider VS. Long-term follow-up of Skylab bone demineralization. Aviat Space Environ Med. 1980;51:1209-13.

364. Carpenter RD, LeBlanc AD, Evans H, Sibonga JD, Lang TF. Long-term changes in the density and structure of the human hip and spine after long-duration spaceflight. Acta Astronaut. 2010;67:71-81.

365. Sibonga JD, Spector ER, Keyak JH, Zwart SR, Smith SM, Lang TF. Use of quantitative computed tomography to assess for clinically-relevant skeletal effects of prolonged spaceflight on astronaut hips. J Clin Densitom. 2020;23:155-64.

366. Whedon GD, Lutwak L, Rambaut PC, Whittle MW, Smith MC, Reid J, Leach C, Stadler CR, Sanford DD. Mineral and nitrogen metabolic studies, experiment M071. In: Johnston RS, Dietlein LF, editors. Biomedical results from Skylab (NASA SP-377). Washington, DC: National Aeronautics and Space Administration; 1977. p. 164-74.

367. Whedon GD. Disuse osteoporosis: physiological aspects. Calcif Tissue Int. 1984;36:S146-50.

368. Whedon GD, Lutwak L, Reid J, Rambaut PC, Whittle MW, Smith MC, Leach CS. Mineral and nitrogen metabolic studies on Skylab orbital space flights. Trans Assoc Am Physicians. 1974;87:95-110.

369. Whedon GD, Lutwak L, Rambaut PC, Whittle MW, Reid J, Smith MC, Leach C, Stadler CR, Sanford DD. Mineral and nitrogen balance study observations: the second manned Skylab mission. Aviat Space Environ Med. 1976;47:391-6.

370. Parfitt AM. Bone effects of space flight: analysis by quantum concept of bone remodelling. Acta Astronaut. 1981;8:1083-90.

371. Rambaut PC, Johnston RS. Prolonged weightlessness and calcium loss in man. Acta Astronaut. 1979;6:1113-22.

372. Grigoriev AI, Oganov VS, Bakulin AV, Poliakov VV, Voronin LI, Morgun VV, Schneider VS, Murashko LV, Novikov VE, LeBlanc A, Shackelford L. [Clinical and physiological evaluation of bone changes among astronauts after long-term space flights]. Aviakosm Ekolog Med. 1998;32:21-5.

373. Minaire P, Meunier P, Edouard C, Bernard J, Courpron P, Bourret J. Quantitative histological data on disuse osteoporosis: comparison with biological data. Calcif Tissue Int. 1974;17:57-73.

374. Giangregorio L, Blimkie CJ. Skeletal adaptations to alterations in weight-bearing activity: a comparison of models of disuse osteoporosis. Sports Med. 2002;32:459-76.

375. Scott JM, Warburton DE, Williams D, Whelan S, Krassioukov A. Challenges, concerns and common problems: physiological consequences of spinal cord injury and microgravity. Spinal Cord. 2011;49:4-16.

376. Leach CS, Rambaut PC, Di Ferrante N. Amino aciduria in weightlessness. Acta Astronaut. 1979;6:1323-33.

377. Seo H, Itoh T, Murata Y, Ohmori S, Kambe F, Mohri M, Sekiguchi C, Matsui N. Changes in urinary excretion of pyridinium cross-links during Spacelab-J. Biol Sci Space. 1997;11:321-6.

378. Eyre DR, Dickson IR, Van Ness K. Collagen cross-linking in human bone and articular cartilage. Age-related changes in the content of mature hydroxypyridinium residues. Biochem J. 1988;252:495-500.

379. Uebelhart D, Gineyts E, Chapuy MC, Delmas PD. Urinary excretion of pyridinium crosslinks: a new marker of bone resorption in metabolic bone disease. Bone Miner. 1990;8:87-96.

380. Robins SP, Woitge H, Hesley R, Ju J, Seyedin S, Seibel MJ. Direct, enzyme-linked immunoassay for urinary deoxypyridinoline as a specific marker for measuring bone resorption. J Bone Miner Res. 1994;9:1643-9.

381. Seyedin SM, Kung VT, Daniloff YN, Hesley RP, Gomez B, Nielsen LA, Rosen HN, Zuk RF. Immunoassay for urinary pyridinoline: the new marker of bone resorption. J Bone Miner Res. 1993;8:635-41.

382. Delmas PD, Schlemmer A, Gineyts E, Riis B, Christiansen C. Urinary excretion of pyridinoline crosslinks correlates with bone turnover measured on iliac crest biopsy in patients with vertebral osteoporosis. J Bone Miner Res. 1991;6:639-44.

383. Demers LM. New biochemical marker for bone disease: Is it a breakthrough? Clin Chem. 1992;38:2169-70.

384. Zittermann A, Heer M, Caillot-Augusso A, Rettberg P, Scheld K, Drummer C, Alexandre C, Horneck G, Vorobiev D, Stehle P. Microgravity inhibits intestinal calcium absorption as shown by a stable strontium test. Eur J Clin Invest. 2000;30:1036-43.

385. Smith SM, Nillen JL, Leblanc A, Lipton A, Demers LM, Lane HW, Leach CS. Collagen cross-link excretion during space flight and bed rest. J Clin Endocrinol Metab. 1998;83:3584-91.

386. Caillot-Augusseau A, Lafage-Proust MH, Soler C, Pernod J, Dubois F, Alexandre C. Bone formation and resorption biological markers in cosmonauts during and after a 180-day space flight (Euromir 95). Clin Chem. 1998;44:578-85.

387. Frost HM. Bone "mass" and the "mechanostat": a proposal. Anat Rec. 1987;219:1-9.

388. Morukov BV, Orlov OI, Grigoriev AI. Calcium homeostasis in prolonged hypokinesia. Physiologist. 1989;32:S37-40.

389. Arnaud SB, Morey-Holton E. Gravity, calcium, and bone: update, 1989. Physiologist. 1990;33(1 Suppl):S-65-S-8.

390. Sorva A, Valvanne J, Tilvis RS. Serum ionized calcium and the prevalence of primary hyperparathyroidism in age cohorts of 75, 80 and 85 years. J Intern Med. 1992;231:309-12.

391. Baecker N, Frings-Meuthen P, Smith SM, Heer M. Short-term high dietary calcium intake during bedrest has no effect on markers of bone turnover in healthy men. Nutrition. 2010;26:522-7.

392. Whitson PA, Pietrzyk RA, Sams CF. Space flight and the risk of renal stones. J Gravit Physiol. 1999;6:P87-8.

393. Pavy-Le Traon A, Heer M, Narici MV, Rittweger J, Vernikos J. From space to Earth: advances in human physiology from 20 years of bed rest studies (1986-2006). Eur J Appl Physiol. 2007;101:143-94.

394. Bloomfield SA. Changes in musculoskeletal structure and function with prolonged bed rest. Med Sci Sports Exerc. 1997;29:197-206.

395. Fortney SM, Schneider VS, Greenleaf JE. The physiology of bed rest. In: Fregly MJ, Blatteis CM, editors. Handbook of Physiology, Section 4: Environmental Physiology. New York: Oxford University Press; 1996. p. 889-942.

396. Hargens AR, Vico L. Long-duration bed rest as an analog to microgravity. J Appl Physiol (1985). 2016; 120:891-903.

397. Baecker N, Tomic A, Mika C, Gotzmann A, Platen P, Gerzer R, Heer M. Bone resorption is induced on the second day of bed rest: results of a controlled crossover trial. J Appl Physiol (1985). 2003;95:977-82.

398. Heer M, Baecker N, Mika C, Boese A, Gerzer R. Immobilization induces a very rapid increase in osteoclast activity. Acta Astronaut. 2005;57:31-6.

399. Baecker N, Frings-Meuthen P, Heer M, Mester J, Liphardt AM. Effects of vibration training on bone metabolism: results from a short-term bed rest study. Eur J Appl Physiol. 2012;112:1741-50.

400. Assimos D. Re: bone metabolism and nutritional status during 30-day head-down tilt bed rest. J Urol. 2013;189:574.

401. Kakurin LI, Lobachik VI, Mikhailov VM, Senkevich YA. Antiorthostatic hypokinesia as a method of weightless simulation. Aviat Space Environ Med. 1976;47:1083-6.

402. Leblanc AD, Schneider VS, Evans HJ, Engelbretson DA, Krebs JM. Bone mineral loss and recovery fter 17 weeks of bed rest. J Bone Miner Res. 1990;5:843-50.

403. Zerwekh JE, Ruml LA, Gottschalk F, Pak CY. The effects of twelve weeks of bed rest on bone histology, biochemical markers of bone turnover, and calcium homeostasis in eleven normal subjects. J Bone Miner Res. 1998;13:1594-601.

404. Vico L, Chappard D, Alexandre C, Palle S, Minaire P, Riffat G, Morukov B, Rakhmanov S. Effects of a 120 day period of bed-rest on bone mass and bone cell activities in man: attempts at countermeasure. Bone Miner. 1987;2:383-94.

405. Spector ER, Smith SM, Sibonga JD. Skeletal effects of long-duration head-down bed rest. Aviat Space Environ Med. 2009;80:A23-8.

406. Belavy DL, Baecker N, Armbrecht G, Beller G, Buehlmeier J, Frings-Meuthen P, Rittweger J, Roth HJ, Heer M, Felsenberg D. Serum sclerostin and DKK1 in relation to exercise against bone loss in experimental bed rest. J Bone Miner Metab. 2016;34:354-65.

407. Berg HE, Eiken O, Miklavcic L, Mekjavic IB. Hip, thigh and calf muscle atrophy and bone loss after 5-week bedrest inactivity. Eur J Appl Physiol. 2007;99:283-9.

408. Armbrecht G, Belavy DL, Gast U, Bongrazio M, Touby F, Beller G, Roth HJ, Perschel FH, Rittweger J, Felsenberg D. Resistive vibration exercise attenuates bone and muscle atrophy in 56 days of bed rest: biochemical markers of bone metabolism. Osteoporos Int. 2010;21:597-607.

409. Armbrecht G, Belavy DL, Backstrom M, Beller G, Alexandre C, Rizzoli R, Felsenberg D. Trabecular and cortical bone density and architecture in women after 60 days of bed rest using high-resolution pQCT: WISE 2005. J Bone Miner Res. 2011;26:2399-410.

410. Belavy DL, Beller G, Armbrecht G, Perschel FH, Fitzner R, Bock O, Borst H, Degner C, Gast U, Felsenberg D. Evidence for an additional effect of whole-body vibration above resistive exercise alone in preventing bone loss during prolonged bed rest. Osteoporos Int. 2011;22:1581-91.

411. Belavy DL, Beller G, Ritter Z, Felsenberg D. Bone structure and density via HR-pQCT in 60d bed-rest, 2-years recovery with and without countermeasures. J Musculoskelet Neuronal Interact. 2011;11:215-26.

412. Donaldson CL, Hulley SB, Vogel JM, Hattner RS, Bayers JH, McMillan DE. Effect of prolonged bed rest on bone mineral. Metabolism. 1970;19:1071-84.

413. LeBlanc A, Schneider V, Spector E, Evans H, Rowe R, Lane H, Demers L, Lipton A. Calcium absorption, endogenous excretion, and endocrine changes during and after long-term bed rest. Bone. 1995;16 (4 suppl):301S-4S.

414. Arnaud SB, Sherrard DJ, Maloney N, Whalen RT, Fung P. Effects of 1-week head-down tilt bed rest on bone formation and the calcium endocrine system. Aviat Space Environ Med. 1992;63:14-20.

415. Hantman DA, Vogel JM, Donaldson CL, Friedman R, Goldsmith RS, Hulley SB. Attempts to prevent disuse osteoporosis by treatment with calcitonin, longitudinal compression and supplementary calcium and phosphate. J Clin Endocrinol Metab. 1973;36:845-58.

416. Jowsey J, Riggs BL, Goldsmith RS, Kelly PJ, Arnaud CD. Effects of prolonged administration of porcine calcitonin in postmenopausal osteoporosis. J Clin Endocrinol Metab. 1971;33:752-8.

417. Arnaud SB, Wolinsky I, Fung P, Vernikos J. Dietary salt and urinary calcium excretion in a human bed rest spaceflight model. Aviat Space Environ Med. 2000;71:1115-9.

418. Schneider VS, MacDonald J. Prevention of disuse osteoporosis: Clodronate therapy. In: DeLuca HF, et al., editor. Osteoporosis. Baltimore: University Park Press; 1981. p. 491.

419. Zwart SR, Oliver SAM, Fesperman JV, Kala G, Krauhs J, Ericson K, Smith SM. Nutritional status assessment before, during, and after long-duration head-down bed rest. Aviat Space Environ Med. 2009;80:A15-22.

420. Smith SM, Zwart SR, Heer M, Lee SM, Baecker N, Meuche S, Macias BR, Shackelford LC, Schneider S, Hargens AR. WISE-2005: supine treadmill exercise within lower body negative pressure and flywheel resistive exercise as a countermeasure to bed rest-induced bone loss in women during 60-day simulated microgravity. Bone. 2008;42:572-81.

421. LeBlanc A, Schneider V, Krebs J, Evans H, Jhingran S, Johnson P. Spinal bone mineral after 5 weeks of bed rest. Calcif Tissue Int. 1987;41:259-61.

422. Kim H, Iwasaki K, Miyake T, Shiozawa T, Nozaki S, Yajima K. Changes in bone turnover markers during 14-day 6 degrees head-down bed rest. J Bone Miner Metab. 2003;21:311-5.

423. Smith SM, Davis-Street JE, Fesperman JV, Calkins DS, Bawa M, Macias BR, Meyer RS, Hargens AR. Evaluation of treadmill exercise in a lower body negative pressure chamber as a countermeasure for weightlessness-induced bone loss: a bed rest study with identical twins. J Bone Miner Res. 2003;18:2223-30.

424. Smith SM, Zwart SR, Heer MA, Baecker N, Evans HJ, Feiveson AH, Shackelford LC, Leblanc AD. Effects of artificial gravity during bed rest on bone metabolism in humans. J Appl Physiol (1985). 2009;107:47-53.

425. Buehlmeier J, Frings-Meuthen P, Mohorko N, Lau P, Mazzucco S, Ferretti JL, Biolo G, Pisot R, Simunic B, Rittweger J. Markers of bone metabolism during 14 days of bed rest in young and older men. J Musculoskelet Neuronal Interact. 2017;17:399-408.

426. Arnaud SB, Fung P, Popova IA, Morey-Holton ER, Grindeland RE. Circulating parathyroid hormone and calcitonin in rats after spaceflight. J Appl Physiol (1985). 1992;73:169S-73S.

427. Morgan JLL, Heer M, Hargens AR, Macias BR, Hudson EK, Shackelford LC, Zwart SR, Smith SM. Sex-specific responses of bone metabolism and renal stone risk during bed rest. Physiol Rep. 2014;2:1-12.

428. Hefferan TE, Evans GL, Lotinun S, Zhang M, Morey-Holton E, Turner RT. Effect of gender on bone turnover in adult rats during simulated weightlessness. J Appl Physiol (1985). 2003;95:1775-80.

429. Navasiolava NM, Custaud MA, Tomilovskaya ES, Larina IM, Mano T, Gauquelin-Koch G, Gharib C, Kozlovskaya IB. Long-term dry immersion: review and prospects. Eur J Appl Physiol. 2011;111:1235-60.

430. Tomilovskaya E, Shigueva T, Sayenko D, Rukavishnikov I, Kozlovskaya I. Dry immersion as a ground-based model of microgravity physiological effects. Front Physiol. 2019;10:284.

431. Kozlovskaya IB. Fundamental and applied objectives of investigation in dry immersion. Hum Physiol. 2010;36:808-12.

432. Linossier MT, Amirova LE, Thomas M, Normand M, Bareille MP, Gauquelin-Koch G, Beck A, Costes-Salon MC, Bonneau C, Gharib C, Custaud MA, Vico L. Effects of short-term dry immersion on bone remodeling markers, insulin and adipokines. PLoS One. 2017;12:e0182970.

433. Morey-Holton ER, Turner RT. Laboratory models of adult human bone loss: Ground-based models that mimic spaceflight. In: Cavanagh PR, Rice AJ, editors. Bone Loss During Spaceflight. Cleveland, OH: Cleveland Clinic Press; 2007. p. 17-24.

434. Keune JA, Branscum AJ, Iwaniec UT, Turner RT. Effects of spaceflight on bone microarchitecture in the axial and appendicular skeleton in growing ovariectomized rats. Sci Rep. 2015;5:18671.

435. Keune JA, Branscum AJ, Wong CP, Iwaniec UT, Turner RT. Effect of leptin deficiency on the skeletal response to hindlimb unloading in adult male mice. Sci Rep. 2019;9:9336.

436. Colleran PN, Wilkerson MK, Bloomfield SA, Suva LJ, Turner RT, Delp MD. Alterations in skeletal perfusion with simulated microgravity: a possible mechanism for bone remodeling. J Appl Physiol (1985). 2000;89:1046-54.

437. Iwaniec UT, Turner RT. Influence of body weight on bone mass, architecture and turnover. J Endocrinol. 2016;230:R115-30.

438. Brent MB, Bruel A, Thomsen JS. Animal models of disuse-induced bone loss: study protocol for a systematic review. Syst Rev. 2020;9:185.

439. Morey ER, Baylink DJ. Inhibition of bone formation during space flight. Science. 1978;201:1138-41.

440. Vico L, Chappard D, Palle S, Bakulin AV, Novikov VE, Alexandre C. Trabecular bone remodeling after seven days of weightlessness exposure (BIOCOSMOS 1667). Am J Physiol. 1988;255:R243-7.

441. Jee WS, Wronski TJ, Morey ER, Kimmel DB. Effects of spaceflight on trabecular bone in rats. Am J Physiol. 1983;244:R310-4.

442. Cann CE, Adachi RR. Bone resorption and mineral excretion in rats during spaceflight. Am J Physiol. 1983;244:R327-31.

443. Wronski TJ, Morey ER. Effect of spaceflight on periosteal bone formation in rats. Am J Physiol. 1983;244:R305-9.

444. Dehority W, Halloran BP, Bikle DD, Curren T, Kostenuik PJ, Wronski TJ, Shen Y, Rabkin B, Bouraoui A, Morey-Holton E. Bone and hormonal changes induced by skeletal unloading in the mature male rat. Am J Physiol. 1999;276:E62-9.

445. Kostenuik PJ, Harris J, Halloran BP, Turner RT, Morey-Holton ER, Bikle DD. Skeletal unloading causes resistance of osteoprogenitor cells to parathyroid hormone and to insulin-like growth factor-I. J Bone Miner Res. 1999;14:21-31.

446. Turner RT, Evans GL, Wakley GK. Spaceflight results in depressed cancellous bone formation in rat humeri. Aviat Space Environ Med. 1995;66:770-4.

447. Smith BJ, King JB, Lucas EA, Akhter MP, Arjmandi BH, Stoecker BJ. Skeletal unloading and dietary copper depletion are detrimental to bone quality of mature rats. J Nutr. 2002;132:190-6.

448. Smith BJ, Lucas EA, Turner RT, Evans GL, Lerner MR, Brackett DJ, Stoecker BJ, Arjmandi BH. Vitamin E provides protection for bone in mature hindlimb unloaded male rats. Calcif Tissue Int. 2005;76:272-9.

449. Keune JA, Philbrick KA, Branscum AJ, Iwaniec UT, Turner RT. Spaceflight-induced vertebral bone loss in ovariectomized rats is associated with increased bone marrow adiposity and no change in bone formation. NPJ Microgravity. 2016;2:16016.

450. Sibonga JD, Pietrzyk R. Evidence Report: Risk of renal stone formation [online]. National Aeronautics and Space Administration. https://humanresearchroadmap.nasa.gov/Evidence/reports/Renal.pdf 2017.

451. Zerwekh JE. Nutrition and renal stone disease in space. Nutrition. 2002;18:857-63.

452. Cintron NM. Inflight assessment of renal stone risk factors. In: Bungo MW, Bagian TM, Bowman MA, Levitan BM, editors. Results of the life sciences DSOs conducted aboard the Space Shuttle 1981-1986. Houston: Space Biomedical Research Institute, Johnson Space Center; 1987. p. 13-7.

453. Whitson PA, Pietrzyk RA, Jones JA, Nelman-Gonzalez M, Hudson EK, Sams CF. Effect of potassium citrate therapy on the risk of renal stone formation during spaceflight. J Urol. 2009;182:2490-6.

454. Whitson PA, Pietrzyk RA, Sams CF. Urine volume and its effects on renal stone risk in astronauts. Aviat Space Environ Med. 2001;72:368-72.

455. National Aeronautics and Space Administration Johnson Space Center. Nutritional status assessment for extended-duration space flight. Report No.: JSC-28566, Revision 1. Houston, TX: Lyndon B. Johnson Space Center; 1999.

456. Kohri K, Yasui T, Okada A. [Space flight/bedrest immobilization and bone. Urolithiasis formation during space flight and long-term bed rest]. Clin Calcium. 2012;22:1821-8.

457. Okada A, Ohshima H, Itoh Y, Yasui T, Tozawa K, Kohri K. Risk of renal stone formation induced by long-term bed rest could be decreased by premedication with bisphosphonate and increased by resistive exercise. Int J Urol. 2008;15:630-5.

458. Watanabe Y, Ohshima H, Mizuno K, Sekiguchi C, Fukunaga M, Kohri K, Rittweger J, Felsenberg D, Matsumoto T, Nakamura T. Intravenous pamidronate prevents femoral bone loss and renal stone formation during 90-day bed rest. J Bone Miner Res. 2004;19:1771-8.

459. Monga M, Macias B, Groppo E, Kostelec M, Hargens A. Renal stone risk in a simulated microgravity environment: impact of treadmill exercise with lower body negative pressure. J Urol. 2006;176:127-31.

460. Pak CY, Skurla C, Harvey J. Graphic display of urinary risk factors for renal stone formation. J Urol. 1985;134:867-70.

461. Smith SM, McCoy T, Gazda D, Morgan JLL, Heer M, Zwart SR. Space flight calcium: implications for astronaut health, spacecraft operations, and Earth. Nutrients. 2012;4:2047-68.

462. Kozlovskaya IB, Yarmanova EN, Yegorov AD, Stepantsov VI, Fomina EV, Tomilovaskaya ES. Russian countermeasure systems for adverse effects of microgravity on long-duration ISS flights. Aerosp Med Hum Perform. 2015;86:A24-A31.

463. LeBlanc A, Schneider V. Countermeasures against space flight related bone loss. Acta Astronaut. 1992;27:89-92.

464. Lang T, Van Loon J, Bloomfield S, Vico L, Chopard A, Rittweger J, Kyparos A, Blottner D, Vuori I, Gerzer R, Cavanagh PR. Towards human exploration of space: the THESEUS review series on muscle and bone research priorities. NPJ Microgravity. 2017;3:8.

465. Shapiro JR, Schneider V. Countermeasure development: future research targets. J Gravit Physiol. 2000;7:P1-4.

466. Petersen N, Jaekel P, Rosenberger A, Weber T, Scott J, Castrucci F, Lambrecht G, Ploutz-Snyder L, Damann V, Kozlovskaya I, Mester J. Exercise in space: the European Space Agency approach to in-flight exercise countermeasures for long-duration missions on ISS. Extrem Physiol Med. 2016;5:9.

467. Hart DA, Zernicke RF. Optimal human functioning requires exercise across the lifespan: Mobility in a 1g environment is intrinsic to the integrity of multiple biological systems. Front Physiol. 2020;11:156.

468. Scott JPR, Weber T, Green DA. Introduction to the Frontiers Research Topic: Optimization of exercise countermeasures for human space flight - Lessons from terrestrial physiology and operational considerations. Front Physiol. 2019;10:173.

469. Hawkey A. The importance of exercising in space. Interdiscip Sci Rev. 2003;28:130-8.

470. Oganov VS, Bogomolov VV. [Human bone system in microgravity: review of research data, hypotheses and predictability of musculoskeletal system state in extended (exploration) missions]. Aviakosm Ekolog Med. 2009;43:3-12.

471. Tesch PA, Berg HE. Resistance training in space. Int J Sports Med. 1997;18 Suppl 4:S322-4.

472. Novotny SC, Perusek GP, Rice AJ, Comstock BA, Bansal A, Cavanagh PR. A harness for enhanced comfort and loading during treadmill exercise in space. Acta Astronaut. 2013;89:205-14.

473. Genc KO, Gopalakrishnan R, Kuklis MM, Maender CC, Rice AJ, Bowersox KD, Cavanagh PR. Foot forces during exercise on the International Space Station. J Biomech. 2010;43:3020-7.

474. Schneider SM, Amonette WE, Blazine K, Bentley J, Lee SM, Loehr JA, Moore AD, Jr., Rapley M, Mulder ER, Smith SM. Training with the International Space Station interim resistive exercise device. Med Sci Sports Exerc. 2003;35:1935-45.

475. Lang T, LeBlanc A, Evans H, Lu Y, Genant H, Yu A. Cortical and trabecular bone mineral loss from the spine and hip in long-duration spaceflight. J Bone Miner Res. 2004;19:1006-12.

476. Loerch LH. Exercise countermeasures on ISS: Summary and future directions. Aerosp Med Hum Perform. 2015;86:A92-A4.

477. Loehr JA, Lee SM, English KL, Sibonga J, Smith SM, Spiering BA, Hagan RD. Musculoskeletal adaptations to training with the advanced resistive exercise device. Med Sci Sports Exerc. 2011;43:146-56.

478. Sibonga J, Matsumoto T, Jones J, Shapiro J, Lang T, Shackelford L, Smith SM, Young M, Keyak J, Kohri K, Ohshima H, Spector E, LeBlanc A. Resistive exercise in astronauts on prolonged spaceflights provides partial protection against spaceflight-induced bone loss. Bone. 2019;128:112037.

479. Shackelford LC, LeBlanc AD, Driscoll TB, Evans HJ, Rianon NJ, Smith SM, Spector E, Feeback DL, Lai D. Resistance exercise as a countermeasure to disuse-induced bone loss. J Appl Physiol (1985). 2004;97:119-29.

480. Belavy DL, Bock O, Borst H, Armbrecht G, Gast U, Degner C, Beller G, Soll H, Salanova M, Habazettl H, Heer M, de Haan A, Stegeman DF, Cerretelli P, Blottner D, Rittweger J, Gelfi C, Kornak U, Felsenberg D. The 2nd Berlin BedRest Study: protocol and implementation. J Musculoskelet Neuronal Interact. 2010;10:207-19.

481. Smith SM, Castaneda-Sceppa C, O'Brien KO, Abrams SA, Gillman P, Brooks NE, Cloutier GJ, Heer M, Zwart SR, Wastney ME. Calcium kinetics during bed rest with artificial gravity and exercise countermeasures. Osteoporos Int. 2014;25:2237-44.

482. Berg HE, Tesch PA. Force and power characteristics of a resistive exercise device for use in space. Acta Astronaut. 1998;42:219-30.

483. Rittweger J, Frost HM, Schiessl H, Ohshima H, Alkner B, Tesch P, Felsenberg D. Muscle atrophy and bone loss after 90 days' bed rest and the effects of flywheel resistive exercise and pamidronate: results from the LTBR study. Bone. 2005;36:1019-29.

484. Ploutz-Snyder LL, Downs M, Goetchius E, Crowell B, English KL, Ploutz-Snyder R, Ryder JW, Dillon EL, Sheffield-Moore M, Scott JM. Exercise training mitigates multisystem deconditioning during bed rest. Med Sci Sports Exerc. 2018;50:1920-8.

485. Belavy DL, Armbrecht G, Gast U, Richardson CA, Hides JA, Felsenberg D. Countermeasures against lumbar spine deconditioning in prolonged bed rest: resistive exercise with and without whole body vibration. J Appl Physiol (1985). 2010;109:1801-11.

486. Wang H, Wan Y, Tam KF, Ling S, Bai Y, Deng Y, Liu Y, Zhang H, Cheung WH, Qin L, Cheng JC, Leung KS, Li Y. Resistive vibration exercise retards bone loss in weight-bearing skeletons during 60 days bed rest. Osteoporos Int. 2012;23:2169-78.

487. Rittweger J, Beller G, Armbrecht G, Mulder E, Buehring B, Gast U, Dimeo F, Schubert H, de Haan A, Stegeman DF, Schiessl H, Felsenberg D. Prevention of bone loss during 56 days of strict bed rest by side-alternating resistive vibration exercise. Bone. 2010;46:137-47.

488. Schneider VS, McDonald J. Skeletal calcium homeostasis and countermeasures to prevent disuse osteoporosis. Calcif Tissue Int. 1984;36 Suppl 1:S151-44.

489. Grigoriev AI, Morukov BV, Oganov VS, Rakhmanov AS, Buravkova LB. Effect of exercise and bisphosphonate on mineral balance and bone density during 360 day antiorthostatic hypokinesia. J Bone Miner Res. 1992;7 Suppl 2:S449-55.

490. Zwart SR, Hargens AR, Lee SM, Macias BR, Watenpaugh DE, Tse K, Smith SM. Lower body negative pressure treadmill exercise as a countermeasure for bed rest-induced bone loss in female identical twins. Bone. 2007;40:529-37.

491. Thomsen JS, Morukov BV, Vico L, Alexandre C, Saparin PI, Gowin W. Cancellous bone structure of iliac crest biopsies following 370 days of head-down bed rest. Aviat Space Environ Med. 2005;76:915-22.

492. Hargens AR, Watenpaugh DE, Lee SMC, Boda WL, Smith SM, Macias B, Groppo E, Schneider S, O'Leary D, Meyer RS, Kawai Y. Physiologic countermeasures for long-duration space flight: review of treadmill exercise within lower body negative pressure. J Adapt Med. 2003;7:2-6.

493. Campbell MR, Charles JB. Historical review of lower body negative pressure research in space medicine. Aerosp Med Hum Perform. 2015;86:633-40.

494. Petersen LG, Hargens A, Bird EM, Ashari N, Saalfeld J, Petersen JCG. Mobile Lower Body Negative Pressure Suit as an Integrative Countermeasure for Spaceflight. Aerosp Med Hum Perform. 2019;90:993-9.

495. Ashari N, Hargens AR. The mobile lower body negative pressure gravity suit for long-duration spaceflight. Front Physiol. 2020;11:977.

496. Petersen LG, Lawley JS, Lilja-Cyron A, Petersen JCG, Howden EJ, Sarma S, Cornwell WK, 3rd, Zhang R, Whitworth LA, Williams MA, Juhler M, Levine BD. Lower body negative pressure to safely reduce intracranial pressure. J Physiol. 2019;597:237-48.

497. Vernikos J. Artificial gravity intermittent centrifugation as a space flight countermeasure. J Gravit Physiol. 1997;4:P13-6.

498. Clément G, Bukley AP, editors. Artificial gravity. New York: Springer; 2007.

499. Clément GR, Charles JB, Paloski WH. Revisiting the needs for artificial gravity during deep space missions. REACH - Reviews in Human Space Exploration. 2016;1:1-10.

500. Clément G. International roadmap for artificial gravity research. NPJ Microgravity. 2017;3:29.

501. Clément G, Pavy-Le Traon A. Centrifugation as a countermeasure during actual and simulated microgravity: a review. Eur J Appl Physiol. 2004;92:235-48.

502. Clément GR, Bukley AP, Paloski WH. Artificial gravity as a countermeasure for mitigating physiological deconditioning during long-duration space missions. Front Syst Neurosci. 2015;9:92.

503. Wolfe JW, Rummel JD. Long-term effects of microgravity and possible countermeasures. Adv Space Res. 1992;12:281-4.

504. Clément G, Paloski WH, Rittweger J, Linnarsson D, Bareille MP, Mulder E, Wuyts FL, Zange J. Centrifugation as a countermeasure during bed rest and dry immersion: What has been learned? J Musculoskelet Neuronal Interact. 2016;16:84-91.

505. Vernikos J, Ludwig DA, Ertl AC, Wade CE, Keil L, O'Hara D. Effect of standing or walking on physiological changes induced by head down bed rest: implications for spaceflight. Aviat Space Environ Med. 1996;67:1069-79.

506. Issekutz B, Jr., Blizzard JJ, Birkhead NC, Rodahl K. Effect of prolonged bed rest on urinary calcium output. J Appl Physiol. 1966;21:1013-20.

507. Greenleaf JE, Chou JL, Stad NJ, Leftheriotis GP, Arndt NF, Jackson CG, Simonson SR, Barnes PR. Short-arm (1.9 m) +2.2 Gz acceleration: isotonic exercise load-O2 uptake relationship. Aviat Space Environ Med. 1999;70:1173-82.

508. Yang Y, Kaplan A, Pierre M, Adams G, Cavanagh P, Takahashi C, Kreitenberg A, Hicks J, Keyak J, Caiozzo V. Space cycle: a human-powered centrifuge that can be used for hypergravity resistance training. Aviat Space Environ Med. 2007;78:2-9.

509. Yang Y, Baker M, Graf S, Larson J, Caiozzo VJ. Hypergravity resistance exercise: the use of artificial gravity as potential countermeasure to microgravity. J Appl Physiol (1985). 2007;103:1879-87.

510. Naumann FL, Bennell KL, Wark JD. The effects of +Gz force on the bone mineral density of fighter pilots. Aviat Space Environ Med. 2001;72:177-81.

511. Naumann FL, Grant MC, Dhaliwal SS. Changes in cervical spine bone mineral density in response to flight training. Aviat Space Environ Med. 2004;75:255-9.

512. Iwase S, Takada H, Watanabe Y, Ishida K, Akima H, Katayama K, Iwase M, Hirayanagi K, Shiozawa T, Hamaoka T, Masuo Y, Custaud MA. Effect of centrifuge-induced artificial gravity and ergometric exercise on cardiovascular deconditioning, myatrophy, and osteoporosis induced by a -6 degrees head-down bedrest. J Gravit Physiol. 2004;11:P243-4.

513. Young LR, Paloski WH. Short radius intermittent centrifugation as a countermeasure to bed-rest and 0-G deconditioning: IMAG pilot study summary and recommendations for research. J Gravit Physiol. 2007;14:P31-3.

514. Stenger MB, Evans JM, Knapp CF, Lee SM, Phillips TR, Perez SA, Moore AD, Jr., Paloski WH, Platts SH. Artificial gravity training reduces bed rest-induced cardiovascular deconditioning. Eur J Appl Physiol. 2012;112:605-16.

515. Symons TB, Sheffield-Moore M, Chinkes DL, Ferrando AA, Paddon-Jones D. Artificial gravity maintains skeletal muscle protein synthesis during 21 days of simulated microgravity. J Appl Physiol (1985). 2009;107:34-8.

516. Rittweger J, Bareille MP, Clément G, Linnarsson D, Paloski WH, Wuyts F, Zange J, Angerer O. Short-arm centrifugation as a partially effective musculoskeletal countermeasure during 5-day head-down tilt bed rest--results from the BRAG1 study. Eur J Appl Physiol. 2015;115:1233-44.

517. Frett T, Mayrhofer M, Schwandtner J, Anken R, Petrat G. An innovative short arm centrifuge for future studies on the effects of artificial gravity on the human body. Microgravity Sci Technol. 2014;26:249-55.

518. Heer M, Baecker N, Zwart SR, Smith SM. Interactions between artificial gravity, affected physiological systems, and nutrition. In: Clement G, Bukley A, editors. Artificial gravity. New York: Springer; 2007. p. 249-70.

519. Slatkovska L, Alibhai SM, Beyene J, Cheung AM. Effect of whole-body vibration on BMD: a systematic review and meta-analysis. Osteoporos Int. 2010;21:1969-80.

520. Holguin N, Uzer G, Chiang FP, Rubin C, Judex S. Brief daily exposure to low-intensity vibration mitigates the degradation of the intervertebral disc in a frequency-specific manner. J Appl Physiol (1985). 2011;111:1846-53.

521. Kiel DP, Hannan MT, Barton BA, Bouxsein ML, Lang TF, Brown KM, Shane E, Magaziner J, Zimmerman S, Rubin CT. Insights from the conduct of a device trial in older persons: low magnitude mechanical stimulation for musculoskeletal health. Clin Trials. 2010;7:354-67.

522. Kiel DP, Hannan MT, Barton BA, Bouxsein ML, Sisson E, Lang T, Allaire B, Dewkett D, Carroll D, Magaziner J, Shane E, Leary ET, Zimmerman S, Rubin CT. Low-magnitude mechanical stimulation to improve bone density in persons of advanced age: A randomized, placebo-controlled trial. J Bone Miner Res. 2015;30:1319-28.

523. Xie L, Rubin C, Judex S. Enhancement of the adolescent murine musculoskeletal system using low-level mechanical vibrations. J Appl Physiol (1985). 2008;104:1056-62.

524. Rubin C, Judex S, Qin YX. Low-level mechanical signals and their potential as a non-pharmacological intervention for osteoporosis. Age Ageing. 2006;35 Suppl 2:ii32-ii6.

525. Rubin C, Pope M, Fritton JC, Magnusson M, Hansson T, McLeod K. Transmissibility of 15-hertz to 35-hertz vibrations to the human hip and lumbar spine: determining the physiologic feasibility of delivering low-level anabolic mechanical stimuli to skeletal regions at greatest risk of fracture because of osteoporosis. Spine. 2003;28:2621-7.

526. Rubin C, Recker R, Cullen D, Ryaby J, McCabe J, McLeod K. Prevention of postmenopausal bone loss by a low-magnitude, high-frequency mechanical stimuli: a clinical trial assessing compliance, efficacy, and safety. J Bone Miner Res. 2004;19:343-51.

527. Rubin C, Turner AS, Bain S, Mallinckrodt C, McLeod K. Anabolism. Low mechanical signals strengthen long bones. Nature. 2001;412:603-4.

528. Rubin C, Turner AS, Mallinckrodt C, Jerome C, McLeod K, Bain S. Mechanical strain, induced noninvasively in the high-frequency domain, is anabolic to cancellous bone, but not cortical bone. Bone. 2002;30:445-52.

529. Rubin CT, Capilla E, Luu YK, Busa B, Crawford H, Nolan DJ, Mittal V, Rosen CJ, Pessin JE, Judex S. Adipogenesis is inhibited by brief, daily exposure to high-frequency, extremely low-magnitude mechanical signals. Proc Natl Acad Sci USA. 2007;104:17879-84.

530. Holguin N, Muir J, Rubin C, Judex S. Short applications of very low-magnitude vibrations attenuate expansion of the intervertebral disc during extended bed rest. Spine J. 2009;9:470-7.

531. Owen PJ, Belavy DL, Rittweger J. Using whole-body vibration for countermeasure exercise. In: Rittweger J, editor. Manual of Vibration Exercise and Vibration Therapy. Switzerland: Springer Nature; 2020. p. 229-44.

532. Belavy DL, Hides JA, Wilson SJ, Stanton W, Dimeo FC, Rittweger J, Felsenberg D, Richardson CA. Resistive simulated weightbearing exercise with whole body vibration reduces lumbar spine deconditioning in bed-rest. Spine (Phila Pa 1976). 2008;33:E121-31.

533. Fleisch H, Russell RG, Bisaz S, Casey PA, Muhlbauer RC. The influence of pyrophosphate analogues (diphosphonates) on the precipitation and dissolution of calcium phosphate in vitro and in vivo. Calcif Tissue Res. 1968:Suppl:10-a.

534. Fleisch H, Russell RG, Francis MD. Diphosphonates inhibit hydroxyapatite dissolution in vitro and bone resorption in tissue culture and in vivo. Science. 1969;165:1262-4.

535. Michael WR, King WR, Francis MD. Effectiveness of diphosphonates in preventing "osteoporosis" of disuse in the rat. Clin Orthop Relat Res. 1971;78:271-6.

536. Fleisch H. Experimental basis for the clinical use of diphosphonates in Paget's disease of bone. Arthritis Rheum. 1980;23:1162-71.

537. Minaire P, Berard E, Meunier PJ, Edouard C, Goedert G, Pilonchery G. Effects of disodium dichloromethylene diphosphonate on bone loss in paraplegic patients. J Clin Invest. 1981;68:1086-92.

538. Shapiro J, Smith B, Beck T, Ballard P, Dapthary M, Brintzenhofeszoc K, Caminis J. Treatment with zoledronic acid ameliorates negative geometric changes in the proximal femur following acute spinal cord injury. Calcif Tissue Int. 2007;80:316-22.

539. Rowe EJ, Hausmann E. The alteration of osteoclast morphology by diphosphonates in bone organ culture. Calcif Tissue Res. 1976;20:53-60.

540. Chappard D, Alexandre C, Palle S, Vico L, Morukov BV, Rodionova SS, Minaire P, Riffat G. Effects of a bisphosphonate (1-hydroxy ethylidene-1,1 bisphosphonic acid) on osteoclast number during prolonged bed rest in healthy humans. Metabolism. 1989;38:822-5.

541. Watts NB, Chesnut CH, 3rd, Genant HK, Harris ST, Jackson RD, Licata AA, Miller PD, Mysiw WJ, Richmond B, Valent D. History of etidronate. Bone. 2020;134:115222.

542. Lockwood DR, Vogel JM, Schneider VS, Hulley SB. Effect of the diphosphonate EHDP on bone mineral metabolism during prolonged bed rest. J Clin Endocrinol Metab. 1975;41:533-41.

543. Schneider VS, Hulley SB, Donaldson CL, Vogel JM, Rosen SN, Hantman DA, Lockwood DR, Seid D, Hyatt KH, Jacobson LB. The prevention of bone mineral changes induced by bed rest: modification by (1) Static compression simulating weight bearing; (2) Combined supplementation of oral calcium and phosphate; (3) calcitonin injections; (4) oscillating compression; (5) the oral diophosphonate-disodium etidronate; (6) Lower body negative presure: NASA 1975. Report No.: NASA Terminal Report for Contract #T-81070; CR-141453.

544. Maheshwari UR, Leybin L, McDonald JT, Schneider VS, Newbrun E, Hodge HC. Effect of dichloromethylene diphosphonate on fluoride balance in healthy men. J Dent Res. 1983;62:559-61.

545. LeBlanc AD, Driscol TB, Shackelford LC, Evans HJ, Rianon NJ, Smith SM, Feeback DL, Lai D. Alendronate as an effective countermeasure to disuse induced bone loss. J Musculoskelet Neuronal Interact. 2002;2:335-43.

546. Leblanc A, Matsumoto T, Jones J, Shapiro J, Lang T, Shackelford L, Smith SM, Evans H, Spector E, Ploutz-Snyder R, Sibonga J, Keyak J, Nakamura T, Kohri K, Ohshima H. Bisphosphonates as a supplement to exercise to protect bone during long-duration spaceflight. Osteoporos Int. 2013;24:2105-14.

547. Li CY, Majeska RJ, Laudier DM, Mann R, Schaffler MB. High-dose risedronate treatment partially preserves cancellous bone mass and microarchitecture during long-term disuse. Bone. 2005;37:287-95.

548. Li CY, Price C, Delisser K, Nasser P, Laudier D, Clément M, Jepsen KJ, Schaffler MB. Long-term disuse osteoporosis seems less sensitive to bisphosphonate treatment than other osteoporosis. J Bone Miner Res. 2005;20:117-24.

549. Wimalawansa SM, Chapa MT, Wei JN, Westlund KN, Quast MJ, Wimalawansa SJ. Reversal of weightlessness-induced musculoskeletal losses with androgens: quantification by MRI. J Appl Physiol (1985). 1999;86:1841-6.

550. Wimalawansa SM, Wimalawansa SJ. Simulated weightlessness-induced attenuation of testosterone production may be responsible for bone loss. Endocrine. 1999;10:253-60.

551. Strollo F. Hormonal changes in humans during spaceflight. Adv Space Biol Med. 1999;7:99-129.

552. Strollo F, Boitani C, Basciani S, Pecorelli L, Palumbo D, Borgia L, Masini MA, More M, Strollo G, Spera G, Uva BM, Riondino G. The pituitary-testicular axis in microgravity: analogies with the aging male syndrome. J Endocrinol Invest. 2005;28:78-83.

553. Strollo F, Masini MA, Pastorino M, Ricci F, Vadrucci S, Cogoli-Greuter M, Uva BM. Microgravity-induced alterations in cultured testicular cells. J Gravit Physiol. 2004;11:P187-8.

554. Strollo F, Riondino G, Harris B, Strollo G, Casarosa E, Mangrossa N, Ferretti C, Luisi M. The effect of microgravity on testicular androgen secretion. Aviat Space Environ Med. 1998;69:133-6.

555. Strollo F, Strollo G, More M, Bollanti L, Ciarmatori A, Longo E, Quintiliani R, Mambro A, Mangrossa N, Ferretti C. Hormonal adaptation to real and simulated microgravity. J Gravit Physiol. 1998;5:P89-92.

556. Strollo F, Strollo G, Morè M, Mangrossa N, Riondino G, Luisi M, Casarosa E. Space flight induces endocrine changes at both the pituitary and peripheral level in the absence of any major chronobiologic disturbances. In: Sahm PR, Keller MH, Schiewe B, editors. Proceedings of the Norderney Symposium on Scientific Results of the German Spacelab Mission D-2. Norderney, Germany: Wissenschaftliche Projectführung D-2; 1995. p. 743-7.

557. Sandal PH, Kim D, Fiebig L, Winnard A, Caplan N, Green DA, Weber T. Effectiveness of nutritional countermeasures in microgravity and its ground-based analogues to ameliorate musculoskeletal and cardiopulmonary deconditioning - a systematic review. PLoS One. 2020;15:e0234412.

558. Zorbas YG, Kakuris KK, Deogenov VA, Yerullis KB. Inadequacy of calcium supplements to normalize muscle calcium deficiency in healthy subjects during prolonged hypokinesia. Nutrition. 2008;24:217-23.

559. Hatton DC, Yue Q, Dierickx J, Roullet C, Otsuka K, Watanabe M, Coste S, Roullet JB, Phanouvang T, Orwoll E, Orwoll S, McCarron DA. Calcium metabolism and cardiovascular function after spaceflight. J Appl Physiol (1985). 2002;92:3-12.

560. Hulley SB, Vogel JM, Donaldson CL, Bayers JH, Friedman RJ, Rosen SN. The effect of supplemental oral phosphate on the bone mineral changes during prolonged bed rest. J Clin Invest. 1971;50:2506-18.

561. Frings-Meuthen P, Bernhardt G, Buehlmeier J, Baecker N, May F, Heer M. The negative effect of unloading exceeds the bone-sparing effect of alkaline supplementation: a bed rest study. Osteoporos Int. 2019;30:431-9.

562. Sun D, Krishnan A, Zaman K, Lawrence R, Bhattacharya A, Fernandes G. Dietary n-3 fatty acids decrease osteoclastogenesis and loss of bone mass in ovariectomized mice. J Bone Miner Res. 2003;18:1206-16.

563. Ellis FR, Holesh S, Ellis JW. Incidence of osteoporosis in vegetarians and omnivores. Am J Clin Nutr. 1972;25:555-8.

564. Ambroszkiewicz J, Chelchowska M, Szamotulska K, Rowicka G, Klemarczyk W, Strucinska M, Gajewska J. The assessment of bone regulatory pathways, bone turnover, and bone mineral density in vegetarian and omnivorous children. Nutrients. 2018;10.

565. Burckhardt P. The role of low acid load in vegetarian diet on bone health: a narrative review. Swiss Med Wkly. 2016;146:w14277.

566. Ho-Pham LT, Vu BQ, Lai TQ, Nguyen ND, Nguyen TV. Vegetarianism, bone loss, fracture and vitamin D: a longitudinal study in Asian vegans and non-vegans. Eur J Clin Nutr. 2012;66:75-82.

567. Lanham-New SA. Is "vegetarianism" a serious risk factor for osteoporotic fracture? Am J Clin Nutr. 2009;90:910-1.

568. Ho-Pham LT, Nguyen ND, Nguyen TV. Effect of vegetarian diets on bone mineral density: a Bayesian meta-analysis. Am J Clin Nutr. 2009;90:943-50.

569. Iguacel I, Miguel-Berges ML, Gomez-Bruton A, Moreno LA, Julian C. Veganism, vegetarianism, bone mineral density, and fracture risk: a systematic review and meta-analysis. Nutr Rev. 2019;77:1-18.

570. Shapses SA. Do we need to Be concerned about bone mineral density in vegetarians and vegans? J Nutr. 2020;150:983-4.

571. Karavasiloglou N, Selinger E, Gojda J, Rohrmann S, Kuhn T. Differences in bone mineral density between adult vegetarians and nonvegetarians become marginal when accounting for differences in anthropometric factors. J Nutr. 2020;150:1266-71.

572. Ferraro PM, Bargagli M, Trinchieri A, Gambaro G. Risk of kidney stones: influence of dietary factors, dietary patterns, and vegetarian-vegan diets. Nutrients. 2020;12.

573. Rodriguez A, Curhan GC, Gambaro G, Taylor EN, Ferraro PM. Mediterranean diet adherence and risk of incident kidney stones. Am J Clin Nutr. 2020.

574. Papageorgiou M, Martin D, Colgan H, Cooper S, Greeves JP, Tang JCY, Fraser WD, Elliott-Sale KJ, Sale C. Bone metabolic responses to low energy availability achieved by diet or exercise in active eumenorrheic women. Bone. 2018;114:181-8.

575. Hawkins J, Cifuentes M, Pleshko NL, Ambia-Sobhan H, Shapses SA. Energy restriction is associated with lower bone mineral density of the tibia and femur in lean but not obese female rats. J Nutr. 2010;140:31-7.

576. McGrath C, Sankaran JS, Misaghian-Xanthos N, Sen B, Xie Z, Styner MA, Zong X, Rubin J, Styner M. Exercise degrades bone in caloric restriction, despite suppression of Marrow Adipose Tissue (MAT). J Bone Miner Res. 2020;35:106-15.

577. Banu J, Orhii PB, Okafor MC, Wang L, Kalu DN. Analysis of the effects of growth hormone, exercise and food restriction on cancellous bone in different bone sites in middle-aged female rats. Mech Ageing Dev. 2001;122:849-64.

578. Banu MJ, Orhii PB, Mejia W, McCarter RJ, Mosekilde L, Thomsen JS, Kalu DN. Analysis of the effects of growth hormone, voluntary exercise, and food restriction on diaphyseal bone in female F344 rats. Bone. 1999;25:469-80.

579. O'Leary TJ, Walsh NP, Casey A, Izard RM, Tang JC, Fraser WD, Greeves JP. Supplementary energy increases bone formation during arduous military training. Med Sci Sports Exerc. 2020.

580. Shapses SA, Sukumar D. Bone metabolism in obesity and weight loss. Annu Rev Nutr. 2012;32:287-309.

581. Schafer AL. Decline in bone mass during weight loss: A cause for concern? J Bone Miner Res. 2016;31:36-9.

582. Wright CS, Li J, Campbell WW. Effects of dietary protein quantity on bone quantity following weight loss: a systematic review and meta-analysis. Adv Nutr. 2019;10:1089-107.

583. Cormick G, Belizan JM. Calcium Intake and Health. Nutrients. 2019;11.

584. Institute of Medicine. Dietary reference intakes for calcium and vitamin D. Washington, DC: National Academy Press; 2011.

585. Schneider VS, LeBlanc A, Huntoon CL. Prevention of space flight induced soft tissue calcification and disuse osteoporosis. Acta Astronaut. 1993;29:139-40.

586. Skulan J, Bullen T, Anbar AD, Puzas JE, Shackelford L, LeBlanc A, Smith SM. Natural calcium isotopic composition of urine as a marker of bone mineral balance. Clin Chem. 2007;53:1155-8.

587. Skulan JL, DePaolo DJ. Calcium isotope fractionation between soft and mineralized tissue as a monitor of calcium use in vertebrates. Proc Natl Acad Sci USA. 1999;96:13709-13.

588. Morgan JLL, Skulan JL, Gordon GW, Romaniello SJ, Smith SM, Anbar AD. Rapidly assessing changes in bone mineral balance using natural stable calcium isotopes. Proc Natl Acad Sci USA. 2012;109:9989-94.

589. Russell WA, Papanastassiou DA, Tombrello TA. Ca isotope fractionation on earth and other solar-system materials. Geochim Cosmochim Acta. 1978;42:1075-90.

590. Morgan JLL, Gordon GW, Arrua RC, Skulan JL, Anbar AD, Bullen TD. High-precision measurement of variations in calcium isotope ratios in urine by multiple collector inductively coupled plasma mass spectrometry. Anal Chem. 2011;83:6956-62.

591. Rosen CJ, Abrams SA, Aloia JF, Brannon PM, Clinton SK, Durazo-Arvizu RA, Gallagher JC, Gallo RL, Jones G, Kovacs CS, Manson JE, Mayne ST, Ross AC, Shapses SA, Taylor CL. IOM committee members respond to Endocrine Society vitamin D guideline. J Clin Endocrinol Metab. 2012;97:1146-52.

592. Ross AC, Manson JE, Abrams SA, Aloia JF, Brannon PM, Clinton SK, Durazo-Arvizu RA, Gallagher JC, Gallo RL, Jones G, Kovacs CS, Mayne ST, Rosen CJ, Shapses SA. The 2011 report on dietary reference intakes for calcium and vitamin D from the Institute of Medicine: what clinicians need to know. J Clin Endocrinol Metab. 2011;96:53-8.

593. Ross AC, Manson JE, Abrams SA, Aloia JF, Brannon PM, Clinton SK, Durazo-Arvizu RA, Gallagher JC, Gallo RL, Jones G, Kovacs CS, Mayne ST, Rosen CJ, Shapses SA. The 2011 Dietary Reference Intakes for calcium and vitamin D: what dietetics practitioners need to know. J Am Diet Assoc. 2011;111:524-7.

594. Taylor CL, Sempos CT, Davis CD, Brannon PM. Vitamin D: Moving forward to address emerging science. Nutrients. 2017;9.

595. Holick MF, Chen TC, Lu Z, Sauter E. Vitamin D and skin physiology: a D-lightful story. J Bone Miner Res. 2007;22 Suppl 2:V28-33.

596. Gilchrest BA. Sun exposure and vitamin D sufficiency. Am J Clin Nutr. 2008;88:570S-7S.

597. Gilchrest BA. Sun protection and Vitamin D: three dimensions of obfuscation. J Steroid Biochem Mol Biol. 2007;103:655-63.

598. Mohr SB, Garland CF, Gorham ED, Grant WB, Garland FC. Relationship between low ultraviolet B irradiance and higher breast cancer risk in 107 countries. Breast J. 2008;14:255-60.

599. Morey-Holton ER, Schnoes HK, DeLuca HF, Phelps ME, Klein RF, Nissenson RH, Arnaud CD. Vitamin D metabolites and bioactive parathyroid hormone levels during Spacelab 2. Aviat Space Environ Med. 1988;59:1038-41.

600. Halloran BP, Bikle DD, Harris J, Foskett HC, Morey-Holton E. Skeletal unloading decreases production of 1,25-dihydroxyvitamin D. Am J Physiol. 1993;264:E712-6.

601. Halloran BP, Bikle DD, Wronski TJ, Globus RK, Levens MJ, Morey-Holton E. The role of 1,25-dihydroxyvitamin D in the inhibition of bone formation induced by skeletal unloading. Endocrinology. 1986;118:948-54.

602. Morey-Holton ER, Globus RK. Hindlimb unloading of growing rats: a model for predicting skeletal changes during space flight. Bone. 1998;22:83S-8S.

603. Smith SM, Gardner KK, Locke J, Zwart SR. Vitamin D supplementation during Antarctic winter. Am J Clin Nutr. 2009;89:1092-8.

604. Zwart SR, Mehta SK, Ploutz-Snyder R, Bourbeau Y, Locke JP, Pierson DL, Smith SM. Response to vitamin D supplementation during Antarctic winter is related to BMI, and supplementation can mitigate Epstein-Barr Virus Reactivation. J Nutr. 2011;141:692-7.

605. Zwart SR, Parsons H, Kimlin M, Innis SM, Locke JP, Smith SM. A 250 µg/week dose of vitamin D was as effective as a 50 µg/d dose in healthy adults, but a regimen of four weekly followed by monthly doses of 1250 µg raised the risk of hypercalciuria. Br J Nutr. 2013;110:1866-72.

606. Zwart SR, Smith SM. Vitamin D and COVID-19: Lessons from spaceflight analogs. J Nutr. 2020;150:2624-7.

607. Bjorkman M, Sorva A, Risteli J, Tilvis R. Vitamin D supplementation has minor effects on parathyroid hormone and bone turnover markers in vitamin D-deficient bedridden older patients. Age Ageing. 2008;37:25-31.

608. EFSA Panel on Dietetic Products Nutrition and Allergies. Scientific opinion on the tolerable upper intake level of vitamin D. EFSA Journal. 2012;10:2813.

609. Sanders KM, Nicholson GC, Ebeling PR. Is high dose vitamin D harmful? Calcif Tissue Int. 2013;92:191-206.

610. Sanders KM, Stuart AL, Williamson EJ, Simpson JA, Kotowicz MA, Young D, Nicholson GC. Annual high-dose oral vitamin D and falls and fractures in older women: a randomized controlled trial. JAMA. 2010;303:1815-22.

611. Allan GM, Cranston L, Lindblad A, McCormack J, Kolber MR, Garrison S, Korownyk C. Vitamin D: A Narrative review examining the evidence for ten beliefs. J Gen Intern Med. 2016;31:780-91.

612. Thys-Jacobs S, Chan FKW, Koberle LMC, et a. Hypercalcemia due to vitamin D toxicity. In: Feldman D, Glorieux FH, Pike JW, editors. Vitamin D. San Diego, CA: Academic Press; 1997. p. 883-901.

613. Hathcock JN, Shao A, Vieth R, Heaney R. Risk assessment for vitamin D. Am J Clin Nutr. 2007;85:6-18.

614. Vieth R. Vitamin D supplementation, 25-hydroxyvitamin D concentrations, and safety. Am J Clin Nutr. 1999;69:842-56.

615. Vieth R. Vitamin D toxicity, policy, and science. J Bone Miner Res. 2007;22 Suppl 2:V64-8.

616. Fusaro M, Gallieni M, Porta C, Nickolas TL, Khairallah P. Vitamin K effects in human health: new insights beyond bone and cardiovascular health. J Nephrol. 2020;33:239-49.

617. Chin KY. The relationship between vitamin K and osteoarthritis: A review of current evidence. Nutrients. 2020;12.

618. Rodriguez-Olleros Rodriguez C, Diaz Curiel M. Vitamin K and bone health: A review on the effects of vitamin K deficiency and supplementation and the effect of non-vitamin K antagonist oral anticoagulants on different bone parameters. J Osteoporos. 2019;2019:2069176.

619. Fusaro M, Mereu MC, Aghi A, Iervasi G, Gallieni M. Vitamin K and bone. Clin Cases Miner Bone Metab. 2017;14:200-6.

620. Gundberg CM. Vitamin K and bone: past, present, and future. J Bone Miner Res. 2009;24:980-2.

621. Bugel S. Vitamin K and bone health in adult humans. Vitam Horm. 2008;78:393-416.

622. Vermeer C, Shearer MJ, Zittermann A, Bolton-Smith C, Szulc P, Hodges S, Walter P, Rambeck W, Stocklin E, Weber P. Beyond deficiency: potential benefits of increased intakes of vitamin K for bone and vascular health. Eur J Nutr. 2004;43:325-35.

623. Palermo A, Tuccinardi D, D'Onofrio L, Watanabe M, Maggi D, Maurizi AR, Greto V, Buzzetti R, Napoli N, Pozzilli P, Manfrini S. Vitamin K and osteoporosis: Myth or reality? Metabolism. 2017;70:57-71.

624. Wolf J, Vermeer C. Potential effect of vitamin K on microgravity-induced bone loss. J Gravit Physiol. 1996;3:29-32.

625. Caillot-Augusseau A, Vico L, Heer M, Voroview D, Souberbielle JC, Zitterman A, Alexandre C, Lafage-Proust MH. Space flight is associated with rapid decreases of undercarboxylated osteocalcin and increases of markers of bone resorption without changes in their circadian variation: Observations in two cosmonauts. Clin Chem. 2000;46:1136-43.

626. Vermeer C, Wolf J, Craciun AM, Knapen MH. Bone markers during a 6-month space flight: effects of vitamin K supplementation. J Gravit Physiol. 1998;5:65-9.

627. Zwart SR, Booth SL, Peterson JW, Wang Z, Smith SM. Vitamin K status in spaceflight and ground-based models of spaceflight. J Bone Miner Res. 2011;26:948-54.

628. Sahni S, Hannan MT, Gagnon D, Blumberg J, Cupples LA, Kiel DP, Tucker KL. High vitamin C intake is associated with lower 4-year bone loss in elderly men. J Nutr. 2008;138:1931-8.

629. New SA, Robins SP, Campbell MK, Martin JC, Garton MJ, Bolton-Smith C, Grubb DA, Lee SJ, Reid DM. Dietary influences on bone mass and bone metabolism: further evidence of a positive link between fruit and vegetable consumption and bone health? Am J Clin Nutr. 2000;71:142-51.

630. New SA, Bolton-Smith C, Grubb DA, Reid DM. Nutritional influences on bone mineral density: a cross-sectional study in premenopausal women. Am J Clin Nutr. 1997;65:1831-9.

631. Macdonald HM, Black AJ, Aucott L, Duthie G, Duthie S, Sandison R, Hardcastle AC, Lanham New SA, Fraser WD, Reid DM. Effect of potassium citrate supplementation or increased fruit and vegetable intake on bone metabolism in healthy postmenopausal women: a randomized controlled trial. Am J Clin Nutr. 2008;88:465-74.

632. Lanham-New SA. The balance of bone health: tipping the scales in favor of potassium-rich, bicarbonate-rich foods. J Nutr. 2008;138:172S-7S.

633. Masse PG, Jougleux JL, Tranchant CC, Dosy J, Caissie M, Coburn SP. Enhancement of calcium/vitamin D supplement efficacy by administering concomitantly three key nutrients essential to bone collagen matrix for the treatment of osteopenia in middle-aged women: a one-year follow-up. J Clin Biochem Nutr. 2010;46:20-9.

634. Sahni S, Hannan MT, Gagnon D, Blumberg J, Cupples LA, Kiel DP, Tucker KL. Protective effect of total and supplemental vitamin C intake on the risk of hip fracture--a 17-year follow-up from the Framingham Osteoporosis Study. Osteoporos Int. 2009;20:1853-61.

635. Morton DJ, Barrett-Connor EL, Schneider DL. Vitamin C supplement use and bone mineral density in postmenopausal women. J Bone Miner Res. 2001;16:135-40.

636. Hall SL, Greendale GA. The relation of dietary vitamin C intake to bone mineral density: results from the PEPI study. Calcif Tissue Int. 1998;63:183-9.

637. Thompson J. Vitamins, minerals and supplements: overview of vitamin C (5). Community Pract. 2007;80:35-6.

638. Yoshida M, Takashima Y, Inoue M, Iwasaki M, Otani T, Sasaki S, Tsugane S, Group JS. Prospective study showing that dietary vitamin C reduced the risk of age-related cataracts in a middle-aged Japanese population. Eur J Nutr. 2007;46:118-24.

639. Watters JL, Satia JA, Kupper LL, Swenberg JA, Schroeder JC, Switzer BR. Associations of antioxidant nutrients and oxidative DNA damage in healthy African-American and White adults. Cancer Epidemiol Biomarkers Prev. 2007;16:1428-36.

640. Tietz NW, Pruden EL, Siggaard-Andersen O. Electrolytes. In: Burtis CA, Ashwood ER, editors. Tietz textbook of clinical chemistry. 2nd ed. Philadelphia, PA: WB Saunders Company; 1994. p. 1887-973.

641. Pitts RF. Ionic composition of body fluids. The physiological basis of diuretic therapy. Springfield, IL: Charles C Thomas Publisher; 1959.

642. Lynn MP, Fouad F, Cook SA, Napoli CA, Ferrario CM. Alterations in cardiac function and cardiopulmonary blood volume in chronic sodium depletion in dogs. Clin Sci (Lond). 1980;59 Suppl 6:393s-5s.

643. Benedict FG. A study of prolonged fasting. Washington, DC: Carnegie Institution of Washington. 1915.

644. Keys AB, Brozek J, Henschel A. The biology of human starvation. Minneapolis: University of Minnesota Press; 1950.

645. Gamble JL, Ross GS, Tisdall FF. The metabolism of fixed base during fasting. J Biol Chem. 1923;57:633-95.

646. Heer M, Zittermann A, Hoetzel D. Role of nutrition during long-term spaceflight. Acta Astronaut. 1995;35:297-311.

647. Lane HW, Leach C, Smith SM. Fluid and electrolyte homeostasis. In: Lane HW, Schoeller DA, editors. Nutrition in spaceflight and weightlessness models. Boca Raton, FL: CRC Press; 2000. p. 119-39.

648. Machnik A, Dahlmann A, Kopp C, Goss J, Wagner H, van Rooijen N, Eckardt KU, Muller DN, Park JK, Luft FC, Kerjaschki D, Titze J. Mononuclear phagocyte system depletion blocks interstitial tonicity-responsive enhancer binding protein/vascular endothelial growth factor C expression and induces salt-sensitive hypertension in rats. Hypertension. 2010;55:755-61.

649. Machnik A, Neuhofer W, Jantsch J, Dahlmann A, Tammela T, Machura K, Park JK, Beck FX, Muller DN, Derer W, Goss J, Ziomber A, Dietsch P, Wagner H, van Rooijen N, Kurtz A, Hilgers KF, Alitalo K, Eckardt KU, Luft FC, Kerjaschki D, Titze J. Macrophages regulate salt-dependent volume and blood pressure by a vascular endothelial growth factor-C-dependent buffering mechanism. Nat Med. 2009;15:545-52.

650. Rakova N, Juttner K, Dahlmann A, Schroder A, Linz P, Kopp C, Rauh M, Goller U, Beck L, Agureev A, Vassilieva G, Lenkova L, Johannes B, Wabel P, Moissl U, Vienken J, Gerzer R, Eckardt KU, Muller DN, Kirsch K, Morukov B, Luft FC, Titze J. Long-term space flight simulation reveals infradian rhythmicity in human Na(+) balance. Cell Metab. 2013;17:125-31.

651. Titze J, Dahlmann A, Lerchl K, Kopp C, Rakova N, Schroder A, Luft FC. Spooky sodium balance. Kidney Int. 2014;85:759-67.

652. Titze J, Krause H, Hecht H, Dietsch P, Rittweger J, Lang R, Kirsch KA, Hilgers KF. Reduced osmotically inactive Na storage capacity and hypertension in the Dahl model. Am J Physiol Renal Physiol. 2002;283:F134-41.

653. Titze J, Shakibaei M, Schafflhuber M, Schulze-Tanzil G, Porst M, Schwind KH, Dietsch P, Hilgers KF. Glycosaminoglycan polymerization may enable osmotically inactive Na+ storage in the skin. Am J Physiol Heart Circ Physiol. 2004;287:H203-8.

654. Ivanova LN, Archibasova VK, Shterental I. [Sodium-depositing function of the skin in white rats]. Fiziol Zh SSSR Im I M Sechenova. 1978;64:358-63.

655. Kitada K, Daub S, Zhang Y, Klein JD, Nakano D, Pedchenko T, Lantier L, LaRocque LM, Marton A, Neubert P, Schroder A, Rakova N, Jantsch J, Dikalova AE, Dikalov SI, Harrison DG, Muller DN, Nishiyama A, Rauh M, Harris RC, Luft FC, Wassermann DH, Sands JM, Titze J. High salt intake reprioritizes osmolyte and energy metabolism for body fluid conservation. J Clin Invest. 2017;127:1944-59.

656. Goulding A. Effects of dietary NaCl supplements on parathyroid function, bone turnover and bone-composition in rats taking restricted amounts of calcium. Miner Electrolyte Metab. 1980;4:203-8.

657. Goulding A, Lim PE. Effects of varying dietary salt intake on the fasting urinary-excretion of sodium, calcium and hydroxyproline in young-women. NZ Med J. 1983;96:853-4.

658. Evans CE, Chughtai AY, Blumsohn A, Giles M, Eastell R. The effect of dietary sodium on calcium metabolism in premenopausal and postmenopausal women. Eur J Clin Nutr. 1997;51:394-9.

659. Castenmiller JJ, Mensink RP, van der Heijden L, Kouwenhoven T, Hautvast JG, de Leeuw PW, Schaafsma G. The effect of dietary sodium on urinary calcium and potassium excretion in normotensive men with different calcium intakes. Am J Clin Nutr. 1985;41:52-60.

660. Cohen AJ, Roe FJ. Review of risk factors for osteoporosis with particular reference to a possible aetiological role of dietary salt. Food Chem Toxicol. 2000;38:237-53.

661. Heer M, Baisch F, Drummer C, Gerzer R. Long-term elevations of dietary sodium produce parallel increases in the renal excretion of urodilatin and sodium. In: Sahm PR, Keller MH, Schiewe B, editors. Proceedings of the Norderney Symposium on Scientific Results of the German Spacelab Mission D-2. Norderney, Germany: Wissenschaftliche Projectführung D-2; 1995. p. 708-14.

662. Ho SC, Chen YM, Woo JLF, Leung SSF, Lam TH, Janus ED. Sodium is the leading dietary factor associated with urinary calcium excretion in Hong Kong Chinese adults. Osteoporos Int. 2001;12:723-31.

663. Nordin BEC, Need AG, Morris HA, Horowitz M. The nature and significance of the relationship between urinary sodium and urinary calcium in women. J Nutr. 1993;123:1615-22.

664. Nordin B, Need A, Morris H, Horowitz M, Cochran M. Sodium and osteoporosis. In: Lesourd B, Rapin C, Sachet P, editors. Osteoporose: pour une prevention nutritionelle du risque? Paris: Centre Recherche et Information Nutritionnelles; 1992. p. 117.

665. Kleeman CR, Bohannan J, Bernstein D, Ling S, Maxwell MH. Effect of variations in sodium intake on calcium excretion in normal humans. Proc Soc Exp Biol Med. 1964;115:29-32.

666. Heer M. Einfluss alimentaer erhoehter Kochsalzzufuhr auf den Wasser- und Elektrolythaushalt des Menschen [dissertation]. Bonn, Germany: University of Bonn; 1996.

667. Agus ZS, Goldfarb S. Renal regulation of calcium balance. In: Seldin DW, Giebisch G, editors. The kidney: physiology and pathophysiology. New York, NY: Raven Press; 1985. p. 1323-35.

668. Costanzo LS, Windhager EE. Effects of PTH, ADH, and cyclic AMP on distal tubular Ca and Na reabsorption. Am J Physiol. 1980;239:F478-85.

669. Meyer WJ, 3rd, Transbol I, Bartter FC, Delea C. Control of calcium absorption: effect of sodium chloride loading and depletion. Metabolism. 1976;25:989-93.

670. Breslau NA, McGuire JL, Zerwekh JE, Pak CY. The role of dietary sodium on renal excretion and intestinal absorption of calcium and on vitamin D metabolism. J Clin Endocrinol Metab. 1982;55:369-73.

671. Ginty F, Flynn A, Cashman KD. The effect of dietary sodium intake on biochemical markers of bone metabolism in young women. Br J Nutr. 1998;79:343-50.

672. Lietz G, Avenell A, Robins SP. Short-term effects of dietary sodium intake on bone metabolism in postmenopausal women measured using urinary deoxypyridinoline excretion. Br J Nutr. 1997;78:73-82.

673. Frings-Meuthen P, Baecker N, Heer M. Low-grade metabolic acidosis may be the cause of sodium chloride-induced exaggerated bone resorption. J Bone Miner Res. 2008;23:517-24.

674. Kwon SJ, Ha YC, Park Y. High dietary sodium intake is associated with low bone mass in postmenopausal women: Korea National Health and Nutrition Examination Survey, 2008-2011. Osteoporos Int. 2017;28:1445-52.

675. Blackwood AM, Sagnella GA, Cook DG, Cappuccio FP. Urinary calcium excretion, sodium intake and blood pressure in a multi-ethnic population: results of the Wandsworth Heart and Stroke Study. J Hum Hypertens. 2001;15:229-37.

676. Harrington M, Bennett T, Jakobsen J, Ovesen L, Brot C, Flynn A, Cashman KD. The effect of a high-protein, high-sodium diet on calcium and bone metabolism in postmenopausal women and its interaction with vitamin D receptor genotype. Br J Nutr. 2004;91:41-51.

677. Harrington M, Bennett T, Jakobsen J, Ovesen L, Brot C, Flynn A, Cashman KD. Effect of a high-protein, high-salt diet on calcium and bone metabolism in postmenopausal women stratified by hormone replacement therapy use. Eur J Clin Nutr. 2004;58:1436-9.

678. Harrington M, Cashman KD. High salt intake appears to increase bone resorption in postmenopausal women but high potassium intake ameliorates this adverse effect. Nutr Rev. 2003;61:179-83.

679. Massey LK, Whiting SJ. Dietary salt, urinary calcium, and bone loss. J Bone Miner Res. 1996;11:731-6.

680. Massey LK, Whiting SJ. Dietary salt, urinary calcium, and kidney stone risk. Nutr Rev. 1995;53:131-9.

681. Sellmeyer DE, Schloetter M, Sebastian A. Potassium citrate prevents increased urine calcium excretion and bone resorption induced by a high sodium chloride diet. J Clin Endocrinol Metab. 2002;87:2008-12.

682. Fatahi S, Namazi N, Larijani B, Azadbakht L. The association of dietary and urinary sodium with bone mineral density and risk of osteoporosis: A systematic review and meta-analysis. J Am Coll Nutr. 2018;37:522-32.

683. Nordin BE, Need AG, Steurer T, Morris HA, Chatterton BE, Horowitz M. Nutrition, osteoporosis, and aging. Ann NY Acad Sci. 1998;854:336-51.

684. Frassetto L, Morris RC, Jr., Sellmeyer DE, Todd K, Sebastian A. Diet, evolution and aging--the pathophysiologic effects of the post-agricultural inversion of the potassium-to-sodium and base-to-chloride ratios in the human diet. Eur J Nutr. 2001;40:200-13.

685. de Wardener HE, MacGregor GA. Harmful effects of dietary salt in addition to hypertension. J Hum Hypertens. 2002;16:213-23.

686. Fellstrom B, Danielson BG, Karlstrom B, Lithell H, Ljunghall S, Vessby B. Dietary habits in renal stone patients compared with healthy subjects. Br J Urol. 1989;63:575-80.

687. Trinchieri A, Mandressi A, Luongo P, Longo G, Pisani E. The influence of diet on urinary risk factors for stones in healthy subjects and idiopathic renal calcium stone formers. Br J Urol. 1991;67:230-6.

688. Sakhaee K, Harvey JA, Padalino PK, Whitson P, Pak CY. The potential role of salt abuse on the risk for kidney stone formation. J Urol. 1993;150:310-2.

689. Matkovic V, Ilich JZ, Andon MB, Hsieh LC, Tzagournis MA, Lagger BJ, Goel PK. Urinary calcium, sodium, and bone mass of young females. Am J Clin Nutr. 1995;62:417-25.

690. Devine A, Criddle RA, Dick IM, Kerr DA, Prince RL. A longitudinal study of the effect of sodium and calcium intakes on regional bone density in postmenopausal women. Am J Clin Nutr. 1995;62:740-5.

691. Frings-Meuthen P, Buehlmeier J, Baecker N, Stehle P, Fimmers R, May F, Kluge G, Heer M. High sodium chloride intake exacerbates immobilization-induced bone resorption and protein losses. J Appl Physiol (1985). 2011;111:537-42.

692. May RC, Kelly RA, Mitch WE. Metabolic acidosis stimulates protein degradation in rat muscle by a glucocorticoid-dependent mechanism. J Clin Invest. 1986;77:614-21.

693. Buehlmeier J, Frings-Meuthen P, Remer T, Maser-Gluth C, Stehle P, Biolo G, Heer M. Alkaline salts to counteract bone resorption and protein wasting induced by high salt intake: results of a randomized controlled trial. J Clin Endocrinol Metab. 2012;97:4789-97.

694. Remer T. High salt intake: detrimental not only for blood pressure, but also for bone health? Endocrine. 2015;49:580-2.

695. Shi L, Sanchez-Guijo A, Hartmann MF, Schonau E, Esche J, Wudy SA, Remer T. Higher glucocorticoid secretion in the physiological range is associated with lower bone strength at the proximal radius in healthy children: importance of protein intake adjustment. J Bone Miner Res. 2015;30:240-8.

696. Compston J. Management of glucocorticoid-induced osteoporosis. Nat Rev Rheumatol. 2010;6:82-8.

697. Cooper MS, Walker EA, Bland R, Fraser WD, Hewison M, Stewart PM. Expression and functional consequences of 11beta-hydroxysteroid dehydrogenase activity in human bone. Bone. 2000;27:375-81.

698. Dovio A, Perazzolo L, Osella G, Ventura M, Termine A, Milano E, Bertolotto A, Angeli A. Immediate fall of bone formation and transient increase of bone resorption in the course of high-dose, short-term glucocorticoid therapy in young patients with multiple sclerosis. J Clin Endocrinol Metab. 2004;89:4923-8.

699. Kuroki Y, Kaji H, Kawano S, Kanda F, Takai Y, Kajikawa M, Sugimoto T. Short-term effects of glucocorticoid therapy on biochemical markers of bone metabolism in Japanese patients: a prospective study. J Bone Miner Metab. 2008;26:271-8.

700. Vormann J, Remer T. Dietary, metabolic, physiologic, and disease-related aspects of acid-base balance: foreword to the contributions of the second International Acid-Base Symposium. J Nutr. 2008;138:413S-4S.

701. Frassetto LA, Morris RC, Jr, Sellmeyer DE, Sebastian A. Adverse effects of sodium chloride on bone in the aging human population resulting from habitual consumption of typical American diets. J Nutr. 2008;138:419S-22S.

702. Burckhardt P. The effect of the alkali load of mineral water on bone metabolism: interventional studies. J Nutr. 2008;138:435S-7S.

703. Arnett TR. Extracellular pH regulates bone cell function. J Nutr. 2008;138:415S-8S.

704. Dawson-Hughes B. Interaction of dietary calcium and protein in bone health in humans. J Nutr. 2003;133:852S-4S.

705. Dawson-Hughes B. Calcium and protein in bone health. Proc Nutr Soc. 2003;62:505-9.

706. Rafferty K, Heaney RP. Nutrient effects on the calcium economy: emphasizing the potassium controversy. J Nutr. 2008;138:166S-71S.

707. Dawson-Hughes B. Challenges in defining the role of dietary protein in bone health. Am J Clin Nutr. 2017;105:1257-8.

708. Frassetto L, Banerjee T, Powe N, Sebastian A. Acid balance, dietary acid load, and bone effects-A controversial subject. Nutrients. 2018;10.

709. Hegsted M, Linkswiler HM. Long-term effects of level of protein intake on calcium metabolism in young adult women. J Nutr. 1981;111:244-51.

710. Borghi L, Schianchi T, Meschi T, Guerra A, Allegri F, Maggiore U, Novarini A. Comparison of two diets for the prevention of recurrent stones in idiopathic hypercalciuria. N Engl J Med. 2002;346:77-84.

711. Dwyer J, Foulkes E, Evans M, Ausman L. Acid/alkaline ash diets: time for assessment and change. J Am Diet Assoc. 1985;85:841-5.

712. Buclin T, Cosma M, Appenzeller M, Jacquet AF, Decosterd LA, Biollaz J, Burckhardt P. Diet acids and alkalis influence calcium retention in bone. Osteoporos Int. 2001;12:493-9.

713. Fenton TR, Eliasziw M, Lyon AW, Tough SC, Hanley DA. Meta-analysis of the quantity of calcium excretion associated with the net acid excretion of the modern diet under the acid-ash diet hypothesis. Am J Clin Nutr. 2008;88:1159-66.

714. Kerstetter JE, O'Brien KO, Caseria DM, Wall DE, Insogna KL. The impact of dietary protein on calcium absorption and kinetic measures of bone turnover in women. J Clin Endocrinol Metab. 2005;90:26-31.

715. Breslau NA, Brinkley L, Hill KD, Pak CY. Relationship of animal protein-rich diet to kidney stone formation and calcium metabolism. J Clin Endocrinol Metab. 1988;66:140-6.

716. Kaneko K, Masaki U, Aikyo M, Yabuki K, Haga A, Matoba C, Sasaki H, Koike G. Urinary calcium and calcium balance in young women affected by high protein diet of soy protein isolate and adding sulfur-containing amino acids and/or potassium. J Nutr Sci Vitaminol (Tokyo). 1990;36:105-16.

717. Zwart SR, Davis-Street JE, Paddon-Jones D, Ferrando AA, Wolfe RR, Smith SM. Amino acid supplementation alters bone metabolism during simulated weightlessness. J Appl Physiol (1985). 2005;99:134-40.

718. Fenton TR, Lyon AW, Eliasziw M, Tough SC, Hanley DA. Meta-analysis of the effect of the acid-ash hypothesis of osteoporosis on calcium balance. J Bone Miner Res. 2009;24:1835-40.

719. Lanham-New SA. Fruit and vegetables: the unexpected natural answer to the question of osteoporosis prevention? Am J Clin Nutr. 2006;83:1254-5.

720. Mitchell PJ, Cooper C, Dawson-Hughes B, Gordon CM, Rizzoli R. Life-course approach to nutrition. Osteoporos Int. 2015;26:2723-42.

721. Dawson-Hughes B, Harris SS, Palermo NJ, Gilhooly CH, Shea MK, Fielding RA, Ceglia L. Potassium bicarbonate supplementation lowers bone turnover and calcium excretion in older men and women: A randomized dose-finding trial. J Bone Miner Res. 2015;30:2103-11.

722. Lemann J, Jr., Gray RW, Pleuss JA. Potassium bicarbonate, but not sodium bicarbonate, reduces urinary calcium excretion and improves calcium balance in healthy men. Kidney Int. 1989;35:688-95.

723. Sebastian A, Harris ST, Ottaway JH, Todd KM, Morris RC, Jr. Improved mineral balance and skeletal metabolism in postmenopausal women treated with potassium bicarbonate. N Engl J Med. 1994;330:1776-81.

724. Frassetto L. Another strategy to help counter the effects of low gravity? Am J Clin Nutr. 2018;107:681-2.

725. Beard J. Iron deficiency alters brain development and functioning. J Nutr. 2003;133:1468S-72S.

726. von Drygalski A, Adamson JW. Iron metabolism in man. JPEN J Parenter Enteral Nutr. 2013;37:599-606.

727. McDermid JM, Lonnerdal B. Iron. Adv Nutr. 2012;3:532-3.

728. Sousa L, Oliveira MM, Pessoa MTC, Barbosa LA. Iron overload: Effects on cellular biochemistry. Clin Chim Acta. 2020;504:180-9.

729. Yang J, Zhang G, Dong D, Shang P. Effects of iron overload and oxidative damage on the musculoskeletal system in the space environment: Data from spaceflights and ground-based simulation models. Int J Mol Sci. 2018;19.

730. Ganz T. Systemic iron homeostasis. Physiol Rev. 2013;93:1721-41.

731. Milne DB, Gallagher SK, Nielsen FH. Response of various indices of iron status to acute iron depletion produced in menstruating women by low iron intake and phlebotomy. Clin Chem. 1990;36:487-91.

732. Prieto J, Barry M, Sherlock S. Serum ferritin in patients with iron overload and with acute and chronic liver diseases. Gastroenterology. 1975;68:525-33.

733. Dallman PR. Iron deficiency and the immune response. Am J Clin Nutr. 1987;46:329-34.

734. Hunnicutt J, He K, Xun P. Dietary iron intake and body iron stores are associated with risk of coronary heart disease in a meta-analysis of prospective cohort studies. J Nutr. 2014;144:359-66.

735. Cook JD. Adaptation in iron metabolism. Am J Clin Nutr. 1990;51:301-8.

736. Finch CA, Huebers H. Perspectives in iron metabolism. N Engl J Med. 1982;306:1520-8.

737. Smith SM. Red blood cell and iron metabolism during space flight. Nutrition. 2002;18:864-6.

738. Leach CS. Biochemical and hematologic changes after short-term space flight. Microgravity Q. 1992;2:69-75.

739. Smith SM, Davis-Street JE, Fontenot TB, Lane HW. Assessment of a portable clinical blood analyzer during space flight. Clin Chem. 1997;43:1056-65.

740. Trudel G, Shafer J, Laneuville O, Ramsay T. Characterizing the effect of exposure to microgravity on anemia: more space is worse. Am J Hematol. 2020;95:267-73.

741. Leach CS, Rambaut PC. Biochemical observations of long duration manned orbital spaceflight. J Am Med Womens Assoc. 1975;30:153-72.

742. Convertino VA. Clinical aspects of the control of plasma volume at microgravity and during return to one gravity. Med Sci Sports Exerc. 1996;28:S45-52.

743. Lane HW, Alfrey CP, Driscoll TB, Smith SM, Nyquist LE. Control of red blood cell mass during spaceflight. J Gravit Physiol. 1996;3:87-8.

744. Beilby J, Olynyk J, Ching S, Prins A, Swanson N, Reed W, Harley H, Garcia-Webb P. Transferrin index: an alternative method for calculating the iron saturation of transferrin. Clin Chem. 1992;38:2078-81.

745. Mendes JF, Arruda SF, Siqueira EM, Ito MK, Silva EF. Iron status and oxidative stress biomarkers in adults: a preliminary study. Nutrition. 2009;25:379-84.

746. Tuomainen TP, Loft S, Nyyssonen K, Punnonen K, Salonen JT, Poulsen HE. Body iron is a contributor to oxidative damage of DNA. Free Radic Res. 2007;41:324-8.

747. Syrovatka P, Kraml P, Potockova J, Fialova L, Vejrazka M, Crkovska J, Andel M. Relationship between increased body iron stores, oxidative stress and insulin resistance in healthy men. Ann Nutr Metab. 2009;54:268-74.

748. Kim BJ, Ahn SH, Bae SJ, Kim EH, Lee SH, Kim HK, Choe JW, Koh JM, Kim GS. Iron overload accelerates bone loss in healthy postmenopausal women and middle-aged men: a 3-year retrospective longitudinal study. J Bone Miner Res. 2012;27:2279-90.

749. Tian Y, Ma X, Yang C, Su P, Yin C, Qian AR. The impact of oxidative stress on the bone system in response to the space special environment. Int J Mol Sci. 2017;18.

750. Dunn CD, Lange RD, Kimzey SL, Johnson PC, Leach CS. Serum erythropoietin titers during prolonged bedrest; relevance to the "anaemia" of space flight. Eur J Appl Physiol Occup Physiol. 1984;52:178-82.

751. Nay K, Koechlin-Ramonatxo C, Rochdi S, Island ML, Orfila L, Treffel L, Bareille MP, Beck A, Gauquelin-Koch G, Ropert M, Loreal O, Derbre F. Simulated microgravity disturbs iron metabolism and distribution in humans: Lessons from dry immersion, an innovative ground-based human model. FASEB J. 2020.

752. Rice L, Ruiz W, Driscoll T, Whitley CE, Tapia R, Hachey DL, Gonzales GF, Alfrey CP. Neocytolysis on descent from altitude: a newly recognized mechanism for the control of red cell mass. Ann Intern Med. 2001;134:652-6.

753. Smith SM, Davis-Street JE, Fesperman JV, Smith MD, Rice BL, Zwart SR. Nutritional assessment during a 14-d saturation dive: the NASA Extreme Environment Mission Operations V Project. J Nutr. 2004;134:1765-71.

754. Bader N, Bosy-Westphal A, Koch A, Mueller MJ. Influence of vitamin C and E supplementation on oxidative stress induced by hyperbaric oxygen in healthy men. Ann Nutr Metab. 2006;50:173-6.

755. Rocco M, Antonelli M, Letizia V, Alampi D, Spadetta G, Passariello M, Conti G, Serio P, Gasparetto A. Lipid peroxidation, circulating cytokine and endothelin 1 levels in healthy volunteers undergoing hyperbaric oxygenation. Minerva Anestesiol. 2001;67:393-400.

756. Alleva R, Nasole E, Di Donato F, Borghi B, Neuzil J, Tomasetti M. alpha-Lipoic acid supplementation inhibits oxidative damage, accelerating chronic wound healing in patients undergoing hyperbaric oxygen therapy. Biochem Biophys Res Commun. 2005;333:404-10.

757. Djurhuus R, Segadal K, Svardal AM. Glutathione in blood cells decreases without DNA breaks after a simulated saturation dive to 250 msw. Aviat Space Environ Med. 2006;77:597-604.

758. Zwart SR, Jessup JM, Ji J, Smith SM. Saturation diving alters folate status and biomarkers of DNA damage and repair. PLoS One. 2012;7:e31058.

759. He X, Hahn P, Iacovelli J, Wong R, King C, Bhisitkul R, Massaro-Giordano M, Dunaief JL. Iron homeostasis and toxicity in retinal degeneration. Prog Retin Eye Res. 2007;26:649-73.

760. Morgan JLL, Ritchie LE, Crucian BE, Theriot C, Wu H, Sams C, Smith SM, Turner ND, Zwart SR. Increased dietary iron and radiation in rats promote oxidative stress, induce localized and systemic immune system responses, and alter colon mucosal environment. FASEB J. 2014;28:1486-98.

761. Sempos CT, Looker AC, Gillum RF, Makuc DM. Body iron stores and the risk of coronary heart disease. N Engl J Med. 1994;330:1119-24.

762. Ascherio A, Willett WC. Are body iron stores related to the risk of coronary heart disease? N Engl J Med. 1994;330:1152-4.

763. Sullivan JL. Stored iron and ischemic heart disease: empirical support for a new paradigm (Editorial Comment). Circulation. 1992;86:1036-7.

764. Lauffer RB. Iron stores and the international variation in mortality from coronary artery disease. Lancet. 1991;2:1288-9.

765. Salonen JT, Nyyssonen K, Korpela H, Tuomilehto J, Seppanen R, Salonen R. High stored iron levels are associated with excess risk of myocardial infarction in eastern Finnish men. Circulation. 1992;86:803-11.

766. Sullivan JL. The iron paradigm of ischemic heart disease. Am Heart J. 1989;117:1177-88.

767. Knekt P, Reunanen A, Takkunen H, Aromaa A, Heliovaara M, Hakulinen T. Body iron stores and risk of cancer. Int J Cancer. 1994;56:379-82.

768. Mainous AG, 3rd, Wells BJ, Koopman RJ, Everett CJ, Gill JM. Iron, lipids, and risk of cancer in the Framingham Offspring cohort. Am J Epidemiol. 2005;161:1115-22.

769. Schreiber WE. Iron, porphyrin, and bilirubin metabolism. In: Kaplan LA, Pesce AJ, editors. Clinical chemistry: Theory, analysis, and correlation. St. Louis, MO: Mosby-Year Books, Inc.; 1996. p. 696-715.

770. Wilson JW, Ott CM, Honer zu Bentrup K, Ramamurthy R, Quick L, Porwollik S, Cheng P, McClelland M, Tsaprailis G, Radabaugh T, Hunt A, Fernandez D, Richter E, Shah M, Kilcoyne M, Joshi L, Nelman-Gonzalez M, Hing S, Parra M, Dumars P, Norwood K, Bober R, Devich J, Ruggles A, Goulart C, Rupert M, Stodieck L, Stafford P, Catella L, Schurr MJ, Buchanan K, Morici L, McCracken J, Allen P, Baker-Coleman C, Hammond T, Vogel J, Nelson R, Pierson DL, Stefanyshyn-Piper HM, Nickerson CA. Space flight alters bacterial gene expression and virulence and reveals a role for global regulator Hfq. Proc Natl Acad Sci USA. 2007;104:16299-304.

771. Payne SM. Iron and virulence in the family Enterobacteriaceae. Crit Rev Microbiol. 1988;16:81-111.

772. Calvo MS, Lamberg-Allardt CJ. Phosphorus. Adv Nutr. 2015;6:860-2.

773. O'Brien KO, Kerstetter JE, Insonga KL. Phosphorus. In: Ross AC, Caballero B, Cousins RJ, Tucker KL, Ziegler TR, editors. Modern nutrition in health and disease, 11th Ed. Philadelphia: Lippincott Williams & Wilkins; 2012. p. p. 150-8.

774. Hu MC, Shiizaki K, Kuro-o M, Moe OW. Fibroblast growth factor 23 and Klotho: physiology and pathophysiology of an endocrine network of mineral metabolism. Annu Rev Physiol. 2013;75:503-33.

775. Calvo MS, Moshfegh AJ, Tucker KL. Assessing the health impact of phosphorus in the food supply: issues and considerations. Adv Nutr. 2014;5:104-13.

776. Chang AR, Lazo M, Appel LJ, Gutierrez OM, Grams ME. High dietary phosphorus intake is associated with all-cause mortality: results from NHANES III. Am J Clin Nutr. 2014;99:320-7.

777. Takeda E, Yamamoto H, Yamanaka-Okumura H, Taketani Y. Increasing dietary phosphorus intake from food additives: potential for negative impact on bone health. Adv Nutr. 2014;5:92-7.

778. Uribarri J, Calvo MS. Dietary phosphorus intake and health. Am J Clin Nutr. 2014;99:247-8.

779. Calvo MS, Uribarri J. Public health impact of dietary phosphorus excess on bone and cardiovascular health in the general population. Am J Clin Nutr. 2013;98:6-15.

780. Calvo MS, Tucker KL. Is phosphorus intake that exceeds dietary requirements a risk factor in bone health? Ann NY Acad Sci. 2013;1301:29-35.

781. Institute of Medicine. Dietary reference intakes for calcium, phosphorus, magnesium, vitamin D, and fluoride. Washington, DC: National Academy Press; 1997.

782. Inniss AM, Rice BL, Smith SM. Dietary support of long-duration head-down bed rest. Aviat Space Environ Med. 2009;80:A9-14. Erratum in Aviat Space Environ Med. 2014;85:768. .

783. Volpe SL. Magnesium in disease prevention and overall health. Adv Nutr. 2013;4:378S-83S.

784. Hayhoe RP, Lentjes MA, Luben RN, Khaw KT, Welch AA. Dietary magnesium and potassium intakes and circulating magnesium are associated with heel bone ultrasound attenuation and osteoporotic fracture risk in the EPIC-Norfolk cohort study. Am J Clin Nutr. 2015;102:376-84.

785. Orchard TS, Larson JC, Alghothani N, Bout-Tabaku S, Cauley JA, Chen Z, Lacroix AZ, Wactawski-Wende J, Jackson RD. Magnesium intake, bone mineral density, and fractures: results from the Women's Health Initiative Observational Study. Am J Clin Nutr. 2014;99:926-33.

786. Severino P, Netti L, Mariani MV, Maraone A, D'Amato A, Scarpati R, Infusino F, Pucci M, Lavalle C, Maestrini V, Mancone M, Fedele F. Prevention of cardiovascular disease: screening for magnesium deficiency. Cardiol Res Pract. 2019;2019:4874921.

787. Chakraborti S, Chakraborti T, Mandal M, Mandal A, Das S, Ghosh S. Protective role of magnesium in cardiovascular diseases: a review. Mol Cell Biochem. 2002;238:163-79.

788. Shils ME. Magnesium. In: Shils ME, Olson JA, Shike M, Ross AC, editors. Modern nutrition in health and disease. 9th ed. Baltimore, MD: Lippincott Williams & Wilkins; 1999. p. 169-92.

789. Belluci MM, de Molon RS, Rossa C, Jr., Tetradis S, Giro G, Cerri PS, Marcantonio E, Jr., Orrico SRP. Severe magnesium deficiency compromises systemic bone mineral density and aggravates inflammatory bone resorption. J Nutr Biochem. 2020;77:108301.

790. Ayuk J, Gittoes NJ. Contemporary view of the clinical relevance of magnesium homeostasis. Ann Clin Biochem. 2014;51:179-88.

791. Shechter M. Magnesium and cardiovascular system. Magnes Res. 2010;23:60-72.

792. Haigney MC, Silver B, Tanglao E, Silverman HS, Hill JD, Shapiro E, Gerstenblith G, Schulman SP. Noninvasive measurement of tissue magnesium and correlation with cardiac levels. Circulation. 1995;92:2190-7.

793. Clarkson PM, Haymes EM. Exercise and mineral status of athletes: calcium, magnesium, phosphorus, and iron. Med Sci Sports Exerc. 1995;27:831-43.

794. Leach CS, Alexander WC, Johnson PC. Endocrine, electrolyte, and fluid volume changes associated with Apollo missions. In: Johnston RS, Dietlein LF, Berry MD, editors. Biomedical results from Apollo (NASA SP-368). Washington, DC: National Aeronautics and Space Administration; 1975. p. 163-84.

795. Leach-Huntoon CS, Schneider H, Cintron NM, Landry R. Combined blood investigations. In: Bungo MW, Bagian TM, Bowman MA, Levitan BM, editors. Results of the life sciences DSOs conducted aboard the Space Shuttle 1981-1986. Houston: Space Biomedical Research Institute, Johnson Space Center; 1987. p. 7-11.

796. Prokhonchukov AA, Zaitsev VP, Shakhunov BA, Zhizhina NA, Kolesnik AG. [Effect of space flight on the concentration of sodium, copper, manganese and magnesium in the bones of the skeleton]. Patol Fiziol Eksp Ter. 1978:65-70.

797. Smith SM, Zwart SR. Magnesium and Space Flight. Nutrients. 2015;7:10209-22.

798. Altarelli M, Ben-Hamouda N, Schneider A, Berger MM. Copper deficiency: Causes, manifestations, and treatment. Nutr Clin Pract. 2019;34:504-13.

799. Collins JF, Klevay LM. Copper. Adv Nutr. 2011;2:520-2.

800. Prohaska JR. Copper. In: Erdman JW, Jr., MacDonald IA, Zeisel SH, editors. Present knowledge in nutrition. 10th ed. Washington, DC: International Life Sciences Institute Press; 2012. p. 540-53.

801. Mezzaroba L, Alfieri DF, Colado Simao AN, Vissoci Reiche EM. The role of zinc, copper, manganese and iron in neurodegenerative diseases. Neurotoxicology. 2019;74:230-41.

802. Bondy SC. Low levels of aluminum can lead to behavioral and morphological changes associated with Alzheimer's disease and age-related neurodegeneration. Neurotoxicology. 2016;52:222-9.

803. Bondy SC. Prolonged exposure to low levels of aluminum leads to changes associated with brain aging and neurodegeneration. Toxicology. 2014;315:1-7.

804. Bondy SC. The neurotoxicity of environmental aluminum is still an issue. Neurotoxicology. 2010;31:575-81.

805. Campbell A, Kumar A, La Rosa FG, Prasad KN, Bondy SC. Aluminum increases levels of beta-amyloid and ubiquitin in neuroblastoma but not in glioma cells. Proc Soc Exp Biol Med. 2000;223:397-402.

806. Brewer GJ. Avoiding Alzheimer's disease: The important causative role of divalent copper ingestion. Exp Biol Med (Maywood). 2019;244:114-9.

807. Zhang J, Cao J, Zhang H, Jiang C, Lin T, Zhou Z, Song Y, Li Y, Liu C, Liu L, Wang B, Tang G, Li J, Zhang Y, Cui Y, Huo Y, Yang Y, Ling W, Yang J, Guo H, Wang X, Xu X, Qin X. Plasma copper and the risk of first stroke in hypertensive patients: a nested case-control study. Am J Clin Nutr. 2019;110:212-20.

808. Eshak ES, Iso H, Yamagishi K, Maruyama K, Umesawa M, Tamakoshi A. Associations between copper and zinc intakes from diet and mortality from cardiovascular disease in a large population-based prospective cohort study. J Nutr Biochem. 2018;56:126-32.

809. Palacios C. The role of nutrients in bone health, from A to Z. Crit Rev Food Sci Nutr. 2006;46:621-8.

810. Davis AT, Franz FP, Courtnay DA, Ullrey DE, Scholten DJ, Dean RE. Plasma vitamin and mineral status in home parenteral nutrition patients. JPEN J Parenter Enteral Nutr. 1987;11:480-5.

811. Arredondo M, Gonzalez M, Olivares M, Pizarro F, Araya M. Ceruloplasmin, an indicator of copper status. Biol Trace Elem Res. 2008;123:261-9.

812. Food and Nutrition Board, Institute of Medicine. Dietary Reference Intakes: a risk assessment model for establishing upper intake levels for nutrients. Washington, DC: National Academies Press; 1998.

813. Milne DB. Copper intake and assessment of copper status. Am J Clin Nutr. 1998;67:1041S-5S.

814. Higuchi S, Higashi A, Nakamura T, Matsuda I. Nutritional copper deficiency in severely handicapped patients on a low copper enteral diet for a prolonged period: estimation of the required dose of dietary copper. J Pediatr Gastroenterol Nutr. 1988;7:583-7.

815. Heacox HN, Gillman PL, Zwart SR, Smith SM. Excretion of zinc and copper increases in men during 3 weeks of bed rest, with or without artificial gravity. J Nutr. 2017;147:1113-20.

816. Krebs JM, Schneider VS, LeBlanc AD, Kuo MC, Spector E, Lane HW. Zinc and copper balances in healthy adult males during and after 17 wk of bed rest. Am J Clin Nutr. 1993;58:897-901.

817. King JC. Zinc: an essential but elusive nutrient. Am J Clin Nutr. 2011;94:679S-84S.

818. Huang L, Drake VJ, Ho E. Zinc. Adv Nutr. 2015;6:224-6.

819. Kaur K, Gupta R, Saraf SA, Saraf SK. Zinc: The metal of life. Comp Rev Food Sci Food Saf. 2014;13:358-76.

820. Yamaguchi M. Role of nutritional zinc in the prevention of osteoporosis. Mol Cell Biochem. 2010;338:241-54.

821. Santos HO, Teixeira FJ, Schoenfeld BJ. Dietary vs. pharmacological doses of zinc: A clinical review. Clin Nutr. 2020;39:1345-53.

822. Lowe NM, Fekete K, Decsi T. Methods of assessment of zinc status in humans: a systematic review. Am J Clin Nutr. 2009;89:2040S-51S.

823. Hennigar SR, Kelley AM, McClung JP. Metallothionein and zinc transporter expression in circulating human blood cells as biomarkers of zinc status: a systematic review. Adv Nutr. 2016;7:735-46.

824. Krebs JM, Schneider VS, LeBlanc AD. Zinc, copper, and nitrogen balances during bed rest and fluoride supplementation in healthy adult males. Am J Clin Nutr. 1988;47:509-14.

825. Kondrashov VS. Cosmonauts and lead: resorption and increased blood lead levels during long term space flight. J Med Toxicol. 2006;2:172-3.

826. Kondrashov V, Rothenberg SJ, Chettle D, Zerwekh J. Evaluation of potentially significant increase of lead in the blood during long-term bed rest and space flight. Physiol Meas. 2005;26:1-12.

827. Garcia HD, Hays SM, Tsuji JS. Modeling of blood lead levels in astronauts exposed to lead from microgravity-accelerated bone loss. Aviat Space Environ Med. 2013;84:1229-34.

7 Muscle

Exposure to microgravity induces loss of muscle volume and performance capabilities such as decrements in maximal force and power production. These effects occur, especially in the legs, during both short- (121, 828-834) and long-duration flights (121, 828, 835-841). As with bone, regional changes in muscle loss appear to be dependent on the muscle's role in counteracting gravity; and thus although the lower extremity and core muscles are significantly affected, upper body muscles are not (842).

This topic has been extensively reviewed (164, 464, 828, 829, 831, 839, 843-851). Interpreting findings reported in the literature can be difficult (833, 843, 846). That is because, as with most physiological systems, a variety of techniques are used to assess multiple aspects of muscle, including exercise tests of functional muscle performance that evaluate multiple muscle groups, single joint evaluations that focus on a single muscle group, muscle biopsies to evaluate cellular changes, and magnetic resonance imaging (MRI) of muscle size. From a nutrition perspective, muscle and protein are almost synonymous; therefore, amino acids and protein biochemistry are studied, along with tracer kinetic studies to evaluate changes in protein metabolism.

Protein Biochemistry

Negative nitrogen balance, a gross indicator of muscle loss, was detected during Space Shuttle flights (852, 853). Potassium and nitrogen balances became increasingly negative throughout the duration of Skylab flights; however, levels of urinary creatinine (a measure of muscle mass) did not change (122, 366) despite volume losses in the leg (121, 840).

Serum concentrations of total protein and albumin were elevated at landing after Skylab missions. After Space Shuttle missions, synthesis of plasma proteins increased at landing but decreased in the week after flight, potentially secondary to competition for amino acid substrates required to replete muscle, RBC, and other proteins after flight (250, 853).

The concentration of urinary albumin is reduced during spaceflight and bed rest (314-316). Levels of urinary albumin excretion are typically low in healthy individuals, reflecting renal protein function.

Levels of amino acid in the urine and plasma do not provide an accurate indication of muscle metabolism, or even protein metabolism; however, in some cases, these are the only available data for this assessment. A general increase in levels of plasma amino acids was noted in cosmonauts after they returned from short- (2-day and 21-day) (854, 855) or long-duration (63-day) flights (856, 857). However, these levels had declined a week after flight (858). The limited data available from Space Shuttle crewmembers indicate a tendency for plasma levels of branched-chain amino acids to increase during flight, relative to preflight levels (859). Crewmembers of short-duration Space Shuttle flights had little or no change in their urinary amino acid profiles during flight (118), whereas Apollo and Skylab crewmembers had increased urinary excretion of the amino acid metabolites creatinine, sarcosine, and 3-methylhistidine during flight (376), suggesting that contractile proteins of skeletal muscle are degraded in weightlessness.

The balance of protein synthesis and protein catabolism affects the amount of protein in the body or in individual tissues. Studies aimed at understanding changes in body protein include measures of both of these factors, in addition to turnover. Directly measuring protein metabolism is not easy, and the results are variable (839, 860). For example, although both decreased protein synthesis and increased protein catabolism will yield a net loss of muscle, the mechanisms involved in these two processes are quite different, and therefore different measures would be required to counter each process.

Studies that used stable isotopes to measure protein turnover indicate that turnover of whole-body protein increases during short-duration spaceflight: although levels of protein synthesis increase, a greater percentage increase occurs in protein breakdown (852, 853). Stein et al. (847, 861) hypothesized that this increase in protein synthesis is related to physiological stress, as indicated by generally (but not consistently) increased levels of urinary cortisol during flight (7, 105, 208). Serum and urine cortisol in ISS crewmembers are shown in Figure 52. Studies of Apollo 17 crewmembers found that excretion of urinary cortisol was higher on days with more physically and mentally demanding mission tasks (862).

Decreased prostaglandin secretion has also been implicated in the loss of muscle tissue during spaceflight, secondary to decreased mechanical stress on muscle (208). Conversely, on long-duration Mir flights, investigators noted decreased rates of protein synthesis (102), secondary to reduced dietary energy intake (158).

The processes that induce muscle loss during spaceflight or bed rest are similar to the processes that induce metabolic breakdown in catabolic patients. This is a critical and confounding issue because inadequate energy intake will lead to these same effects. Therefore, because most astronauts do not meet energy intake requirements and they lose body mass, and it is unknown whether (or the extent of) loss of muscle mass results from the effects of spaceflight alone, or to what degree inadequate dietary intake confounds this loss.

Ground Analog Studies

Bed rest is the most common model used for studying changes in muscle and protein during disuse. Many studies have shown decrements in muscle mass,

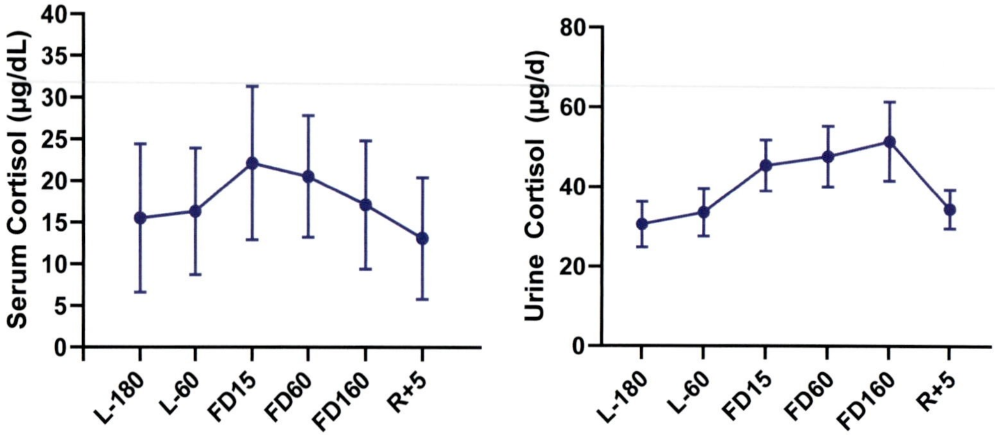

Figure 52. Serum and urine cortisol in 13 astronauts before, during, and after ISS missions. Adapted from (863).

strength, and performance in this analog (829, 832, 864-875). A recent bed rest study assessed whether feeding patterns affected muscle loss and metabolism; no difference in muscle loss or glucose metabolism was detected when food was delivered using nasogastric tube feeding, either continuously or in four bolus administrations per day (876).

Dry immersion is another method of invoking muscle disuse. Muscle changes may be induced faster during dry immersion than during bed rest; however, long-duration dry immersion studies are more difficult to implement than long-duration bed rest studies (429-431, 877-884). Unilateral limb suspension (ULLS) can also be used to induce muscle changes as a result of disuse. These studies incur significantly less expense than bed rest studies and the subjects have more freedom (885-889). Loss of muscle mass and strength in the suspended limb is the same as losses induced in the same muscle during bed rest, although changes are restricted to the immobilized muscle whereas bed rest induces muscle loss through the body (890-892). These models all provide a means to collect data that would be difficult if not impossible to collect from large groups of subjects during actual spaceflight. However, it is important to remember that model systems are just that, and that they likely do not provide an exact replica of the physiological changes that occur during spaceflight (893).

Spaceflight-induced loss of muscle mass and muscle strength may be related to changes in whole body protein turnover. Many studies have documented a decrease in protein synthesis during bed rest (515, 894-901). Evidence of increased rates of protein catabolism during bed rest is more limited, as reviewed by Bodine (846). The loss of muscle loss with disuse is associated with increased oxidative stress, as reviewed by Powers et al. (902).

Muscle Loss Countermeasures

Mechanical

Exercise is perhaps the most obvious measure to maintain muscle, bone, and cardiovascular health (464, 467, 469, 829, 845, 848, 884, 903-910). On Mir flights, crewmembers differed significantly with respect to frequency and intensity of their in-flight exercise (related to such factors as mission requirements and personal habits). However, all subjects lost almost 20% of the volume of their leg muscles, as detected immediately after flight using MRI (841).

The ISS has the size and volume to accommodate a suite of exercise equipment that includes a treadmill, a cycle ergometer (Figure 57), and resistive exercise devices (476, 911, 912). On early ISS missions, the exercise regimens generally did not help to maintain muscle or bone mass (475) or muscle mass or strength (906). When a second-generation treadmill and an advanced resistance exercise device were launched in 2008 (Figure 53), ISS crewmembers were able to maintain bone and increase their lean body mass (124, 147); however, these countermeasures did not fully protect muscle strength.

Many types of exercise devices and protocols have been proposed to aid in maintaining musculoskeletal and cardiovascular health during flight, including resistance exercise using traditional resistance (479, 886, 898), rowing (913), flywheel devices (871, 914-918), jumping systems (919), and treadmill exercise within a LBNP system (920), or combinations of the above (921, 922).

Given that ISS crews use multiple exercise devices, it will be important to assess the effects of exercise protocols that involve combined use of these devices. Combined resistance and aerobic exercise protocols have shown promise for protecting muscle

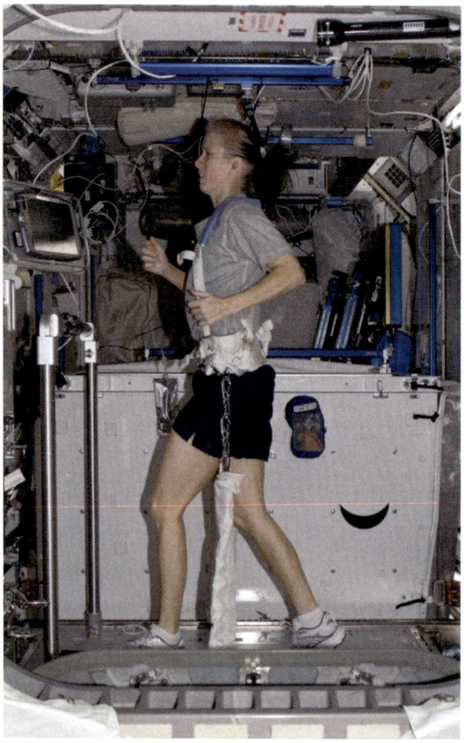

Figure 53. NASA astronaut Shannon Walker, equipped with a bungee harness, exercises on the Combined Operational Load Bearing External Resistance Treadmill (COLBERT) in Node 3 of the ISS. Photo Credit: NASA.

(and the cardiovascular system) during bed rest (923, 924). A shorter, more-intense combined exercise regimen has been proposed as a way to save time while protecting muscle, bone, and cardiovascular health. Although ground results were promising (484), initial spaceflight results suggest these regimens did not provide additional physiological benefit, but did save crew time (925, 926).

Whole-body vibration alone or while performing resistive exercise may provide a viable musculoskeletal countermeasure (485, 526, 531, 532, 927-931), particularly when strenuous exercise is not advised due to increased risk for injury—for instance, in older people. As mentioned earlier, mechanical stimulation is a prerequisite to avoid degradation of muscle and bone. According to Frost's mechanostat theory (387, 932), a certain individual level of mechanical stimulation has to be achieved to maintain muscle and bone mass and muscle strength, and that lowering or increasing that level of mechanical stimulation will affect the response. The vibration magnitude during whole-body vibration training seems to be one of the key factors. Vibration magnitude is defined as the vibration frequency (Hz) times the amplitude or displacement (mm) (929). This is most likely the reason why whole-body vibration training with a frequency of 20 Hz has not always been effective for protecting muscle and bone (399), whereas whole-body vibration while performing resistive exercise seemed to be more effective. When young, healthy male subjects performed this combined protocol during bed rest studies of 56 or 60 days (485, 931), they were able to attenuate atrophy of their muscle and bone and deconditioning of their lumbar spine, and prevent accumulation of fat in their vertebral marrow (408, 410, 411, 485, 531, 933-935). Although the efficacy, vibration dose, frequency, and duration of whole-body vibration exercise have not been thoroughly researched, this does not seem a viable countermeasure for use inflight given the associated risks.

Electrical stimulation is another way to invoke muscle activity in cases of disuse (936, 937), as reviewed by Dirks et al. (938). However, electrical stimulation maintains muscle mass but not strength (939), and electrical stimulation is likely a much-less-effective countermeasure than exercise, which provides many additional benefits.

Blood flow restriction in combination with either resistance or vibration exercise has been advocated as a countermeasure for muscle loss (940-942); however, results have been varied (886, 943). As reviewed by Behringer and Willberg, blood flow restriction may provide a potential way to augment exercise, but concerns about safety and utility in microgravity require further study (941). Whether the recent findings of thrombosis (944, 945) during flight dampen enthusiasm for this technique is not yet known.

Pharmacological

Exogenous testosterone is commonly suggested as a pharmacological method to mitigate spaceflight-included muscle (and/or bone) loss, because testosterone concentration can decrease in humans (551-556, 946, 947) and animals (549, 550) during flight, and in cellular models of spaceflight. Among the potential confounding factors for the reduced levels of testosterone is inadequate energy intake. Decreases in testosterone have been observed in exercising bed rest subjects, whereas sedentary controls had no change in testosterone (948). A recent study in rats showed that suppression of testosterone (via orchiectomy) did not exacerbate disuse-induced muscle loss (949).

The initial in-flight testosterone data from human spaceflight were from three astronauts on Skylab 4, an 84-day mission (950), followed by one in-flight data point from four astronauts on Space Shuttle mission STS-55, which flew in 1993. On the Space Shuttle mission, circulating testosterone levels were decreased after 4 or 5 days of flight relative to preflight levels, when measured in serum, saliva, and urine. Serum cortisol, cortisol biorhythms, and dehydroepiandrosterone-sulfate concentrations in these four astronauts were unchanged during flight (947, 951).

A significant confounding issue is that these crewmembers were consuming only about 60% to 85% of their basal metabolic energy requirements during the flight (113). Estimates of spaceflight energy requirements calculated with the WHO equation typically use an activity factor of 1.7 (i.e., 1.7 x basal metabolic rate) (1, 40). This factor is based on data documenting that total energy requirements are unchanged during flight (101) or, in some cases, are even increased with heavy exercise (102), relative to before flight. Even if lower estimates of activity were used, the result would reveal significant energy deficit in crewmembers on the STS-55 mission, especially during the days of sample collections (113). Indeed, energy intake, which was very carefully documented on these missions, was below even basal requirements. Energy deficits, both short- and long-term, are associated with lower circulating testosterone (free and total) (952-954). Thus, the discrepancy between the long-duration data presented here (Figure 54) and the earlier reports of effects observed during the first week of flight could be explained simply by inadequate energy intake.

Data from ISS show that testosterone and related hormones are unchanged by real or simulated weightlessness, apart from transient effects on landing day (209). Furthermore, Skylab missions reported urinary testosterone from three crewmembers at two in-flight data points, and found that testosterone excretion was increased relative to the preflight period (209, 950).

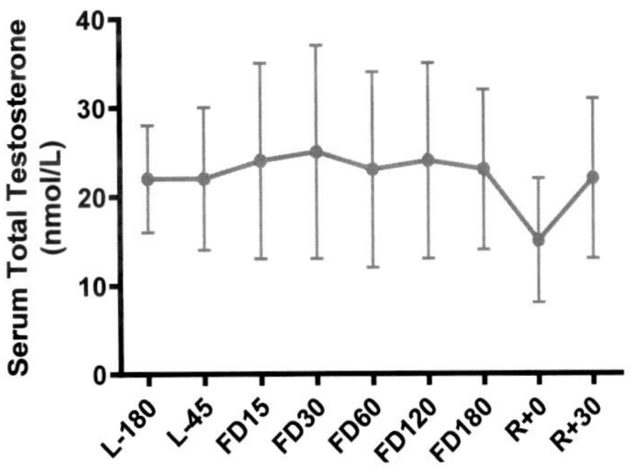

Figure 54. Serum total testosterone concentrations before, during, and after flight on the ISS. Although circulating concentrations decreased significantly after flight (at R+0), no other time point differed significantly from the preflight mean. Data are mean ± SD. Data are from Smith et al. (209).

Plasma data from the three Skylab missions (N=9) are reported to have shown "a trend toward lower values after the mission" (950). Although we do not have urinary testosterone data on all crewmembers, these reports from the 1970s confirm the findings from the ISS (209).

Several ground-analog studies demonstrate that bed rest has no effect on circulating testosterone concentrations in sedentary subjects (209, 897, 948, 955-957). In one such study, consistent decreases in serum testosterone were observed after subjects had been in the bed rest facility for 7 days (while they were still ambulatory) and then another decrease occurred when testosterone was measured 5 days after re-ambulation. The pre-bed rest change is likely related to stress and decreased ambulation while subjects were in the bed rest facility, and the post-bed rest change was probably related to body fluid shifts during and after bed rest. No changes in testosterone occurred during bed rest (209).

Bed rest subjects are typically required to consume energy at a level to maintain body mass. If energy deficits are indeed part of the observed decrease in testosterone during the Space Shuttle flights previously reported, this may also explain the difference between those flight data and bed rest study data, reported herein and elsewhere. Although we showed an intermittent decrease in total and free testosterone in bed rest subjects with or without an artificial gravity (i.e., centrifugation) protocol (254), this study had combined the two pre-bed rest collection sessions. When these sessions were analyzed separately because of our results in the later bed rest study, it turned out that testosterone concentrations were indeed higher only at the first data collection point (BR-10) than during or after bed rest (209) (Figure 55).

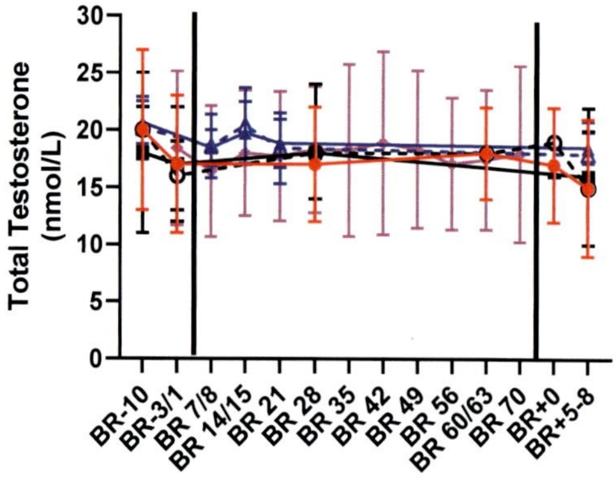

Figure 55. Serum total serum testosterone concentrations in subjects in multiple bed rest studies: data from a 21-day bed rest testing an artificial gravity countermeasure are shown with blue triangles, filled symbols and solid line = control, n=7, open symbols and dashed line = AG, n=8 (254). Note: pre-bed rest data assigned to BR-10; control subjects in 60- to 90-day bed rest studies are shown with red circles and solid line, n=15 (209); control subjects in a 70-day bed rest study are shown with purple diamonds and solid line (957); control subjects in a 30-day bed rest study are shown with black squares and solid line, n=8 (209); subjects treated with vibration for 60- to 90-day bed rest are shown with open black circles and dashed line, n=7 (209). Vertical lines represent the beginning and end of bed rest. All data are mean ± SD.

One criticism of sedentary bed rest studies as an analog for spaceflight is that astronauts are not sedentary, especially on long-duration missions, when they exercise extensively. Wade et al. reported that in a 4-week study, bed rest subjects with intensive exercise protocols had lower non-fasting circulating plasma testosterone concentrations than non-exercising bed rested controls (948). They reported a small loss of (non-fasting) post-breakfast body mass (948, 958), and reported that caloric and liquid intakes were designed to maintain body mass. Despite the exercise, which was described as including an expenditure of 214 or 446 kcal/d (5 times a week), actual intakes in the exercise groups were only 155 or 212 kcal/d greater than those of the no-exercise group (958). A bed rest study of exercise with and without testosterone administration showed some beneficial effects on metabolism and an enhanced muscle response (957, 959), with the steroid adding some protections beyond exercise itself. In another bed rest study, exogenous testosterone administration maintained muscle mass and protein balance, but with no effect on muscle strength (956).

In a 30-day study, Zorbas et al. showed that serum testosterone decreased during bed rest only in trained subjects, whereas it did not change in untrained subjects during bed rest (960). Interestingly, when conditioned subjects were "hyperhydrated" by saline ingestion during bed rest, testosterone did not change relative to the pre-bed rest period. In a shorter, 3-day bed rest, no differences in plasma testosterone were observed before or after exercise in typically untrained or trained individuals, either cyclists or weight trainers (961). Astronauts on ISS missions are typically relatively fit before flight and exercise heavily during flight, using treadmill, cycle, and resistive exercise devices.

As reviewed by Tou (962), in studies of rats with sample collections after spaceflight, serum (963) and urinary (964) testosterone were generally decreased relative to the preflight period (965). Unfortunately, in-flight biological samples are typically not available, given the difficulties with collection procedures in the microgravity environment. These postflight conclusions are consistent with data reported on landing day after a short-duration spaceflight (209).

In ground-based rodent models, short-duration (7-12 d) unloading generally results in reduced circulating testosterone concentrations and an associated loss of bone and muscle mass (549, 550, 966). One study of unilateral limb immobilized rats found that androgen deficiency did not exacerbate muscle loss of immobilization (i.e., that these two factors are not additive) (949).

Unloading of longer-duration (6 weeks) in rats resulted in impaired spermatogenesis, but had no effect on circulating testosterone concentrations (967). Similarly, the production of testosterone by rat testes after actual spaceflight is diminished, as is response to stimulation by luteinizing hormone (968). Contradicting these findings, another study showed no change in circulating testosterone in suspended rats after suspension for 1 or 3 weeks, but it did show an increase in testosterone of suspended animals after 8 weeks, despite reduced testicular weight (969). One critical confounding factor in the hind-limb suspended rat model is that not all studies take (surgical) precautions to prevent ascension of the testicles into the abdominal cavity, which can significantly affect testosterone production and the interpretation of the study. Some, but not all, studies have accounted for this, and this limitation contributes to inconsistencies in the literature.

Rotating cell culture vessels have also been used as an analog of weightlessness, with some limitations, as with all analogs. Cultured testicular fragments exposed to this environment, compared with static 1g cultures, have maintained cellular architecture and have increased both proliferation and testosterone secretion (970), but with altered testicular physiology (971), including impaired Leydig cell responsiveness to luteinizing hormone stimulation. Whether the lack of change in circulating testosterone observed in the studies reported herein obscured alterations in testicular physiology is unclear, but it seems imprudent to make that leap without additional data.

Administration of testosterone to suspended rats mitigates muscle and bone losses (549). The bone data in rats are confounded by differential effects on growing and adult rats (447); however, these results are of interest nonetheless. Testosterone administration to elderly individuals has shown that the bone response to testosterone depended on the initial circulating testosterone concentrations (972). That is, subjects who had normal blood concentrations of testosterone had less or no response to testosterone administration. Given these data, there is little rationale for providing testosterone during flight to mitigate bone loss.

Hypergravity, induced by centrifugation, has been shown to result in increased urinary testosterone excretion in monkeys (946), as well as in rats (964, 966). Hypergravity has also been found to affect tissues of rats and some other endocrine variables, but increased gravitational force had no effect on circulating testosterone (963). On the basis of these data, authors have suggested that the response to gravity is roughly linear, from hypergravity (increased), to unit gravity, to microgravity (decreased) (946, 963). Intriguing as this concept may be, the data presented herein do not support it.

As is understandable, the proposed use of exogenous steroids is somewhat controversial. Muscle physiologists argue that despite the lack of change in endogenous steroids, exogenous androgens may prove a viable countermeasure nonetheless. Treatments with such androgens have been reported to improve physical performance, muscle mass, and muscle strength in both young athletes and older sedentary men (973). The interaction of endocrine factors, aging (including middle age), the spaceflight environment, and the use of exercise to replace loading is not well understood.

In summary, circulating testosterone and related hormones are unchanged by real or simulated weightlessness, apart from transient effects after flight. The interrelationships of energy balance, exercise, stress response, and endocrine function are complicated, and evaluation of available literature must be done so carefully to assess study design, dietary intake, controls and countermeasure treatments, and fitness of subjects. As we contemplate space exploration beyond low-Earth orbit, endocrine data will be critical for understanding human adaptation in this unique environment, and potentially for helping to counteract the negative effects of spaceflight on the human body.

Nutritional

Use of protein and amino acid supplementation has long been studied as a potential means to mitigate muscle loss associated with spaceflight (865, 974, 975); however, results have been inconclusive at best (976). Noteworthy, feeding Skylab crewmembers energy and protein equivalent to those given to a comparison bed rest group did not prevent negative nitrogen balance and loss of leg muscle strength observed during flight (366, 836, 840).

In a 2011 review, Stein and Blanc evaluated the literature from bed rest studies (977), and found that the effect (or lack thereof) of amino acids on muscle depended greatly on protein intake and energy provision. Specifically, if nominal protein intake (i.e., in both treatment and control groups) was at levels greater than 1.1 to 1.2 g protein/kg body mass/d, then supplemental amino acids had no effect. If control subjects were provided with ≤0.8 g protein/kg body mass/d while the supplemented group consumed >1.0 g protein/kg body mass/d, then the supplement appeared to have a beneficial effect. We review many of these studies in this report, and attempt to highlight details and differences that potentially contribute to the varied effects.

Two recent studies were conducted using unilateral leg immobilization. One fed subjects eucaloric diets with high (1.6 g protein/kg body weight), low (0.5 g protein/kg body weight), or no/very low (0.15 g protein/kg body weight) for 3 days, and found no difference in protein intake on loss of muscle mass or strength (978). The other fed high-dose leucine (15 gm/d) and found no protection of muscle strength (979). The latter paper was accompanied by an editorial concluding that these protein and amino acid supplementation studies had run their course (976).

Feeding a bed rest group adequate energy with higher protein reversed nitrogen losses (899). These subjects consumed isocaloric diets, with either 0.6 or 1.0 g protein/kg body weight (899). Given the lower protein intakes are below the RDA of 0.8 g/kg body weight, these findings aren't surprising. Typical intakes of protein during flight exceed the RDA (as with most Western diets). Recent updates to the spaceflight nutritional requirements have used protein recommendations set for "high intensity athletes," and target 1.2-1.8 g/kg body weight.

A series of studies evaluated amino acid supplementation in bed rest and other ground models (980). Supplementation of essential amino acids (16.5 g) and carbohydrate (30 g sucrose) three times per day maintained muscle mass and strength via maintenance of protein synthetic pathways during 28-day bed rest (981, 982), compared to those not receiving the supplements. The sucrose was added "to improve palatability" of the supplement; in turn, the supplement provided 558 kcals/d to the treatment group. Including exogenous hypercortisolemia as a treatment group improved the relative effect of essential AA/carbohydrate supplementation when compared to the bed rest with hypercortisolemia (982-984).

A 10-day bed rest study of older individuals (group average age: 68 years and 71 years) receiving placebo or essential amino acid supplementation (45 g/d) had minimal effect on muscle parameters when pre-bed rest differences among subjects were taken into account (985). A 7-day bed rest of older (60- to 80-year-old) individuals supplemented with either leucine (14.6 g/d on average) or alanine (13.2 g/d on average) found positive effects of leucine on maintenance of muscle mass, but not of strength or function (986) when compared to alanine. The difference in dose amounts was related to differences in body mass of the subjects between groups, and the doses were per kg body mass. Similarly, provision of a whey protein isolate supplement in a eucaloric diet had some effect on muscle mass, but not on function (973). In this study and others, individual response variability highlights concern of the nature of the effect and potential for confounding factors.

A 28-day bed rest study evaluating the timing of amino acid administration provided subjects with 15 g of essential amino acids with carbohydrate (35 g sucrose) before or 3 hours after exercise, with findings suggesting that exercise plus the supplement is better than the supplement alone (987-989). Although this essential amino acid supplement was similar to the regimen described above, it was given only once per day, and 6 days per week (to align with exercise sessions). The supplement was also given to all treatment groups. The supplement plus exercise ameliorated, but did not eliminate, loss of muscle mass and strength (987, 989) as well as metabolic changes (e.g., altered lipid profiles) (988).

Protein/amino acid supplementation was one countermeasure that was tested in the Women in Space Exploration study (WISE-2005) (990), a 60-day bed rest study with female subjects. The control group consumed 1 g protein/kg body mass, and the treatment group consumed 1.45 g protein/kg body mass with an additional 0.72 gm branched chain amino acids (leucine, isoleucine, and valine) daily. By design, the diet during bed rest was hypocaloric, and subjects in this study were not required to eat all of their food, resulting in body mass loss and increased subject variability (248). Nonetheless, this approach did not mitigate losses of muscle mass or strength (923, 991, 992). As reviewed in Chapter 6, excess protein is a concern for bone health, as documented in this study as well (248, 409), in part related to effects of amino acid oxidation on acid/base balance, specifically driving pH lower.

To address this acidogenic effect, some studies have employed providing a source of base to counteract the acid. In a pair of bed rest studies, 19 and 21 days, Bosutti et al. evaluated effects of bed rest on muscle fatigue and metabolism, and the ability of a whey protein (0.6 g/kg/d in addition to the baseline 1.2 g/kg body weight protein, provided isocalorically in place of carbohydrate and fat) plus potassium bicarbonate supplement to counteract any decrements (993, 994). Although muscle volume was reduced, resistance to fatigue was not affected by bed rest alone, or by the countermeasure (993). Oxidative capacity was reduced with bed rest. A similar 21-day bed rest study evaluated whey protein and potassium bicarbonate supplementation, with no mitigation of muscle atrophy or on the effects of bed rest on cartilage (995, 996).

Using a single leg immobilization model in healthy older men (average age 69 years), Dirks et al. tested a nutritional supplement that provided 300 kcal/d, and specifically included protein (41.4 g total protein per day, including 21.2 g essential amino acids), carbohydrate (18.8 g/d), and fat (6 g/), along with vitamins and minerals (997). The supplement (and inherent additional caloric intake) did not mitigate loss of muscle mass and strength.

Although many continue to argue for the importance and benefit of protein as a spaceflight countermeasure, or for different sources of protein, or specific amino acid mixtures, or the timing of protein intake relative to exercise (as described in the review of a subset of this literature provided here), clear evidence supporting this is simply not available. The existing studies are often too short to allow an understanding of long-term effects and adaptation, and are often not completely controlled with respect to treatment groups. This presents a confounding factor that is often ignored, given that protein (or amino acids) provide not only a nitrogen source, but moreover, an energy source. Studies often compare protein supplementation to controls getting no supplement, and the caloric intake difference could explain (i.e., confound) effects. Few if any studies evaluate the simple effect of providing more food (i.e., a balanced diet) would offer similar benefit. Providing protein supplements to subjects that are losing weight because of hypocaloric provisions seems an ill-fated approach to the maintenance of muscle. Well-controlled, balanced, long-term studies are required to conclusively define the effect of protein intake on musculoskeletal health.

From the data to date, if crewmembers consume enough energy and protein, with adequate exercise, then supplemental amino acids (or other variants of protein supplementation) provide no benefit and, at worst case, they may actually be detrimental, as described in Chapter 6.

Nutrients Associated with Muscle Health

Energy and protein are key nutritional components when it comes to muscle health. Energy was described in detail in Chapter 4, and protein was also discussed in Chapter 7, as well as being discussed above in relation to counteracting muscle loss.

Potassium

As the most plentiful intracellular cation, potassium has a significant role in several physiological processes (39, 998, 999). It is crucial to regulation of acid-base balance, energy metabolism, blood pressure, membrane transport, and distribution of fluid within the body. It is also involved in the transmission of nerve impulses and cardiac function (1000). Potassium metabolism that is disordered because of excessive or deficient circulating levels has negative consequences for cardiac, muscle, and neurological function.

Deficiency of potassium leads to hypokalemia, muscle weakness, constipation, and fatigue, or even death. No evidence of adverse effects is associated with toxicity of potassium from naturally occurring sources. However, supplemental intake may cause hyperkalemia (and associated weakness, cardiac arrest, and paralysis), metabolic acidosis (700), decreased neuromuscular function, or even death.

Serum and urinary levels of potassium were both decreased after spaceflight in Apollo crewmembers (1001), and evidence exists that a similar decrease occurred in Skylab crewmembers (122). Loss of both total body potassium and exchangeable potassium was observed in Apollo crewmembers (1001). Increased levels of urinary potassium during spaceflight may be related to muscle disuse atrophy and inadequate intake (647).

In the initial days of bed rest, excess dietary sodium was shown to be potassium-depleting (Heer, et al., unpublished observations). Loss of lean body mass, along with high sodium intake, may also result in potassium depletion.

Figure 56. Front to back: Expedition 34 crew astronaut Tom Marshburn and cosmonauts Roman Romanenko and Evgeny Tarelkin with floating fruit and vegetables in ISS Node 1. Photo Credit: NASA.

References for Chapter 7

1. Smith SM, Zwart SR, Kloeris V, Heer M. Nutritional biochemistry of space flight. New York: Nova Science Publishers; 2009.

7. Leach CS, Alfrey CP, Suki WN, Leonard JI, Rambaut PC, Inners LD, Smith SM, Lane HW, Krauhs JM. Regulation of body fluid compartments during short-term spaceflight. J Appl Physiol (1985). 1996;81:105-16.

39. National Academies of Sciences, Engineering, and Medicine. Dietary Reference Intakes for sodium and potassium. Washington, DC: The National Academies Press. 2019.

40. World Health Organization. Energy and protein requirements. Report of a joint FAO/WHO/UNU expert consultation. Geneva, Switzerland: World Health Organization; 1985.

101. Lane HW, Gretebeck RJ, Schoeller DA, Davis-Street J, Socki RA, Gibson EK. Comparison of ground-based and space flight energy expenditure and water turnover in middle-aged healthy male US astronauts. Am J Clin Nutr. 1997;65:4-12.

102. Stein TP, Leskiw MJ, Schluter MD, Hoyt RW, Lane HW, Gretebeck RE, LeBlanc AD. Energy expenditure and balance during spaceflight on the space shuttle. Am J Physiol. 1999;276:R1739-48.

105. Stein TP, Schluter MD, Leskiw MJ. Cortisol, insulin and leptin during space flight and bed rest. J Gravit Physiol. 1999;6:P85-6.

113. Heer M, Boerger A, Kamps N, Mika C, Korr C, Drummer C. Nutrient supply during recent European missions. Pflugers Arch. 2000;441:R8-14.

118. Stein TP, Schluter MD. Excretion of amino acids by humans during space flight. Acta Astronaut. 1998;42:205-14.

121. Rambaut PC, Leach CS, Leonard JI. Observations in energy balance in man during spaceflight. Am J Physiol. 1977;233:R208-12.

122. Leach CS, Rambaut PC. Biochemical responses of the Skylab crewmen: an overview. In: Johnston RS, Dietlein LF, editors. Biomedical results from Skylab (NASA SP-377). Washington, DC: National Aeronautics and Space Administration; 1977. p. 204-16.

124. Smith SM, Heer MA, Shackelford LC, Sibonga JD, Ploutz-Snyder L, Zwart SR. Benefits for bone from resistance exercise and nutrition in long-duration spaceflight: evidence from biochemistry and densitometry. J Bone Miner Res. 2012;27:1896-906.

147. Smith SM, Zwart SR, Heer M, Hudson EK, Shackelford L, Morgan JLL. Men and women in space: bone loss and kidney stone risk after long-duration spaceflight. J Bone Miner Res. 2014;29:1639-45.

158. Stein TP, Leskiw MJ, Schluter MD, Donaldson MR, Larina I. Protein kinetics during and after long-duration spaceflight on MIR. Am J Physiol. 1999;276:E1014-21.

164. Ferrando AA, Paddon-Jones D, Wolfe RR. Alterations in protein metabolism during space flight and inactivity. Nutrition. 2002;18:837-41.

208. Stein TP, Schluter MD, Moldawer LL. Endocrine relationships during human spaceflight. Am J Physiol. 1999;276:E155-62.

209. Smith SM, Heer M, Wang Z, Huntoon CL, Zwart SR. Long-duration space flight and bed rest effects on testosterone and other steroids. J Clin Endocrinol Metab. 2012;97:270-8.

248. Heer M, Baecker N, Frings-Meuthen P, Graf S, Zwart SR, Biolo G, Smith SM. Effects of high-protein intake on bone turnover in long-term bed rest in women. Appl Physiol Nutr Metab. 2017;42:537-46.

250. Stein TP, Schluter MD. Plasma protein synthesis after spaceflight. Aviat Space Environ Med. 2006;77:745-8.

254. Zwart SR, Crawford GE, Gillman PL, Kala G, Rodgers AS, Rogers A, Inniss AM, Rice BL, Ericson K, Coburn S, Bourbeau Y, Hudson E, Mathew G, Dekerlegand DE, Sams CF, Heer MA, Paloski WH, Smith SM. Effects of 21 days of bed rest, with or without artificial gravity, on nutritional status of humans. J Appl Physiol (1985). 2009;107:54-62.

314. Cirillo M, De Santo NG, Heer M, Norsk P, Elmann-Larsen B, Bellini L, Stellato D, Drummer C. Urinary albumin in space missions. J Gravit Physiol. 2002;9:P193-4.

315. Cirillo M, De Santo NG, Heer M, Norsk P, Elmann-Larsen B, Bellini L, Stellato D, Drummer C. Low urinary albumin excretion in astronauts during space missions. Nephron Physiol. 2003;93:102-5.

316. Cirillo M, Stellato D, Heer M, Drummer C, Bellini L, De Santo NG. Urinary albumin in head-down bed rest. J Gravit Physiol. 2002;9:P195-6.

366. Whedon GD, Lutwak L, Rambaut PC, Whittle MW, Smith MC, Reid J, Leach C, Stadler CR, Sanford DD. Mineral and nitrogen metabolic studies, experiment M071. In: Johnston RS, Dietlein LF, editors. Biomedical results from Skylab (NASA SP-377). Washington, DC: National Aeronautics and Space Administration; 1977. p. 164-74.

376. Leach CS, Rambaut PC, Di Ferrante N. Amino aciduria in weightlessness. Acta Astronaut. 1979;6:1323-33.

387. Frost HM. Bone "mass" and the "mechanostat": a proposal. Anat Rec. 1987;219:1-9.

399. Baecker N, Frings-Meuthen P, Heer M, Mester J, Liphardt AM. Effects of vibration training on bone metabolism: results from a short-term bed rest study. Eur J Appl Physiol. 2012;112:1741-50.

408. Armbrecht G, Belavy DL, Gast U, Bongrazio M, Touby F, Beller G, Roth HJ, Perschel FH, Rittweger J, Felsenberg D. Resistive vibration exercise attenuates bone and muscle atrophy in 56 days of bed rest: biochemical markers of bone metabolism. Osteoporos Int. 2010;21:597-607.

409. Armbrecht G, Belavy DL, Backstrom M, Beller G, Alexandre C, Rizzoli R, Felsenberg D. Trabecular and cortical bone density and architecture in women after 60 days of bed rest using high-resolution pQCT: WISE 2005. J Bone Miner Res. 2011;26:2399-410.

410. Belavy DL, Beller G, Armbrecht G, Perschel FH, Fitzner R, Bock O, Borst H, Degner C, Gast U, Felsenberg D. Evidence for an additional effect of whole-body vibration above resistive exercise alone in preventing bone loss during prolonged bed rest. Osteoporos Int. 2011;22:1581-91.

411. Belavy DL, Beller G, Ritter Z, Felsenberg D. Bone structure and density via HR-pQCT in 60d bed-rest, 2-years recovery with and without countermeasures. J Musculoskelet Neuronal Interact. 2011;11:215-26.

429. Navasiolava NM, Custaud MA, Tomilovskaya ES, Larina IM, Mano T, Gauquelin-Koch G, Gharib C, Kozlovskaya IB. Long-term dry immersion: review and prospects. Eur J Appl Physiol. 2011;111:1235-60.

430. Tomilovskaya E, Shigueva T, Sayenko D, Rukavishnikov I, Kozlovskaya I. Dry immersion as a ground-based model of microgravity physiological effects. Front Physiol. 2019;10:284.

431. Kozlovskaya IB. Fundamental and applied objectives of investigation in dry immersion. Hum Physiol. 2010;36:808-12.

447. Smith BJ, King JB, Lucas EA, Akhter MP, Arjmandi BH, Stoecker BJ. Skeletal unloading and dietary copper depletion are detrimental to bone quality of mature rats. J Nutr. 2002;132:190-6.

464. Lang T, Van Loon J, Bloomfield S, Vico L, Chopard A, Rittweger J, Kyparos A, Blottner D, Vuori I, Gerzer R, Cavanagh PR. Towards human exploration of space: the THESEUS review series on muscle and bone research priorities. NPJ Microgravity. 2017;3:8.

467. Hart DA, Zernicke RF. Optimal human functioning requires exercise across the lifespan: Mobility in a 1g environment is intrinsic to the integrity of multiple biological systems. Front Physiol. 2020;11:156.

469. Hawkey A. The importance of exercising in space. Interdiscip Sci Rev. 2003;28:130-8.

475. Lang T, LeBlanc A, Evans H, Lu Y, Genant H, Yu A. Cortical and trabecular bone mineral loss from the spine and hip in long-duration spaceflight. J Bone Miner Res. 2004;19:1006-12.

476. Loerch LH. Exercise countermeasures on ISS: Summary and future directions. Aerosp Med Hum Perform. 2015;86:A92-A4.

479. Shackelford LC, LeBlanc AD, Driscoll TB, Evans HJ, Rianon NJ, Smith SM, Spector E, Feeback DL, Lai D. Resistance exercise as a countermeasure to disuse-induced bone loss. J Appl Physiol (1985). 2004;97:119-29.

484. Ploutz-Snyder LL, Downs M, Goetchius E, Crowell B, English KL, Ploutz-Snyder R, Ryder JW, Dillon EL, Sheffield-Moore M, Scott JM. Exercise training mitigates multisystem deconditioning during bed rest. Med Sci Sports Exerc. 2018;50:1920-8.

485. Belavy DL, Armbrecht G, Gast U, Richardson CA, Hides JA, Felsenberg D. Countermeasures against lumbar spine deconditioning in prolonged bed rest: resistive exercise with and without whole body vibration. J Appl Physiol (1985). 2010;109:1801-11.

515. Symons TB, Sheffield-Moore M, Chinkes DL, Ferrando AA, Paddon-Jones D. Artificial gravity maintains skeletal muscle protein synthesis during 21 days of simulated microgravity. J Appl Physiol (1985). 2009;107:34-8.

526. Rubin C, Recker R, Cullen D, Ryaby J, McCabe J, McLeod K. Prevention of postmenopausal bone loss by a low-magnitude, high-frequency mechanical stimuli: a clinical trial assessing compliance, efficacy, and safety. J Bone Miner Res. 2004;19:343-51.

531. Owen PJ, Belavy DL, Rittweger J. Using whole-body vibration for countermeasure exercise. In: Rittweger J, editor. Manual of Vibration Exercise and Vibration Therapy. Switzerland: Springer Nature; 2020. p. 229-44.

532. Belavy DL, Hides JA, Wilson SJ, Stanton W, Dimeo FC, Rittweger J, Felsenberg D, Richardson CA. Resistive simulated weightbearing exercise with whole body vibration reduces lumbar spine deconditioning in bed-rest. Spine (Phila Pa 1976). 2008;33:E121-31.

549. Wimalawansa SM, Chapa MT, Wei JN, Westlund KN, Quast MJ, Wimalawansa SJ. Reversal of weightlessness-induced musculoskeletal losses with androgens: quantification by MRI. J Appl Physiol (1985). 1999;86:1841-6.

550. Wimalawansa SM, Wimalawansa SJ. Simulated weightlessness-induced attenuation of testosterone production may be responsible for bone loss. Endocrine. 1999;10:253-60.

551. Strollo F. Hormonal changes in humans during spaceflight. Adv Space Biol Med. 1999;7:99-129.

552. Strollo F, Boitani C, Basciani S, Pecorelli L, Palumbo D, Borgia L, Masini MA, More M, Strollo G, Spera G, Uva BM, Riondino G. The pituitary-testicular axis in microgravity: analogies with the aging male syndrome. J Endocrinol Invest. 2005;28:78-83.

553. Strollo F, Masini MA, Pastorino M, Ricci F, Vadrucci S, Cogoli-Greuter M, Uva BM. Microgravity-induced alterations in cultured testicular cells. J Gravit Physiol. 2004;11:P187-8.

554. Strollo F, Riondino G, Harris B, Strollo G, Casarosa E, Mangrossa N, Ferretti C, Luisi M. The effect of microgravity on testicular androgen secretion. Aviat Space Environ Med. 1998;69:133-6.

555. Strollo F, Strollo G, More M, Bollanti L, Ciarmatori A, Longo E, Quintiliani R, Mambro A, Mangrossa N, Ferretti C. Hormonal adaptation to real and simulated microgravity. J Gravit Physiol. 1998;5:P89-92.

556. Strollo F, Strollo G, Morè M, Mangrossa N, Riondino G, Luisi M, Casarosa E. Space flight induces endocrine changes at both the pituitary and peripheral level in the absence of any major chronobiologic disturbances. In: Sahm PR, Keller MH, Schiewe B, editors. Proceedings of the Norderney Symposium on Scientific Results of the German Spacelab Mission D-2. Norderney, Germany: Wissenschaftliche Projectführung D-2; 1995. p. 743-7.

647. Lane HW, Leach C, Smith SM. Fluid and electrolyte homeostasis. In: Lane HW, Schoeller DA, editors. Nutrition in spaceflight and weightlessness models. Boca Raton, FL: CRC Press; 2000. p. 119-39.

700. Vormann J, Remer T. Dietary, metabolic, physiologic, and disease-related aspects of acid-base balance: foreword to the contributions of the second International Acid-Base Symposium. J Nutr. 2008;138:413S-4S.

828. Fitts RH, Riley DR, Widrick JJ. Physiology of a microgravity environment invited review: microgravity and skeletal muscle. J Appl Physiol (1985). 2000;89:823-39.

829. Adams GR, Caiozzo VJ, Baldwin KM. Skeletal muscle unweighting: spaceflight and ground-based models. J Appl Physiol (1985). 2003;95:2185-201.

830. LeBlanc A, Rowe R, Schneider V, Evans H, Hedrick T. Regional muscle loss after short duration spaceflight. Aviat Space Environ Med. 1995;66:1151-4.

831. Desplanches D. Structural and functional adaptations of skeletal muscle to weightlessness. Int J Sports Med. 1997;18 Suppl 4:S259-64.

832. Grogor'eva LS, Kozlovskaia IB. [Effect of weightlessness and hypokinesia on the velocity-strength properties of human muscles]. Kosm Biol Aviakosm Med. 1987;21:27-30.

833. Tesch PA, Berg HE, Bring D, Evans HJ, LeBlanc AD. Effects of 17-day spaceflight on knee extensor muscle function and size. Eur J Appl Physiol. 2005;93:463-8.

834. Widrick JJ, Knuth ST, Norenberg KM, Romatowski JG, Bain JL, Riley DA, Karhanek M, Trappe SW, Trappe TA, Costill DL, Fitts RH. Effect of a 17 day spaceflight on contractile properties of human soleus muscle fibres. J Physiol. 1999;516 (Pt 3):915-30.

835. Gopalakrishnan R, Genc KO, Rice AJ, Lee SM, Evans HJ, Maender CC, Ilaslan H, Cavanagh PR. Muscle volume, strength, endurance, and exercise loads during 6-month missions in space. Aviat Space Environ Med. 2010;81:91-102.

836. Michel EL, Rummel JA, Sawin CF, Buderer MC, Lem JD. Results of Skylab medical experiment M-171 - Metabolic Activity. In: Johnston RS, Dietlein LF, editors. Biomedical results from Skylab (NASA SP-377). Washington, DC: National Aeronautics and Space Administration; 1977. p. 372-87.

837. Antonutto G, Capelli C, Girardis M, Zamparo P, di Prampero PE. Effects of microgravity on maximal power of lower limbs during very short efforts in humans. J Appl Physiol (1985). 1999;86:85-92.

838. Zange J, Muller K, Schuber M, Wackerhage H, Hoffmann U, Gunther RW, Adam G, Neuerburg JM, Sinitsyn VE, Bacharev AO, Belichenko OI. Changes in calf muscle performance, energy metabolism, and muscle volume caused by long-term stay on space station MIR. Int J Sports Med. 1997;18 Suppl 4:S308-9.

839. Bajotto G, Shimomura Y. Determinants of disuse-induced skeletal muscle atrophy: exercise and nutrition countermeasures to prevent protein loss. J Nutr Sci Vitaminol (Tokyo). 2006;52:233-47.

840. Thornton WE, Rummel JA. Muscle deconditioning and its prevention in space flight. In: Johnston RS, Dietlein LF, editors. Biomedical results from Skylab (NASA SP-377). Washington, DC: National Aeronautics and Space Administration; 1977. p. 191-7.

841. LeBlanc A, Lin C, Shackelford L, Sinitsyn V, Evans H, Belichenko O, Schenkman B, Kozlovskaya I, Oganov V, Bakulin A, Hedrick T, Feeback D. Muscle volume, MRI relaxation times (T2), and body composition after spaceflight. J Appl Physiol (1985). 2000;89:2158-64.

842. McNamara KP, Greene KA, Tooze JA, Dang J, Khattab K, Lenchik L, Weaver AA. Neck muscle changes following long-duration spaceflight. Front Physiol. 2019;10:1115.

843. Narici MV, de Boer MD. Disuse of the musculo-skeletal system in space and on earth. Eur J Appl Physiol. 2011;111:403-20.

844. Convertino VA. Physiological adaptations to weightlessness: effects on exercise and work performance. Exerc Sport Sci Rev. 1990;18:119-66.

845. Baldwin KM. Effect of spaceflight on the functional, biochemical, and metabolic properties of skeletal muscle. Med Sci Sports Exerc. 1996;28:983-7.

846. Bodine SC. Disuse-induced muscle wasting. Int J Biochem Cell Biol. 2013;45:2200-8.

847. Stein TP. Nutrition and muscle loss in humans during spaceflight. Adv Space Biol Med. 1999;7:49-97.

848. di Prampero PE, Narici MV. Muscles in microgravity: from fibres to human motion. J Biomech. 2003;36:403-12.

849. Bachl N, Baron R, Tschan H, Mossaheb M, Bumba W, Hildebrand F, Knauf M, Witt M, Albrecht R, Kozlovskaya I, Charitonov N. [Principles of muscle efficiency in weightlessness]. Wien Med Wochenschr. 1993;143:588-610.

850. Hackney KJ, English KL. Protein and essential amino acids to protect musculoskeletal health during spaceflight: Evidence of a paradox? Life (Basel). 2014;4:295-317.

851. Ferrando AA. Protein metabolism during space flight. Diabetes Nutr Metab. 2000;13:30-4.

852. Stein TP, Leskiw MJ, Schluter MD. Diet and nitrogen metabolism during spaceflight on the shuttle. J Appl Physiol (1985). 1996;81:82-97.

853. Stein TP, Leskiw MJ, Schluter MD. Effect of spaceflight on human protein metabolism. Am J Physiol. 1993;264:E824-8.

854. Popov IG, Latskevich AA. [Free amino acids in the blood of the "Salyut-5" crew members before and after a 21-day space flight (2d expedition)]. Kosm Biol Aviakosm Med. 1983;17:15-21.

855. Vlasova TF, Miroshnikova EB, Ushakova AS. [Free amino acids in the blood before and after short-term space flight]. Kosm Biol Aviakosm Med. 1983;17:43-5.

856. Ushakov AS, Vlasova TF. Free amino acids in human blood plasma during space flights. Aviat Space Environ Med. 1976;47:1061-4.

857. Ushakov AS, Vlasova TF. Amino acid spectrum of human blood plasma during space flight and in antiorthostatic hypokinesia. Life Sci Space Res. 1976;14:257-62.

858. Popov IG, Latskevich AA. [Blood amino acids in astronauts before and after a 211-day space flight]. Kosm Biol Aviakosm Med. 1984;18:10-5.

859. Stein TP, Schluter MD. Plasma amino acids during human spaceflight. Aviat Space Environ Med. 1999;70:250-5.

860. Smith GI, Patterson BW, Mittendorfer B. Human muscle protein turnover--why is it so variable? J Appl Physiol (1985). 2011;110:480-91.

861. Stein TP. Protein and muscle homeostasis: the role of nutrition. In: Lane HW, Schoeller DA, editors. Nutrition in spaceflight and weightlessness models. Boca Raton, FL: CRC Press; 2000. p. 141-77.

862. Leach CS, Rambaut PC, Johnson PC. Adrenocortical responses of the Apollo 17 crew members. Aerosp Med. 1974;45:529-34.

863. Lee SMC, Ribeiro LC, Martin DS, Zwart SR, Feiveson AH, Laurie SS, Macias BR, Crucian BE, Krieger S, Weber D, Grune T, Platts SH, Smith SM, Stenger MB. Arterial structure and function during and after long-duration spaceflight. J Appl Physiol (1985). 2020;129:108-23.

864. Dirks ML, Wall BT, van de Valk B, Holloway TM, Holloway GP, Chabowski A, Goossens GH, van Loon LJ. One week of bed rest leads to substantial muscle atrophy and induces whole-body insulin resistance in the absence of skeletal muscle lipid accumulation. Diabetes. 2016;65:2862-75.

865. Ferrando AA, Paddon-Jones D, Wolfe RR. Bed rest and myopathies. Curr Opin Clin Nutr Metab Care. 2006;9:410-5.

866. Paddon-Jones D, Sheffield-Moore M, Cree MG, Hewlings SJ, Aarsland A, Wolfe RR, Ferrando AA. Atrophy and impaired muscle protein synthesis during prolonged inactivity and stress. J Clin Endocrinol Metab. 2006;91:4836-41.

867. Winnard A, Scott J, Waters N, Vance M, Caplan N. Effect of time on human muscle outcomes during simulated microgravity exposure without countermeasures - systematic review. Front Physiol. 2019;10:1046.

868. Milesi S, Capelli C, Denoth J, Hutchinson T, di Prampero PE, Stussi E. Effects of 17 days bed rest on the maximal isometric torque of the flexors and extensors of the ankle. J Gravit Physiol. 1997;4:P125-6.

869. Berg HE, Larsson L, Tesch PA. Lower limb skeletal muscle function after 6 wk of bed rest. J Appl Physiol (1985). 1997;82:182-8.

870. Dudley GA, Gollnick PD, Convertino VA, Buchanan P. Changes of muscle function and size with bedrest. Physiologist. 1989;32:S65-6.

871. Reeves ND, Maganaris CN, Ferretti G, Narici MV. Influence of 90-day simulated microgravity on human tendon mechanical properties and the effect of resistive countermeasures. J Appl Physiol (1985). 2005;98:2278-86.

872. LeBlanc A, Rowe R, Evans H, West S, Shackelford L, Schneider V. Muscle atrophy during long duration bed rest. Int J Sports Med. 1997;18 Suppl 4:S283-5.

873. LeBlanc AD, Schneider VS, Evans HJ, Pientok C, Rowe R, Spector E. Regional changes in muscle mass following 17 weeks of bed rest. J Appl Physiol (1985). 1992;73:2172-8.

874. Buehring B, Belavy DL, Michaelis I, Gast U, Felsenberg D, Rittweger J. Changes in lower extremity muscle function after 56 days of bed rest. J Appl Physiol (1985). 2011;111:87-94.

875. Widrick JJ, Romatowski JG, Bain JL, Trappe SW, Trappe TA, Thompson JL, Costill DL, Riley DA, Fitts RH. Effect of 17 days of bed rest on peak isometric force and unloaded shortening velocity of human soleus fibers. Am J Physiol. 1997;273:C1690-9.

876. Dirks ML, Smeets JSJ, Holwerda AM, Kouw IWK, Marzuca-Nassr GN, Gijsen AP, Holloway GP, Verdijk LB, van Loon LJC. Dietary feeding pattern does not modulate the loss of muscle mass or the decline in metabolic health during short-term bed rest. Am J Physiol Endocrinol Metab. 2019;316:E536-E45.

877. Acket B, Amirova L, Gerdelat A, Cintas P, Custaud MA, Pavy-LeTraon A. Dry immersion as a model of deafferentation: A neurophysiology study using somatosensory evoked potentials. PLoS One. 2018;13:e0201704.

878. Berendeeva TA, Rykova MP, Antropova EN, Larina IM, Morukov BV. [Human immunity system status during 7-day dry immersion]. Aviakosm Ekolog Med. 2009;43:36-42.

879. De Abreu S, Amirova L, Murphy R, Wallace R, Twomey L, Gauquelin-Koch G, Raverot V, Larcher F, Custaud MA, Navasiolava N. Multi-system deconditioning in 3-day dry immersion without daily raise. Front Physiol. 2017;8:799.

880. Shenkman BS, Kozlovskaya IB. Cellular responses of human postural muscle to dry immersion. Front Physiol. 2019;10:187.

881. Shenkman BS, Kozlovskaya IB, Nemirovskaya TL, Tcheglova IA. Human muscle atrophy in supportlessness: effects of short-term exposure to dry immersion. J Gravit Physiol. 1997;4:P137-8.

882. Vilchinskaya NA, Mirzoev TM, Lomonosova YN, Kozlovskaya IB, Shenkman BS. Human muscle signaling responses to 3-day head-out dry immersion. J Musculoskelet Neuronal Interact. 2015;15:286-93.

883. Treffel L, Massabuau N, Zuj K, Custaud MA, Gauquelin-Koch G, Blanc S, Gharib C, Millet C. Pain and vertebral dysfunction in dry immersion: A model of microgravity simulation different from bed rest studies. Pain Res Manag. 2017;2017:9602131.

884. Ploutz-Snyder L. Evaluating countermeasures in spaceflight analogs. J Appl Physiol (1985). 2016;120:915-21.

885. Wall BT, Dirks ML, Snijders T, Senden JM, Dolmans J, van Loon LJ. Substantial skeletal muscle loss occurs during only 5 days of disuse. Acta Physiol (Oxf). 2014;210:600-11.

886. Hackney KJ, Downs ME, Ploutz-Snyder L. Blood flow restricted exercise compared to high load resistance exercise during unloading. Aerosp Med Hum Perform. 2016;87:688-96.

887. Carrithers JA, Tesch PA, Trieschmann J, Ekberg A, Trappe TA. Skeletal muscle protein composition following 5 weeks of ULLS and resistance exercise countermeasures. J Gravit Physiol. 2002;9:P155-6.

888. Tesch PA, Lundberg TR, Fernandez-Gonzalo R. Unilateral lower limb suspension: From subject selection to "omic" responses. J Appl Physiol (1985). 2016;120:1207-14.

889. Trappe TA, Carrithers JA, Ekberg A, Trieschmann J, Tesch PA. The influence of 5 weeks of ULLS and resistance exercise on vastus lateralis and soleus myosin heavy chain distribution. J Gravit Physiol. 2002;9:P127-8.

890. Dirks ML, Backx EM, Wall BT, Verdijk LB, van Loon LJ. May bed rest cause greater muscle loss than limb immobilization? Acta Physiol (Oxf). 2016;218:10-2.

891. Wall BT, Dirks ML, Snijders T, Stephens FB, Senden JM, Verscheijden ML, van Loon LJ. Short-term muscle disuse atrophy is not associated with increased intramuscular lipid deposition or a decline in the maximal activity of key mitochondrial enzymes in young and older males. Exp Gerontol. 2015;61:76-83.

892. Wall BT, Dirks ML, Snijders T, van Dijk JW, Fritsch M, Verdijk LB, van Loon LJ. Short-term muscle disuse lowers myofibrillar protein synthesis rates and induces anabolic resistance to protein ingestion. Am J Physiol Endocrinol Metab. 2016;310:E137-47.

893. Widrick JJ, Trappe SW, Romatowski JG, Riley DA, Costill DL, Fitts RH. Unilateral lower limb suspension does not mimic bed rest or spaceflight effects on human muscle fiber function. J Appl Physiol (1985). 2002;93:354-60.

894. Biolo G, Ciocchi B, Lebenstedt M, Barazzoni R, Zanetti M, Platen P, Heer M, Guarnieri G. Short-term bed rest impairs amino acid-induced protein anabolism in humans. J Physiol. 2004;558:381-8.

895. Biolo G, Ciocchi B, Lebenstedt M, Heer M, Guarnieri G. Sensitivity of whole body protein synthesis to amino acid administration during short-term bed rest. J Gravit Physiol. 2002;9:P197-8.

896. Drummond MJ, Dickinson JM, Fry CS, Walker DK, Gundermann DM, Reidy PT, Timmerman KL, Markofski MM, Paddon-Jones D, Rasmussen BB, Volpi E. Bed rest impairs skeletal muscle amino acid transporter expression, mTORC1 signaling, and protein synthesis in response to essential amino acids in older adults. Am J Physiol Endocrinol Metab. 2012;302:E1113-22.

897. Ferrando AA, Lane HW, Stuart CA, Davis-Street J, Wolfe RR. Prolonged bed rest decreases skeletal muscle and whole body protein synthesis. Am J Physiol. 1996;270:E627-33.

898. Ferrando AA, Tipton KD, Bamman MM, Wolfe RR. Resistance exercise maintains skeletal muscle protein synthesis during bed rest. J Appl Physiol (1985). 1997;82:807-10.

899. Stuart CA, Shangraw RE, Peters EJ, Wolfe RR. Effect of dietary protein on bed-rest-related changes in whole-body-protein synthesis. Am J Clin Nutr. 1990;52:509-14.

900. Glover EI, Phillips SM, Oates BR, Tang JE, Tarnopolsky MA, Selby A, Smith K, Rennie MJ. Immobilization induces anabolic resistance in human myofibrillar protein synthesis with low and high dose amino acid infusion. J Physiol. 2008;586:6049-61.

901. Kortebein P, Ferrando A, Lombeida J, Wolfe R, Evans WJ. Effect of 10 days of bed rest on skeletal muscle in healthy older adults. JAMA. 2007;297:1772-4.

902. Powers SK, Kavazis AN, McClung JM. Oxidative stress and disuse muscle atrophy. J Appl Physiol (1985). 2007;102:2389-97.

903. Greenleaf JE, Bulbulian R, Bernauer EM, Haskell WL, Moore T. Exercise-training protocols for astronauts in microgravity. J Appl Physiol (1985). 1989;67:2191-204.

904. Davis SA, Davis BL. Exercise equipment used in microgravity: challenges and opportunities. Curr Sports Med Rep. 2012;11:142-7.

905. Baldwin KM. Future research directions in seeking countermeasures to weightlessness. J Gravit Physiol. 1995;2:P51-3.

906. Trappe S, Costill D, Gallagher P, Creer A, Peters JR, Evans H, Riley DA, Fitts RH. Exercise in space: human skeletal muscle after 6 months aboard the International Space Station. J Appl Physiol (1985). 2009;106:1159-68.

907. Ralston GW, Kilgore L, Wyatt FB, Dutheil F, Jaekel P, Buchan DS, Baker JS. Re-examination of 1- vs. 3-sets of resistance exercise for pre-spaceflight muscle conditioning: A systematic review and meta-analysis. Front Physiol. 2019;10:864.

908. Hackney KJ, Scott JM, Hanson AM, English KL, Downs ME, Ploutz-Snyder LL. The astronaut-athlete: Optimizing human performance in space. J Strength Cond Res. 2015;29:3531-45.

909. Hawkey A. The physical price of a ticket into space. J Br Interplanet Soc. 2003;56:152-9.

910. Hawkey A. Physiological and biomechanical considerations for a human Mars mission. J Br Interplanet Soc. 2005;58:117-30.

911. Hayes J. The first decade of ISS exercise: Lessons learned on Expeditions 1-25. Aerosp Med Hum Perform. 2015;86:A1-A6.

912. Korth DW. Exercise countermeasure hardware evolution on ISS: the first decade. Aerosp Med Hum Perform. 2015;86:A7-A13.

913. Krainski F, Hastings JL, Heinicke K, Romain N, Pacini EL, Snell PG, Wyrick P, Palmer MD, Haller RG, Levine BD. The effect of rowing ergometry and resistive exercise on skeletal muscle structure and function during bed rest. J Appl Physiol (1985). 2014;116:1569-81.

914. Tesch PA, Ekberg A, Lindquist DM, Trieschmann JT. Muscle hypertrophy following 5-week resistance training using a non-gravity-dependent exercise system. Acta Physiol Scand. 2004;180:89-98.

915. Alkner BA, Berg HE, Kozlovskaya I, Sayenko D, Tesch PA. Effects of strength training, using a gravity-independent exercise system, performed during 110 days of simulated space station confinement. Eur J Appl Physiol. 2003;90:44-9.

916. Alkner BA, Tesch PA. Knee extensor and plantar flexor muscle size and function following 90 days of bed rest with or without resistance exercise. Eur J Appl Physiol. 2004;93:294-305.

917. Rittweger J, Felsenberg D, Maganaris C, Ferretti JL. Vertical jump performance after 90 days bed rest with and without flywheel resistive exercise, including a 180 days follow-up. Eur J Appl Physiol. 2007;100:427-36.

918. Belavy DL, Ohshima H, Rittweger J, Felsenberg D. High-intensity flywheel exercise and recovery of atrophy after 90 days bed--rest. BMJ Open Sport Exerc Med. 2017;3:e000196.

919. Ritzmann R, Freyler K, Kummel J, Gruber M, Belavy DL, Felsenberg D, Gollhofer A, Kramer A, Ambrecht G. High intensity jump exercise preserves posture control, gait, and functional mobility during 60 days of bed-rest: An RCT including 90 days of follow-up. Front Physiol. 2018;9:1713.

920. Macias BR, Groppo ER, Eastlack RK, Watenpaugh DE, Lee SM, Schneider SM, Boda WL, Smith SM, Cutuk A, Pedowitz RA, Meyer RS, Hargens AR. Space exercise and Earth benefits. Curr Pharm Biotechnol. 2005;6:305-17.

921. Streeper T, Cavanagh PR, Hanson AM, Carpenter RD, Saeed I, Kornak J, Frassetto L, Grodsinsky C, Funk J, Lee SMC, Spiering BA, Bloomberg J, Mulavara A, Sibonga J, Lang T. Development of an integrated countermeasure device for use in long-duration spaceflight. Acta Astronaut. 2011;68:2029-37.

922. Schwandt DF, Whalen RT, Watenpaugh DE, Parazynski SE, Hargens AR. Development of exercise devices to minimize musculoskeletal and cardiovascular deconditioning in microgravity. Physiologist. 1991;34 Suppl 1:S189-90.

923. Lee SM, Schneider SM, Feiveson AH, Macias BR, Smith SM, Watenpaugh DE, Hargens AR. WISE-2005: Countermeasures to prevent muscle deconditioning during bed rest in women. J Appl Physiol (1985). 2014;116:654-67.

924. Ploutz-Snyder LL, Downs M, Ryder J, Hackney K, Scott J, Buxton R, Goetchius E, Crowell B. Integrated resistance and aerobic exercise protects fitness during bed rest. Med Sci Sports Exerc. 2014;46:358-68.

925. English KL, Downs M, Goetchius E, Buxton R, Ryder JW, Ploutz-Snyder R, Guilliams M, Scott JM, Ploutz-Snyder LL. High intensity training during spaceflight: results from the NASA Sprint Study. NPJ Microgravity. 2020;6:21.

926. Scott JM, Downs M, Buxton R, Goetchius E, Crowell B, Ploutz-Snyder R, Hackney KJ, Ryder J, English K, Ploutz-Snyder LL. Disuse-induced muscle loss and rehabilitation: the National Aeronautics and Space Administration bed rest study. Crit Care Explor. 2020;2:e0269.

927. Bleeker MW, De Groot PC, Rongen GA, Rittweger J, Felsenberg D, Smits P, Hopman MT. Vascular adaptation to deconditioning and the effect of an exercise countermeasure: results of the Berlin Bed Rest study. J Appl Physiol (1985). 2005;99:1293-300.

928. Zange J, Mester J, Heer M, Kluge G, Liphardt AM. 20-Hz whole body vibration training fails to counteract the decrease in leg muscle volume caused by 14 days of 6 degrees head down tilt bed rest. Eur J Appl Physiol. 2009;105:271-7.

929. Mikhael M, Orr R, Fiatarone Singh MA. The effect of whole body vibration exposure on muscle or bone morphology and function in older adults: a systematic review of the literature. Maturitas. 2010;66:150-7.

930. Prisby RD, Lafage-Proust MH, Malaval L, Belli A, Vico L. Effects of whole body vibration on the skeleton and other organ systems in man and animal models: what we know and what we need to know. Ageing Res Rev. 2008;7:319-29.

931. Rittweger J, Belavy D, Hunek P, Gast U, Boerst H, Feilcke B, Armbrecht G, Mulder E, Schubert H, Richardson C, de Haan A, Stegeman DF, Schiessl H, Felsenberg D. Highly demanding resistive vibration exercise program is tolerated during 56 days of strict bed-rest. Int J Sports Med. 2006;27:553-9.

932. Frost HM. Bone's mechanostat: a 2003 update. Anat Rec A Discov Mol Cell Evol Biol. 2003;275:1081-101.

933. Belavy DL, Miokovic T, Armbrecht G, Rittweger J, Felsenberg D. Resistive vibration exercise reduces lower limb muscle atrophy during 56-day bed-rest. J Musculoskelet Neuronal Interact. 2009;9:225-35.

934. Trudel G, Coletta E, Cameron I, Belavy DL, Lecompte M, Armbrecht G, Felsenberg D, Uhthoff HK. Resistive exercises, with or without whole body vibration, prevent vertebral marrow fat accumulation during 60 days of head-down tilt bed rest in men. J Appl Physiol (1985). 2012;112:1824-31.

935. Ogawa M, Belavy DL, Yoshiko A, Armbrecht G, Miokovic T, Felsenberg D, Akima H. Effects of 8 weeks of bed rest with or without resistance exercise intervention on the volume of the muscle tissue and the adipose tissues of the thigh. Physiol Rep. 2020;8:e14560.

936. Dirks ML, Groen BB, Franssen R, van Kranenburg J, van Loon LJ. Neuromuscular electrical stimulation prior to presleep protein feeding stimulates the use of protein-derived amino acids for overnight muscle protein synthesis. J Appl Physiol (1985). 2017;122:20-7.

937. Dirks ML, Hansen D, Van Assche A, Dendale P, Van Loon LJ. Neuromuscular electrical stimulation prevents muscle wasting in critically ill comatose patients. Clin Sci (Lond). 2015;128:357-65.

938. Dirks ML, Wall BT, van Loon LJC. Interventional strategies to combat muscle disuse atrophy in humans: focus on neuromuscular electrical stimulation and dietary protein. J Appl Physiol (1985). 2018;125:850-61.

939. Dirks ML, Wall BT, Snijders T, Ottenbros CL, Verdijk LB, van Loon LJ. Neuromuscular electrical stimulation prevents muscle disuse atrophy during leg immobilization in humans. Acta Physiol (Oxf). 2014;210:628-41.

940. Willis SJ, Borrani F, Millet GP. High-intensity exercise with blood flow restriction or in hypoxia as valuable spaceflight countermeasures? Front Physiol. 2019;10:1266.

941. Behringer M, Willberg C. Application of blood flow restriction to optimize exercise countermeasures for human space flight. Front Physiol. 2019;10:33.

942. Hackney KJ, Everett M, Scott JM, Ploutz-Snyder L. Blood flow-restricted exercise in space. Extrem Physiol Med. 2012;1:12.

943. Cai ZY, Wang WY, Lin JD, Wu CM. Effects of whole body vibration training combined with blood flow restriction on muscle adaptation. Eur J Sport Sci. 2020:1-9.

944. Aunon-Chancellor SM, Pattarini JM, Moll S, Sargsyan A. Venous thrombosis during spaceflight. N Engl J Med. 2020;382:89-90.

945. Marshall-Goebel K, Laurie SS, Alferova IV, Arbeille P, Aunon-Chancellor SM, Ebert DJ, Lee SMC, Macias BR, Martin DS, Pattarini JM, Ploutz-Snyder R, Ribeiro LC, Tarver WJ, Dulchavsky SA, Hargens AR, Stenger MB. Assessment of jugular venous blood flow stasis and thrombosis during spaceflight. JAMA Netw Open. 2019;2:e1915011.

946. Strollo F, Barger L, Fuller C. Testosterone urinary excretion rate increases during hypergravity in male monkeys. J Gravit Physiol. 2000;7:P181-2.

947. Strollo F, Strollo G, More M, Ferretti C, Mangrossa N, Casarosa E, Luisi M, Riondino G. Changes in human adrenal and gonadal function onboard Spacelab. J Gravit Physiol. 1997;4:P103-4.

948. Wade CE, Stanford KI, Stein TP, Greenleaf JE. Intensive exercise training suppresses testosterone during bed rest. J Appl Physiol (1985). 2005;99:59-63.

949. Hanson ED, Betik AC, Timpani CA, Tarle J, Zhang X, Hayes A. Testosterone suppression does not exacerbate disuse atrophy and impairs muscle recovery that is not rescued by high protein. J Appl Physiol (1985). 2020;129:5-16.

950. Space Science Board. Endocrinology. Life beyond the Earth's environment: the biology of living organisms in space. Washington, D.C.: National Academy of Sciences; 1979. p. 65.

951. Strollo F, Norsk P, Roecker L, Strollo G, More M, Bollanti L, Riondino G, Scano A. Indirect evidence of CNS adrenergic pathways activation during spaceflight. Aviat Space Environ Med. 1998;69:777-80.

952. Alemany JA, Nindl BC, Kellogg MD, Tharion WJ, Young AJ, Montain SJ. Effects of dietary protein content on IGF-I, testosterone, and body composition during 8 days of severe energy deficit and arduous physical activity. J Appl Physiol (1985). 2008;105:58-64.

953. Kyrolainen H, Karinkanta J, Santtila M, Koski H, Mantysaari M, Pullinen T. Hormonal responses during a prolonged military field exercise with variable exercise intensity. Eur J Appl Physiol. 2008;102:539-46.

954. Cangemi R, Friedmann AJ, Holloszy JO, Fontana L. Long-term effects of calorie restriction on serum sex-hormone concentrations in men. Aging Cell. 2010;9:236-42.

955. Murdaca G, Setti M, Brenci S, Fenoglio D, Lantieri P, Indiveri F, Puppo F. Modifications of immunological and neuro-endocrine parameters induced by antiorthostatic bed-rest in human healthy volunteers. Minerva Med. 2003;94:363-78.

956. Zachwieja JJ, Smith SR, Lovejoy JC, Rood JC, Windhauser MM, Bray GA. Testosterone administration preserves protein balance but not muscle strength during 28 days of bed rest. J Clin Endocrinol Metab. 1999;84:207-12.

957. Dillon EL, Sheffield-Moore M, Durham WJ, Ploutz-Snyder LL, Ryder JW, Danesi CP, Randolph KM, Gilkison CR, Urban RJ. Efficacy of testosterone plus NASA exercise countermeasures during head-down bed rest. Med Sci Sports Exerc. 2018;50:1929-39.

958. Greenleaf JE, Bernauer EM, Ertl AC, Trowbridge TS, Wade CE. Work capacity during 30 days of bed rest with isotonic and isokinetic exercise training. J Appl Physiol (1985). 1989;67:1820-6.

959. Downs ME, Scott JM, Ploutz-Snyder LL, Ploutz-Snyder R, Goetchius E, Buxton RE, Danesi CP, Randolph KM, Urban RJ, Sheffield-Moore M, Dillon EL. Exercise and testosterone countermeasures to mitigate metabolic changes during bed rest. Life Sci Space Res (Amst). 2020;26:97-104.

960. Zorbas YG, Naexu KA, Federenko YF. Blood serum biochemical changes in physically conditioned and unconditioned subjects during bed rest and chronic hyperhydration. Clin Exp Pharmacol Physiol. 1992;19:137-45.

961. Smorawinski J, Nazar K, Kaciuba-Uscilko H, Kaminska E, Cybulski G, Kodrzycka A, Bicz B, Greenleaf JE. Effects of 3-day bed rest on physiological responses to graded exercise in athletes and sedentary men. J Appl Physiol (1985). 2001;91:249-57.

962. Tou J, Ronca A, Grindeland R, Wade C. Models to study gravitational biology of Mammalian reproduction. Biol Reprod. 2002;67:1681-7.

963. Vasques M, Lang C, Grindeland RE, Roy RR, Daunton N, Bigbee AJ, Wade CE. Comparison of hyper- and microgravity on rat muscle, organ weights and selected plasma constituents. Aviat Space Environ Med. 1998;69:A2-8.

964. Ortiz RM, Wade CE, Morey-Holton E. Urinary excretion of LH and testosterone from male rats during exposure to increased gravity: post-spaceflight and centrifugation. Proc Soc Exp Biol Med. 2000;225:98-102.

965. Amann RP, Deaver DR, Zirkin BR, Grills GS, Sapp WJ, Veeramachaneni DN, Clemens JW, Banerjee SD, Folmer J, Gruppi CM, Wolgemuth DJ, Williams CS. Effects of microgravity or simulated launch on testicular function in rats. J Appl Physiol (1985). 1992;73:174S-85S.

966. Ortiz RM, Wang TJ, Wade CE. Influence of centrifugation and hindlimb suspension on testosterone and corticosterone excretion in rats. Aviat Space Environ Med. 1999;70:499-504.

967. Tash JS, Johnson DC, Enders GC. Long-term (6-wk) hindlimb suspension inhibits spermatogenesis in adult male rats. J Appl Physiol (1985). 2002;92:1191-8.

968. Macho L, Kvetnansky R, Fickova M, Popova IA, Grigoriev A. Effects of exposure to space flight on endocrine regulations in experimental animals. Endocr Regul. 2001;35:101-14.

969. Royland JE, Weber LJ, Fitzpatrick M. Testes size and testosterone levels in a model for weightlessness. Life Sci. 1994;54:545-54.

970. Ricci G, Catizone A, Esposito R, Galdieri M. Microgravity effect on testicular functions. J Gravit Physiol. 2004;11:P61-2.

971. Ricci G, Esposito R, Catizone A, Galdieri M. Direct effects of microgravity on testicular function: analysis of hystological, molecular and physiologic parameters. J Endocrinol Invest. 2008;31:229-37.

972. Clarke BL, Khosla S. Androgens and bone. Steroids. 2009;74:296-305.

973. Sheffield-Moore M, Dillon EL, Casperson SL, Gilkison CR, Paddon-Jones D, Durham WJ, Grady JJ, Urban RJ. A randomized pilot study of monthly cycled testosterone replacement or continuous testosterone replacement versus placebo in older men. J Clin Endocrinol Metab. 2011;96:E1831-7.

974. Paddon-Jones D. Interplay of stress and physical inactivity on muscle loss: Nutritional countermeasures. J Nutr. 2006;136:2123-6.

975. Galvan E, Arentson-Lantz E, Lamon S, Paddon-Jones D. Protecting skeletal muscle with protein and amino acid during periods of disuse. Nutrients. 2016;8.

976. Millward DJ. Limiting deconditioned muscle atrophy and strength loss with appropriate nutrition: can it be done? Am J Clin Nutr. 2020;112:499-500.

977. Stein TP, Blanc S. Does protein supplementation prevent muscle disuse atrophy and loss of strength? Crit Rev Food Sci Nutr. 2011;51:828-34.

978. Kilroe SP, Fulford J, Jackman S, Holwerda A, Gijsen A, van Loon L, Wall BT. Dietary protein intake does not modulate daily myofibrillar protein synthesis rates or loss of muscle mass and function during short-term immobilization in young men: a randomized controlled trial. Am J Clin Nutr. 2020.

979. Edwards SJ, Smeuninx B, McKendry J, Nishimura Y, Luo D, Marshall RN, Perkins M, Ramsay J, Joanisse S, Philp A, Breen L. High-dose leucine supplementation does not prevent muscle atrophy or strength loss over 7 days of immobilization in healthy young males. Am J Clin Nutr. 2020;112:1368-81.

980. Paddon-Jones D, Wolfe RR, Ferrando AA. Amino acid supplementation for reversing bed rest and steroid myopathies. J Nutr. 2005;135:1809S-12S.

981. Paddon-Jones D, Sheffield-Moore M, Urban RJ, Sanford AP, Aarsland A, Wolfe RR, Ferrando AA. Essential amino acid and carbohydrate supplementation ameliorates muscle protein loss in humans during 28 days bedrest. J Clin Endocrinol Metab. 2004;89:4351-8.

982. Paddon-Jones D, Sheffield-Moore M, Urban RJ, Aarsland A, Wolfe RR, Ferrando AA. The catabolic effects of prolonged inactivity and acute hypercortisolemia are offset by dietary supplementation. J Clin Endocrinol Metab. 2005;90:1453-9.

983. Fitts RH, Romatowski JG, Peters JR, Paddon-Jones D, Wolfe RR, Ferrando AA. The deleterious effects of bed rest on human skeletal muscle fibers are exacerbated by hypercortisolemia and ameliorated by dietary supplementation. Am J Physiol Cell Physiol. 2007;293:C313-20.

984. Cree MG, Paddon-Jones D, Newcomer BR, Ronsen O, Aarsland A, Wolfe RR, Ferrando A. Twenty-eight-day bed rest with hypercortisolemia induces peripheral insulin resistance and increases intramuscular triglycerides. Metabolism. 2010;59:703-10.

985. Ferrando AA, Paddon-Jones D, Hays NP, Kortebein P, Ronsen O, Williams RH, McComb A, Symons TB, Wolfe RR, Evans W. EAA supplementation to increase nitrogen intake improves muscle function during bed rest in the elderly. Clin Nutr. 2010;29:18-23.

986. Arentson-Lantz EJ, Fiebig KN, Anderson-Catania KJ, Deer RR, Wacher A, Fry CS, Lamon S, Paddon-Jones D. Countering disuse atrophy in older adults with low-volume leucine supplementation. J Appl Physiol (1985). 2020;128:967-77.

987. Brooks N, Cloutier GJ, Cadena SM, Layne JE, Nelsen CA, Freed AM, Roubenoff R, Castaneda-Sceppa C. Resistance training and timed essential amino acids protect against the loss of muscle mass and strength during 28 days of bed rest and energy deficit. J Appl Physiol (1985). 2008;105:241-8.

988. Brooks NE, Cadena SM, Cloutier G, Vega-Lopez S, Roubenoff R, Castaneda-Sceppa C. Influence of exercise on the metabolic profile caused by 28 days of bed rest with energy deficit and amino acid supplementation in healthy men. Int J Med Sci. 2014;11:1248-57.

989. Brooks NE, Cadena SM, Vannier E, Cloutier G, Carambula S, Myburgh KH, Roubenoff R, Castaneda-Sceppa C. Effects of resistance exercise combined with essential amino acid supplementation and energy deficit on markers of skeletal muscle atrophy and regeneration during bed rest and active recovery. Muscle Nerve. 2010;42:927-35.

990. Jost PD. Simulating human space physiology with bed rest. Hippokratia. 2008;12 Suppl 1:37-40.

991. Trappe TA, Burd NA, Louis ES, Lee GA, Trappe SW. Influence of concurrent exercise or nutrition countermeasures on thigh and calf muscle size and function during 60 days of bed rest in women. Acta Physiol (Oxf). 2007;191:147-59.

992. Lemoine JK, Haus JM, Trappe SW, Trappe TA. Muscle proteins during 60-day bedrest in women: impact of exercise or nutrition. Muscle Nerve. 2009;39:463-71.

993. Bosutti A, Mulder E, Zange J, Buhlmeier J, Ganse B, Degens H. Effects of 21 days of bed rest and whey protein supplementation on plantar flexor muscle fatigue resistance during repeated shortening contractions. Eur J Appl Physiol. 2020;120:969-83.

994. Bosutti A, Salanova M, Blottner D, Buehlmeier J, Mulder E, Rittweger J, Yap MH, Ganse B, Degens H. Whey protein with potassium bicarbonate supplement attenuates the reduction in muscle oxidative capacity during 19 days of bed rest. J Appl Physiol (1985). 2016;121:838-48.

995. Liphardt AM, Bolte V, Eckstein F, Wirth W, Brüggemann GP, Niehoff A. Response of thigh muscle cross□sectional area to 21□days of bed rest with exercise and nutrition countermeasures. Translational Sports Medicine. 2019;3:93-106.

996. Liphardt AM, Mundermann A, Andriacchi TP, Achtzehn S, Heer M, Mester J. Sensitivity of serum concentration of cartilage biomarkers to 21-days of bed rest. J Orthop Res. 2018;36:1465-71.

997. Dirks ML, Wall BT, Nilwik R, Weerts DH, Verdijk LB, van Loon LJ. Skeletal muscle disuse atrophy is not attenuated by dietary protein supplementation in healthy older men. J Nutr. 2014;144:1196-203.

998. Preuss HG, Clouatre DL. Sodium, chloride, and potassium. In: Erdman JW, Jr., MacDonald IA, Zeisel SH, editors. Present knowledge in nutrition. 8th ed. Washington, DC: International Life Sciences Institute Press; 2010. p. 475-92.

999. Lanham-New SA, Lambert H, Frassetto L. Potassium. Adv Nutr. 2012;3:820-1.

1000. Kleinman LI, Lorenz JM. Physiology and pathophysiology of body water and electrolytes. In: Kaplan LA, Pesce AJ, editors. Clinical chemistry: Theory, analysis, and correlation. St. Louis, MO: CV Mosby Company; 1984. p. 363-86.

1001. Alexander WC, Leach CS, Fischer CL. Clinical biochemistry. In: Johnston RS, Dietlein LF, Berry CA, editors. Biomedical results of Apollo (NASA SP-368). Washington, DC: National Aeronautics and Space Administration; 1975. p. 185-96.

European Space Agency astronaut Tim Peake uses hardware for the Vascular Echo experiment. Photo Credit: NASA.

8 Cardiovascular

Cardiovascular health is a concern for space travelers, and is one of the most studied aspects of human physiology during actual and simulated flight. Although a brief overview is presented here, along with a focus on nutritional aspects of cardiovascular health, the overarching topic of cardiovascular health in space has been reviewed in the scientific literature (1002-1009), and in evidence books analogous to this one (1010-1012).

Studies on the ISS have shown mixed results, with some, but not all, investigations finding evidence of vascular changes (1013, 1014). Recent studies identified few changes in arterial structure and function, but noted accompanying metabolic changes (e.g., insulin resistance) and oxidative stress and inflammation (863, 1015, 1016). Whether these differences represent individual variability in responses among astronaut cohorts in different experiments, or differences in techniques, timing, or other factors remains unknown.

As discussed in Chapter 12, exposure to ionizing radiation during spaceflight can produce reactive oxygen species (ROS) and reactive nitrogen species (RNS), which can induce oxidative stress and damage. Oxygen participates in high-energy electron transfers during biological reduction/oxidation (aka redox) reactions such as the synthesis of adenosine-5-triphosphate (1017). Because of their biochemistry, proteins, lipids, and DNA are all susceptible to oxidative damage from ROS and RNS. ROS and RNS are produced by endogenous and exogenous sources and the body has antioxidant systems to remove them. As reviewed by Tahimic and Globus, ROS and RNS play a role in regulating tissue function and structural integrity, including specifically vascular and bone health (1018). These reactive species are known to contribute to atherogenic processes (1019). Oxidative stress and inflammation in general are known risk factors for the development of cardiovascular disease and has been extensively reviewed (1020). Several studies conducted during spaceflight provide evidence that oxidative damage markers are elevated during flight (10, 863, 1021). Plasma inflammatory cytokines are also elevated in most crewmembers during flight (1022). ROS generation during spaceflight seems to be from radiation exposure and through upregulation of oxidative enzymes and downregulation of antioxidant enzymes, all of which are associated with concerns for cardiovascular health (1023). Whether the oxidative damage and inflammation observed in crewmembers contributes greatly to cardiovascular changes is still not well understood. One study with 13 crewmembers on long-duration missions to the ISS did observe increased oxidative damage and inflammation; however, no changes occurred in common carotid artery and brachial artery structure and function (863). Long-term follow-up continues to assess residual effects of spaceflight on cardiovascular health.

The findings from these studies may have significant implications for future missions (1024). As described later in this book, oxidative stress is a multifaceted issue that affects many systems; given the radiation concerns of exploration-class missions (1011, 1025), and space radiation concerns related to cardiovascular health in particular (1026-1029), this issue will draw greater attention in the future.

Although bed rest, specifically using -6° head-down tilt, is a common model for cardiovascular adaptation to spaceflight (1030), the resulting fluid shift does not appear to be the same (303, 396), as reviewed in Chapter 5. Comparisons of bed rest and dry immersion had found generally similar effects, albeit with some differences in magnitude, over a much shorter duration of dry immersion (3 days) compared to bed rest (21 days) (430, 1031).

Exercise is a common countermeasure for many systems, but especially for cardiovascular health. A recent 21-day bed rest study of resistive vibration exercise, with or without a protein supplement (whey protein, 1.8 g/kg body weight), with controls, revealed that it had no effect on cardiovascular deconditioning (1032). An earlier study of rowing and resistance exercise training revealed that it did protect against cardiovascular degradation and, when coupled with an oral fluid/salt load before reambulation, protected against orthostatic intolerance (1033).

The role of nutrition in cardiovascular adaptation to spaceflight has not been well characterized. Diet and nutrition obviously play a huge role in cardiovascular disease development on Earth. The space food system, as described in Chapter 3, provides excess cholesterol and saturated fat, with insufficient quantities of fruits and vegetables, omega-3 fatty acids, and specific vitamins (e.g., choline) and minerals (e.g., copper, selenium) and other phytochemicals with known cardiovascular benefits. The Food Physiology study–both flight and ground-based aspects–will help define the role of enhanced nutrition on immune function and biochemistry. Although cardiovascular health was not a primary end point, the dietary modifications implemented here are also expected to provide benefits for many systems, cardiovascular included.

Figure 57. NASA astronaut Catherine (Cady) Coleman exercises on the Cycle Ergometer with Vibration Isolation System (CEVIS) in the U.S. Laboratory module on the ISS. Photo Credit: NASA.

Nutrients Associated with Cardiovascular Health

Energy

As discussed in Chapter 4, cardio vascular deconditioning is associated with restricted energy consumption during bed rest (161, 162). Insufficient energy intake is associated with greater plasma volume loss (Figure 58). The spaceflight data came from the work of Dr. William Carpentier, who evaluated crewmember medical records from the Mercury, Gemini, and Apollo programs (88).

Dr. Carpentier's data from astronauts in the early U.S. space programs have been integrated and modeled to predict postflight heart rate response to LBNP, standing, and tilt from factors including flight duration, plasma volume loss or energy intake, and preflight resting heart rate. Project Mercury data documented effects of weight loss corresponding to changes in heart rate and, moreover, that these effects were more related to time in the pressure suit than time in microgravity (88). These data clearly link energy intake and plasma volume loss with cardiovascular health during and after spaceflight, as reviewed in more detail in (154).

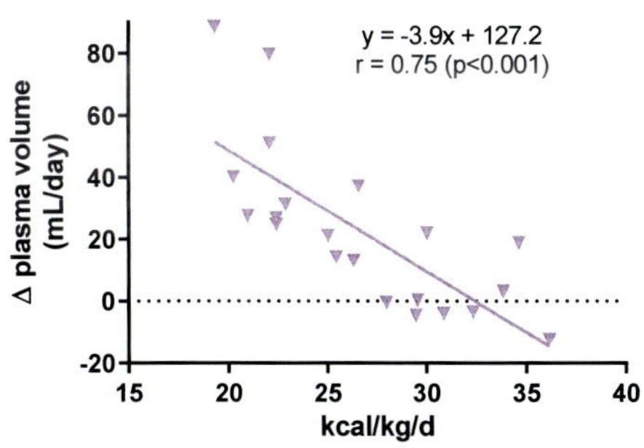

Figure 58. Relationship between energy intake (kcal/kg body mass/d) and change in plasma volume loss (mL/d) during Apollo missions. N = 21. Data are courtesy of William Carpentier.

One piece of the spaceflight puzzle that is still missing is the effect of longer flight durations. That is, the data presented in Figure 58 were generated from short-term flights, and this relationship may change on longer ISS missions. Given the inference that energy intake should be greater than 33 kcal/kg body mass to avoid plasma volume loss, we evaluated ISS intake data (Figure 59) and found that few crewmembers are meeting this threshold.

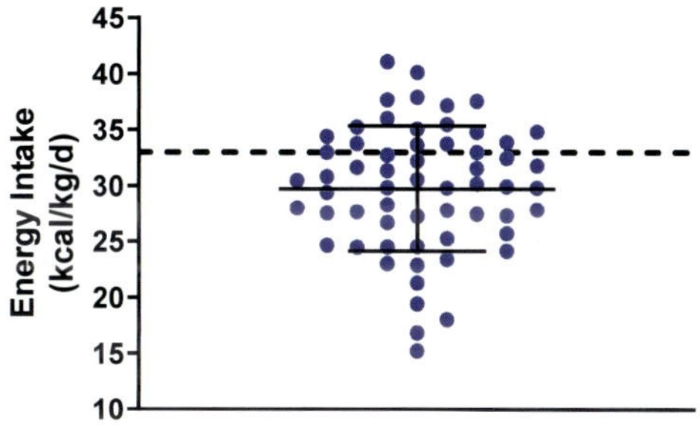

Figure 59. Energy intake during ISS missions (N=60). Each point represents an individual crewmember and is his or her reported average daily energy intake over the course of the mission, expressed per kg body mass. The dashed line represents 33 kcal/kg body mass.

Similar findings relating energy intake and cardiovascular deficits were obtained from bed rest studies to evaluate the effects of hypocaloric diets on many physiological systems (159, 1034). The cardiovascular data showed that caloric restriction during bed rest led to decrements in cardiovascular physiology (specifically, performance on a stand test or during lower body negative pressure), thus exceeding the decrements that occurred during bed rest when subjects received adequate calories (161, 162). Interestingly, caloric restriction (and low-fat diet) were associated with mitigating bed rest effects on endothelial function and circulating lipids (1035).

Magnesium

As detailed in Chapter 6, magnesium has benefits for metabolism of bone and calcium and for reduction of renal stone risk. In addition, magnesium has been shown to have effects on the cardiovascular system (783, 1036-1038). Specifically, lower plasma magnesium concentrations are associated with atherosclerosis, and magnesium supplementation can lower serum lipids (1039-1042). Although consistently decreased magnesium excretion after flight is a concern for many reasons, and ensuring adequate intake during and after flight is important, the available evidence does not bear out concerns about magnesium during flight (797).

Antioxidants and Oxidative Stress

Reducing inflammation and oxidative stress through diet during spaceflight may be a viable countermeasure to help minimize cardiovascular risk factors during spaceflight. Although dietary antioxidants have yet to be tested during flight, their beneficial effects on oxidative stress and damage associated with space radiation have been shown in many ground-based studies (1043-1045). Beyond individual nutrients, overall dietary patterns that are rich in antioxidants, such as the Mediterranean diet in the general population, have been reviewed and are associated with lower inflammation and protective against cardiovascular events (1046).

Omega-3 Fatty Acids

Omega-3 fatty acids have beneficial impact on cardiovascular health on Earth (1047); however, such effects have not been evaluated during spaceflight. Nonetheless, the initial efforts being made to increase fish and omega-3 fatty acid intake in astronauts for the benefit of other systems (bone, muscle) will likely have positive effects here as well. As reviewed in Chapters 4 and 6, although dietary intake of omega-3 fatty acids is beneficial (1048, 1049), there is little-to-no evidence in support of omega-3 supplements for cardiovascular health for the general population (1050-1054).

Figure 60. A Salmo-rita (salmon and hot sauce on a tortilla) floats near the Galley Table in the Unity Node 1 on the ISS. Photo Credit: NASA.

Overall Diet Effects on Cardiovascular Health

Although individual nutrients are easier to study in a controlled, experimental fashion, the effect of overall dietary quality is one topic that is continuing to gain ground, particularly as studies of individual supplements fail to produce the "magic" supplement. Overall dietary quality, including the intake of fruits and vegetables, fish (omega-3 and vitamin D), and foods rich in phytochemicals and lower in sodium, has broad health—specifically, cardiovascular—effects (1055-1061). Shivappa et al. (1062) have described a dietary inflammatory index that consists of pro-inflammatory and anti-inflammatory dietary components that predicts six inflammatory cytokines and C-reactive protein. Many studies have documented how dietary inflammatory index is associated with cardiovascular risk factors (1063-1071).

Dr. Douglas' Food Physiology experiment is designed to evaluate the effects of an enhanced diet on immune function, microbiome, and nutritional biochemistry. The ground-based portion of this study was completed in 45-d HERA missions (data are currently being analyzed, publications should begin to appear in 2021). The flight portion of this experiment started in 2020.

Figure 61. NASA astronaut Jessica Meir harvests Mizuna mustard plant leaves from plants in the Vegetable Production System (Veggie) for Veg-04B experiment plant harvesting operations. Photo Credit: NASA.

References for Chapter 8

10. Zwart SR, Morgan JLL, Smith SM. Iron status and its relations with oxidative damage and bone loss during long-duration space flight on the International Space Station. Am J Clin Nutr. 2013;98:217-23.

88. Carpentier WR, Charles JB, Shelhamer M, Hackler AS, Johnson TL, Domingo CMM, Sutton JP, Scott GBI, Wotring VE. Biomedical findings from NASA's Project Mercury: a case series. NPJ Microgravity. 2018;4:6.

154. Smith SM, Zwart SR, Heer M. Human adaptation to spaceflight: The role of nutrition (NP-2014-10-018-JSC). Houston, TX: National Aeronautics and Space Administration Lyndon B. Johnson Space Center; 2014.

159. Biolo G, Ciocchi B, Stulle M, Bosutti A, Barazzoni R, Zanetti M, Antonione R, Lebenstedt M, Platen P, Heer M, Guarnieri G. Calorie restriction accelerates the catabolism of lean body mass during 2 wk of bed rest. Am J Clin Nutr. 2007;86:366-72.

161. Florian JP, Baisch FJ, Heer M, Pawelczyk JA. Caloric restriction decreases orthostatic tolerance independently from 6 degrees head-down bedrest. PLoS One. 2015;10:e0118812.

162. Florian JP, Baisch FJ, Heer M, Pawelczyk JA. Caloric restriction diminishes the pressor response to static exercise. Extrem Physiol Med. 2016;5:2.

303. Norsk P. Cardiovascular and fluid volume control in humans in space. Curr Pharm Biotechnol. 2005;6:325-30.

396. Hargens AR, Vico L. Long-duration bed rest as an analog to microgravity. J Appl Physiol (1985). 2016;120:891-903.

430. Tomilovskaya E, Shigueva T, Sayenko D, Rukavishnikov I, Kozlovskaya I. Dry immersion as a ground-based model of microgravity physiological effects. Front Physiol. 2019;10:284.

783. Volpe SL. Magnesium in disease prevention and overall health. Adv Nutr. 2013;4:378S-83S.

797. Smith SM, Zwart SR. Magnesium and Space Flight. Nutrients. 2015;7:10209-22.

863. Lee SMC, Ribeiro LC, Martin DS, Zwart SR, Feiveson AH, Laurie SS, Macias BR, Crucian BE, Krieger S, Weber D, Grune T, Platts SH, Smith SM, Stenger MB. Arterial structure and function during and after long-duration spaceflight. J Appl Physiol (1985). 2020;129:108-23.

1002. Hughson RL, Helm A, Durante M. Heart in space: effect of the extraterrestrial environment on the cardiovascular system. Nat Rev Cardiol. 2018;15:167-80.

1003. Shen M, Frishman WH. Effects of spaceflight on cardiovascular physiology and health. Cardiol Rev. 2019;27:122-6.

1004. Norsk P. Adaptation of the cardiovascular system to weightlessness: Surprises, paradoxes and implications for deep space missions. Acta Physiol (Oxf). 2020;228:e13434.

1005. Norsk P. Blood pressure regulation IV: adaptive responses to weightlessness. Eur J Appl Physiol. 2014;114:481-97.

1006. Hargens AR, Richardson S. Cardiovascular adaptations, fluid shifts, and countermeasures related to space flight. Respir Physiol Neurobiol. 2009;169 Suppl 1:S30-3.

1007. Hughson RL. Recent findings in cardiovascular physiology with space travel. Respir Physiol Neurobiol. 2009;169 Suppl 1:S38-41.

1008. Platts SH, Bairey Merz CN, Barr Y, Fu Q, Gulati M, Hughson R, Levine BD, Mehran R, Stachenfeld N, Wenger NK. Effects of sex and gender on adaptation to space: cardiovascular alterations. J Womens Health (Larchmt). 2014;23:950-5.

1009. Navasiolava N, Yuan M, Murphy R, Robin A, Coupe M, Wang L, Alameddine A, Gauquelin-Koch G, Gharib C, Li Y, Custaud MA. Vascular and microvascular dysfunction induced by microgravity and its analogs in humans: Mechanisms and countermeasures. Front Physiol. 2020;11:952.

1010. Stenger MB, Platts SH, Lee SMC, Westby CM, Phillips TR, Arzeno NM, Johnston S, Mulegeta L. Evidence Report: Risk of orthostatic intolerance during re-exposure to gravity [online]. National Aeronautics and Space Administration. https://humanresearchroadmap.nasa.gov/Evidence/reports/ORTHO.pdf. 2015.

1011. Patel Z, Huff J, Saha J, Wang M, Blattnig SR, Wu H. Evidence Report: Risk of cardiovascular disease and other degenerative tissue effects from radiation exposure. [online]. National Aeronautics and Space Administration. https://humanresearchroadmap.nasa.gov/Evidence/other/Degen.pdf. 2016.

1012. Lee SMC, Stenger MB, Laurie SS, Macias BR. Evidence Report: Risk of cardiac rhythm problems during spaceflight [online]. National Aeronautics and Space Administration. https://humanresearchroadmap.nasa.gov/evidence/other/Arrhythmia.pdf. 2017.

1013. Arbeille P, Provost R, Zuj K. Carotid and femoral arterial wall distensibility during long-duration spaceflight. Aerosp Med Hum Perform. 2017;88:924-30.

1014. Arbeille P, Provost R, Zuj K. Carotid and femoral artery intima-media thickness during 6 months of spaceflight. Aerosp Med Hum Perform. 2016;87:449-53.

1015. Greaves DK, Roberstson AD, Patterson CA, Au JS, Hughson RL. Evidence for increased cardiovascular risk to crew during long duration space missions. J Appl Physiol (1985). 2020;129:1111-2.

1016. Lee SMC, Laurie SS, Macias BR, Zwart SR, Smith SM, Stenger MB. Reply to Greaves et al. J Appl Physiol (1985). 2020;129:1113.

1017. Droge W. Free radicals in the physiological control of cell function. Physiol Rev. 2002;82:47-95.

1018. Tahimic CGT, Globus RK. Redox signaling and its impact on skeletal and vascular responses to spaceflight. Int J Mol Sci. 2017;18.

1019. Khosravi M, Poursaleh A, Ghasempour G, Farhad S, Najafi M. The effects of oxidative stress on the development of atherosclerosis. Biol Chem. 2019;400:711-32.

1020. Senoner T, Dichtl W. Oxidative stress in cardiovascular diseases: Still a therapeutic target? Nutrients. 2019;11.

1021. Stein TP. Space flight and oxidative stress. Nutrition. 2002;18:867-71.

1022. Crucian BE, Zwart SR, Mehta S, Uchakin P, Quiriarte HD, Pierson D, Sams CF, Smith SM. Plasma cytokine concentrations indicate that in vivo hormonal regulation of immunity is altered during long-duration spaceflight. J Interferon Cytokine Res. 2014;34:778-86.

1023. Takahashi K, Okumura H, Guo R, Naruse K. Effect of oxidative stress on cardiovascular system in response to gravity. Int J Mol Sci. 2017;18.

1024. Gallo C, Ridolfi L, Scarsoglio S. Cardiovascular deconditioning during long-term spaceflight through multiscale modeling. NPJ Microgravity. 2020;6:27.

1025. Rikhi R, Samra G, Arustamyan M, Patel J, Zhou L, Bungo B, Moudgil R. Radiation induced cardiovascular disease: An odyssey of bedside-bench-bedside approach. Life Sciences in Space Research. 2020;27:49-55.

1026. Abbasi J. Do Apollo astronaut deaths shine a light on deep space radiation and cardiovascular disease? JAMA. 2016;316:2469-70.

1027. Boerma M, Nelson GA, Sridharan V, Mao XW, Koturbash I, Hauer-Jensen M. Space radiation and cardiovascular disease risk. World J Cardiol. 2015;7:882-8.

1028. Delp MD, Charvat JM, Limoli CL, Globus RK, Ghosh P. Apollo lunar astronauts show higher cardiovascular disease mortality: Possible deep space radiation effects on the vascular endothelium. Sci Rep. 2016;6:29901.

1029. Elgart SR, Little MP, Chappell LJ, Milder CM, Shavers MR, Huff JL, Patel ZS. Radiation exposure and mortality from cardiovascular disease and cancer in early NASA astronauts. Sci Rep. 2018;8:8480.

1030. Arbeille P, Shoemaker K, Kerbeci P, Schneider S, Hargens A, Hughson R. Aortic, cerebral and lower limb arterial and venous response to orthostatic stress after a 60-day bedrest. Eur J Appl Physiol. 2012;112:277-84.

1031. Amirova L, Navasiolava N, Rukavishvikov I, Gauquelin-Koch G, Gharib C, Kozlovskaya I, Custaud MA, Tomilovskaya E. Cardiovascular system under simulated weightlessness: Head-down bed rest vs. dry immersion. Front Physiol. 2020;11:395.

1032. Guinet P, MacNamara JP, Berry M, Larcher F, Bareille M-P, Custaud M-A, Pavy-Le Traon A, Levine BD, Navasiolava N. MNX (Medium Duration Nutrition and Resistance-Vibration Exercise) bed-rest: Effect of resistance vibration exercise alone or combined with whey protein supplementation on cardiovascular system in 21-day head-down bed rest. Front Physiol. 2020;11.

1033. Hastings JL, Krainski F, Snell PG, Pacini EL, Jain M, Bhella PS, Shibata S, Fu Q, Palmer MD, Levine BD. Effect of rowing ergometry and oral volume loading on cardiovascular structure and function during bed rest. J Appl Physiol (1985). 2012;112:1735-43.

1034. Bosutti A, Malaponte G, Zanetti M, Castellino P, Heer M, Guarnieri G, Biolo G. Calorie restriction modulates inactivity-induced changes in the inflammatory markers C-reactive protein and pentraxin-3. J Clin Endocrinol Metab. 2008;93:3226-9.

1035. Hesse C, Siedler H, Luntz SP, Arendt BM, Goerlich R, Fricker R, Heer M, Haefeli WE. Modulation of endothelial and smooth muscle function by bed rest and hypoenergetic, low-fat nutrition. J Appl Physiol (1985). 2005;99:2196-203.

1036. Nie ZL, Wang ZM, Zhou B, Tang ZP, Wang SK. Magnesium intake and incidence of stroke: meta-analysis of cohort studies. Nutr Metab Cardiovasc Dis. 2013;23:169-76.

1037. Altura BM, Altura BT. New perspectives on the role of magnesium in the pathophysiology of the cardiovascular system. I. Clinical aspects. Magnesium. 1985;4:226-44.

1038. Altura BM, Altura BT. Cardiovascular risk factors and magnesium: relationships to atherosclerosis, ischemic heart disease and hypertension. Schriftenr Ver Wasser Boden Lufthyg. 1993;88:451-73.

1039. Iskra M, Patelski J, Majewski W. Concentrations of calcium, magnesium, zinc and copper in relation to free fatty acids and cholesterol in serum of atherosclerotic men. J Trace Elem Electrolytes Health Dis. 1993;7:185-8.

1040. Kirsten R, Heintz B, Nelson K, Sieberth HG, Oremek G, Hasford J, Speck U. Magnesium pyridoxal 5-phosphate glutamate reduces hyperlipidaemia in patients with chronic renal insufficiency. Eur J Clin Pharmacol. 1988;34:133-7.

1041. Singh RB, Rastogi SS, Mani UV, Seth J, Devi L. Does dietary magnesium modulate blood lipids? Biol Trace Elem Res. 1991;30:59-64.

1042. Cambray S, Ibarz M, Bermudez-Lopez M, Marti-Antonio M, Bozic M, Fernandez E, Valdivielso JM. Magnesium levels modify the effect of lipid parameters on carotid intima media thickness. Nutrients. 2020;12.

1043. Guan J, Stewart J, Ware JH, Zhou Z, Donahue JJ, Kennedy AR. Effects of dietary supplements on the space radiation-induced reduction in total antioxidant status in CBA mice. Radiat Res. 2006;165:373-8.

1044. Guan J, Wan XS, Zhou Z, Ware J, Donahue JJ, Biaglow JE, Kennedy AR. Effects of dietary supplements on space radiation-induced oxidative stress in Sprague-Dawley rats. Radiat Res. 2004;162:572-9.

1045. Kennedy AR, Ware JH, Guan J, Donahue JJ, Biaglow JE, Zhou Z, Stewart J, Vazquez M, Wan XS. Selenomethionine protects against adverse biological effects induced by space radiation. Free Radic Biol Med. 2004;36:259-66.

1046. Tuttolomondo A, Simonetta I, Daidone M, Mogavero A, Ortello A, Pinto A. Metabolic and vascular effect of the mediterranean diet. Int J Mol Sci. 2019;20.

1047. Abdelhamid AS, Brown TJ, Brainard JS, Biswas P, Thorpe GC, Moore HJ, Deane KH, Summerbell CD, Worthington HV, Song F, Hooper L. Omega-3 fatty acids for the primary and secondary prevention of cardiovascular disease. Cochrane Database Syst Rev. 2020;3:CD003177.

1048. Psota TL, Gebauer SK, Kris-Etherton P. Dietary omega-3 fatty acid intake and cardiovascular risk. Am J Cardiol. 2006;98:3i-18i.

1049. Rimm EB, Appel LJ, Chiuve SE, Djousse L, Engler MB, Kris-Etherton PM, Mozaffarian D, Siscovick DS, Lichtenstein AH, American Heart Association Nutrition Committee of the Council on L, Cardiometabolic H, Council on E, Prevention, Council on Cardiovascular Disease in the Y, Council on C, Stroke N, Council on Clinical C. Seafood long-chain n-3 polyunsaturated fatty acids and cardiovascular disease: A science advisory From the American Heart Association. Circulation. 2018;138:e35-e47.

1050. Abbasi J. Another nail in the coffin for fish oil supplements. JAMA. 2018;319:1851-2.

1051. He K. Fish, long-chain omega-3 polyunsaturated fatty acids and prevention of cardiovascular disease--eat fish or take fish oil supplement? Prog Cardiovasc Dis. 2009;52:95-114.

1052. Rangel-Huerta OD, Gil A. Omega 3 fatty acids in cardiovascular disease risk factors: An updated systematic review of randomised clinical trials. Clin Nutr. 2018;37:72-7.

1053. Blacher J, Czernichow S, Paillard F, Ducimetiere P, Hercberg S, Galan P, Group SFOSR. Cardiovascular effects of B-vitamins and/or N-3 fatty acids: the SU.FOL.OM3 trial. Int J Cardiol. 2013;167:508-13.

1054. Aung T, Halsey J, Kromhout D, Gerstein HC, Marchioli R, Tavazzi L, Geleijnse JM, Rauch B, Ness A, Galan P, Chew EY, Bosch J, Collins R, Lewington S, Armitage J, Clarke R, Omega-3 Treatment Trialists C. Associations of omega-3 fatty acid supplement use with cardiovascular disease risks: Meta-analysis of 10 trials involving 77917 individuals. JAMA Cardiol. 2018;3:225-34.

1055. Meier T, Grafe K, Senn F, Sur P, Stangl GI, Dawczynski C, Marz W, Kleber ME, Lorkowski S. Cardiovascular mortality attributable to dietary risk factors in 51 countries in the WHO European Region from 1990 to 2016: a systematic analysis of the Global Burden of Disease Study. Eur J Epidemiol. 2019;34:37-55.

1056. Bellavia A, Larsson SC, Bottai M, Wolk A, Orsini N. Fruit and vegetable consumption and all-cause mortality: a dose-response analysis. Am J Clin Nutr. 2013;98:454-9.

1057. Boeing H, Bechthold A, Bub A, Ellinger S, Haller D, Kroke A, Leschik-Bonnet E, Muller MJ, Oberritter H, Schulze M, Stehle P, Watzl B. Critical review: vegetables and fruit in the prevention of chronic diseases. Eur J Nutr. 2012;51:637-63.

1058. Cocate PG, Natali AJ, de Oliveira A, Longo GZ, Alfenas Rde C, Peluzio Mdo C, E CDS, Buthers JM, de Oliveira LL, Hermsdorff HH. Fruit and vegetable intake and related nutrients are associated with oxidative stress markers in middle-aged men. Nutrition. 2014;30:660-5.

1059. Leenders M, Sluijs I, Ros MM, Boshuizen HC, Siersema PD, Ferrari P, Weikert C, Tjonneland A, Olsen A, Boutron-Ruault MC, Clavel-Chapelon F, Nailler L, Teucher B, Li K, Boeing H, Bergmann MM, Trichopoulou A, Lagiou P, Trichopoulos D, Palli D, Pala V, Panico S, Tumino R, Sacerdote C, Peeters PH, van Gils CH, Lund E, Engeset D, Redondo ML, Agudo A, Sanchez MJ, Navarro C, Ardanaz E, Sonestedt E, Ericson U, Nilsson LM, Khaw KT, Wareham NJ, Key TJ, Crowe FL, Romieu I, Gunter MJ, Gallo V, Overvad K, Riboli E, Bueno-de-Mesquita HB. Fruit and vegetable consumption and mortality: European prospective investigation into cancer and nutrition. Am J Epidemiol. 2013;178:590-602.

1060. Macready AL, George TW, Chong MF, Alimbetov DS, Jin Y, Vidal A, Spencer JP, Kennedy OB, Tuohy KM, Minihane AM, Gordon MH, Lovegrove JA, Group FS. Flavonoid-rich fruit and vegetables improve microvascular reactivity and inflammatory status in men at risk of cardiovascular disease--FLAVURS: a randomized controlled trial. Am J Clin Nutr. 2014;99:479-89.

1061. Oyebode O, Gordon-Dseagu V, Walker A, Mindell JS. Fruit and vegetable consumption and all-cause, cancer and CVD mortality: analysis of Health Survey for England data. J Epidemiol Community Health. 2014;68:856-62.

1062. Shivappa N, Steck SE, Hurley TG, Hussey JR, Hebert JR. Designing and developing a literature-derived, population-based dietary inflammatory index. Public Health Nutr. 2013:1-8.

1063. Agraib LM, Azab M, Al-Shudifat AE, Allehdan SS, Shivappa N, Hebert JR, Tayyem R. Dietary inflammatory index and odds of coronary artery disease in a case-control study from Jordan. Nutrition. 2019;63-64:98-105.

1064. Garcia-Arellano A, Ramallal R, Ruiz-Canela M, Salas-Salvado J, Corella D, Shivappa N, Schroder H, Hebert JR, Ros E, Gomez-Garcia E, Estruch R, Lapetra J, Aros F, Fiol M, Serra-Majem L, Pinto X, Babio N, Gonzalez JI, Fito M, Martinez JA, Martinez-Gonzalez MA, Predimed I. Dietary inflammatory index and incidence of cardiovascular disease in the PREDIMED study. Nutrients. 2015;7:4124-38.

1065. Hodge AM, Bassett JK, Dugue PA, Shivappa N, Hebert JR, Milne RL, English DR, Giles GG. Dietary inflammatory index or Mediterranean diet score as risk factors for total and cardiovascular mortality. Nutr Metab Cardiovasc Dis. 2018;28:461-9.

1066. Sanchez-Villegas A, Ruiz-Canela M, de la Fuente-Arrillaga C, Gea A, Shivappa N, Hebert JR, Martinez-Gonzalez MA. Dietary inflammatory index, cardiometabolic conditions and depression in the Seguimiento Universidad de Navarra cohort study. Br J Nutr. 2015;114:1471-9.

1067. Shin D, Lee KW, Brann L, Shivappa N, Hebert JR. Dietary inflammatory index is positively associated with serum high-sensitivity C-reactive protein in a Korean adult population. Nutrition. 2019;63-64:155-61.

1068. Shivappa N, Bonaccio M, Hebert JR, Di Castelnuovo A, Costanzo S, Ruggiero E, Pounis G, Donati MB, de Gaetano G, Iacoviello L, Moli-sani study I. Association of proinflammatory diet with low-grade inflammation: results from the Moli-sani study. Nutrition. 2018;54:182-8.

1069. Shivappa N, Godos J, Hebert JR, Wirth MD, Piuri G, Speciani AF, Grosso G. Dietary inflammatory index and cardiovascular risk and mortality-A meta-analysis. Nutrients. 2018;10.

1070. Shivappa N, Steck SE, Hussey JR, Ma Y, Hebert JR. Inflammatory potential of diet and all-cause, cardiovascular, and cancer mortality in National Health and Nutrition Examination Survey III Study. Eur J Nutr. 2017;56:683-92.

1071. Vissers LET, Waller M, van der Schouw YT, Hebert JR, Shivappa N, Schoenaker D, Mishra GD. A pro-inflammatory diet is associated with increased risk of developing hypertension among middle-aged women. Nutr Metab Cardiovasc Dis. 2017;27:564-70.

Expedition 61 Flight Engineer Christina Koch is shown with a New Year's Eve meal in the Zvezda Service Module. Photo Credit: NASA.

9

Nutrition has significant importance for brain function, and is even more critical during space travel where factors such as microgravity and radiation can affect both brain structure and function. Understanding how nutrition supports brain function in astronauts, and how nutrition can counteract these effects, may be critical for enabling exploration missions beyond low-Earth orbit.

Radiation and Central Nervous System, Behavior/Performance, and Sensorimotor Function

Radiation exposure during deep space missions is unavoidable and it could affect many physiological systems including the central nervous system (CNS), behavior, and sensorimotor function (14). Radiation can affect the brain and induce neuroinflammation by activating microglia, producing oxidative stress, inducing mitochondrial dysfunction that leads to altered energy production in the brain, and directly effecting the permeability of the blood-brain barrier. Increased neuroinflammation is associated with progressive neuronal loss and with increased risk of decrements in behavior and cognitive performance. Evidence indicates that specific nutrients and/or dietary intake patterns can mitigate neuroinflammation; thus, nutrition could protect against neuroinflammatory processes caused by the hazards of spaceflight.

The brain requires micro- and macronutrients to build and maintain structure and function, not only during development but also throughout adulthood. The human brain accounts for about 2% of the weight of an average human; however, it consumes 20% to 25% of the body's total energy (1072). The half-lives of proteins in the brain vary from a few hours to more than 20 days, depending on their location. This turnover is necessary to ensure that synapses (structures that allow chemical or electrical impulses to travel from one nerve cell to another) remain flexible (1073). Maintaining synaptic plasticity is essential for memory and learning (1074). Nutritional deficits can affect the pathophysiology of mood disorders, including depression, which could in turn affect an astronaut's performance during an exploration mission. B vitamins such as thiamin, riboflavin, niacin, and folate are associated with abstract thought processes, whereas vitamin C status can affect visuo-spatial performance (1075). Vitamins A, E, B_{12}, and B_6 are associated with both visuo-spatial memory and abstract thought processes (1075). These vitamins also play a role in cognition and degenerative diseases (1076-1081).

Although each of these vitamins has an individual role in cerebral function, nutrients are generally consumed in a food matrix and they interact with other nutrients and compounds. Historical events remind us of the importance of individual nutrients—for example, the associations between vitamin C deficiency and scurvy, thiamin and beriberi, vitamin D and rickets, and iodine and goiter (1074). Research studies that focus on single nutrients often do not reach the same conclusions as studies focusing on diets as a whole (1082). Although delivery of individual nutrients will continue to serve medical needs in certain instances, high-quality diets rich in nutrients known to be involved in cerebral health is the preferred long-term approach for sustaining a healthy brain over a lifetime. Chapter 11 includes more detail on microbiome and brain, mood, and behavior.

The fact that high-LET radiation affects cognition and behavior is becoming increasingly evident. Rodents irradiated with acute doses of accelerated particles have changes in cognition and behavior that involve altered learning and memory, anxiety, social behavior, and fear/startle responses (13). After young animals were exposed to high-LET radiation, they develop changes in neuronal signal transduction and accompanying changes in motor performance that are similar to effects seen in aging animals (1083). Mice exposed to either protons alone, or a combination of protons and heavy ions, had acute and chronic cognitive impairment as assessed by a novel object recognition task (1084), and this response was believed to be mediated by changes in or by the hippocampus. Exposure to high-LET radiation can also alter patterns of gene expression and change networks in the hippocampus that affect spatial memory (1084, 1085). Kiffer and colleagues recently completed a comprehensive review of behavioral and cognitive changes in animals that were irradiated with either a single type of charged particle (56Fe, 48Ti, 28Si, 16O, 12C, or protons) or a mixed radiation field (14). By far, 56Fe is the most well studied type of charged particle radiation for assessing behavior outcomes. This type of radiation exposure clearly has behavioral and cognitive consequences in mice and rats. Doses of 56Fe ranging from 0.05 to 5 Gy affected behavior or cognition at many time points after irradiation (14).

Figure 62. NASA astronaut Kjell Lindgren is photographed with a bag of assorted fruit (oranges, lemons, grapefruits) floating in the Node 2 module after being unpacked from the Kounotori H-II Transfer Vehicle 5. Photo Credit: NASA.

Nutrition Countermeasures

A single antioxidant may not be effective for countering the effects of oxidative stress or neuroinflammation because these processes are complex and simultaneously involve many biological cascades. Differences in effectiveness of dietary components may be due to the differences in their bioactive compounds. All berries contain phenolics, anthocyanins, and flavonols; however, blueberries contain more proanthocyanins, whereas strawberries contain more ellagitannins (1086). These variations can affect antioxidant properties and their capacity to cross the blood-brain barrier (1086-1088). Numerous large-scale epidemiological studies show improvements in disease state by diet but not with individual supplements (1050, 1089-1093), which underscores the importance of phytochemicals in whole foods. Similarly, although an abundance of data show that individual nutrients are radioprotective (1094-1099), whole foods with an equivalent dose of the specific nutrient may confer more radioprotection than a supplement because the myriad phytochemicals in foods also have radioprotective effects (1100). Detailed reviews have been published on the many radioprotective effects of phytochemicals (1101-1103).

Flavonoids are a subclass of phenolics that have a structure with two aromatic rings attached by three carbons, usually in a heterocyclic ring (57). Flavonoids have strong antioxidant properties because they can bind to heavy metals and scavenge free radicals (1104). Berries are especially rich in phytochemicals and have beneficial effects on cognitive and motor behaviors (1105, 1106). Luteolin, a flavonoid found in citrus fruit, and diosmin, a citrus flavone derivative that is structurally similar to luteolin, reduced formation of amyloid plaque peptides in a mouse model of Alzheimer's disease (1107). The suggested mechanism of diosmin action is through glycogen synthase kinase 3 inhibition, which affects formation of presenilin-1 phosphorylation and amyloid plaques (1107). Other specific polyphenols such as naringenin, which is also found in citrus fruits, inhibit activation of amyloid β-induced microglia (1108). A recent systematic review discusses how plant flavonoids and other phenolics affect human health (1109). Some of the beneficial effects of flavonoids include their antioxidant, anti-inflammatory, and antibacterial actions, and their actions in protecting against cancer, cardio and immune dysfunction, and ultraviolet radiation damage. Flavonoid-rich diets are associated with enhanced cognitive capabilities and are believed to slow the progression of neurodegenerative disease such as Alzheimer's disease (1110-1112). It is thought that flavonoids relay their neuroprotective effects by maintaining the quality and number of neurons through inhibition of neuroinflammation and oxidative stress, thus averting the trigger or advancement of the disease that causes the decline in cognitive function (1104). Cheki and colleagues (1113) provide a convenient list of the radioprotective effects of phytochemicals that have been tested at various doses of ionizing radiation. They determined that phytochemicals can protect against the effects of ionizing radiation at doses of 1-5 Gy, which is within the realm of possibility of a total mission dose during a Mars mission.

References for Chapter 9

13. Cekanaviciute E, Rosi S, Costes SV. Central nervous system responses to simulated galactic cosmic rays. Int J Mol Sci. 2018;19.

14. Kiffer F, Boerma M, Allen A. Behavioral effects of space radiation: A comprehensive review of animal studies. Life Sci Space Res (Amst). 2019;21:1-21.

57. Liu RH. Health-promoting components of fruits and vegetables in the diet. Adv Nutr. 2013;4:384S-92S.

1050. Abbasi J. Another nail in the coffin for fish oil supplements. JAMA. 2018;319:1851-2.

1072. Mink JW, Blumenschine RJ, Adams DB. Ratio of central nervous system to body metabolism in vertebrates: its constancy and functional basis. Am J Physiol. 1981;241:R203-12.

1073. Dorrbaum AR, Kochen L, Langer JD, Schuman EM. Local and global influences on protein turnover in neurons and glia. Elife. 2018;7.

1074. Goyal MS, Iannotti LL, Raichle ME. Brain nutrition: A life span approach. Annu Rev Nutr. 2018;38:381-99.

1075. La Rue A, Koehler KM, Wayne SJ, Chiulli SJ, Haaland KY, Garry PJ. Nutritional status and cognitive functioning in a normally aging sample: a 6-y reassessment. Am J Clin Nutr. 1997;65:20-9.

1076. Craenen K, Verslegers M, Baatout S, Abderrafi Benotmane M. An appraisal of folates as key factors in cognition and ageing-related diseases. Crit Rev Food Sci Nutr. 2019:1-18.

1077. Annweiler C, Schott AM, Rolland Y, Blain H, Herrmann FR, Beauchet O. Dietary intake of vitamin D and cognition in older women: a large population-based study. Neurology. 2010;75:1810-6.

1078. Constans T, Mondon K, Annweiler C, Hommet C. [Vitamin D and cognition in the elderly]. Psychol Neuropsychiatr Vieil. 2010;8:255-62.

1079. Jannusch K, Jockwitz C, Bidmon HJ, Moebus S, Amunts K, Caspers S. A complex interplay of vitamin B_1 and B_6 metabolism with cognition, brain structure, and functional connectivity in older adults. Front Neurosci. 2017;11:596.

1080. Przybelski RJ, Binkley NC. Is vitamin D important for preserving cognition? A positive correlation of serum 25-hydroxyvitamin D concentration with cognitive function. Arch Biochem Biophys. 2007;460:202-5.

1081. van der Schaft J, Koek HL, Dijkstra E, Verhaar HJ, van der Schouw YT, Emmelot-Vonk MH. The association between vitamin D and cognition: A systematic review. Ageing Res Rev. 2013;12:1013-23.

1082. Thorning TK, Bertram HC, Bonjour JP, de Groot L, Dupont D, Feeney E, Ipsen R, Lecerf JM, Mackie A, McKinley MC, Michalski MC, Remond D, Riserus U, Soedamah-Muthu SS, Tholstrup T, Weaver C, Astrup A, Givens I. Whole dairy matrix or single nutrients in assessment of health effects: current evidence and knowledge gaps. Am J Clin Nutr. 2017;105:1033-45.

1083. Joseph JA, Shukitt-Hale B, McEwen J, Rabin BM. CNS-induced deficits of heavy particle irradiation in space: the aging connection. Adv Space Res. 2000;25:2057-64.

1084. Raber J, Allen AR, Sharma S, Allen B, Rosi S, Olsen RH, Davis MJ, Eiwaz M, Fike JR, Nelson GA. Effects of proton and combined proton and (56)Fe radiation on the hippocampus. Radiat Res. 2016;185:20-30.

1085. Impey S, Jopson T, Pelz C, Tafessu A, Fareh F, Zuloaga D, Marzulla T, Riparip LK, Stewart B, Rosi S, Turker MS, Raber J. Short- and long-term effects of (56)Fe irradiation on cognition and hippocampal DNA methylation and gene expression. BMC Genomics. 2016;17:825.

1086. Prior RL, Cao G, Martin A, Sofic E, McEwen J, O'Brien C, Lischner N, Ehlenfeldt M, Kalt W, Krewer M. Antioxidant capacity as influenced by total phenolic and anthocyanin content, maturity and variety of Vaccinium species. . J Agric Food Chem. 1998;46:2586-93.

1087. Wang H, Cao G, Prior R. Total antioxidant capacity of fruits. J Agric Food Chem. 1996;44:701-5.

1088. Youdim KA, Joseph JA. A possible emerging role of phytochemicals in improving age-related neurological dysfunctions: a multiplicity of effects. Free Radic Biol Med. 2001;30:583-94.

1089. Schwingshackl L, Boeing H, Stelmach-Mardas M, Gottschald M, Dietrich S, Hoffmann G, Chaimani A. Dietary supplements and risk of cause-specific death, cardiovascular disease, and cancer: a systematic review and meta-analysis of primary prevention trials. Adv Nutr. 2017;8:27-39.

1090. Chen F, Du M, Blumberg JB, Ho Chui KK, Ruan M, Rogers G, Shan Z, Zeng L, Zhang FF. Association among dietary supplement use, nutrient intake, and mortality among U.S. adults: A cohort study. Ann Intern Med. 2019;170:604-13.

1091. Ashor AW, Brown R, Keenan PD, Willis ND, Siervo M, Mathers JC. Limited evidence for a beneficial effect of vitamin C supplementation on biomarkers of cardiovascular diseases: an umbrella review of systematic reviews and meta-analyses. Nutr Res. 2019;61:1-12.

1092. Kim J, Choi J, Kwon SY, McEvoy JW, Blaha MJ, Blumenthal RS, Guallar E, Zhao D, Michos ED. Association of multivitamin and mineral supplementation and risk of cardiovascular disease: A systematic review and meta-analysis. Circ Cardiovasc Qual Outcomes. 2018;11:e004224.

1093. Collins F. NIH Director's Blog: Study finds no benefit for dietary supplements. 2019 [accessed 2020]; Available from: https://directorsblog.nih.gov/2019/04/16/study-finds-no-benefit-for-dietary-supplements/.

1094. Salvadori DM, Ribeiro LR, Xiao Y, Boei JJ, Natarajan AT. Radioprotection of beta-carotene evaluated on mouse somatic and germ cells. Mutat Res. 1996;356:163-70.

1095. Srinivasan V, Weiss JF. Radioprotection by vitamin E: injectable vitamin E administered alone or with WR-3689 enhances survival of irradiated mice. Int J Radiat Oncol Biol Phys. 1992;23:841-5.

1096. Pote MS, Gandhi NM, Mishra KP. Antiatherogenic and radioprotective role of folic acid in whole body gamma-irradiated mice. Mol Cell Biochem. 2006;292:19-25.

1097. Singh VK, Kulkarni S, Fatanmi OO, Wise SY, Newman VL, Romaine PL, Hendrickson H, Gulani J, Ghosh SP, Kumar KS, Hauer-Jensen M. Radioprotective efficacy of gamma-tocotrienol in nonhuman primates. Radiat Res. 2016;185:285-98.

1098. Gonzalez E, Cruces MP, Pimentel E, Sanchez P. Evidence that the radioprotector effect of ascorbic acid depends on the radiation dose rate. Environ Toxicol Pharmacol. 2018;62:210-4.

1099. Rostami A, Moosavi SA, Dianat Moghadam H, Bolookat ER. Micronuclei assessment of the radioprotective effects of melatonin and vitamin C in human lymphocytes. Cell J. 2016;18:46-51.

1100. Fischer N, Seo EJ, Efferth T. Prevention from radiation damage by natural products. Phytomedicine. 2018;47:192-200.

1101. Jagetia GC. Radioprotective potential of plants and herbs agains the effects of ionizing radiation. J Clin Biochem Nutr. 2007;40:74-81.

1102. Hosseinimehr SJ. Trends in the development of radioprotective agents. Drug Discov Today. 2007;12:794-805.

1103. Herman F, Westfall S, Brathwaite J, Pasinetti GM. Suppression of presymptomatic oxidative stress and inflammation in neurodegeneration by grape-derived polyphenols. Front Pharmacol. 2018;9:867.

1104. Ayaz M, Sadiq A, Junaid M, Ullah F, Ovais M, Ullah I, Ahmed J, Shahid M. Flavonoids as prospective neuroprotectants and their therapeutic propensity in aging associated neurological disorders. Front Aging Neurosci. 2019;11:155.

1105. Miller MG, Shukitt-Hale B. Berry fruit enhances beneficial signaling in the brain. J Agric Food Chem. 2012;60:5709-15.

1106. Power R, Prado-Cabrero A, Mulcahy R, Howard A, Nolan JM. The role of nutrition for the aging population: implications for cognition and alzheimer's disease. Annu Rev Food Sci Technol. 2019;10:619-39.

1107. Rezai-Zadeh K, Douglas Shytle R, Bai Y, Tian J, Hou H, Mori T, Zeng J, Obregon D, Town T, Tan J. Flavonoid-mediated presenilin-1 phosphorylation reduces Alzheimer's disease beta-amyloid production. J Cell Mol Med. 2009;13:574-88.

1108. Yang Z, Kuboyama T, Tohda C. Naringenin promotes microglial M2 polarization and Abeta degradation enzyme expression. Phytother Res. 2019;33:1114-21.

1109. Tungmunnithum D, Thongboonyou A, Pholboon A, Yangsabai A. Flavonoids and other phenolic compounds from medicinal plants for pharmaceutical and medical aspects: An overview. Medicines (Basel). 2018;5.

1110. Bakoyiannis I, Daskalopoulou A, Pergialiotis V, Perrea D. Phytochemicals and cognitive health: Are flavonoids doing the trick? Biomed Pharmacother. 2019;109:1488-97.

1111. Socci V, Tempesta D, Desideri G, De Gennaro L, Ferrara M. Enhancing human cognition with cocoa flavonoids. Front Nutr. 2017;4:19.

1112. Spencer JP. The impact of fruit flavonoids on memory and cognition. Br J Nutr. 2010;104 Suppl 3:S40-7.

1113. Cheki M, Mihandoost E, Shirazi A, Mahmoudzadeh A. Prophylactic role of some plants and phytochemicals against radio-genotoxicity in human lymphocytes. J Cancer Res Ther. 2016;12:1234-42.

In the International Space Station's Harmony node, European Space Agency astronaut Alexander Gerst, Expedition 40 flight engineer, performs an eye exam for the Ocular Health experiment. Photo Credit: NASA.

10 Ocular

Nutrition is known to be an important factor for ophthalmic health in general. This chapter will review the available literature on this topic and general nutrition in ophthalmic health, along with ongoing research to understand and counteract the effects of spaceflight. The harsh environment of spaceflight affects vision and ocular health. Some of the environmental aspects that can contribute to changes in ocular health are radiation exposure, cephalad shifts of body fluid, spacecraft cabin and spacesuit gas mixtures, and the spaceflight food system. Astronauts have an increased risk to develop cataracts, one of the ocular pathologies, as has been documented.

Cataracts are opacities of the lens and have a multifactorial etiology. Diet, genetics, and environmental stressors can all play a role in initiating oxidative damage that can lead to cataract formation. Several studies have confirmed that astronauts and cosmonauts have an increased risk of cataract formation after spaceflight (1114-1117). Cucinotta et al. (1115) identified an increased risk of all types of cataracts (including posterior subcapsular, cortical, and nuclear) among astronauts with higher exposure to radiation. Longitudinal follow-up studies have been conducted and it was determined that progression of cortical cataracts, but not posterior subcapsular or nuclear cataracts, is related to space radiation exposure (1116, 1118). Although radiation exposure is a large driving force for the oxidative damage that leads to some types of cataracts, the longitudinal study provided evidence that intake of specific nutrients may provide some protective effects (1116). In the first report of the NASA Study of Cataract in Astronauts, nutritional intake estimates were obtained from a questionnaire, and the data provided evidence that beta-carotene and lycopene intake had a protective effect for some types of cataracts in astronauts (1116). As reviewed by Agte and Tarwadi, numerous ground-based studies have provided evidence for associations between micronutrients and antioxidants (either blood levels or estimated intakes) and cataracts (1119).

Although epidemiological data support the idea that lower nutritional status—particularly vitamin A, riboflavin, vitamin E, beta-carotene, zinc, and vitamin C status—is associated with cataract risk (1120-1123), it is not known whether altered micronutrient and antioxidant intake during spaceflight could minimize cataract incidence related to space radiation. Further interventional study and better estimates of in-flight nutrient intake along with nutrient status assessments will help to answer these important questions in the future.

Spaceflight Associated Neuro-ocular Syndrome

In addition to a general increase in cataract risk (1115, 1116, 1118), some crewmembers have experienced ocular changes after long-duration spaceflight. Spaceflight Associated Neuro-ocular Syndrome (SANS) is characterized as the occurrence of optic disc edema, flattening of the posterior region of the sclera, hyperopic refractive error shifts, and choroidal and retinal folds (1124, 1125).

Although the precise mechanism is not yet fully understood, out of several published theories, some suggest an involvement of a cephalad fluid shift (1, 289, 1124). Other possible contributing factors include elevated cabin CO_2 exposure or local intraorbital (choridal and optic nerve sheath) changes. Elevated intracranial pressure has also been postulated to be a contributing factor; however, so far there are no supporting data for this proposed mechanism, and astronauts typically do not report any other symptoms associated with elevated intracranial pressure (1126, 1127). It is important to note that not all crewmembers who have flown on long-duration missions develop SANS (1126), thus it is likely that the cause is multifactorial. The impact of a cephalad fluid shift on one crewmember may be different than for another crewmember. One hypothesis to explain different responses to a fluid shift is genetic differences. Biochemical and genetic evidence confirms that the folate- and vitamin B_{12}-dependent pathway are involved (1128, 1129), as described in detail below.

Mader and colleagues first described seven cases among long-duration crewmembers on the ISS who had evidence of ophthalmic changes after flight, including optic disc edema, globe flattening, choroidal folds, and hyperopic shifts (1125). The definition of SANS has changed over the years, related to additional data and expanded assessment technology, and is still under some debate. With additional cases having been identified, the incidence of optic disc edema based upon fundoscopy is approximately 15% (1126), and some maintain a much higher incidence rate based on ocular coherence tomography imagery (1126, 1130).

Myasnikov and Stepanova reported evidence of postflight optic disc edema among Russian cosmonauts and one case (out of 10) with signs of intracranial hypertension, although they note the measurements were made before and after (not during) flight (1131).

Figure 63. NASA astronaut Karen Nyberg performs fundoscopy in the Destiny laboratory of the ISS. Photo Credit: NASA.

Spaceflight Associated Neuro-ocular Syndrome, Vitamins, and One Carbon Biochemistry

SANS only affects a subset of astronauts (31). Although no single cause has been documented, the fact that not all astronauts develop SANS increases the likelihood that this is multifactorial. Physiological (e.g., headward fluid shift, intracranial hypertension), environmental (e.g., CO_2, radiation), dietary (e.g., sodium, fluid), and genetic influences have all been posited to have a role or influence on this syndrome (31, 1132).

In astronauts, vitamin B_{12}-dependent one-carbon metabolic pathway intermediates, including homocysteine, were significantly higher in affected astronauts before, during, and after flight (Figure 64). Although the four one-carbon metabolites we measured were significantly higher, serum folate was significantly lower in affected astronauts during flight (19, 1128).

In addition to biochemical intermediates in the one-carbon metabolic pathway, one-carbon pathway genetic variations in astronauts are linked to SANS outcomes (1129, 1133). Specifically, the G and C alleles for MTRR A66G and SHMT1 C1420T polymorphisms, respectively, both contributed to the odds of SANS pathologies (e.g., choroidal folds, cotton wool spots, optic disc edema) after flight (1129) (Figure 65).

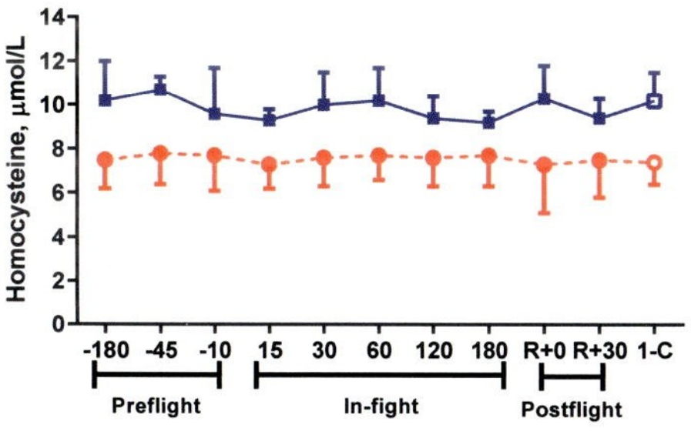

Figure 64. Homocysteine is significantly higher ($P<0.001$) in astronauts with ophthalmic findings (blue squares) than in those without ophthalmic findings (red circles) (1128). The "1C" sample (open symbols) was collected 2 to 6 years after flight as part of the experiment evaluating one-carbon pathway SNPs (1129).

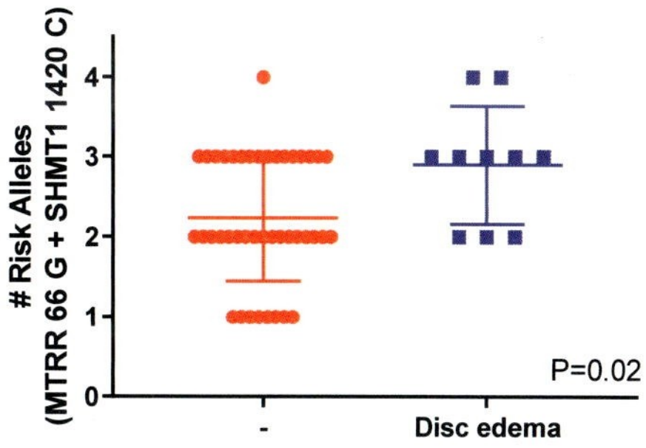

Figure 65. The presence of more risk alleles (i.e., G and C alleles for MTRR A66G and SHMT1 C1420T) was significantly related to incidence of optic disc edema in astronauts after 4 – to 6-month space missions.

In a ground-analog study, one-carbon pathway genetics are associated with acute response to head-down tilt and CO_2 exposure (1134). In a pilot study with eight subjects, a multiple regression model significantly predicted end-tidal CO_2 from the number of G alleles for MTRR 66 with vitamin B_{12} status as a covariate (1134) (Figure 66).

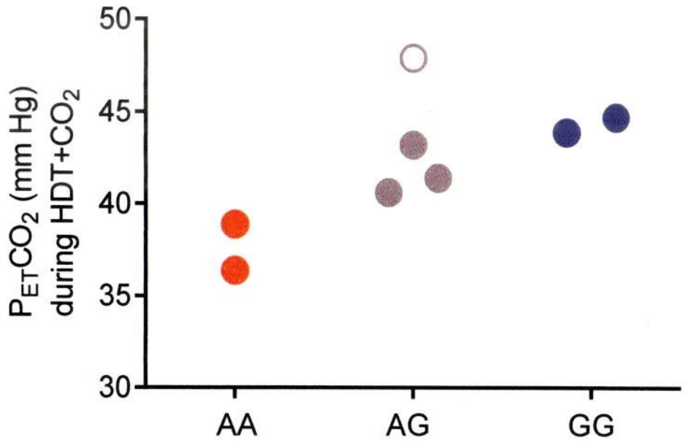

Figure 66. Relationship between MTRR A66G genotype and end tidal CO_2. The individual with AG genotype denoted by the open circle was vitamin B_{12} deficient. Adapted from (1134).

In a ground-analog study conducted in Germany (the "VaPER" study), optic disc edema was observed in 5 of 11 subjects during and after a 30-day head-down tilt bed rest with 0.5% CO_2 exposure (1135); the degree of optic disc edema was correlated with the total number of G and C alleles for MTRR 66 and SHMT1 1420 SNPs, respectively. Although work is ongoing to determine whether the strict head-down tilt and/or 0.5% CO_2 were causative, the fact that only 45% of the bed rest subjects developed optic disc edema further supports a role for genetics contributing to divergent responses among subjects–in this case, during well-controlled studies. The change in total retinal thickness, a quantitative measure of optic disc edema, was greater in subjects with 3 to 4 risk alleles than those with 1 to 2 risk alleles during and after bed rest (1136) and (Figure 67).

It is also worth noting that folate status in the VaPER bed rest subjects was much lower than those of subjects in head-down tilt bed rest studies conducted at the University of Texas Medical Branch (UTMB) in Galveston (Figure 68). This is likely due to lack of folate fortification of the food supply in Europe, a process initiated in the United States more than 20 years ago. None of the UTMB subjects in bed rest studies up to 70 days experienced optic disc edema (1137-1139). Another difference was noted between these studies: UTMB subjects were allowed use of a small head pillow and were allowed to prop themselves up on one elbow during meals. This change was implemented in the VaPER study based on concerns that the pillow, or leaning on an elbow to eat, might reduce the fluid shift pressures at the level of the eye (1127).

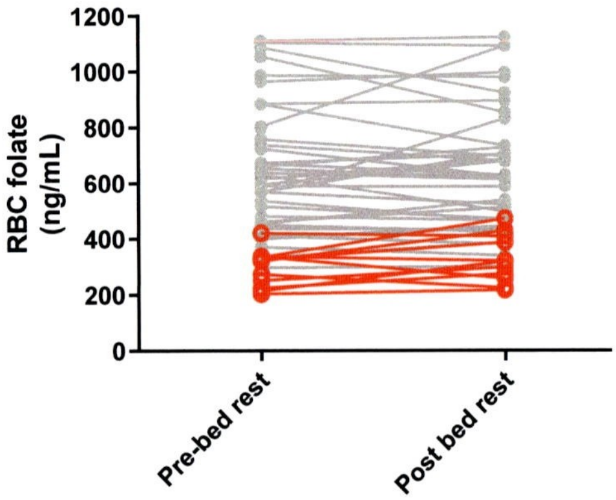

Figure 68. Red blood cell folate in VaPER subjects (red symbols/lines) and UTMB 30-day bed rest subjects (gray symbols/lines) before and after bed rest. Data adapted and expanded from (262).

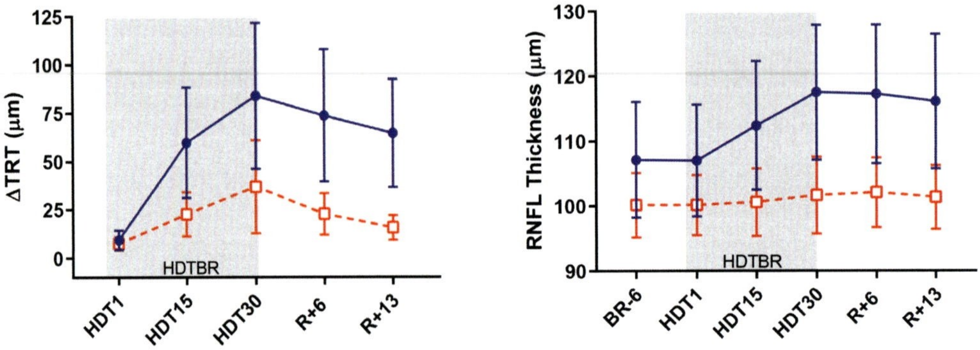

Figure 67. Change in peripapillary total retina thickness in subjects with 3 to 4 (n=4) or 0 to 2 (n=7) risk alleles, after 1, 15, and 30 days of head-down tilt bed rest and 6 and 13 days of recovery (left). Peripapillary retinal nerve fiber layer means showing a difference between the two genetic categories at all time points (BR-6, 6 days before head-down tilt bed rest began) (right). Data are means ± 95% CI. Adapted from (1136).

How could one-carbon pathway function contribute to optic disc edema and SANS?

Based on biochemical and genetic data, there is an undeniable association between altered one-carbon pathway function and SANS incidence (1128, 1129). The mechanism for how one-carbon metabolism might induce SANS is unknown, as is the mechanism for SANS. One hypothesized mechanism has been published (1136, 1140, 1141) and is detailed in Figure 64. Briefly, we hypothesize that because one-carbon metabolic pathway genetic variants can impair efficiency of the pathway, a resulting decrease in cofactor availability (including folate) occurs, which ultimately affects endothelial nitric oxide synthase (eNOS) coupling, nitric oxide synthesis, and peroxynitrite formation. This is explained in further detail below.

One Carbon Metabolism

Before detailing the hypothesis, it is necessary to understand the importance of the one-carbon metabolic pathway and its role in nitric oxide production. One-carbon metabolism is a universal metabolic pathway that serves to activate and transfer single carbon units for biosynthetic processes including purine and thymidylate biosynthesis, and for remethylation of homocysteine to methionine. A subsection of the pathway is shown in Figure 69.

Several B vitamins act as cofactors in the one-carbon metabolic pathway, including folate, vitamin B_{12}, vitamin B_6, and riboflavin. No cell can survive without these B vitamins, given the pathway's key role in DNA and RNA synthesis. These processes are therefore sensitive to vitamin status. For one example related to folate: all cellular forms of folate are

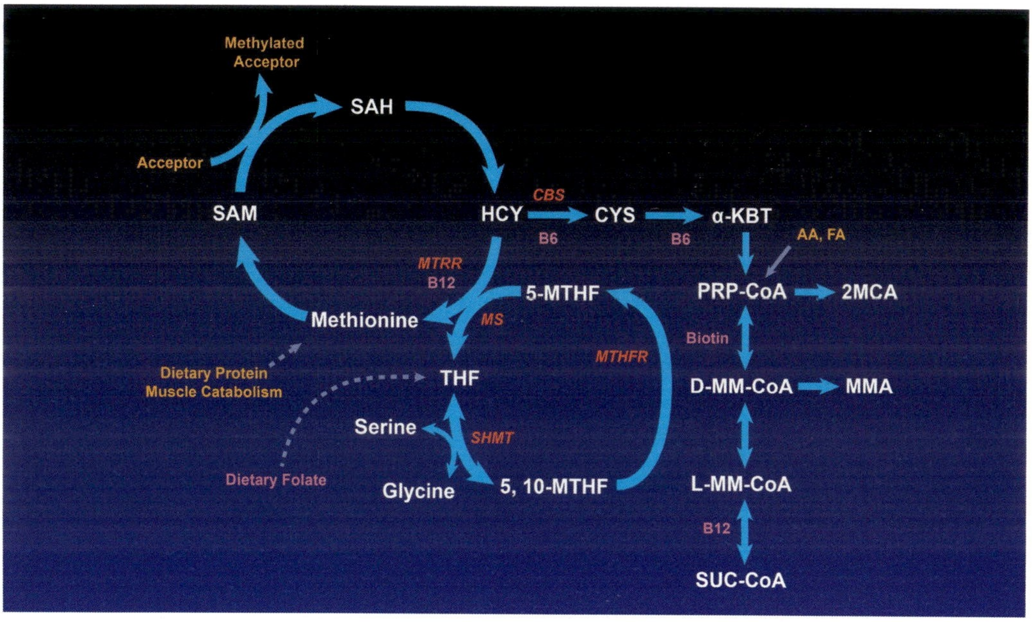

Figure 69. Overview of one-carbon metabolism. AA = amino acids; CBS = cystathionine ß-synthase; CYS = cystathionine; FA = fatty acids; HCY = homocysteine; αKBT = α-ketobutyrate; MCA = methylcitric acid; MM-CoA = methylmalonyl coenzyme A (CoA); MMA = methylmalonic acid; MS = methionine synthase; 5-MTHF = 5-methyltetrahydrofolate; 5,10-MTHF = 5,10-methylenetetrahydrofolate; MTHFR = methylenetetrahydrofolate reductase; MTRR = 5-methyltetrahydrofolate homocysteine methyltransferase reductase; PRP-CoA = propionyl CoA; SAH = S-adenosylhomocysteine; SAM = S-adenosylmethionine; SUC-CoA = succinyl CoA; THF = tetrahydrofolate. Image Credit: NASA.

expected to be protein bound, given binding constants (i.e., Kd values) in the nanomolar range. Folate-dependent anabolic pathways must compete for a rate-limiting pool of folate (1142) and are thus sensitive to primary folate deficiency. Furthermore, genetic variation that alters B-vitamin cofactors through any folate-dependent pathway influences the entire one-carbon metabolic pathway (1143). Clinical deficiencies of these B vitamins lead to hematologic and neurologic symptoms in adults, and folate insufficiency during development involves failure of neural tube closure early in pregnancy (1144-1146). Folate, vitamin B_{12}, and vitamin B_6 insufficiency due to either diet or genetic variants that alter pathway function and efficiency can lead to increased circulating homocysteine (1147). Animal studies show that folate deficiency or homocysteine exposure during development contributes to not only neural tube defects, but also negatively impacts normal eye development and can cause optic cup modifications (1148, 1149). Elevated homocysteine has been reported in numerous ocular conditions, including macular degeneration, diabetic retinopathy, macular edema, pseudoexfoliation glaucoma, and retinal venous and arterial occlusions (1150, 1151). Impaired nitric oxide metabolism is found to be one of the main effects of homocysteine toxicity (1152).

Role of One-Carbon Metabolism and Nitric Oxide in Endothelial Function

The vascular endothelium is a monolayer of cells that control vascular tone. Vascular tone is modulated by the synthesis and release of endothelium-derived relaxing factors (e.g., nitric oxide) and endothelium-derived contracting factors (1153). In healthy endothelium, nitric oxide is synthesized by a constitutively expressed enzyme: eNOS. Nitric oxide is an important vasodilator that maintains vascular health and function through its anti-thrombotic, anti-inflammatory, anti-angiogenic properties. It also plays an important role in inhibiting platelet adhesion and aggregation, leukocyte adhesion, and smooth muscle cell proliferation, which are events that contribute to atherosclerosis (1154). Endothelial dysfunction is mainly caused by reduced production or action of endothelium-derived relaxing factors and can be an early indicator of cardiovascular disease (1153). A hallmark of cardiovascular disease is the reduced ability of the endothelium to produce nitric oxide, resulting in increased vascular stiffness (1155, 1156).

The eNOS enzyme is a dimer that relies on tetrahydrobiopterin (BH_4) as a cofactor to couple the oxidation of L-arginine to the reduction of molecular oxygen to produce nitric oxide. The eNOS dimer can be decoupled when there is too little substrate or cofactor available. When eNOS is decoupled, superoxide radicals are produced instead of nitric oxide, and peroxynitrite forms (1157). Oxidative stress itself can directly oxidize BH_4 to dihydrobiopterin (BH_2) to deplete the supply of BH_4 or it can decrease de novo synthesis of BH_4 (1158). During spaceflight, astronauts are exposed to several sources of oxidative stress, including a low, chronic exposure to ionizing radiation. As reviewed by Pathak et al. (1159), in vitro studies show that ionizing radiation-induced oxidation can lead to decreased BH_4. Oxidation of BH_4 to BH_2 leads to decoupling of eNOS because BH_2 can compete for eNOS binding with BH_4 (1159). The formation of peroxynitrite can directly oxidize BH_4 to BH_2 (1160), thus creating a cycle that produces even more superoxide radicals. A deficiency of nitric oxide and excess peroxynitrite are both markers of endothelial dysfunction (1159).

Folate status can affect endothelial function through several direct actions. First, 5-methyltetrahydrofolate (5-MTHF), the primary circulating form of folate, can decrease superoxide generation in the vascular wall (1161). Both in vitro and in vivo studies show that 5-MTHF can reduce superoxide production and increase nitric oxide synthesis (1161-1163). The mechanism of action for increasing nitric oxide synthesis includes 5-MTHF acting to preserve the coupling of eNOS with consumption of nicotinamide adenine dinucleotide phosphate (NADPH) (1164). Second, 5-MTHF preserves eNOS coupling by increasing availability of BH_4 through its role in stabilizing BH_4 and facilitating its binding to eNOS (1161, 1165). Third, 5-MTHF plays a role in upregulating dihydrofolate reductase (DHFR), an enzyme that recycles BH_2 to BH_4 (as illustrated in Figure 64) (1166). This preservation of eNOS coupling is associated with improved endothelial function (1164). Finally, 5-MTHF can directly scavenge peroxynitrite radicals that otherwise oxidize BH_4 (1161).

There is debate over the role of homocysteine in cardiovascular health (1167), and it appears that some of the reasons behind the disparate results in the field could be due to population-specific genetic and dietary intake differences. One example is a link found between the MTHFR C677T polymorphism and increased risk of venous thromboembolism; however, the association is not found in North America where dietary intakes of folate is higher due to fortification practices (1168).

Several studies have documented that high doses of folic acid can mitigate endothelial dysfunction as assessed by flow-mediated dilation in patients with cardiovascular disease, amenorrheic runners, or known endothelial dysfunction (1169-1173). In a thorough review by Stanhewicz and Kenney (1174), they present evidence from several folic acid supplementation trials, and summarized that daily doses of ≥5 mg folic acid are efficacious in improving flow mediated dilation. In comparison, the current RDA for folate is 0.4 mg/d (266). They report that doses lower than 5 mg/d may lower plasma homocysteine, but they are not effective in improving flow-mediated dilation (1174). In many studies showing improved vascular endothelial function with folate or folic acid supplementation, no relationship exists between homocysteine concentration and endothelial function, suggesting that the protective effects of folate on endothelial function are likely not mediated through homocysteine (1163, 1169, 1175). Supportive of these studies showing improvement in flow-mediated dilation, local 5-MTHF administration as well as folic acid treatment improved vasodilator function in healthy older adults' skin through nitric oxide-dependent mechanisms (1176). Furthermore, folic acid supplementation (5 mg/d for 6 weeks) increased nitric oxide-dependent vasodilation of non-cutaneous vascular beds (1177). In older adults, folic acid supplementation improved skeletal muscle blood flow (1177). These studies support endothelial dysfunction as a systemic condition, and an improvement in endothelial function includes an improvement in microvascular function.

Endothelial Dysfunction: Nitric Oxide, Peroxynitrite, and sclera/lamina cribrosa integrity

Endothelial dysfunction from decoupled eNOS and increased peroxynitrite formation could be exacerbated, during spaceflight, by other factor(s) known to affect endothelial dysfunction (e.g., fluid shifts, CO_2, radiation exposure, insulin sensitivity) (1140). There are multiple potential downstream implications of decoupled eNOS.

Peroxynitrite formation from an inefficient one-carbon metabolism pathway may influence risk for optic disc edema through an effect on elasticity of the extracellular matrix near the optic disc (lamina cribrosa) or sclera, possibly affecting the optic cup shape and/or rendering some individuals more vulnerable to pressure from a headward fluid shift during head-down tilt bed rest or spaceflight. The sclera is a dense layer of connective tissue that defines the shape and size of the eye. It is a strong framework that supports the retina so that it can withstand forces of intraocular pressure (sclera and lamina cribrosa) and intracranial pressure (lamina cribrosa), while providing a pathway for aqueous drainage and protecting the eye from trauma (1178). Scleral tissue contains about 50% collagen by weight (1179), embedded in a matrix of proteoglycans and non-collagenous glycoproteins. Scleral tissue remodeling is an ongoing dynamic process involving both synthesis and degradation of component elements. Matrix metalloproteinases (MMPs) are zinc-dependent proteolytic enzymes that degrade extracellular matrix components, including structural components such as collagen and elastin. There are several types of MMPs, and the ones found in scleral tissue include MMP-1, MMP-2, MMP-3, and MMP-9 (1178). Most vascular and scleral MMPs are constitutively latent because of the presence of inhibitors (e.g., NO) (1180). When activators are present, including peroxynitrite or even increased mechanical strain (1181), MMPs are activated and degradation is instigated. One study found high levels of active MMP-2 and MMP-9 (as opposed to latent forms of MMPs) in the optic nerve and optic rim area. The authors suggest that the high turnover of collagen within the optic nerve area may be an important mechanism for maintaining elasticity of the lamina cribrosa (1182). Additionally, cells in the optic nerve head and sclera have mechanosensory capabilities and respond to hydrostatic pressure by upregulating MMP-2 activity (1181, 1183). Osteocalcin can increase expression of matrix metalloproteinase proteins (1184) that contribute to soft tissue turnover. Inefficient one-carbon pathway function, and specifically reduced MTRR activity (due to the presence of the MTRR 66 G allele), is associated with higher circulating osteocalcin concentrations (1185). Interestingly, the MTRR 66 G variant that has been described above as a risk allele for optic disc edema in spaceflight and bed rest, has 4-fold lower activity than the wild type variant (1186). In addition to peroxynitrite affecting MMP activation, low folate status and higher homocysteine can directly activate MMP-9, thus affecting NO bioavailability, resulting in constrictive vascular remodeling, and reduced arterial compliance (1187-1189), and folic acid supplementation can attenuate an increase in MMP-9 activation due to a genetically-induced slower one-carbon pathway (1190). Activation of MMPs in the sclera could decrease firmness and elasticity and affect response to headward fluid shifts during HDT bed rest and spaceflight. As an aside, neural tube defects are a common result in offspring where there is maternal folate deficiency (1191), and maintaining closure of the neural tube during mammalian formation requires MMPs to be inactive (1192). In other words, an optimal folate status is necessary to maintain MMPs in their latent state to maintain closure of neural tubes during development, providing evidence that folate can directly impact extracellular matrix structure. Further evidence for the role of folate in collagen metabolism: folic acid supplementation increases collagen fiber density resulting in skin firmness (1193).

One more factor that can contribute to endothelial dysfunction and/or sclera structural differences is insulin resistance. Insulin resistance is documented in astronauts (192) and bed rest subjects (187, 206). There is also evidence to suggest altered insulin responsiveness and carbohydrate metabolism in astronauts who experienced optic disc edema, with a lower myo-inositol:chiro-inositol ratio (1129). Advanced glycation end products (AGEs) are another factor that can affect extracellular matrix stiffness. AGEs are generated through non-enzymatic reactions between sugars and proteins, lipids, or DNA. AGEs also result from diets rich in animal protein and fat, particularly where the meat has been cooked at high temperatures (1194). AGEs can affect sclera structure because they promote collagen crosslinking (1195, 1196), making it stiffer. Cell culture studies of interstitial tissue demonstrate that impaired glucose metabolism may affect crosslink formation through manipulation of MMP activation, in particular MMP-2 (1197). Serum MMP-2 has been measured in astronauts (192), but caution must be used in interpreting those results because it is known that serum (but not plasma) MMP measurements primarily reflect release of proteases by leukocytes during the clotting process in the blood collection tube (the use of anticoagulant can prevent this in vitro serum artifact) (1198-1201).

Taken together, a potential impact of the contributing factors that lead to endothelial dysfunction could result in SANS pathologies through multiple mechanisms. One potential impact is that endothelial dysfunction could lead to leakier vasculature and edema, which could block cerebrospinal fluid drainage and increase subarachnoid space pressure, impinging on the optic nerve and eye (1140, 1141). Additionally, there is the potential for structural alterations in sclera and lamina cribrosa as the result of oxidative stress and matrix

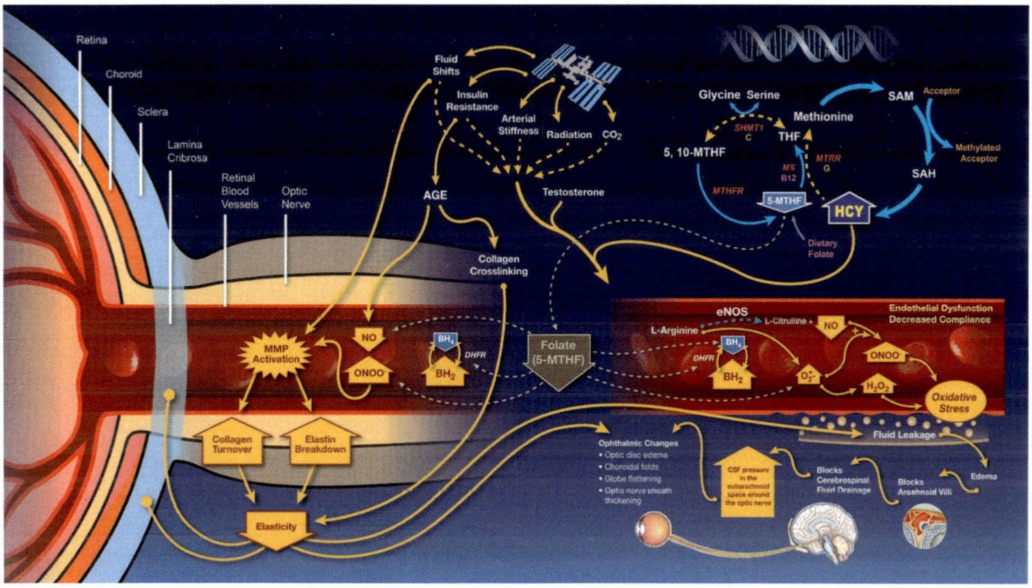

Figure 70. Depiction of hypothesized multi-hit mechanism relating one-carbon pathway genetics with ocular pathologies. Genetics and B-vitamin status lead to endothelial dysfunction and leaking microvasculature; the resulting edema could block cerebrospinal fluid (CSF) drainage, increasing subarachnoid space CSF pressure impinging on the optic nerve and eye (1140, 1141). Similarly, uncoupled eNOS yields increased oxidative stressors, including peroxynitrite. Peroxynitrite may affect the elasticity of the lamina cribrosa or sclera, affecting the optic cup shape and rendering some individuals vulnerable to pressure from a headward fluid shift during head-down tilt bed rest or spaceflight. MMPs are zinc-dependent proteolytic enzymes that degrade extracellular matrix components, including structural components such as collagen and elastin. Most vascular and scleral MMPs are constitutively latent because of the presence of inhibitors, including nitric oxide (1180). Cells in the optic nerve head and sclera have mechanosensory capabilities and respond to hydrostatic pressure by activating MMPs (1181). Additionally, low folate status and higher homocysteine can directly activate MMPs, affect nitric oxide bioavailability and production, cause constrictive vascular remodeling, and reduce arterial compliance (1188). Connective tissue remodeling could lead to changes in elasticity, fluid leakage, and ultimately ophthalmic changes. Adapted from (1136).

metalloproteinase (MMP) activation, altering scleral elasticity and thus making it more susceptible to develop ocular pathologies when exposed to spaceflight-induced fluid shifts and/or intracranial hypertension. These hypotheses are characterized in Figure 70, adapted from (1136).

Nutrients Associated with Ocular Health

Folate

Folate is the general term used to describe the vitamin folate and compounds that have activity similar to that of folate, (1202, 1203). Folic acid is the synthetic form of the vitamin used in vitamin supplements and fortified food products; however, it is not found to occur naturally in food. The reduction of folic acid and dihydrofolate by a cytosolic enzyme dihydrofolate reductase produces the active form of folate, tetrahydrofolate (THF). Tetrahydrofolate accepts single-carbon groups from reactions in amino acid metabolism to form active derivatives of THF (1202). This pathway is called one-carbon metabolism, and it not only requires folate, but also vitamin B_{12}, and vitamin B_6. The pathway is required for purine and pyrimidine synthesis, amino acid metabolism, and synthesis of the methylating agent S-adenosylmethionine (SAM) (Figure 63). Alterations in the efficiency of this pathway due to various single nucleotide polymorphism variants or low B-vitamin availability can lead to a buildup of certain intermediates, including homocysteine. Factors such as genetic polymorphisms, pharmacological agents, and dietary intake and status of folate, vitamin B_6, and vitamin B_{12} can influence plasma homocysteine concentration (1204, 1205).

Much of the homocysteine literature has focused on its association with coronary artery disease, stroke, and migraines (1204, 1206, 1207); however, some studies show associations of homocysteine with ophthalmic health issues. Issues such as age-related macular degeneration result from lipid deposits under the retinal pigment epithelium (1208) and decreased retinal vessel functionality (1209), and some theorize that age-related macular degeneration is similar to the development of cardiovascular disease (1210). Because homocysteine is a risk factor for cardiovascular disease, many have looked at relationships between homocysteine, or other metabolites and vitamins in the one-carbon metabolism pathway, and ophthalmic health issues such as age-related macular degeneration, dry eye, glaucoma, retinopathy, pseudoexfoliative glaucoma maculopathy, cataract, retinal vessel atherosclerosis, and optic neuropathy (1211-1216). For instance, a meta-analysis showed that elevated plasma homocysteine was associated with an increased risk of primary open-angle glaucoma (1217). Other meta-analyses have shown that increased serum homocysteine and low vitamin B_{12} status were independently associated with increased risk for age-related macular degeneration (1214, 1218). Daily supplementation with folate, vitamin B_6, and vitamin B_{12} is associated with a 30% to 40% decreased risk for age-related macular degeneration (1219).

Deficiency of folate leads to megaloblastic anemia. Low folate intake will cause RBC folate concentrations to diminish within 4 months. Bone marrow cells become megaloblastic (that is, they take on a nucleated, embryonic form), and anemia occurs after 4 to 5 months of low folate intake (1220). Folate deficiency in humans has been described as a 4-stage process (1221, 1222), including changes in serum folate (Stage 1), changes in RBC folate (Stage 2), defective DNA synthesis and elevated homocysteine (Stage 3), and clinical folate deficiency (Stage 4), manifested by macroovalocytosis (many large, oval cells in the blood), elevated mean corpuscular (RBC) volume, and large, nucleated embryonic cells.

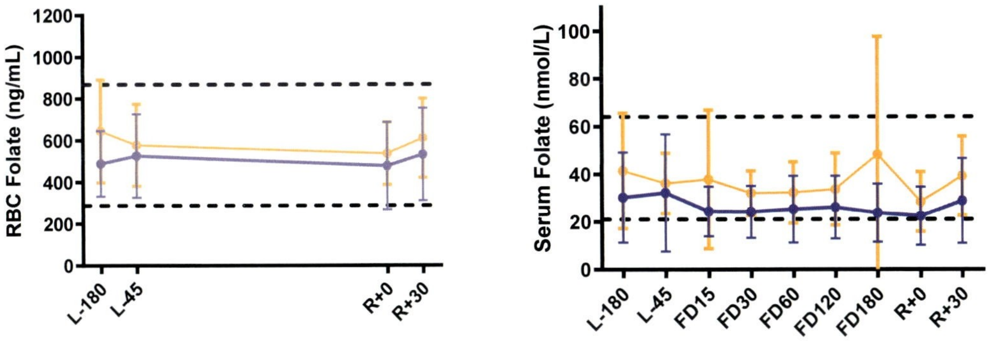

Figure 71. RBC (left) and serum folate (right) before, during, and after long-duration spaceflight (data are mean ± SD). Note: RBC folate data are not available during flight because of sample processing requirements.

Early spaceflight data showed a reduction in RBC folate after long-duration missions (110, 111). Serum folate is variable among crewmembers, but generally does not change during flight (Figure 71). Interestingly, serum folate was lower during spaceflight in crewmembers with SANS compared to those that did not have SANS (1128).

Vitamin B_{12}

Vitamin B_{12} functions in many enzymatic reactions, and deficiencies result in anemia, as well as neurological disorders. Vitamin B_{12} works as a cofactor for three different enzymatic reactions: 1) the conversion of homocysteine to methionine; 2) the conversion of L-methylmalonyl-coenzyme A (CoA) to succinyl-CoA; and 3) the isomerization of L-leucine and ß-leucine. Vitamin B_{12} deficiency may cause the accumulation of folate in the serum because of a reduction in B_{12}-dependent methyltransferase, also known as the methyl-folate trap (1223). Vitamin B_{12} also functions in the synthesis of choline, which can be converted to the neurotransmitter acetylcholine.

Unlike other water-soluble vitamins, vitamin B_{12} can be stored in the body for years. It is stored predominantly in the liver; however, smaller amounts can be found in the muscles, kidneys, bones, heart, brain, and spleen. About 2 to 5 mg of vitamin B_{12} is stored in the body (266). The size of B_{12} stores remains relatively stable, partly because urinary and fecal excretion decrease in direct relationship to decreases in the body pools. The half-life of vitamin B_{12} in humans is 350 to 400 days (266).

No evidence of toxicity has been found with vitamin B_{12} supplementation in amounts greater than the RDA (266), and no adverse effects have been reported to be caused by an excess of vitamin B_{12} (1224). If a person went for many years without adequate intake and/or supplementation, body stores could be depleted. Other factors that could contribute to a vitamin B_{12} deficiency include a decrease in gastric acidity, the presence of atrophic gastritis, and uncontrolled growth of bacteria accompanied by malabsorption of food- bound B_{12} (1225). Deficiency of vitamin B_{12} leads to pernicious anemia and demyelination of the central nervous system, effects on cognition and neurodegenerative diseases (1226-1228), and can lead to death (1229).

Methylmalonic acid is generally unchanged during spaceflight, suggesting that vitamin B_{12} deficiency is not a significant issue during flight. However, blood concentrations of methylmalonic acid were shown to be higher in crewmembers who experienced vision-related issues after flight than in those who did not have such issues (1128). This difference was evident before, during, and after spaceflight. Several studies support the notion that perturbations in the vitamin B_{12} metabolic pathway can cause ophthalmic health issues such as optic neuropathy and age-related macular degeneration (1211-1214).

Riboflavin

Riboflavin has been discussed in the Energy section, but it is also relevant to ocular health, mainly due to its antioxidant properties. Riboflavin status influences antioxidant enzymes such as superoxide dismutase, catalase, and glutathione peroxidase. Glutathione reductase requires riboflavin in the form of FAD to convert oxidized glutathione to the reduced form (1230).

Among other B vitamins, riboflavin has been used in dietary supplements for protecting against or treating cataracts (1230, 1231). Cataract formation among elderly is associated with riboflavin deficiency, but this does not appear to be the case for the general population (1232). Riboflavin status can affect glutathione concentration in the lens of the eye, and glutathione is protective against oxidative damage (1233).

Riboflavin status is low among Russian cosmonauts during intensive preflight training (1234). An initial look at riboflavin status from astronauts before and after 4- to 6-month missions to the ISS, as assessed by RBC glutathione reductase, showed no evidence of reduced riboflavin status after flight (111). We documented that a lower B-vitamin status (folate, B_6, and riboflavin, in particular) combined with the presence of specific genetic variants in the one-carbon metabolic pathway was associated with greater risk of ocular changes after flight (1129). Riboflavin status can affect the efficiency of enzymes in that pathway and can affect metabolite concentrations including homocysteine (1235).

Vitamin A

Another important vitamin involved in vision health is vitamin A. Vitamin A is a general term that refers to a family of fat-soluble compounds that are structurally similar to retinol and share its biological activity. Among these are retinol, α-carotene, β-carotene, and retinyl palmitate. Vitamin A or carotenoids can be found in dark green leafy vegetables and in vegetables and fruits that are yellow, orange, or red. Vitamin A plays a fundamental role in the retinal response to light. Inadequate vitamin A can result in night blindness, delayed light and dark adaptation, and dry eye (1236).

Beyond its essential role in the visual process, vitamin A is directly involved in gene expression, reproduction, embryonic development, and immunity. Vitamin A and β-carotene serve as biological antioxidants and have been shown, in multiple studies, to reduce the risk of cancer and coronary heart disease (1237, 1238). Vitamin A also plays a role, albeit sometimes indirectly, in the function of almost all of the body's organs (1239). Oxidative stress is increased during spaceflight, and this could affect cardiovascular health and cancer risk, as described in other sections of this book. Vitamin A status may play a critical role in maintaining antioxidant health during spaceflight; however, as with many antioxidants, the desire to supplement with high doses in the hope of staving off one disease is high, but is unwarranted and potentially counterproductive. Excess vitamin A, in levels on the order of twice the recommended daily intake, has been shown to increase bone resorption and fracture risk (809, 1240-1242). Furthermore, supplementation with β-carotene should be done with caution (either alone or with vitamin A or in combination with vitamin E), because of unanticipated outcomes of an increased risk of lung cancer in smokers (1243, 1244). This increased risk among smokers might be related to pro-oxidant actions of ß-carotene in the lung.

When considering pre- and post-spaceflight data, there is a significant interaction between the effects of landing site and spaceflight on serum levels of both retinol and retinol-binding protein (111). Russian landings are different from U.S. landings in that blood samples are usually collected later (8 to 24 hours after landing) than on Space Shuttle missions (2 to 4 hours after landing) because of the logistics of the landing site and crew return to data collection facilities. This time delay is important, as crewmembers begin to eat and drink soon after landing, and the spaceflight fluid shift (described in Chapter 5) begins to readapt to gravity immediately. Serum retinol decreased from 0.73 ± 0.17 μg/mL to 0.59 ± 0.13 μg/mL when landings were in Russia, and increased from 0.52 ± 0.09 μg/mL to 0.63 ± 0.12 μg/mL when landings were in the United States. Similarly, retinol-binding protein decreased from 61.4 ± 5.6 to 50.9 ± 8.4 mg/L when landings were in Russia, and increased from 49.2 ± 9.2 to 53.0 ± 8.7 mg/L when landings were in the United States. These differences in landing sites could be related to the time delay in sample collection, the fact that crew-members might have consumed food during the time delay, or even variations in the stress response at different sites. These data, however, do not provide evidence that there is a deficiency of any sort for vitamin A.

In-flight vitamin A data have been collected as part of Nutrition experiments on the ISS. Figure 72 shows that no significant changes in retinol or ß-carotene occur during spaceflight.

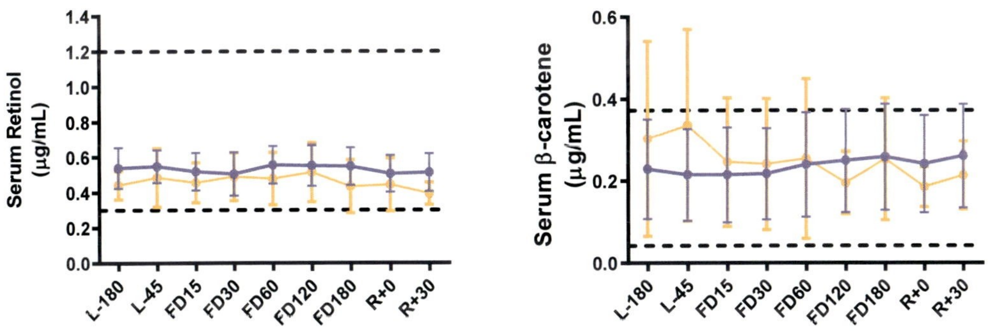

Figure 72. Serum retinol (left) and ß-carotene (right) before, during, and after long-duration spaceflight. Dashed lines represent normal range. Data are mean ± SD.

References for Chapter 10

1. Smith SM, Zwart SR, Kloeris V, Heer M. Nutritional biochemistry of space flight. New York: Nova Science Publishers; 2009.

19. Garrett-Bakelman FE, Darshi M, Green SJ, Gur RC, Lin L, Macias BR, McKenna MJ, Meydan C, Mishra T, Nasrini J, Piening BD, Rizzardi LF, Sharma K, Siamwala JH, Taylor L, Vitaterna MH, Afkarian M, Afshinnekoo E, Ahadi S, Ambati A, Arya M, Bezdan D, Callahan CM, Chen S, Choi AMK, Chlipala GE, Contrepois K, Covington M, Crucian BE, De Vivo I, Dinges DF, Ebert DJ, Feinberg JI, Gandara JA, George KA, Goutsias J, Grills GS, Hargens AR, Heer M, Hillary RP, Hoofnagle AN, Hook VYH, Jenkinson G, Jiang P, Keshavarzian A, Laurie SS, Lee-McMullen B, Lumpkins SB, MacKay M, Maienschein-Cline MG, Melnick AM, Moore TM, Nakahira K, Patel HH, Pietrzyk R, Rao V, Saito R, Salins DN, Schilling JM, Sears DD, Sheridan CK, Stenger MB, Tryggvadottir R, Urban AE, Vaisar T, Van Espen B, Zhang J, Ziegler MG, Zwart SR, Charles JB, Kundrot CE, Scott GBI, Bailey SM, Basner M, Feinberg AP, Lee SMC, Mason CE, Mignot E, Rana BK, Smith SM, Snyder MP, Turek FW. The NASA Twins Study: A multidimensional analysis of a year-long human spaceflight. Science. 2019;364.

31. Stenger MB, Tarver WJ, Brunstetter T, Gibson CR, Laurie SS, Macias BR, Mader TH, Otto C, Smith SM, Zwart SR. Evidence Report: Risk of spaceflight associated neuro-ocular syndrome (SANS) [online]. National Aeronautics and Space Administration. https://humanresearchroadmap.nasa.gov/evidence/reports/SANS.pdf. 2017.

110. Smith SM, Davis-Street JE, Rice BL, Nillen JL, Gillman PL, Block G. Nutritional status assessment in semiclosed environments: ground-based and space flight studies in humans. J Nutr. 2001;131:2053-61.

111. Smith SM, Zwart SR, Block G, Rice BL, Davis-Street JE. The nutritional status of astronauts is altered after long-term space flight aboard the International Space Station. J Nutr. 2005;135:437-43.

187. Kenny HC, Rudwill F, Breen L, Salanova M, Blottner D, Heise T, Heer M, Blanc S, O'Gorman DJ. Bed rest and resistive vibration exercise unveil novel links between skeletal muscle mitochondrial function and insulin resistance. Diabetologia. 2017;60:1491-501.

192. Hughson RL, Robertson AD, Arbeille P, Shoemaker JK, Rush JW, Fraser KS, Greaves DK. Increased postflight carotid artery stiffness and inflight insulin resistance resulting from 6-mo spaceflight in male and female astronauts. Am J Physiol Heart Circ Physiol. 2016;310:H628-38.

206. Mazzucco S, Agostini F, Biolo G. Inactivity-mediated insulin resistance is associated with upregulated pro-inflammatory fatty acids in human cell membranes. Clin Nutr. 2010;29:386-90.

262. Morgan JLL, Zwart SR, Heer M, Ploutz-Snyder R, Ericson K, Smith SM. Bone metabolism and nutritional status during 30-day head-down-tilt bed rest. J Appl Physiol (1985). 2012;113:1519-29.

266. Institute of Medicine. Dietary reference intakes for thiamin, riboflavin, niacin, vitamin B_6, folate, vitamin B_{12}, pantothenic acid, biotin, and choline. Washington, DC: National Academy Press; 2000.

289. Smith SM, Krauhs JM, Leach CS. Regulation of body fluid volume and electrolyte concentrations in spaceflight. Adv Space Biol Med. 1997;6:123-65.

809. Palacios C. The role of nutrients in bone health, from A to Z. Crit Rev Food Sci Nutr. 2006;46:621-8.

1114. Rastegar N, Eckart P, Mertz M. Radiation-induced cataract in astronauts and cosmonauts. Graefes Arch Clin Exp Ophthalmol. 2002;240:543-7.

1115. Cucinotta FA, Manuel FK, Jones J, Iszard G, Murrey J, Djojonegro B, Wear M. Space radiation and cataracts in astronauts. Radiat Res. 2001;156:460-6.

1116. Chylack LT, Jr., Peterson LE, Feiveson AH, Wear ML, Manuel FK, Tung WH, Hardy DS, Marak LJ, Cucinotta FA. NASA study of cataract in astronauts (NASCA). Report 1: cross-sectional study of the relationship of exposure to space radiation and risk of lens opacity. Radiat Res. 2009;172:10-20.

1117. Jones JA, McCarten M, Manuel K, Djojonegoro B, Murray J, Feiversen A, Wear M. Cataract formation mechanisms and risk in aviation and space crews. Aviat Space Environ Med. 2007;78:A56-66.

1118. Chylack LT, Jr., Feiveson AH, Peterson LE, Tung WH, Wear ML, Marak LJ, Hardy DS, Chappell LJ, Cucinotta FA. NASCA Report 2: longitudinal study of relationship of exposure to space radiation and risk of lens opacity. Radiat Res. 2012;178:25-32.

1119. Agte V, Tarwadi K. The importance of nutrition in the prevention of ocular disease with special reference to cataract. Ophthalmic Res. 2010;44:166-72.

1120. Tan AG, Mitchell P, Flood VM, Burlutsky G, Rochtchina E, Cumming RG, Wang JJ. Antioxidant nutrient intake and the long-term incidence of age-related cataract: the Blue Mountains Eye Study. Am J Clin Nutr. 2008;87:1899-905.

1121. Leske MC, Wu SY, Hyman L, Sperduto R, Underwood B, Chylack LT, Milton RC, Srivastava S, Ansari N. Biochemical factors in the lens opacities. Case-control study. The Lens Opacities Case-Control Study Group. Arch Ophthalmol. 1995;113:1113-9.

1122. Taylor A, Hobbs M. 2001 assessment of nutritional influences on risk for cataract. Nutrition. 2001;17:845-57.

1123. Wang A, Han J, Jiang Y, Zhang D. Association of vitamin A and beta-carotene with risk for age-related cataract: A meta-analysis. Nutrition. 2014;30:1113-21.

1124. Lee AG, Mader TH, Gibson CR, Tarver W, Rabiei P, Riascos RF, Galdamez LA, Brunstetter T. Spaceflight associated neuro-ocular syndrome (SANS) and the neuro-ophthalmologic effects of microgravity: a review and an update. NPJ Microgravity. 2020;6:7.

1125. Mader TH, Gibson CR, Pass AF, Kramer LA, Lee AG, Fogarty J, Tarver WJ, Dervay JP, Hamilton DR, Sargsyan A, Phillips JL, Tran D, Lipsky W, Choi J, Stern C, Kuyumjian R, Polk JD. Optic disc edema, globe flattening, choroidal folds, and hyperopic shifts observed in astronauts after long-duration space flight. Ophthalmology. 2011;118:2058-69.

1126. Laurie SS, Lee SMC, Macias BR, Patel N, Stern C, Young M, Stenger MB. Optic disc edema and choroidal engorgement in astronauts during spaceflight and individuals exposed to bed rest. JAMA Ophthalmol. 2020;138:165-72.

1127. Lawley JS, Petersen LG, Howden EJ, Sarma S, Cornwell WK, Zhang R, Whitworth LA, Williams MA, Levine BD. Effect of gravity and microgravity on intracranial pressure. J Physiol. 2017;595:2115-27.

1128. Zwart SR, Gibson CR, Mader TH, Ericson K, Ploutz-Snyder R, Heer M, Smith SM. Vision changes after spaceflight are related to alterations in folate- and vitamin B-12-dependent one-carbon metabolism. J Nutr. 2012;142:427-31.

1129. Zwart SR, Gregory JF, Zeisel SH, Gibson CR, Mader TH, Kinchen JM, Ueland PM, Ploutz-Snyder R, Heer MA, Smith SM. Genotype, B-vitamin status, and androgens affect spaceflight-induced ophthalmic changes. FASEB J. 2016;30:141-8.

1130. Macias BR, Patel NB, Gibson CR, Samuels BC, Laurie SS, Otto C, Ferguson CR, Lee SMC, Ploutz-Snyder R, Kramer LA, Mader TH, Brunstetter T, Stenger MB. Association of long-duration spaceflight with anterior and posterior ocular structure changes in astronauts and their recovery. JAMA Ophthalmol. 2020;138:553-9.

1131. Myasnikov VI, Stepanova SI. Features of cerebral hemodynamics in cosmonauts before and after flight on the Mir orbital station. Orbital Station Mir. Moscow: Institute for Biomedical Problems; 2008. p. 300-5.

1132. Buckey JC, Phillips SD, Anderson AP, Chepko AB, Archambault-Leger V, Gui J, Fellows AM. Microgravity-induced ocular changes are related to body weight. Am J Physiol Regul Integr Comp Physiol. 2018;315:R496-R9.

1133. Zwart SR, Gibson CR, Smith SM. Spaceflight ophthalmic changes, diet, and vitamin metabolism. In: Preedy VR, editor. Handbook of diet, nutrition and the eye. Waltham: Academic Press; 2014. p. 393-9.

1134. Laurie SS, Vizzeri G, Taibbi G, Ferguson CR, Hu X, Lee SMC, Ploutz-Snyder R, Smith SM, Zwart SR, Stenger MB. Effects of short-term mild hypercapnia during head-down tilt on intracranial pressure and ocular structures in healthy human subjects. Physiol Rep. 2017;5:e13302.

1135. Laurie SS, Macias BR, Dunn JT, Young M, Stern C, Lee SMC, Stenger MB. Optic disc edema after 30 days of strict head-down tilt bed rest. Ophthalmology. 2019;126:467-8.

1136. Zwart SR, Laurie SS, Chen JJ, Macias BR, Lee SMC, Stenger M, Grantham B, Carey K, Young M, Smith SM. Association of genetics and B vitamin status with the magnitude of optic disc edema during 30-day strict head-down tilt bed rest. JAMA Ophthalmol. 2019;137:1195-200.

1137. Taibbi G, Cromwell RL, Zanello SB, Yarbough PO, Ploutz-Snyder RJ, Godley BF, Vizzeri G. Ocular outcomes comparison between 14- and 70-day head-down-tilt bed rest. Invest Ophthalmol Vis Sci. 2016;57:495-501.

1138. Taibbi G, Cromwell RL, Zanello SB, Yarbough PO, Ploutz-Snyder RJ, Godley BF, Vizzeri G. Ophthalmological evaluation of integrated resistance and aerobic training during 70-day bed rest. Aerosp Med Hum Perform. 2017;88:633-40.

1139. Taibbi G, Kaplowitz K, Cromwell RL, Godley BF, Zanello SB, Vizzeri G. Effects of 30-day head-down bed rest on ocular structures and visual function in a healthy subject. Aviat Space Environ Med. 2013;84:148-54.

1140. Zwart SR, Gibson CR, Gregory JF, Mader TH, Stover PJ, Zeisel SH, Smith SM. Astronaut ophthalmic syndrome. FASEB J. 2017;31:3746-56.

1141. Smith SM, Zwart SR. Spaceflight-related ocular changes: the potential role of genetics, and the potential of B vitamins as a countermeasure. Curr Opin Clin Nutr Metab Care. 2018;21:481-8.

1142. Herbig K, Chiang EP, Lee LR, Hills J, Shane B, Stover PJ. Cytoplasmic serine hydroxymethyltransferase mediates competition between folate-dependent deoxyribonucleotide and S-adenosylmethionine biosyntheses. J Biol Chem. 2002;277:38381-9.

1143. Stover PJ. One-carbon metabolism-genome interactions in folate-associated pathologies. J Nutr. 2009;139:2402-5.

1144. Ducker GS, Rabinowitz JD. One-carbon metabolism in health and disease. Cell Metab. 2017;25:27-42.

1145. Allen LH, Miller JW, de Groot L, Rosenberg IH, Smith AD, Refsum H, Raiten DJ. Biomarkers of Nutrition for Development (BOND): Vitamin B-12 review. J Nutr. 2018;148:1995S-2027S.

1146. Molloy AM, Pangilinan F, Brody LC. Genetic risk factors for folate-responsive neural tube defects. Annu Rev Nutr. 2017;37:269-91.

1147. Zaric BL, Obradovic M, Bajic V, Haidara MA, Jovanovic M, Isenovic ER. Homocysteine and hyperhomocysteinaemia. Curr Med Chem. 2019;26:2948-61.

1148. Maestro de las Casas C, Epeldegui M, Tudela C, Varela-Moreiras G, Perez-Miguelsanz J. High exogenous homocysteine modifies eye development in early chick embryos. Birth Defects Res A Clin Mol Teratol. 2003;67:35-40.

1149. Maestro-de-las-Casas C, Perez-Miguelsanz J, Lopez-Gordillo Y, Maldonado E, Partearroyo T, Varela-Moreiras G, Martinez-Alvarez C. Maternal folic acid-deficient diet causes congenital malformations in the mouse eye. Birth Defects Res A Clin Mol Teratol. 2013;97:587-96.

1150. Li J, Zhang H, Shi M, Yan L, Xie M. Homocysteine is linked to macular edema in type 2 diabetes. Curr Eye Res. 2014;39:730-5.

1151. Ajith TA, Ranimenon. Homocysteine in ocular diseases. Clin Chim Acta. 2015;450:316-21.

1152. Perna AF, Ingrosso D, De Santo NG. Homocysteine and oxidative stress. Amino Acids. 2003;25:409-17.

1153. Godo S, Shimokawa H. Endothelial functions. Arterioscler Thromb Vasc Biol. 2017;37:e108-e14.

1154. Flammer AJ, Anderson T, Celermajer DS, Creager MA, Deanfield J, Ganz P, Hamburg NM, Luscher TF, Shechter M, Taddei S, Vita JA, Lerman A. The assessment of endothelial function: from research into clinical practice. Circulation. 2012;126:753-67.

1155. Kietadisorn R, Juni RP, Moens AL. Tackling endothelial dysfunction by modulating NOS uncoupling: new insights into its pathogenesis and therapeutic possibilities. Am J Physiol Endocrinol Metab. 2012;302:E481-95.

1156. Siragusa M, Fleming I. The eNOS signalosome and its link to endothelial dysfunction. Pflugers Arch. 2016;468:1125-37.

1157. Katusic ZS. Vascular endothelial dysfunction: does tetrahydrobiopterin play a role? Am J Physiol Heart Circ Physiol. 2001;281:H981-6.

1158. Vasquez-Vivar J, Kalyanaraman B, Martasek P, Hogg N, Masters BS, Karoui H, Tordo P, Pritchard KA, Jr. Superoxide generation by endothelial nitric oxide synthase: the influence of cofactors. Proc Natl Acad Sci USA. 1998;95:9220-5.

1159. Pathak R, Cheema AK, Boca SM, Krager KJ, Hauer-Jensen M, Aykin-Burns N. Modulation of radiation response by the tetrahydrobiopterin pathway. Antioxidants (Basel). 2015;4:68-81.

1160. Kohnen SL, Mouithys-Mickalad AA, Deby-Dupont GP, Deby CM, Lamy ML, Noels AF. Oxidation of tetrahydrobiopterin by peroxynitrite or oxoferryl species occurs by a radical pathway. Free Radic Res. 2001;35:709-21.

1161. Antoniades C, Shirodaria C, Warrick N, Cai S, de Bono J, Lee J, Leeson P, Neubauer S, Ratnatunga C, Pillai R, Refsum H, Channon KM. 5-methyltetrahydrofolate rapidly improves endothelial function and decreases superoxide production in human vessels: effects on vascular tetrahydrobiopterin availability and endothelial nitric oxide synthase coupling. Circulation. 2006;114:1193-201.

1162. Verhaar MC, Stroes E, Rabelink TJ. Folates and cardiovascular disease. Arterioscler Thromb Vasc Biol. 2002;22:6-13.

1163. Antoniades C, Shirodaria C, Leeson P, Baarholm OA, Van-Assche T, Cunnington C, Pillai R, Ratnatunga C, Tousoulis D, Stefanadis C, Refsum H, Channon KM. MTHFR 677 C>T Polymorphism reveals functional importance for 5-methyltetrahydrofolate, not homocysteine, in regulation of vascular redox state and endothelial function in human atherosclerosis. Circulation. 2009;119:2507-15.

1164. Moens AL, Champion HC, Claeys MJ, Tavazzi B, Kaminski PM, Wolin MS, Borgonjon DJ, Van Nassauw L, Haile A, Zviman M, Bedja D, Wuyts FL, Elsaesser RS, Cos P, Gabrielson KL, Lazzarino G, Paolocci N, Timmermans JP, Vrints CJ, Kass DA. High-dose folic acid pretreatment blunts cardiac dysfunction during ischemia coupled to maintenance of high-energy phosphates and reduces postreperfusion injury. Circulation. 2008;117:1810-9.

1165. Moens AL, Vrints CJ, Claeys MJ, Timmermans JP, Champion HC, Kass DA. Mechanisms and potential therapeutic targets for folic acid in cardiovascular disease. Am J Physiol Heart Circ Physiol. 2008;294:H1971-7.

1166. Chalupsky K, Kracun D, Kanchev I, Bertram K, Gorlach A. Folic acid promotes recycling of tetrahydrobiopterin and protects against hypoxia-induced pulmonary hypertension by recoupling endothelial nitric oxide synthase. Antioxid Redox Signal. 2015;23:1076-91.

1167. Helfand M, Buckley DI, Freeman M, Fu R, Rogers K, Fleming C, Humphrey LL. Emerging risk factors for coronary heart disease: a summary of systematic reviews conducted for the U.S. Preventive Services Task Force. Ann Intern Med. 2009;151:496-507.

1168. Den Heijer M, Lewington S, Clarke R. Homocysteine, MTHFR and risk of venous thrombosis: a meta-analysis of published epidemiological studies. J Thromb Haemost. 2005;3:292-9.

1169. Verhaar MC, Wever RM, Kastelein JJ, van Dam T, Koomans HA, Rabelink TJ. 5-methyltetrahydrofolate, the active form of folic acid, restores endothelial function in familial hypercholesterolemia. Circulation. 1998;97:237-41.

1170. Title LM, Ur E, Giddens K, McQueen MJ, Nassar BA. Folic acid improves endothelial dysfunction in type 2 diabetes--an effect independent of homocysteine-lowering. Vasc Med. 2006;11:101-9.

1171. Doshi SN, McDowell IF, Moat SJ, Payne N, Durrant HJ, Lewis MJ, Goodfellow J. Folic acid improves endothelial function in coronary artery disease via mechanisms largely independent of homocysteine lowering. Circulation. 2002;105:22-6.

1172. Hoch AZ, Lynch SL, Jurva JW, Schimke JE, Gutterman DD. Folic acid supplementation improves vascular function in amenorrheic runners. Clin J Sport Med. 2010;20:205-10.

1173. Hoch AZ, Papanek P, Szabo A, Widlansky ME, Gutterman DD. Folic acid supplementation improves vascular function in professional dancers with endothelial dysfunction. PM R. 2011;3:1005-12.

1174. Stanhewicz AE, Kenney WL. Role of folic acid in nitric oxide bioavailability and vascular endothelial function. Nutr Rev. 2017;75:61-70.

1175. Verhaar MC, Wever RM, Kastelein JJ, van Loon D, Milstien S, Koomans HA, Rabelink TJ. Effects of oral folic acid supplementation on endothelial function in familial hypercholesterolemia. A randomized placebo-controlled trial. Circulation. 1999;100:335-8.

1176. Stanhewicz AE, Alexander LM, Kenney WL. Folic acid supplementation improves microvascular function in older adults through nitric oxide-dependent mechanisms. Clin Sci (Lond). 2015;129:159-67.

1177. Romero SA, Gagnon D, Adams AN, Moralez G, Kouda K, Jaffery MF, Cramer MN, Crandall CG. Folic acid ingestion improves skeletal muscle blood flow during graded handgrip and plantar flexion exercise in aged humans. Am J Physiol Heart Circ Physiol. 2017;313:H658-H66.

1178. Harper AR, Summers JA. The dynamic sclera: extracellular matrix remodeling in normal ocular growth and myopia development. Exp Eye Res. 2015;133:100-11.

1179. Keeley FW, Morin JD, Vesely S. Characterization of collagen from normal human sclera. Exp Eye Res. 1984;39:533-42.

1180. Chen H-H, Wang DL. Nitric Oxide Inhibits Matrix Metalloproteinase-2 Expression via the Induction of Activating Transcription Factor 3 in Endothelial Cells. Mol Pharmacol. 2004;65:1130-40.

1181. Shelton L, Rada JS. Effects of cyclic mechanical stretch on extracellular matrix synthesis by human scleral fibroblasts. Exp Eye Res. 2007;84:314-22.

1182. Hussain AA, Lee Y, Zhang JJ, Marshall J. Characterization of the gelatinase system of the laminar human optic nerve, and surrounding annulus of Bruch's membrane, choroid, and sclera. Invest Ophthalmol Vis Sci. 2014;55:2358-64.

1183. Kirwan RP, Crean JK, Fenerty CH, Clark AF, O'Brien CJ. Effect of cyclical mechanical stretch and exogenous transforming growth factor-beta1 on matrix metalloproteinase-2 activity in lamina cribrosa cells from the human optic nerve head. J Glaucoma. 2004;13:327-34.

1184. Varga F, Rumpler M, Spitzer S, Karlic H, Klaushofer K. Osteocalcin attenuates T3- and increases vitamin D3-induced expression of MMP-13 in mouse osteoblasts. Endocr J. 2009;56:441-50.

1185. Kim DJ, Park BL, Koh JM, Kim GS, Kim LH, Cheong HS, Shin HD, Hong JM, Kim TH, Shin HI, Park EK, Kim SY. Methionine synthase reductase polymorphisms are associated with serum osteocalcin levels in postmenopausal women. Exp Mol Med. 2006;38:519-24.

1186. Olteanu H, Banerjee R. Human methionine synthase reductase, a soluble P-450 reductase-like dual flavoprotein, is sufficient for NADPH-dependent methionine synthase activation. J Biol Chem. 2001;276:35558-63.

1187. Munjal C, Givvimani S, Qipshidze N, Tyagi N, Falcone JC, Tyagi SC. Mesenteric vascular remodeling in hyperhomocysteinemia. Mol Cell Biochem. 2011;348:99-108.

1188. Arcaro G, Fava C, Dagradi R, Faccini G, Gaino S, Degan M, Lechi C, Lechi A, Minuz P. Acute hyperhomocysteinemia induces a reduction in arterial distensibility and compliance. J Hypertens. 2004;22:775-81.

1189. Fu WY, Dudman NP, Perry MA, Wang XL. Homocysteine attenuates hemodynamic responses to nitric oxide in vivo. Atherosclerosis. 2002;161:169-76.

1190. Tyagi N, Kandel M, Munjal C, Qipshidze N, Vacek JC, Pushpakumar SB, Metreveli N, Tyagi SC. Homocysteine mediated decrease in bone blood flow and remodeling: role of folic acid. J Orthop Res. 2011;29:1511-6.

1191. Crider KS, Qi YP, Devine O, Tinker SC, Berry RJ. Modeling the impact of folic acid fortification and supplementation on red blood cell folate concentrations and predicted neural tube defect risk in the United States: have we reached optimal prevention? Am J Clin Nutr. 2018;107:1027-34.

1192. Shinotsuka N, Yamaguchi Y, Nakazato K, Matsumoto Y, Mochizuki A, Miura M. Caspases and matrix metalloproteases facilitate collective behavior of non-neural ectoderm after hindbrain neuropore closure. BMC Dev Biol. 2018;18:17.

1193. Fischer F, Achterberg V, Marz A, Puschmann S, Rahn CD, Lutz V, Kruger A, Schwengler H, Jaspers S, Koop U, Blatt T, Wenck H, Gallinat S. Folic acid and creatine improve the firmness of human skin in vivo. J Cosmet Dermatol. 2011;10:15-23.

1194. Sharma C, Kaur A, Thind SS, Singh B, Raina S. Advanced glycation End-products (AGEs): an emerging concern for processed food industries. J Food Sci Technol. 2015;52:7561-76.

1195. Hegab Z, Gibbons S, Neyses L, Mamas MA. Role of advanced glycation end products in cardiovascular disease. World J Cardiol. 2012;4:90-102.

1196. Sharma Y, Saxena S, Mishra A, Saxena A, Natu SM. Advanced glycation end products and diabetic retinopathy. J Ocul Biol Dis Infor. 2012;5:63-9.

1197. Kuzuya M, Asai T, Kanda S, Maeda K, Cheng XW, Iguchi A. Glycation cross-links inhibit matrix metalloproteinase-2 activation in vascular smooth muscle cells cultured on collagen lattice. Diabetologia. 2001;44:433-6.

1198. Jung K, Meisser A, Bischof P. Blood sampling as critical preanalytical determinant to use circulating MMP and TIMP as surrogate markers for pathological processes. Int J Cancer. 2005;116:1000-1; author reply 2-3.

1199. Mannello F, Luchetti F, Canonico B, Papa S. Effect of anticoagulants and cell separation media as preanalytical determinants on zymographic analysis of plasma matrix metalloproteinases. Clin Chem. 2003;49:1956-7.

1200. Verspaget HW, Kuyvenhoven JP, van Hoek B. Preanalytical conditions and circulating matrix metalloproteinases. Transplantation. 2005;79:745-6.

1201. Zucker S, Cao J. Measurement of matrix metalloproteinases in serum of patients with melanoma: snarled in technical pitfalls. Clin Cancer Res. 2005;11:5069-70.

1202. Bailey LB, Caudill MA. Folate. In: Erdman JW, Jr., MacDonald IA, Zeisel SH, editors. Present knowledge in nutrition. 9th ed. Washington, DC: International Life Sciences Institute; 2010. p. 321-42.

1203. Chan YM, Bailey R, O'Connor DL. Folate. Adv Nutr. 2013;4:123-5.

1204. Nygard O, Vollset SE, Refsum H, Stensvold I, Tverdal A, Nordrehaug JE, Ueland M, Kvale G. Total plasma homocysteine and cardiovascular risk profile. The Hordaland Homocysteine Study. JAMA. 1995;274:1526-33.

1205. Finkelstein JD. The metabolism of homocysteine: pathways and regulation. Eur J Pediatr. 1998;157 Suppl 2:S40-4.

1206. Pizza V, Agresta A, Agresta A, Lamaida E, Lamaida N, Infante F, Capasso A. Migraine and genetic polymorphisms: an overview. Open Neurol J. 2012;6:65-70.

1207. Homocysteine Studies Collaboration. Homocysteine and risk of ischemic heart disease and stroke: a meta-analysis. JAMA. 2002;288:2015-22.

1208. Ebrahimi KB, Handa JT. Lipids, lipoproteins, and age-related macular degeneration. J Lipids. 2011;2011:802059.

1209. Burgansky-Eliash Z, Barash H, Nelson D, Grinvald A, Sorkin A, Loewenstein A, Barak A. Retinal blood flow velocity in patients with age-related macular degeneration. Curr Eye Res. 2014;39:304-11.

1210. Evans J. Should we be taking B vitamins to prevent age-related macular degeneration? Not yet, but worth doing more research. Am J Clin Nutr. 2013;98:4-5.

1211. Roda M, di Geronimo N, Pellegrini M, Schiavi C. Nutritional optic neuropathies: State of the art and emerging evidences. Nutrients. 2020;12.

1212. Chu C, Scanlon P. Vitamin B_{12} deficiency optic neuropathy detected by asymptomatic screening. BMJ case reports. 2011 3083013]; 2011: Available from: https://www.ncbi.nlm.nih.gov/pmc/articles/PMC3083013/.

1213. Jalil A, Usmani HA, Khan MI, Blakely EL, Taylor RW, Vassallo G, Ashworth J. Bilateral paediatric optic neuropathy precipitated by vitamin B_{12} deficiency and a novel mitochondrial DNA mutation. Int Ophthalmol. 2013;33:687-90.

1214. Gopinath B, Flood VM, Rochtchina E, Wang JJ, Mitchell P. Homocysteine, folate, vitamin B-12, and 10-y incidence of age-related macular degeneration. Am J Clin Nutr. 2013;98:129-35.

1215. Sekeryapan B, Oner V, Kirbas A, Turkyilmaz K, Durmus M. Plasma homocysteine levels in dry eye patients. Cornea. 2013;32:e94-6.

1216. George AK, Majumder A, Ice H, Homme RP, Eyob W, Tyagi SC, Singh M. Genes and genetics in hyperhomocysteinemia and the "1-carbon metabolism": implications for retinal structure and eye functions. Can J Physiol Pharmacol. 2020;98:51-60.

1217. Xu F, Zhao X, Zeng SM, Li L, Zhong HB, Li M. Homocysteine, B vitamins, methylenetetrahydrofolate reductase gene, and risk of primary open-angle glaucoma: a meta-analysis. Ophthalmology. 2012;119:2493-9.

1218. Rochtchina E, Wang JJ, Flood VM, Mitchell P. Elevated serum homocysteine, low serum vitamin B_{12}, folate, and age-related macular degeneration: the Blue Mountains Eye Study. Am J Ophthalmol. 2007;143:344-6.

1219. Christen WG, Glynn RJ, Chew EY, Albert CM, Manson JE. Folic acid, pyridoxine, and cyanocobalamin combination treatment and age-related macular degeneration in women: the Women's Antioxidant and Folic Acid Cardiovascular Study. Arch Intern Med. 2009;169:335-41.

1220. Groff J, Gropper S. Advanced nutrition and human metabolism, 3rd edition. St. Paul, MN: Wadsworth Publishing; 2000.

1221. Herbert V. Development of human folate deficiency. In: Picciano MF, Sotokstad ELR, Gregory JFI, editors. Folic acid metabolism in health and disease. New York: Wiley-Liss; 1990. p. 195-210.

1222. Herbert V. Folic acid. In: Shils ME, Olson JA, Shike M, Ross AC, editors. Modern nutrition in health and disease. 9th ed. Baltimore, MD: Lippincott Williams & Wilkins; 1999.

1223. Shin YS, Beuhring KU, Stokstad EL. The relationships between vitamin B_{12} and folic acid and the effect of methionine on folate metabolism. Mol Cell Biochem. 1975;9:97-108.

1224. EFSA Panel on Dietetic Products Nutrition and Allergies. Overview on Tolerable Upper Intake Levels as derived by the Scientific Committee on Food (SCF). 2018 [Version 4]; Available from: https://www.efsa.europa.eu/sites/default/files/assets/UL_Summary_tables.pdf.

1225. van Asselt DZ, van den Broek WJ, Lamers CB, Corstens FH, Hoefnagels WH. Free and protein-bound cobalamin absorption in healthy middle-aged and older subjects. J Am Geriatr Soc. 1996;44:949-53.

1226. O'Connor DMA, Laird EJ, Carey D, O'Halloran AM, Clarke R, Kenny RA, Molloy AM. Plasma concentrations of vitamin B_{12} and folate and global cognitive function in an older population: cross-sectional findings from The Irish Longitudinal Study on Ageing (TILDA). Br J Nutr. 2020;124:602-10.

1227. Schaffner A, Li X, Gomez-Llorente Y, Leandrou E, Memou A, Clemente N, Yao C, Afsari F, Zhi L, Pan N, Morohashi K, Hua X, Zhou MM, Wang C, Zhang H, Chen SG, Elliott CJ, Rideout H, Ubarretxena-Belandia I, Yue Z. Vitamin B_{12} modulates Parkinson's disease LRRK2 kinase activity through allosteric regulation and confers neuroprotection. Cell Res. 2019;29:313-29.

1228. Ma F, Zhou X, Li Q, Zhao J, Song A, An P, Du Y, Xu W, Huang G. Effects of folic acid and vitamin B_{12}, alone and in combination on cognitive function and inflammatory factors in the elderly with mild cognitive impairment: A single-blind experimental design. Curr Alzheimer Res. 2019;16:622-32.

1229. Stabler SP. Vitamin B_{12}. In: Erdman JW, Jr., MacDonald IA, Zeisel SH, editors. Present knowledge in nutrition. 9th ed. Washington, DC: International Life Sciences Institute Press; 2010. p. 343-57.

1230. Suwannasom N, Kao I, Pruss A, Georgieva R, Baumler H. Riboflavin: The health benefits of a forgotten natural vitamin. Int J Mol Sci. 2020;21.

1231. Kuzniarz M, Mitchell P, Cumming RG, Flood VM. Use of vitamin supplements and cataract: the Blue Mountains Eye Study. Am J Ophthalmol. 2001;132:19-26.

1232. Skalka HW, Prchal JT. Cataracts and riboflavin deficiency. Am J Clin Nutr. 1981;34:861-3.

1233. Horwitz J, Dovrat A, Straatsma BR, Revilla PJ, Lightfoot DO. Glutathione reductase in human lens epithelium: FAD-induced in vitro activation. Curr Eye Res. 1987;6:1249-56.

1234. Belakovskii MS, Radchenko ND, Bogdanov NG, Spirichev VB. [Vitamin metabolism in cosmonauts during pre-flight training]. Kosm Biol Aviakosm Med. 1983;17:8-10.

1235. Garcia-Minguillan CJ, Fernandez-Ballart JD, Ceruelo S, Rios L, Bueno O, Berrocal-Zaragoza MI, Molloy AM, Ueland PM, Meyer K, Murphy MM. Riboflavin status modifies the effects of methylenetetrahydrofolate reductase (MTHFR) and methionine synthase reductase (MTRR) polymorphisms on homocysteine. Genes Nutr. 2014;9:435.

1236. Whatham A, Bartlett H, Eperjesi F, Blumenthal C, Allen J, Suttle C, Gaskin K. Vitamin and mineral deficiencies in the developed world and their effect on the eye and vision. Ophthalmic Physiol Opt. 2008;28:1-12.

1237. van Poppel G, Goldbohm RA. Epidemiologic evidence for beta-carotene and cancer prevention. Am J Clin Nutr. 1995;62:1393S-402S.

1238. Kohlmeier L, Hastings SB. Epidemiologic evidence of a role of carotenoids in cardiovascular disease prevention. Am J Clin Nutr. 1995;62:1370S-6S.

1239. Olson JA. Vitamin A, retinoids, and carotenoids. In: Shils ME, Olson JA, Shike M, editors. Modern nutrition in health and disease. 8th ed. Malvern, PA: Lea & Febiger; 1994. p. 287-307.

1240. Michaelsson K, Lithell H, Vessby B, Melhus H. Serum retinol levels and the risk of fracture. N Engl J Med. 2003;348:287-94.

1241. Melhus H, Michaelsson K, Kindmark A, Bergstrom R, Holmberg L, Mallmin H, Wolk A, Ljunghall S. Excessive dietary intake of vitamin A is associated with reduced bone mineral density and increased risk for hip fracture. Ann Intern Med. 1998;129:770-8.

1242. Jackson HA, Sheehan AH. Effect of vitamin A on fracture risk. Ann Pharmacother. 2005;39:2086-90.

1243. Omenn GS, Goodman GE, Thornquist MD, Balmes J, Cullen MR, Glass A, Keogh JP, Meyskens FL, Jr., Valanis B, Williams JH, Jr., Barnhart S, Cherniack MG, Brodkin CA, Hammar S. Risk factors for lung cancer and for intervention effects in CARET, the Beta-Carotene and Retinol Efficacy Trial. J Natl Cancer Inst. 1996;88:1550-9.

1244. ATBC Cancer Prevention Study Group. The alpha-tocopherol, beta-carotene lung cancer prevention study: design, methods, participant characteristics, and compliance. Ann Epidemiol. 1994;4:1-10.

Expedition 62 special delivery of a limited shelf life Space Charcuterie includes brie cheese, dry salami nuggets, cube of cheese, dried figs and nuts. Photo Credit: NASA.

11 Immune

Adequate nutrition is required for nominal immune system function and for provision of all components needed to generate an effective immune response (1245, 1246). Nutrients act as antioxidants and as cofactors (1247). Historically, crews generally have lower dietary intake during spaceflight than they do under normal conditions on the ground (1). It is well known from ground research that a lack of macronutrients or selected micronutrients, such as zinc, selenium, and the antioxidant vitamins, can have profound effects on immune function (1248-1251). Such a lack of nutrients also leads to deregulation of the balanced host response (1252). Disruption of nutritional balance and dietary intake of astronauts during spaceflight, which is often accompanied by a stress response, might influence their immune response (1253, 1254). However, detailed information on the effects of many micronutrients during spaceflight are mandatory before specific nutritional recommendations can be made, especially with respect to their relationship with immune system function.

Diet, Gastrointestinal Microbiota, and Immune Response

The composition and dynamic of the gut microbiota is tightly linked to dietary habits, the ability to respond to dietary intervention, and the potential to modulate immune dysregulation (1255-1262). Dietary shifts have the ability to rapidly alter the composition of the gastrointestinal microbiome, resulting microbial metabolites, and the effect on the immune system (1259, 1263, 1264). Microbiota, their components, or their metabolites interact with receptors on intestinal epithelial cells or immune cells in the lamina propria, inducing strain-dependent responses that may impact both the innate and adaptive immune system. Mechanisms have been demonstrated that link some strains with immune benefits such as immune tolerance, anti-inflammatory effects, and integrity of the epithelial barrier (1265-1267).

The metabolites available in diets rich in diverse plant-based foods can promote a varied microbiome, both enriching beneficial species and metabolic capabilities, and reducing inflammation-associated species (1268, 1269). Plant foods provide a diverse variety of fibers and prebiotics (defined as "dietary substrates that are selectively utilized by host microorganisms conferring a health benefit") that are nondigestible to humans, and require a wide variety of microbial enzymes for hydrolysis (1268, 1270). Key products include short chain fatty acids—predominantly butyrate, acetate, and propionate—that may regulate inflammatory response (1261). Butyrate supplies the majority of the energy needs of colonocytes, and has been associated with normal colonocyte growth, anti-inflammatory effects, multiple mechanisms that may protect against infection, and tumor suppression (1266, 1271). Increasing intake of fruits and vegetables has been associated with significantly higher butyrate production. African children consuming a plant-based high-fiber diet had a gut microbiota significantly enriched in Bacteroides and lower in Firmicutes, with reduced numbers of pathogenic bacteria and twice the production of butyrate, acetate, and propionate compared to European children consuming a low-fiber, high-protein Western diet (1272). Healthy adults consuming a plant-based diet for 4 days produced nearly twice as much butyrate as the same adults on an animal-based diet for the same time (1273). These results indicate that differences in short chain fatty acid production may be induced by diet after only a few days.

Similarly, plant-derived polyphenols, including flavonoids, require microbial enzymes for the production of many beneficial substrates, some of which are associated with anti-inflammatory effects (59, 1274, 1275). One example, 3,4-dihydroxybenzoic (protocatechuic) acid (PCA) is a microbial metabolite that can be produced from several polyphenols, with benefits that may include anti-inflammatory and anticarcinogenic effects (1275, 1276).

Despite links between diet, microbiota, the immune system, and disease state, defining a healthy microbiome is complex, as composition and responses vary by individual (1277, 1278). However, dysbiosis of the microbiota, which can include loss of beneficial bacteria or overgrowth of detrimental bacteria, has been associated with inflammation, loss of epithelial barrier integrity, and disease (1265, 1279). Dietary components such as fat, sugar, and high animal protein have been associated with alterations to the composition of the gut microbiome that may be linked to disease and inflammatory conditions (1264). For instance, low gastrointestinal microflora diversity has been linked to diets enriched in fat and sugars (1280), and also to metabolic disorders such as obesity and inflammatory bowel disease (1281, 1282).

Few spaceflight studies have evaluated the microbiome to date (1283). However, alterations in the microbiome of astronauts have been reported, and associations with the inflammatory immune response in spaceflight have been suggested (1284). These results were not evaluated in relation to diet. Therefore, the effect of diet, as well as its ability to provide a countermeasure to microbiome changes may be an important consideration in spaceflight (1283). However, even if the dietary substrates are present, beneficial end products cannot be produced in the absence of the necessary bacteria (1268, 1269). Probiotic supplements may provide a benefit in cases where bacteria are depleted, such as through antibiotic use. It has previously been suggested that probiotics may benefit some of the conditions that have manifested in spaceflight (1283, 1285); however, they have not been systematically evaluated in spaceflight to date.

In addition to immune interactions, the microbiota and associated metabolites have been increasingly linked with stress and psychological health (1286). The gastrointestinal microbiome may also influence the brain, mood, and behavior through interaction with the gut-brain axis (66), the immune system (1286-1288), or through production of odorants that act as social cues (1289). Although human studies in these areas are limited, a preliminary investigation in a confined 105-day human analog study indicated a potential relationship between gastrointestinal microbial composition and mood (1290). Microorganisms with probiotic psychiatric effects, meaning they can produce a mental health benefit if consumed in adequate amounts, have been described as “psychobiotics” (1291). Evidence from both animal studies and human clinical trials supports that ingestion of psychobiotics, many of which are associated with foods and supplements, can reduce symptoms of stress, anxiety, and depression (1285, 1292, 1293). Considering the substantial impact that the microbiome may have on cognitive function, neuro-inflammation, and behavior, the impacts that the spaceflight diet and individual crew food selection may have on the gastrointestinal composition warrants further investigation.

Although current data indicate a strong link between the interaction of the diet, the microbiome, and immune response, the diet may directly impact innate immunity completely independent of the microbiome (1265). This was effectively demonstrated in a recent study, where a Western diet was associated with increased sepsis severity and mortality in both colonized and germ-free mice (1294).

Figure 73. NASA astronaut Chris Cassidy processes a fecal sample as part of the Food Physiology experiment. Photo Credit: NASA.

Skin

The skin is an active immune organ that provides a physical barrier between internal organs and toxins and microbes in the environment. When the epidermal layer of skin is disrupted, there is a local release of cytokines in the epidermal layer with subsequent systemic absorption through the upper dermis (1295). This is an early signal to the host immune system that the skin barrier has been disrupted.

Skin is a target organ involved in food or medication hypersensitivity responses including rash or atopic dermatitis. In addition to hypersensitivity reactions, dermatologic conditions can result from nutritional deficiencies, metabolic disorders, or even nutrient excess, and can help provide diagnostic clues (1296). Deficiencies of zinc, vitamin A, vitamin B_6, vitamin C, riboflavin, and niacin are all associated with dermatological symptoms (1297). Although these are usually rare, they can happen in individuals with restricted diets (e.g., vegetarian) or in individuals who have issues with absorption of nutrients for various reasons. Beyond deficiencies or toxicities, specific nutrients can be used in the treatment of some dermatologic conditions including psoriasis, which is an inflammatory condition that can be aggravated by an inflammatory diet (1296).

The most common reported medical events during spaceflight are dermatological in nature (1298). These manifestations include contact dermatitis, eczematous patches, viral reactivation, and skin infections. There is evidence that skin microbiome changes during long-duration missions to the ISS (1284), which may be a contributing factor. Nutritional deficiencies or insufficiencies could also be a contributing factor and should be considered in future analyses. Unfortunately, biomarkers of nutritional status are not routinely collected during flight unless there is a scientific study specifically looking at those markers.

Nutrients Associated with Immune and Dermatologic Health

Energy

As discussed earlier, some crewmembers have an insufficient energy intake, which can lead to more extensive free radical propagation because of diminished protein-based antioxidant defense mechanisms (1, 1021). On the other hand, caloric restriction with otherwise optimal nutrition in healthy, non-obese subjects has been shown to reduce oxidative stress (1299). On the Mir and the Life and Microgravity Science Space Shuttle mission, space travelers who consumed inadequate energy intake had significant increases in urinary excretion of 8-iso-prostaglandin-F2α and 8OHdG, which are markers for oxidative damage (1300). In the NASA Twins study, where one twin stayed on the ISS for 1 year and the other one being the control on Earth, these biomarkers were not consistently increased although the twin who stayed in space lost about 8% of the preflight body mass, thus suggesting insufficient energy intake inflight (19). In spaceflight, other factors inducing oxidative stress such as changes in metabolism, inflammation status, and radiation need to be considered when interpreting effects on the antioxidant defense mechanisms.

Protein and Amino Acids

Stein et al. suggest that spaceflight triggers a stress response similar to the one triggered by stress induced by injury (1301). Protein and amino acid deficiencies can have profound effects on a variety of immune system functions (1302, 1303). Increasing protein intake and/or supplementing certain amino acids may have a positive impact on the immune system function. Whey protein containing high levels of leucine, for instance, could enhance natural killer (NK) cell function and IL-12 concentration (1304) and improve immune function in sarcopenic older adults (1305) and cancer patients (1306). Lactoferrin, an essential glycoprotein extracted from milk or whey, demonstrated improvement of the innate immune system and functioning as a bactericide (1307). Improved antiviral responses have also been obtained in studies involving the elderly (1308). Although further studies are needed, provision of protein- and/or peptide-rich foods and/or supplements might be a means to maintain immune system function on exploration missions.

With respect to specific amino acids, arginine is necessary for normal T-cell function and may become essential in catabolic states. Supplementary dietary arginine has been shown to have useful effects on cellular immunity in animal studies, showing increased size of the thymus, enhanced lymphocyte proliferation in response to mitogen and alloantigen, augmented macrophage and killer cell lysis, and increased lymphocyte interleukin 2 production and receptor activity (1309). Supplementation of arginine led to improved wound healing and immune responses in elderly subjects (1310). Patients following an arthroplasty had lower C-reactive protein levels and could leave the hospital earlier when arginine was part of an immune supplement (1311). Judging by these observations it might seem promising to supplement arginine during long-term missions; however, up to now, no studies have been carried out to test arginine as a measure to improve immune response during space missions.

Another amino acid beneficial for the immune system is glutamine. Glutamine is the most abundant free amino acid in the body. It can inhibit NF-κB activation and cytokine expression after sepsis (1312). Some of the beneficial effects of glutamine are its antioxidant effects and its actions as a precursor to glutathione, an energy substrate for lymphocytes and neutrophils, and as a stimulator of nucleotide synthesis (1313, 1314). Glutathione is the most abundant endogenous antioxidant and plays a central role in antioxidant defense. Glutamine seems to have a significant beneficial effect on mortality, length of hospital stay, and infectious morbidity in critical illness (1314). Positive results of glutamine supplementation have been shown in critically ill patients in whom supplemental glutamine reduced complications and mortality rates in addition to having a stimulating action on the immune system (1315, 1316). However, up to now, supplementation of glutamine as a pharmaconutrient has not been tested in spaceflight or spaceflight analogs (e.g., bed rest). However, as was reviewed in Chapter 7, studies often compare protein supplementation to controls getting no supplement, and the caloric intake difference could explain (i.e., confound) effects. Few, if any, studies evaluate whether the simple effect of providing more food (i.e., a balanced diet) would offer similar benefit.

Vitamin D

As described in Chapter 6, the classical function of vitamin D is to regulate calcium homeostasis and thus bone formation and resorption. However, recent publications show that vitamin D also exerts non-skeletal biological activities including immunomodulation (1317, 1318). The latter seems to be mediated by the (nuclear) vitamin D receptor (VDR) expressed in antigen-presenting cells and activated T cells (1319). Vitamin D and the VDR are required for the blood to have normal numbers of regulatory T cells.

The discovery that VDR is inducible in lymphocytes suggests a role for 1,25$(OH)_2D_3$ in the immune system (1320). Even the enzyme 25$(OH)D_3$-1-α-hydroxylase is expressed by active macrophages, making them able to synthesize and secrete 1,25$(OH)_2D_3$ (1321). However, in macrophages, the enzyme is mainly activated by immune signals such as interferon-γ rather than by parathyroid hormone, which is the activator in the kidney (695). Moreover, the active vitamin D metabolite 1,25$(OH)_2D_3$ can also be modulated by alternative mechanisms to increase the ability of peripheral blood mononuclear cells from sensitized human donors to resist microbes (here mycobacteria). Martineau et al. found that 1,25$(OH)_2D_3$ suppressed both bacillus Calmette-Guérin, a live attenuated strain of *Mycobacterium bovis* used in vaccines, and *Mycobacterium tuberculosis* in infected cell cultures, likely through "nonclassical" mechanisms including the induction of antimicrobial peptides (1322, 1323). Kondo et al. found that vitamin D supplementation improved the sensitivity of the treatment response to pegylated interferon α/ribavirin therapy in chronic hepatitis C patients (1324). Im et al. (1325) observed in patients with Coronavirus disease 2019 (COVID-19) a vitamin D and selenium deficiency suggesting that this may decrease immune defense against the virus and may cause progression to a severe disease. People might therefore benefit from higher Vitamin D levels—for instance by supplementing vitamin D—and have a reduced risk to get infected (1326-1328). This is in line with the conclusions drawn from spaceflight analog studies (606) (Figure 74).

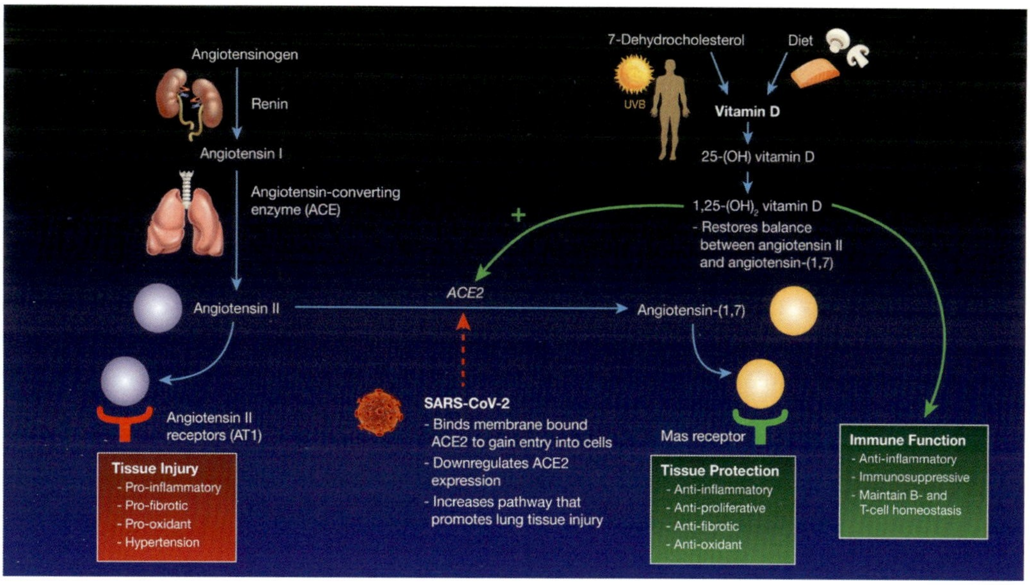

Figure 74. Vitamin D actions on the Renin-Angiotensin Aldosterone System, and how vitamin D might promote tissue protection from SARS-CoV-2 infection. Adapted from (606).

Vitamin D might also be linked to the regulation of glutathione synthesis, as shown in in vitro studies, resulting in reduced oxidative stress and TGF-β levels (1329). When human monocytes were supplemented with calcitriol, they increased glutathione syntheses (1329), demonstrating an immune-enhancing effect.

Studies during or after spaceflight have shown numerous changes in astronauts' immune status, including altered distribution of circulating leukocytes, altered production of cytokines, decreased activity of NK cells, decreased function of granulocytes, decreased activation of T cells, altered levels of immunoglobulins, reactivation of latent viruses, altered virus-specific immunity, expression of Epstein-Barr virus immediate early and late genes, and altered neuroendocrine responses (19, 1330-1334). Cell culture studies in microgravity demonstrated a temporary immunosuppression, which could promote infections by respective pathogens (1335). When including the molecular drivers for the immunosuppressive state, it turned out that the molecular architecture links energy metabolism and immunodeficiency in microgravity. Based on that, a hypocaloric nutrition in space could lead to a dysregulation of protein metabolism and impairment of host immunity (1336).

Furthermore, evidence exists that among individuals wintering over in the Antarctic for 6 months, who have high serum cortisol, a higher vitamin D status is related to a lower probability of viral shedding in saliva (604). In that study, an interactive effect occurred between cortisol and vitamin D. Subjects with lower serum 25-hydroxyvitamin D and with the highest quartile of serum cortisol (22.5 µg/dL or higher) had more evidence of shedding Epstein-Barr virus (EBV) in saliva than did individuals in the lowest quartile of cortisol (13.1 µg/dL or below, Figure 75). Thus, a low vitamin D status of astronauts during space missions might have an impact on their immune status.

Although improvements of immunity and the reactivation of latent herpesviruses have been demonstrated lately onboard the ISS based on dietary, operational, and stress-relieving countermeasures (49), studies are still mandatory to distinguish between the effects of vitamin D deficiency and of microgravity.

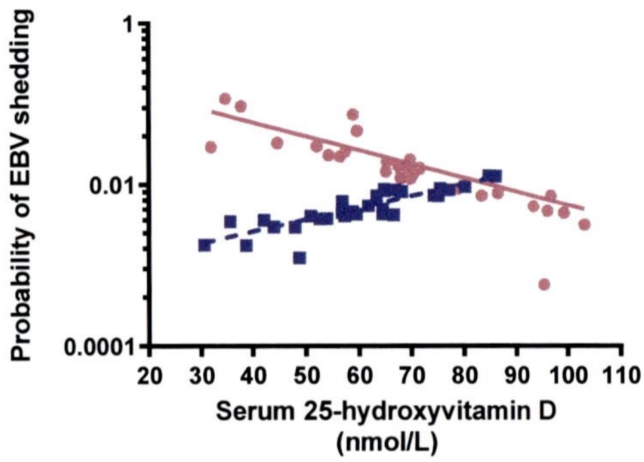

Figure 75. An interaction between serum cortisol, vitamin D status, and the probability of EBV shedding. Data from all 41 participants in the Antarctic study are included in the graph. The data were statistically analyzed using the continuous data set of cortisol data. The data are split into the two subgroups for presentation purposes. The graph is from Zwart et al. (604).

Vitamin B_{12}

Vitamin B_{12} was described in detail in Chapter 10. With regard to the immune system, vitamin B_{12} deficiency may lead to alterations of immunological indicators, such as a reduction of lymphocytes and suppression of NK cell activity, both of which can be reversed by supplementation with vitamin B_{12} (1337). In one study, for 4 months elderly subjects (aged 70 years) received—in addition to the regular diet—a special nutritional formula that provided, among other nutrients, 120 IU vitamin E, 3.8 mg vitamin B_{12}, and 400 mg folic acid. NK-cell cytotoxic activity increased in supplemented subjects, indicating increased innate immunity in elderly people (1338). Vitamin B_{12} deficiency can also manifest as skin hyperpigmentation or skin lesions. Restoration of vitamin B_{12} status can resolve these symptoms (1339).

Riboflavin

People with diets low in dairy and meat products are at risk for a riboflavin deficiency. Symptoms include angular stomatitis, glossitis, cheilosis, and dermatitis (1297). Skin dyscrasias similar to those associated with deficiencies in essential fatty acids are also found with marginal riboflavin deficiencies (263).

Vitamin B_6

Cutaneous manifestation of a vitamin B_6 deficiency include seborrheic dermatitis and eczema. These changes are likely due to impaired synthesis of proline from ornithine and the resulting suppression of collagen neogenesis in the skin (1340).

Biotin

Biotin is a required cofactor for pyruvate carboxylase, acetyl-CoA carboxylase isoforms 1 and 2, propionyl-CoA carboxylase, and ß-methylcrotonyl-CoA carboxylase (1341, 1342). The five biotin-dependent enzymes are involved in carbohydrate, fatty acid, and amino acid metabolism (1341, 1342). The primary role of biotin is to transfer CO_2 units from one compound to another. Biotin exists in a free state or bound to proteins. About 81% of biotin in the human body is free biotin in serum, and 10% is free in tissues (1343).

Despite the observation that frank signs of deficiency are rare, there is growing appreciation of genetic, physiologic, and pharmacologic conditions that marginally impair biotin status (1344-1346). This suggests that the lack of physiologic manifestations of biotin deficiency may not be a reliable measure to gauge biotin status. Marginal changes in biotin status have been shown to affect a range of metabolic factors, from carboxylase activity to the expression of non-biotin-dependent enzymes such as glucokinase, ornithine transcarbamylase, and phosphoenolpyruvate carboxykinase (1347-1349).

Biotin status has never been measured during or after long-duration spaceflight; however, it is unlikely there are any frank biotin deficiencies, which would present as neurological and dermatological manifestations.

Sodium

High sodium intake is correlated with the development of hypertension in sodium-sensitive people. We have shown in spaceflight, as well as in ambulatory conditions on Earth, that at an intake level of about 4000 mg/d, sodium is retained without being accompanied by fluid retention (123, 299, 1350). A hypothesis that might explain how sodium can be bound in an osmotically inactive way has been brought forward by Titze et al. (653, 1351) and proposes that sodium can be stored on proteoglycans in interstitial sites. This uniquely bound sodium can induce a state of local hypertonicity in the skin interstitium. In a further study, they suggest that the local hypertonicity is sensed by macrophages, which then activate a transcription factor (tonicity enhanced binding protein), which in turn induces vascular endothelial growth factor C signaling (648, 649, 1352). High cutaneous sodium content may also facilitate T helper 2 cell mediated atopic dermatitis (1353). Therefore, high dietary sodium intake can be considered proinflammatory. Additionally, high sodium intake has shown systemic immunosuppressive effects, which lead to an impaired antibacterial immune defense (1354). Further studies in microgravity should distinguish between the effects of microgravity and high sodium intake on the immune system.

Vitamin A

Vitamin A plays a well-known role in immune function and protection against infections (1355-1358). A vitamin A deficiency impairs mucosal barriers and diminishes the function of neutrophils, macrophages, and NK cells (1359); it may affect host defenses directly (1360) or indirectly through its role in epithelial cell differentiation and host barrier function (1357). The considerable immunity benefits of vitamin A, which would contribute to reducing the risk of various pathogen-mediated diseases, warrant a recommendation to supplement individuals with minimal or poor vitamin A status. Supplementing vitamin A after training in rats led to increased total serum antioxidant capacity; however, concurrently, expression of superoxide dismutase-1 was down regulated and upregulation of superoxide dismutase-2 induced by exercise was blunted by vitamin A (1361). Additionally, IL-10 and heat shock protein 70 expression, which are both positive for tissue damage protection after exercise, were decreased (1361, 1362). In obese mice, supplementing vitamin A following vaccination with inactivated influenza virus improved antibody responses and reduced blood concentration of inflammatory cytokines (1363). When supplementing young children (6 to 23 months) together with the measles vaccine, significant sex differences were found (1364). Additionally, previous supplementation with vitamin A affected the immunological responses (1364). In a study in healthy-aged subjects, vitamin A supplementation did not affect lymphocyte proliferation (1365). However, whether immunity benefits accrue from providing additional vitamin A to those with sufficient status is not known (1366). Whether vitamin A supplementation would be a desired measure to improve immune response in spaceflight has not been investigated up to now and needs to be thoroughly thought through.

Vitamin C

Ascorbic acid (vitamin C) is an essential component of every living cell. Although discussed in more detail in the Oxidative Stress section of the book, the role of vitamin C in maintaining a healthy immune system is discussed briefly here. The concentration of vitamin C is very high in leukocytes. The vitamin is used rapidly during infection to prevent oxidative damage. Vitamin C is a regulator of redox and metabolic checkpoints that control activation and survival of immune cells (1252). A deficiency in vitamin C status is associated with reduced immune function (1367) and, due to its role in the formation of collagen, clinical manifestations of scurvy are cutaneous findings including follicular hyperkeratosis with fragmented corkscrew hair and perifollicular hemorrhages (1368). Vitamin C has been shown to stimulate the immune system by enhancing T-lymphocyte proliferation in response to infection, and increasing cytokine production and synthesis of immunoglobulins (1369). Vitamin C stimulates neutrophil migration to the site of infection, enhances phagocytosis and oxidant generation, and microbial killing (1370). The antiviral effects of vitamin C are carried out by promoting lymphocyte activity, modulating cytokines, and reducing inflammation (reviewed in (1371).

Supplementation of very high doses of vitamin C in patients with shingles led to a lower incidence of postherpetic neuralgia (reviewed in (1371). In analog studies such as (short- or long-duration) bed rest, no significant change in vitamin C could be shown (262, 419); however, a trend for an increase was apparent. This might be related to dietary vitamin C intake during the study relative to the intake before the study (419). Up to now, however, the antioxidant role of vitamin C has not been tested in spaceflight.

Vitamin E

Vitamin E is a lipid-soluble, chain-breaking antioxidant found in body tissues, and is also the first line of defense against lipid peroxidation reactions. Eight naturally occurring compounds have vitamin E activity: four tocopherol derivatives (α-, γ-, δ-, and ß-tocopherol) and four tocotrienol derivatives (α-, γ-, δ-, and ß-tocotrienol) (1372, 1373). The tocopherols that are most abundant in biological systems are α- and γ-tocopherol; however, small amounts of δ-tocopherol and γ-tocopheryl quinine are also present. About 90% of the tocopherol found in human plasma is in the form of α-tocopherol (1374). Vitamin E can support monocyte/macrophage-mediated responses (1375). Vitamin E and selenium have synergistic functions in tissues to reduce damage to lipid membranes by the formation of ROS during infections. The ability of vitamin E to scavenge lipid-soluble free radicals depends to some extent on the status of two other antioxidant compounds, vitamin C and glutathione, which are involved in reducing oxidized vitamin E back to a reusable (i.e., able to be oxidized) form. Additionally, vitamin E may improve T-cell function by decreasing production of prostaglandin E2 by macrophages by modulating the amino acid cascade initiated by lipoxygenase and/or cyclooxygenase (213). Furthermore, vitamin E influences lymphocyte maturation, possibly by stabilizing membranes and allowing enhanced binding of antigen-presenting cells to immature T cells through increased expression of intercellular adhesion molecule-1.

After ISS crewmembers spent 4 to 6 months in space, their plasma γ-tocopherol was 50% less than preflight levels (111). No change in α-tocopherol occurred in these subjects. Vitamin E data have not yet been investigated in light of immune function changes during spaceflight.

Copper

Copper has wide-ranging functions in the body, including a catalytic cofactor for oxidation-reduction reactions for copper enzymes. Copper enzymes are involved in several metabolic pathways such as energy production and iron metabolism. Copper deficiency may lead to anemia and neurological alterations (798). Many functions of copper are considered vital for spaceflight (179, 1376-1379). This might have direct or indirect (when alterations are induced by psychological stress or radiation stress) implications for nutrition and nutritional status being possible causes (or effects) of alterations in immune system function (1). In a 3-week bed rest study where artificial gravity was applied for 1 hour per day as a countermeasure, no change in urinary copper excretion was observed (815). Urinary excretion during 180 days of spaceflight did not change either, whether different mechanical loading during exercise or bisphosphonate was applied (815). Nonetheless, to date, no further information is available about copper metabolism during spaceflight.

Zinc

In addition to its many essential functions in growth and development, zinc is essential for the function of cells of the immune system (1380). It has an important role in promotion of wound healing and in maintenance of intestinal integrity. Zinc is also involved in the synthesis of ROS-turning enzymes and thereby takes part in antioxidant reactions (1381) On the other hand, the synthesis of the proinflammatory markers Il-6 and TNF-α in zinc-deficient monocytes were lower, thus suggesting a strengthening of the innate defense (1382). A zinc deficiency can manifest with cutaneous changes such as periorificial lesions and angular cheilitis (1297). Eczematous annular plaques develop in areas with substantial amounts of friction (1297). A deficiency of zinc is also associated with reduced concentrations of insulin-like growth factor 1 and reduced rates of protein synthesis. Therefore, zinc deficiency could be especially detrimental during immobility. However, zinc status of astronauts, as assessed by mean serum zinc and urinary zinc excretion (admittedly, not the best markers of zinc status), did not change after long-duration spaceflight (1, 815). Practicing different exercise regimes leading to different mechanical loads or supplementing bisphosphonates did not change urinary zinc excretion either (815). In a 3-week bed rest study, however, urinary and fecal zinc excretion increased with and without application of artificial gravity (1 hour per day) as a countermeasure leading to zinc losses during bed rest (815). Notably, zinc losses tended to be higher in the artificial gravity group (815). No data are available on the use of zinc supplementation as a countermeasure during spaceflight.

Selenium

Comparable to zinc, the physiological role of selenium is a cofactor of enzymes exerting their effects as antioxidants. Selenocysteine and selenomethionine are incorporated into selenoproteins, which function alongside others as antioxidants. Selenium deficiency may lead to increased oxidative stress, reduced immune function, and chronic low level of inflammation (1381). Selenium should only be supplemented after thorough analysis of the selenium status because selenium supplementation seems to be associated with increased mortality (1383). Supplementing supraphysiological amounts of selenium does not seem to lead to further optimization of the immune status (reviewed in (1382)).

Polyphenols

The polyphenol family—according to their chemical structure—can be subclassed into flavonoids, phenolic acids, tannins, and stilbenes. Naturally occurring polyphenols such as resveratrol, quercetin, curcumin, and catechins have shown antioxidant and anti-inflammatory effects (1384). These effects seem to be modulated through different pathways such as protein kinase-dependent pathways activated by NF-κB or mitogens, as well as through preventing the generation of ROS by iron binding (1385). Curcumin, quercetin, and epigallocatechingallate may induce epigenetic changes within cells (1386, 1387). Additionally, polyphenols seem to activate sirtuin 1 directly or indirectly and thereby are beneficial—besides having other functions—for regulation of oxidative stress, inflammation, and autoimmunity. Accumulating evidence has shown that polyphenols such as resveratrol, curcumin, catechins, and quercetins have a regulatory role in immune function in vitro and in vivo (1388-1394). Regarding the effect of polyphenols on their capability to prevent allergies, these are the most studied natural compounds. They seem to dampen the onset of allergic inflammation by affecting the interference with T-helper cell activation (1395, 1396). Based on these results, polyphenol supplementation might be a promising countermeasure to counteract oxidative stress and changes in immune function in spaceflight; however, oxidative stress is not merely negative. During exercise, for instance, mitochondria produce ROS as one product of oxidative phosphorylation. The increased ROS production is one signal to induce adaptation processes. This adaptation is one of the positive functions of ROS because it induces mitochondrial, cell- and system-wide adaptations (1397). In this context, the ROS increase reduces the incidents of diseases and extends life expectancy (1397).

Polyphenols might also have beneficial effects in prevention of immune dysfunction during long-term space missions, particularly because body iron stores are higher during spaceflight. However, the role of polyphenols in sirtuin-1-mediated or iron-related regulation in immune function remains to be studied. To prove any effects of antioxidants, the ESA sponsored a 60-day bed rest study, which has been finished recently. The antioxidant cocktail evaluated consisted of an antioxidant and anti-inflammatory food supplement (i.e., a mixture of natural polyphenolic extracts from edible plants) that was supplied in the form of capsules. The respective experiments will address effects of the cocktail on metabolism, the cardiovascular system, muscles, bones, immunology, the neurosensory system, and sleep. At this juncture, no results have been obtained during spaceflight; however, a recently initiated flight study will examine the role of increasing polyphenol intake, along with other dietary modifications, on immune health and nutritional status.

Iron

As mentioned previously, the maintenance of iron homeostasis is extremely important for human health. Iron is known to be involved in immune system function—specifically, adaptive and innate immune response—and both iron overload and iron deficiency affect immune function. As reviewed by Dao and Meydani, iron overload can affect susceptibility to infection (1398). Conversely, iron deficiency affects the function of certain immune cells, including neutrophils and NK cells, and production of cytokines (1398).

As with any nutrient, supplementation must be used with caution because in areas of the world where infection rates are high, such as malaria-endemic regions, iron supplementation can actually increase risk of infection, suggesting that the supplemented iron provides an environment for pathogens to thrive (1399). Others have shown that iron deficiency can help protect against some types of infections (1400). Evidence from short- (weeks) and long-duration (months) space missions shows that RBC mass decreases during flight because of neocytolysis (9, 1401). An early hypothesis for the cause of decreased RBC mass was that RBC synthesis in space was understimulated relative to synthesis on the ground (1402). Decreased release of mature RBCs into the circulation is associated with a decrease in circulating erythropoietin concentrations. Serum erythropoietin concentrations decrease in the first few days of spaceflight; however, return to preflight levels later in the flight and iron turnover is unchanged during flight (9, 1403), indicating that synthesis of RBCs and hemoglobin is unchanged.

The decreased RBC mass, increased serum ferritin, decreased transferrin receptors, and increased serum iron all provide evidence for increased iron storage during spaceflight. Furthermore, the space food system provides almost three times the recommended intake (1). Iron plays an ambiguous role in human health: not only do humans require it for survival, but microorganisms (including pathogens) also require iron acquisition from the environment for their survival. Cells of the innate immune system have genes that regulate proteins that can modulate iron homeostasis at the cellular and systemic level to restrict iron availability to invading microorganisms. One such protein is hepcidin, a key regulator of iron homeostasis and a critical factor in the anemia of inflammation (1404, 1405). Hepcidin has been shown to be endogenously expressed by innate immune cells—macrophages and neutrophils. It plays a role in making iron less available by increasing intracellular iron sequestration and decreasing circulating iron concentrations, and it is influenced by cytokines IL-6 and IL-1 (1406, 1407). Iron, on the other hand, catalyzes the formation of ROS and thereby may contribute to bone loss in microgravity (reviewed in (729)). It is also associated with certain optic neuropathies and retinal degeneration (1408, 1409). Studies suggest that some types of radiation exposure and oxidative stress can release ferrous iron (Fe^{2+}) from ferritin (1410), further adding to the load of free iron in the body. Independently, both radiation exposure and high dietary iron load promote a state of oxidative stress with increased risk of pathophysiological outcomes (1411, 1412). In a recent study in rats, the effect of high dietary iron intake and whole-body radiation exposure was analyzed (1409). They found evidence of increased DNA damage (i.e., increased 8-OH-dG) in the high iron intake group, the radiation group, and in the combined treatment group. An attenuation of radiation-induced DNA oxidation in the retina of animals under the high-iron diet was observed (1409). Studies need to be done to determine the role of increased iron stores on immune function and reactivation of latent viruses during spaceflight.

Polyunsaturated Fatty Acids

Polyunsaturated fatty acids, such as omega-3 and omega-6 fatty acids may exert different effects on the immune system. Omega-3 fatty acids may protect from oxidative damage and radiation-related risks (212, 1413), both of which are concerns for space travelers. Omega-6 fatty acids are rather proinflammatory whereas omega-3 fatty acids have anti-inflammatory properties (reviewed in (1414)). The mode of action of polyunsaturated fatty acids seem to be through multiple pathways. The main ones (reviewed in (1414)) seem to be: 1) Providing substrates for biosynthesis of inflammatory eicosanoid mediators, providing precursors for the production of specific leukotrienes, anti-inflammatory lipids or the production of pro-inflammatory mediators, other kinds of leukotrienes. 2) Interactions with cell surface receptors with immune cells such as peroxisome proliferation activating receptor (PPAR) and Toll-like receptors and thereby affecting the transcription of respective pro- and anti-inflammatory cytokines. PPAR-γ seems to affect the inflammatory response through NF-κB. This transcription factor affects transcription of genes involved in cell cycle regulation and inflammatory processes. NF-κB is activated by arachidonic acid, an omega-6 fatty acid, and specifically by prostaglandin E2. The suppression of NF-κB induced pro-inflammatory responses by eicosapentaenoic acid (omega-3 fatty acid), however, seems to be independent of PPAR-γ (1415). 3) Affecting lymphocyte proliferation and cytokine profiles. Omega-3 fatty acids, for instance, promote an acute immune response by reducing TNFα syntheses and/or can stimulate IL-4 production (reviewed in (1414)). We have reported elevated NF-κB after short-duration spaceflight (231). The effects of omega-3 fatty acids on inflammatory cytokines, and specifically TNFα, are well documented on the ground (231, 1416-1418), but warrant further studies during spaceflight.

In summary, astronauts in space are generally not optimally nourished, particularly with regard to nutrients supporting the immune system. Dietary intake tailored to the astronauts' needs may be beneficial for their immune system function. Furthermore, the environmental stress of spaceflight can lead to changes in immune response as well as in the nutritional needs of the individual astronaut. Nutrition for optimal immune response and other functions is required to support optimal astronaut health during long-duration missions. However, it is important to be aware that "one size does not fit all." An immune nutrient intake profile that is appropriate for one astronaut or one condition may be of minimal benefit for another individual or condition, and could be harmful in other settings. This implies that genetics and other impact factors need to be considered to develop a personalized optimal immunonutrition. Although further research both on the ground and in spaceflight may continue to advance the science of personalized nutrition, the constraints of spaceflight resources and prepositioned food systems make it even more important to understand the benefits of standardized whole food diets to the health and performance of the astronauts. The use of basic clinical pharmacology, genetics, molecular biology, and clinical research principles in the study of nutritional therapy during spaceflight and analog studies will lead to answers on how to administer the right nutrients, in the right amounts, at the right time during space travelers' missions.

References for Chapter 11

1. Smith SM, Zwart SR, Kloeris V, Heer M. Nutritional biochemistry of space flight. New York: Nova Science Publishers; 2009.

9. Alfrey CP, Udden MM, Leach-Huntoon C, Driscoll T, Pickett MH. Control of red blood cell mass in spaceflight. J Appl Physiol (1985). 1996;81:98-104.

19. Garrett-Bakelman FE, Darshi M, Green SJ, Gur RC, Lin L, Macias BR, McKenna MJ, Meydan C, Mishra T, Nasrini J, Piening BD, Rizzardi LF, Sharma K, Siamwala JH, Taylor L, Vitaterna MH, Afkarian M, Afshinnekoo E, Ahadi S, Ambati A, Arya M, Bezdan D, Callahan CM, Chen S, Choi AMK, Chlipala GE, Contrepois K, Covington M, Crucian BE, De Vivo I, Dinges DF, Ebert DJ, Feinberg JI, Gandara JA, George KA, Goutsias J, Grills GS, Hargens AR, Heer M, Hillary RP, Hoofnagle AN, Hook VYH, Jenkinson G, Jiang P, Keshavarzian A, Laurie SS, Lee-McMullen B, Lumpkins SB, MacKay M, Maienschein-Cline MG, Melnick AM, Moore TM, Nakahira K, Patel HH, Pietrzyk R, Rao V, Saito R, Salins DN, Schilling JM, Sears DD, Sheridan CK, Stenger MB, Tryggvadottir R, Urban AE, Vaisar T, Van Espen B, Zhang J, Ziegler MG, Zwart SR, Charles JB, Kundrot CE, Scott GBI, Bailey SM, Basner M, Feinberg AP, Lee SMC, Mason CE, Mignot E, Rana BK, Smith SM, Snyder MP, Turek FW. The NASA Twins Study: A multidimensional analysis of a year-long human spaceflight. Science. 2019;364.

49. Crucian BE, Makedonas G, Sams CF, Pierson DL, Simpson R, Stowe RP, Smith SM, Zwart SR, Krieger SS, Rooney B, Douglas G, Downs M, Nelman-Gonzalez M, Williams TJ, Mehta S. Countermeasures-based improvements in stress, immune system dysregulation and latent herpesvirus reactivation onboard the International Space Station - relevance for deep space missions and terrestrial medicine. Neurosci Biobehav Rev. 2020;115:68-76.

59. Kawabata K, Yoshioka Y, Terao J. Role of intestinal microbiota in the bioavailability and physiological functions of dietary polyphenols. Molecules. 2019;24.

66. Cryan JF, O'Riordan KJ, Cowan CSM, Sandhu KV, Bastiaanssen TFS, Boehme M, Codagnone MG, Cussotto S, Fulling C, Golubeva AV, Guzzetta KE, Jaggar M, Long-Smith CM, Lyte JM, Martin JA, Molinero-Perez A, Moloney G, Morelli E, Morillas E, O'Connor R, Cruz-Pereira JS, Peterson VL, Rea K, Ritz NL, Sherwin E, Spichak S, Teichman EM, van de Wouw M, Ventura-Silva AP, Wallace-Fitzsimons SE, Hyland N, Clarke G, Dinan TG. The microbiota-gut-brain axis. Physiol Rev. 2019;99:1877-2013.

111. Smith SM, Zwart SR, Block G, Rice BL, Davis-Street JE. The nutritional status of astronauts is altered after long-term space flight aboard the International Space Station. J Nutr. 2005;135:437-43.

123. Drummer C, Hesse C, Baisch F, Norsk P, Elmann-Larsen B, Gerzer R, Heer M. Water and sodium balances and their relation to body mass changes in microgravity. Eur J Clin Invest. 2000;30:1066-75.

179. Levine DS, Greenleaf JE. Immunosuppression during spaceflight deconditioning. Aviat Space Environ Med. 1998;69:172-7.

212. Turner ND, Braby LA, Ford J, Lupton JR. Opportunities for nutritional amelioration of radiation-induced cellular damage. Nutrition. 2002;18:904-12.

213. Chapkin RS, Davidson LA, Ly L, Weeks BR, Lupton JR, McMurray DN. Immunomodulatory effects of (n-3) fatty acids: putative link to inflammation and colon cancer. J Nutr. 2007;137:200S-4S.

231. Zwart SR, Pierson D, Mehta S, Gonda S, Smith SM. Capacity of omega-3 fatty acids or eicosapentaenoic acid to counteract weightlessness-induced bone loss by inhibiting NF-kappaB activation: from cells to bed rest to astronauts. J Bone Miner Res. 2010;25:1049-57.

262. Morgan JLL, Zwart SR, Heer M, Ploutz-Snyder R, Ericson K, Smith SM. Bone metabolism and nutritional status during 30-day head-down-tilt bed rest. J Appl Physiol (1985). 2012;113:1519-29.

263. Pinto JT, Zempleni J. Riboflavin. Adv Nutr. 2016;7:973-5.

299. Heer M, Frings-Meuthen P, Titze J, Boschmann M, Frisch S, Baecker N, Beck L. Increasing sodium intake from a previous low or high intake affects water, electrolyte and acid-base balance differently. Br J Nutr. 2009;101:1286-94.

419. Zwart SR, Oliver SAM, Fesperman JV, Kala G, Krauhs J, Ericson K, Smith SM. Nutritional status assessment before, during, and after long-duration head-down bed rest. Aviat Space Environ Med. 2009;80:A15-22.

604. Zwart SR, Mehta SK, Ploutz-Snyder R, Bourbeau Y, Locke JP, Pierson DL, Smith SM. Response to vitamin D supplementation during Antarctic winter is related to BMI, and supplementation can mitigate Epstein-Barr Virus Reactivation. J Nutr. 2011;141:692-7.

606. Zwart SR, Smith SM. Vitamin D and COVID-19: Lessons from spaceflight analogs. J Nutr. 2020;150:2624-7.

648. Machnik A, Dahlmann A, Kopp C, Goss J, Wagner H, van Rooijen N, Eckardt KU, Muller DN, Park JK, Luft FC, Kerjaschki D, Titze J. Mononuclear phagocyte system depletion blocks interstitial tonicity-responsive enhancer binding protein/vascular endothelial growth factor C expression and induces salt-sensitive hypertension in rats. Hypertension. 2010;55:755-61.

649. Machnik A, Neuhofer W, Jantsch J, Dahlmann A, Tammela T, Machura K, Park JK, Beck FX, Muller DN, Derer W, Goss J, Ziomber A, Dietsch P, Wagner H, van Rooijen N, Kurtz A, Hilgers KF, Alitalo K, Eckardt KU, Luft FC, Kerjaschki D, Titze J. Macrophages regulate salt-dependent volume and blood pressure by a vascular endothelial growth factor-C-dependent buffering mechanism. Nat Med. 2009;15:545-52.

653. Titze J, Shakibaei M, Schafflhuber M, Schulze-Tanzil G, Porst M, Schwind KH, Dietsch P, Hilgers KF. Glycosaminoglycan polymerization may enable osmotically inactive Na+ storage in the skin. Am J Physiol Heart Circ Physiol. 2004;287:H203-8.

729. Yang J, Zhang G, Dong D, Shang P. Effects of iron overload and oxidative damage on the musculoskeletal system in the space environment: Data from spaceflights and ground-based simulation models. Int J Mol Sci. 2018;19.

798. Altarelli M, Ben-Hamouda N, Schneider A, Berger MM. Copper deficiency: Causes, manifestations, and treatment. Nutr Clin Pract. 2019;34:504-13.

815. Heacox HN, Gillman PL, Zwart SR, Smith SM. Excretion of zinc and copper increases in men during 3 weeks of bed rest, with or without artificial gravity. J Nutr. 2017;147:1113-20.

1021. Stein TP. Space flight and oxidative stress. Nutrition. 2002;18:867-71.

1245. Beisel WR. History of nutritional immunology: introduction and overview. J Nutr. 1992;122:591-6.

1246. Mizock BA. Immunonutrition and critical illness: an update. Nutrition. 2010;26:701-7.

1247. Cunningham-Rundles S, McNeeley DF, Moon A. Mechanisms of nutrient modulation of the immune response. J Allergy Clin Immunol. 2005;115:1119-28; quiz 29.

1248. Chandra RK, Kumari S. Effects of nutrition on the immune system. Nutrition. 1994;10:207-10.

1249. Chandra RK. Nutrient regulation of immune functions. Forum Nutr. 2003;56:147-8.

1250. Chandra RK. Nutrition and the immune system: an introduction. Am J Clin Nutr. 1997;66:460S-3S.

1251. Keith ME, Jeejeebhoy KN. Immunonutrition. Baillieres Clin Endocrinol Metab. 1997;11:709-38.

1252. Wintergerst ES, Maggini S, Hornig DH. Contribution of selected vitamins and trace elements to immune function. Ann Nutr Metab. 2007;51:301-23.

1253. Sonnenfeld G, Shearer WT. Immune function during space flight. Nutrition. 2002;18:899-903.

1254. Sonnenfeld G. The immune system in space, including Earth-based benefits of space-based research. Curr Pharm Biotechnol. 2005;6:343-9.

1255. Korpela K, Flint HJ, Johnstone AM, Lappi J, Poutanen K, Dewulf E, Delzenne N, de Vos WM, Salonen A. Gut microbiota signatures predict host and microbiota responses to dietary interventions in obese individuals. PLoS One. 2014;9:e90702.

1256. Zeng H, Lazarova DL, Bordonaro M. Mechanisms linking dietary fiber, gut microbiota and colon cancer prevention. World J Gastrointest Oncol. 2014;6:41-51.

1257. Cani PD, Delzenne NM. The gut microbiome as therapeutic target. Pharmacol Ther. 2011;130:202-12.

1258. Jacobs DM, Gaudier E, van Duynhoven J, Vaughan EE. Non-digestible food ingredients, colonic microbiota and the impact on gut health and immunity: a role for metabolomics. Curr Drug Metab. 2009;10:41-54.

1259. Kau AL, Ahern PP, Griffin NW, Goodman AL, Gordon JI. Human nutrition, the gut microbiome and the immune system. Nature. 2011;474:327-36.

1260. Lozupone CA, Stombaugh JI, Gordon JI, Jansson JK, Knight R. Diversity, stability and resilience of the human gut microbiota. Nature. 2012;489:220-30.

1261. Maslowski KM, Vieira AT, Ng A, Kranich J, Sierro F, Yu D, Schilter HC, Rolph MS, Mackay F, Artis D, Xavier RJ, Teixeira MM, Mackay CR. Regulation of inflammatory responses by gut microbiota and chemoattractant receptor GPR43. Nature. 2009;461:1282-6.

1262. Singh RK, Chang HW, Yan D, Lee KM, Ucmak D, Wong K, Abrouk M, Farahnik B, Nakamura M, Zhu TH, Bhutani T, Liao W. Influence of diet on the gut microbiome and implications for human health. J Transl Med. 2017;15:73.

1263. Turnbaugh PJ, Ridaura VK, Faith JJ, Rey FE, Knight R, Gordon JI. The effect of diet on the human gut microbiome: a metagenomic analysis in humanized gnotobiotic mice. Sci Transl Med. 2009;1:6ra14.

1264. Wu GD, Chen J, Hoffmann C, Bittinger K, Chen YY, Keilbaugh SA, Bewtra M, Knights D, Walters WA, Knight R, Sinha R, Gilroy E, Gupta K, Baldassano R, Nessel L, Li H, Bushman FD, Lewis JD. Linking long-term dietary patterns with gut microbial enterotypes. Science. 2011;334:105-8.

1265. Alexander M, Turnbaugh PJ. Deconstructing mechanisms of diet-microbiome-immune interactions. Immunity. 2020;53:264-76.

1266. Kayama H, Okumura R, Takeda K. Interaction between the microbiota, epithelia, and immune cells in the intestine. Annu Rev Immunol. 2020;38:23-48.

1267. Million M, Tomas J, Wagner C, Lelouard H, Raoult D, Gorvel J-P. New insights in gut microbiota and mucosal immunity of the small intestine. Hum Microbiome J. 2018;7:23-32.

1268. Holscher HD. Dietary fiber and prebiotics and the gastrointestinal microbiota. Gut microbes. 2017;8:172-84.

1269. Holscher HD, Bauer LL, Gourineni V, Pelkman CL, Fahey GC, Jr., Swanson KS. Agave inulin supplementation affects the fecal microbiota of healthy adults participating in a randomized, double-blind, placebo-controlled, crossover trial. J Nutr. 2015;145:2025-32.

1270. La Fata G, Rastall RA, Lacroix C, Harmsen HJ, Mohajeri MH, Weber P, Steinert RE. Recent development of prebiotic research—statement from an expert workshop. Nutrients. 2017;9:1376.

1271. Bultman SJ. Emerging roles of the microbiome in cancer. Carcinogenesis. 2014;35:249-55.

1272. De Filippo C, Cavalieri D, Di Paola M, Ramazzotti M, Poullet JB, Massart S, Collini S, Pieraccini G, Lionetti P. Impact of diet in shaping gut microbiota revealed by a comparative study in children from Europe and rural Africa. Proc Natl Acad Sci USA. 2010;107:14691-6.

1273. David LA, Maurice CF, Carmody RN, Gootenberg DB, Button JE, Wolfe BE, Ling AV, Devlin AS, Varma Y, Fischbach MA, Biddinger SB, Dutton RJ, Turnbaugh PJ. Diet rapidly and reproducibly alters the human gut microbiome. Nature. 2014;505:559-63.

1274. Duda-Chodak A, Tarko T, Satora P, Sroka P. Interaction of dietary compounds, especially polyphenols, with the intestinal microbiota: a review. Eur J Nutr. 2015;54:325-41.

1275. Murota K, Nakamura Y, Uehara M. Flavonoid metabolism: The interaction of metabolites and gut microbiota. Biosci Biotechnol Biochem. 2018;82:600-10.

1276. Masella R, Santangelo C, D'Archivio M, Li Volti G, Giovannini C, Galvano F. Protocatechuic acid and human disease prevention: biological activities and molecular mechanisms. Curr Med Chem. 2012;19:2901-17.

1277. Johnson AJ, Vangay P, Al-Ghalith GA, Hillmann BM, Ward TL, Shields-Cutler RR, Kim AD, Shmagel AK, Syed AN, Personalized Microbiome Class S, Walter J, Menon R, Koecher K, Knights D. Daily sampling reveals personalized diet-microbiome associations in humans. Cell Host Microbe. 2019;25:789-802 e5.

1278. McBurney MI, Davis C, Fraser CM, Schneeman BO, Huttenhower C, Verbeke K, Walter J, Latulippe ME. Establishing what constitutes a healthy human gut microbiome: State of the science, regulatory considerations, and future directions. J Nutr. 2019;149:1882-95.

1279. Petersen C, Round JL. Defining dysbiosis and its influence on host immunity and disease. Cell Microbiol. 2014;16:1024-33.

1280. Yatsunenko T, Rey FE, Manary MJ, Trehan I, Dominguez-Bello MG, Contreras M, Magris M, Hidalgo G, Baldassano RN, Anokhin AP, Heath AC, Warner B, Reeder J, Kuczynski J, Caporaso JG, Lozupone CA, Lauber C, Clemente JC, Knights D, Knight R, Gordon JI. Human gut microbiome viewed across age and geography. Nature. 2012;486:222-7.

1281. Turnbaugh PJ, Backhed F, Fulton L, Gordon JI. Diet-induced obesity is linked to marked but reversible alterations in the mouse distal gut microbiome. Cell Host Microbe. 2008;3:213-23.

1282. Willing BP, Dicksved J, Halfvarson J, Andersson AF, Lucio M, Zheng Z, Jarnerot G, Tysk C, Jansson JK, Engstrand L. A pyrosequencing study in twins shows that gastrointestinal microbial profiles vary with inflammatory bowel disease phenotypes. Gastroenterology. 2010;139:1844-54 e1.

1283. Turroni S, Magnani M, Kc P, Lesnik P, Vidal H, Heer M. Gut microbiome and space travelers' health: State of the art and possible pro/prebiotic strategies for long-term space missions. Front Physiol. 2020;11.

1284. Voorhies AA, Mark Ott C, Mehta S, Pierson DL, Crucian BE, Feiveson A, Oubre CM, Torralba M, Moncera K, Zhang Y, Zurek E, Lorenzi HA. Study of the impact of long-duration space missions at the International Space Station on the astronaut microbiome. Sci Rep. 2019;9:9911.

1285. Douglas GL, Voorhies AA. Evidence based selection of probiotic strains to promote astronaut health or alleviate symptoms of illness on long duration spaceflight missions. Beneficial microbes. 2017:1-12.

1286. Cruz-Pereira JS, Rea K, Nolan YM, O'Leary OF, Dinan TG, Cryan JF. Depression's unholy trinity: Dysregulated stress, immunity, and the microbiome. Annu Rev Psychol. 2020;71:49-78.

1287. Rothhammer V, Borucki DM, Tjon EC, Takenaka MC, Chao C-C, Ardura-Fabregat A, de Lima KA, Gutiérrez-Vázquez C, Hewson P, Staszewski O. Microglial control of astrocytes in response to microbial metabolites. Nature. 2018:1.

1288. Sylvia KE, Demas GE. A gut feeling: Microbiome-brain-immune interactions modulate social and affective behaviors. Horm Behav. 2018;99:41-9.

1289. Bienenstock J, Kunze WA, Forsythe P. Disruptive physiology: olfaction and the microbiome-gut-brain axis. Biol Rev Camb Philos Soc. 2018;93:390-403.

1290. Li L, Su Q, Xie B, Duan L, Zhao W, Hu D, Wu R, Liu H. Gut microbes in correlation with mood: case study in a closed experimental human life support system. Neurogastroenterol Motil. 2016;28:1233-40.

1291. Dinan TG, Stanton C, Cryan JF. Psychobiotics: a novel class of psychotropic. Biol Psychiatry. 2013;74:720-6.

1292. Sampson TR, Mazmanian SK. Control of brain development, function, and behavior by the microbiome. Cell Host Microbe. 2015;17:565-76.

1293. Stilling RM, Dinan TG, Cryan JF. Microbial genes, brain & behaviour–epigenetic regulation of the gut–brain axis. Genes, Brain and Behavior. 2014;13:69-86.

1294. Napier BA, Andres-Terre M, Massis LM, Hryckowian AJ, Higginbottom SK, Cumnock K, Casey KM, Haileselassie B, Lugo KA, Schneider DS. Western diet regulates immune status and the response to LPS-driven sepsis independent of diet-associated microbiome. Proceedings of the National Academy of Sciences. 2019;116:3688-94.

1295. Salmon JK, Armstrong CA, Ansel JC. The skin as an immune organ. West J Med. 1994;160:146-52.

1296. Basavaraj KH, Seemanthini C, Rashmi R. Diet in dermatology: present perspectives. Indian J Dermatol. 2010;55:205-10.

1297. Galimberti F, Mesinkovska NA. Skin findings associated with nutritional deficiencies. Cleve Clin J Med. 2016;83:731-9.

1298. Dunn C, Boyd M, Orengo I. Dermatologic manifestations in spaceflight: a review. Dermatol Online J. 2018;24.

1299. Broskey NT, Marlatt KL, Most J, Erickson ML, Irving BA, Redman LM. The panacea of human aging: Calorie restriction versus exercise. Exerc Sport Sci Rev. 2019;47:169-75.

1300. Stein TP, Leskiw MJ. Oxidant damage during and after spaceflight. Am J Physiol Endocrinol Metab. 2000;278:E375-82.

1301. Stein TP, Gaprindashvili T. Spaceflight and protein metabolism, with special reference to humans. Am J Clin Nutr. 1994;60:806S-19S.

1302. Chandra RK, Chandra S, Gupta S. Antibody affinity and immune complexes after immunization with tetanus toxoid in protein-energy malnutrition. Am J Clin Nutr. 1984;40:131-4.

1303. Guadagni M, Biolo G. Effects of inflammation and/or inactivity on the need for dietary protein. Curr Opin Clin Nutr Metab Care. 2009;12:617-22.

1304. Kang M, Oh NS, Kim M, Ahn HY, Yoo HJ, Sun M, Kang SH, Yang HJ, Kwon DY, Lee JH. Supplementation of fermented Maillard-reactive whey protein enhances immunity by increasing NK cell activity. Food Funct. 2017;8:1718-25.

1305. Liberman K, Njemini R, Luiking Y, Forti LN, Verlaan S, Bauer JM, Memelink R, Brandt K, Donini LM, Maggio M, Mets T, Wijers SLJ, Sieber C, Cederholm T, Bautmans I. Thirteen weeks of supplementation of vitamin D and leucine-enriched whey protein nutritional supplement attenuates chronic low-grade inflammation in sarcopenic older adults: the PROVIDE study. Aging Clin Exp Res. 2019;31:845-54.

1306. Bumrungpert A, Pavadhgul P, Nunthanawanich P, Sirikanchanarod A, Adulbhan A. Whey protein supplementation improves nutritional status, glutathione levels, and immune function in cancer patients: A randomized, double-blind controlled trial. J Med Food. 2018;21:612-6.

1307. Lu J, Francis J, Doster RS, Haley KP, Craft KM, Moore RE, Chambers SA, Aronoff DM, Osteen K, Damo SM, Manning S, Townsend SD, Gaddy JA. Lactoferrin: A critical mediator of both host immune response and antimicrobial activity in response to streptococcal infections. ACS Infect Dis. 2020;6:1615-23.

1308. van Splunter M, Perdijk O, Fick-Brinkhof H, Feitsma AL, Floris-Vollenbroek EG, Meijer B, Brugman S, Savelkoul HFJ, van Hoffen E, van Neerven RJJ. Bovine lactoferrin enhances TLR7-mediated responses in plasmacytoid dendritic cells in elderly women: Results from a nutritional intervention study with bovine lactoferrin, GOS and vitamin D. Front Immunol. 2018;9:2677.

1309. Kirk SJ, Barbul A. Role of arginine in trauma, sepsis, and immunity. JPEN J Parenter Enteral Nutr. 1990;14:226S-9S.

1310. Kirk SJ, Hurson M, Regan MC, Holt DR, Wasserkrug HL, Barbul A. Arginine stimulates wound healing and immune function in elderly human beings. Surgery. 1993;114:155-9; discussion 60.

1311. Alito MA, de Aguilar-Nascimento JE. Multimodal perioperative care plus immunonutrition versus traditional care in total hip arthroplasty: a randomized pilot study. Nutr J. 2016;15:34.

1312. Singleton KD, Wischmeyer PE. Glutamine attenuates inflammation and NF-kappaB activation via Cullin-1 deneddylation. Biochem Biophys Res Commun. 2008;373:445-9.

1313. Wischmeyer PE. Glutamine: mode of action in critical illness. Crit Care Med. 2007;35:S541-4.

1314. Wischmeyer PE. Glutamine: role in critical illness and ongoing clinical trials. Curr Opin Gastroenterol. 2008;24:190-7.

1315. Mondello S, Italiano D, Giacobbe MS, Mondello P, Trimarchi G, Aloisi C, Bramanti P, Spina E. Glutamine-supplemented total parenteral nutrition improves immunological status in anorectic patients. Nutrition. 2010;26:677-81.

1316. Novak F, Heyland DK, Avenell A, Drover JW, Su X. Glutamine supplementation in serious illness: a systematic review of the evidence. Crit Care Med. 2002;30:2022-9.

1317. Lang PO, Aspinall R. Vitamin D status and the host resistance to infections: What it is currently (not) understood. Clin Ther. 2017;39:930-45.

1318. Pincikova T, Paquin-Proulx D, Sandberg JK, Flodstrom-Tullberg M, Hjelte L. Vitamin D treatment modulates immune activation in cystic fibrosis. Clin Exp Immunol. 2017;189:359-71.

1319. van Etten E, Mathieu C. Immunoregulation by 1,25-dihydroxyvitamin D3: basic concepts. J Steroid Biochem Mol Biol. 2005;97:93-101.

1320. Mathieu C, Adorini L. The coming of age of 1,25-dihydroxyvitamin D(3) analogs as immunomodulatory agents. Trends Mol Med. 2002;8:174-9.

1321. Hewison M, Freeman L, Hughes SV, Evans KN, Bland R, Eliopoulos AG, Kilby MD, Moss PA, Chakraverty R. Differential regulation of vitamin D receptor and its ligand in human monocyte-derived dendritic cells. J Immunol. 2003;170:5382-90.

1322. Martineau AR, Wilkinson KA, Newton SM, Floto RA, Norman AW, Skolimowska K, Davidson RN, Sorensen OE, Kampmann B, Griffiths CJ, Wilkinson RJ. IFN-gamma- and TNF-independent vitamin D-inducible human suppression of mycobacteria: the role of cathelicidin LL-37. J Immunol. 2007;178:7190-8.

1323. Martineau AR, Wilkinson RJ, Wilkinson KA, Newton SM, Kampmann B, Hall BM, Packe GE, Davidson RN, Eldridge SM, Maunsell ZJ, Rainbow SJ, Berry JL, Griffiths CJ. A single dose of vitamin D enhances immunity to mycobacteria. Am J Respir Crit Care Med. 2007;176:208-13.

1324. Kondo Y, Kato T, Kimura O, Iwata T, Ninomiya M, Kakazu E, Miura M, Akahane T, Miyazaki Y, Kobayashi T, Ishii M, Kisara N, Sasaki K, Nakayama H, Igarashi T, Obara N, Ueno Y, Morosawa T, Shimosegawa T. 1(OH) vitamin D3 supplementation improves the sensitivity of the immune-response during Peg-IFN/RBV therapy in chronic hepatitis C patients-case controlled trial. PLoS One. 2013;8:e63672.

1325. Im JH, Je YS, Baek J, Chung MH, Kwon HY, Lee JS. Nutritional status of patients with coronavirus disease 2019 (COVID-19). Int J Infect Dis. 2020.

1326. Alipio MM. Vitamin D supplementation could possibly improve clinical outcomes of patients infected with coronavirus-2019 (COVID-2019) SSRN Electron J. 2020:Apr 9.

1327. Grant WB, Lahore H, McDonnell SL, Baggerly CA, French CB, Aliano JL, Bhattoa HP. Evidence that vitamin D supplementation could reduce risk of influenza and COVID-19 infections and deaths. Nutrients. 2020;12.

1328. Grant WB, Lahore H, Rockwell MS. The benefits of vitamin D supplementation for athletes: better performance and reduced risk of COVID-19. Nutrients. 2020;12.

1329. Ricca C, Aillon A, Viano M, Bergandi L, Aldieri E, Silvagno F. Vitamin D inhibits the epithelial-mesenchymal transition by a negative feedback regulation of TGF-beta activity. J Steroid Biochem Mol Biol. 2019;187:97-105.

1330. Rooney BV, Crucian BE, Pierson DL, Laudenslager ML, Mehta SK. Herpes virus reactivation in astronauts during spaceflight and its application on Earth. Front Microbiol. 2019;10:16.

1331. Agha NH, Baker FL, Kunz HE, Spielmann G, Mylabathula PL, Rooney BV, Mehta SK, Pierson DL, Laughlin MS, Markofski MM, Crucian BE, Simpson RJ. Salivary antimicrobial proteins and stress biomarkers are elevated during a 6-month mission to the International Space Station. J Appl Physiol (1985). 2020;128:264-75.

1332. Bigley AB, Agha NH, Baker FL, Spielmann G, Kunz HE, Mylabathula PL, Rooney BV, Laughlin MS, Mehta SK, Pierson DL, Crucian BE, Simpson RJ. NK cell function is impaired during long-duration spaceflight. J Appl Physiol (1985). 2019;126:842-53.

1333. Buchheim JI, Matzel S, Rykova M, Vassilieva G, Ponomarev S, Nichiporuk I, Horl M, Moser D, Biere K, Feuerecker M, Schelling G, Thieme D, Kaufmann I, Thiel M, Choukér A. Stress related shift toward inflammaging in cosmonauts after long-duration space flight. Front Physiol. 2019;10:85.

1334. Choukér A. Stress challenges and immunity in space: from mechanisms to monitoring and preventive strategies, 2nd edition. Berlin: Springer International Publishing; 2020.

1335. Chakraborty N, Gautam A, Muhie S, Miller SA, Jett M, Hammamieh R. An integrated omics analysis: impact of microgravity on host response to lipopolysaccharide in vitro. BMC Genomics. 2014;15:659.

1336. Chakraborty N, Cheema A, Gautam A, Donohue D, Hoke A, Conley C, Jett M, Hammamieh R. Gene-metabolite profile integration to understand the cause of spaceflight induced immunodeficiency. NPJ Microgravity. 2018;4:4.

1337. Tamura J, Kubota K, Murakami H, Sawamura M, Matsushima T, Tamura T, Saitoh T, Kurabayshi H, Naruse T. Immunomodulation by vitamin B_{12}: augmentation of CD8+ T lymphocytes and natural killer (NK) cell activity in vitamin B_{12}-deficient patients by methyl-B_{12} treatment. Clin Exp Immunol. 1999;116:28-32.

1338. Bunout D, Barrera G, Hirsch S, Gattas V, de la Maza MP, Haschke F, Steenhout P, Klassen P, Hager C, Avendano M, Petermann M, Munoz C. Effects of a nutritional supplement on the immune response and cytokine production in free-living Chilean elderly. JPEN J Parenter Enteral Nutr. 2004;28:348-54.

1339. Kannan R, Ng MJ. Cutaneous lesions and vitamin B_{12} deficiency: an often-forgotten link. Can Fam Physician. 2008;54:529-32.

1340. Inubushi T, Takasawa T, Tuboi Y, Watanabe N, Aki K, Katunuma N. Changes of glucose metabolism and skin-collagen neogenesis in vitamin B_6 deficiency. Biofactors. 2005;23:59-67.

1341. Zempleni J, Kuroishi T. Biotin. Adv Nutr. 2012;3:213-4.

1342. Zempleni J, Wijeratne SSK, Kuroishi T. Biotin. In: Erdman JW, Jr., MacDonald IA, Zeisel SH, editors. Present knowledge in nutrition. 9th ed. Washington, DC: International Life Sciences Institute Press; 2010. p. 359-74.

1343. Mock DM, Malik MI. Distribution of biotin in human plasma: most of the biotin is not bound to protein. Am J Clin Nutr. 1992;56:427-32.

1344. Rathman SC, Gregory JF, 3rd, McMahon RJ. Pharmacological biotin supplementation maintains biotin status and function in rats administered dietary carbamazepine. J Nutr. 2003;133:2857-62.

1345. Krause KH, Bonjour JP, Berlit P, Kynast G, Schmidt-Gayk H, Schellenberg B. Effect of long-term treatment with antiepileptic drugs on the vitamin status. Drug Nutr Interact. 1988;5:317-43.

1346. Mock DM, Stadler DD, Stratton SL, Mock NI. Biotin status assessed longitudinally in pregnant women. J Nutr. 1997;127:710-6.

1347. Maeda Y, Kawata S, Inui Y, Fukuda K, Igura T, Matsuzawa Y. Biotin deficiency decreases ornithine transcarbamylase activity and mRNA in rat liver. J Nutr. 1996;126:61-6.

1348. Borboni P, Magnaterra R, Rabini RA, Staffolani R, Porzio O, Sesti G, Fusco A, Mazzanti L, Lauro R, Marlier LN. Effect of biotin on glucokinase activity, mRNA expression and insulin release in cultured beta-cells. Acta Diabetol. 1996;33:154-8.

1349. Dakshinamurti K, Li W. Transcriptional regulation of liver phosphoenolpyruvate carboxykinase by biotin in diabetic rats. Mol Cell Biochem. 1994;132:127-32.

1350. Heer M, Baisch F, Kropp J, Gerzer R, Drummer C. High dietary sodium chloride consumption may not induce body fluid retention in humans. Am J Physiol Renal Physiol. 2000;278:F585-95.

1351. Titze J, Lang R, Ilies C, Schwind KH, Kirsch KA, Dietsch P, Luft FC, Hilgers KF. Osmotically inactive skin Na+ storage in rats. Am J Physiol Renal Physiol. 2003;285:F1108-17.

1352. Marvar PJ, Gordon FJ, Harrison DG. Blood pressure control: salt gets under your skin. Nat Med. 2009; 15:487-8.

1353. Matthias J, Maul J, Noster R, Meinl H, Chao YY, Gerstenberg H, Jeschke F, Gasparoni G, Welle A, Walter J, Nordstrom K, Eberhardt K, Renisch D, Donakonda S, Knolle P, Soll D, Grabbe S, Garzorz-Stark N, Eyerich K, Biedermann T, Baumjohann D, Zielinski CE. Sodium chloride is an ionic checkpoint for human TH2 cells and shapes the atopic skin microenvironment. Sci Transl Med. 2019;11.

1354. Jobin K, Stumpf NE, Schwab S, Eichler M, Neubert P, Rauh M, Adamowski M, Babyak O, Hinze D, Sivalingam S, Weisheit C, Hochheiser K, Schmidt SV, Meissner M, Garbi N, Abdullah Z, Wenzel U, Holzel M, Jantsch J, Kurts C. A high-salt diet compromises antibacterial neutrophil responses through hormonal perturbation. Sci Transl Med. 2020;12.

1355. Chen Q, Ross AC. Vitamin A and immune function: retinoic acid modulates population dynamics in antigen receptor and CD38-stimulated splenic B cells. Proc Natl Acad Sci USA. 2005;102:14142-9.

1356. Ross AC. Vitamin A and retinoic acid in T cell-related immunity. Am J Clin Nutr. 2012;96:1166S-72S.

1357. Ross AC. Vitamin A status: relationship to immunity and the antibody response. Proc Soc Exp Biol Med. 1992;200:303-20.

1358. Stephensen CB. Vitamin A, infection, and immune function. Annu Rev Nutr. 2001;21:167-92.

1359. Stephensen CB. Examining the effect of a nutrition intervention on immune function in healthy humans: what do we mean by immune function and who is really healthy anyway? Am J Clin Nutr. 2001;74:565-6.

1360. Semba RD. The role of vitamin A and related retinoids in immune function. Nutr Rev. 1998;56:S38-48.

1361. Petiz LL, Girardi CS, Bortolin RC, Kunzler A, Gasparotto J, Rabelo TK, Matte C, Moreira JC, Gelain DP. Vitamin A oral supplementation induces oxidative stress and suppresses IL-10 and HSP70 in skeletal muscle of trained rats. Nutrients. 2017;9.

1362. Petiz LL, Kunzler A, Bortolin RC, Gasparotto J, Matte C, Moreira JCF, Gelain DP. Role of vitamin A oral supplementation on oxidative stress and inflammatory response in the liver of trained rats. Appl Physiol Nutr Metab. 2017;42:1192-200.

1363. Penkert RR, Cortez V, Karlsson EA, Livingston B, Surman SL, Li Y, Catharine Ross A, Schultz-Cherry S, Hurwitz JL. Vitamin A corrects tissue deficits in diet-induced obese mice and reduces influenza infection after vaccination and challenge. Obesity (Silver Spring). 2020;28:1631-6.

1364. Jensen KJ, Fisker AB, Andersen A, Sartono E, Yazdanbakhsh M, Aaby P, Erikstrup C, Benn CS. The effects of vitamin A supplementation with measles vaccine on leucocyte counts and in vitro cytokine production. Br J Nutr. 2016;115:619-28.

1365. Bouamama S, Merzouk H, Medjdoub A, Merzouk-Saidi A, Merzouk SA. Effects of exogenous vitamins A, C, and E and NADH supplementation on proliferation, cytokines release, and cell redox status of lymphocytes from healthy aged subjects. Appl Physiol Nutr Metab. 2017;42:579-87.

1366. Field CJ, Johnson IR, Schley PD. Nutrients and their role in host resistance to infection. J Leukoc Biol. 2002;71:16-32.

1367. Schwager J, Schulze J. Modulation of interleukin production by ascorbic acid. Vet Immunol Immunopathol. 1998;64:45-57.

1368. Hirschmann JV, Raugi GJ. Adult scurvy. J Am Acad Dermatol. 1999;41:895-906; quiz 7-10.

1369. Jeng KC, Yang CS, Siu WY, Tsai YS, Liao WJ, Kuo JS. Supplementation with vitamins C and E enhances cytokine production by peripheral blood mononuclear cells in healthy adults. Am J Clin Nutr. 1996;64:960-5.

1370. Carr AC, Maggini S. Vitamin C and immune function. Nutrients. 2017;9.

1371. Colunga Biancatelli RML, Berrill M, Catravas JD, Marik PE. Quercetin and vitamin C: An experimental, synergistic therapy for the prevention and treatment of SARS-CoV-2 related disease (COVID-19). Front Immunol. 2020;11:1451.

1372. Traber MG. Vitamin E inadequacy in humans: causes and consequences. Adv Nutr. 2014;5:503-14.

1373. Traber MG. Vitamin E. In: Erdman JW, Jr., MacDonald IA, Zeisel SH, editors. Present knowledge in nutrition. 7th ed. Washington, DC: International Life Sciences Institute; 2010. p. 214-29.

1374. Institute of Medicine. Dietary reference intakes for vitamin C, vitamin E, selenium, and carotenoids. Washington, DC: National Academy Press; 2000.

1375. Park OJ, Kim HY, Kim WK, Kim YJ, Kim SH. Effect of vitamin E supplementation on antioxidant defense systems and humoral immune responses in young, middle-aged and elderly Korean women. J Nutr Sci Vitaminol (Tokyo). 2003;49:94-9.

1376. Taylor GR, Konstantinova I, Sonnenfeld G, Jennings R. Changes in the immune system during and after spaceflight. Adv Space Biol Med. 1997;6:1-32.

1377. Borchers AT, Keen CL, Gershwin ME. Microgravity and immune responsiveness: implications for space travel. Nutrition. 2002;18:889-98.

1378. Tipton CM, Greenleaf JE, Jackson CG. Neuroendocrine and immune system responses with spaceflights. Med Sci Sports Exerc. 1996;28:988-98.

1379. Crucian BE, Stowe RP, Pierson DL, Sams CF. Immune system dysregulation following short- vs long-duration spaceflight. Aviat Space Environ Med. 2008;79:835-43.

1380. Wintergerst ES, Maggini S, Hornig DH. Immune-enhancing role of vitamin C and zinc and effect on clinical conditions. Ann Nutr Metab. 2006;50:85-94.

1381. Steinbrenner H, Klotz LO. [Selenium and zinc: "antioxidants" for healthy aging?]. Z Gerontol Geriatr. 2020;53:295-302.

1382. Elmadfa I, Meyer AL. The role of the status of selected micronutrients in shaping the immune function. Endocr Metab Immune Disord Drug Targets. 2019;19:1100-15.

1383. Rayman MP, Winther KH, Pastor-Barriuso R, Cold F, Thvilum M, Stranges S, Guallar E, Cold S. Effect of long-term selenium supplementation on mortality: Results from a multiple-dose, randomised controlled trial. Free Radic Biol Med. 2018;127:46-54.

1384. Chung S, Yao H, Caito S, Hwang JW, Arunachalam G, Rahman I. Regulation of SIRT1 in cellular functions: role of polyphenols. Arch Biochem Biophys. 2010;501:79-90.

1385. Perron NR, Brumaghim JL. A review of the antioxidant mechanisms of polyphenol compounds related to iron binding. Cell Biochem Biophys. 2009;53:75-100.

1386. Ding S, Jiang H, Fang J. Regulation of immune function by polyphenols. J Immunol Res. 2018;2018:1264074.

1387. Cuevas A, Saavedra N, Salazar LA, Abdalla DS. Modulation of immune function by polyphenols: possible contribution of epigenetic factors. Nutrients. 2013;5:2314-32.

1388. Gao X, Deeb D, Media J, Divine G, Jiang H, Chapman RA, Gautam SC. Immunomodulatory activity of resveratrol: discrepant in vitro and in vivo immunological effects. Biochem Pharmacol. 2003;66:2427-35.

1389. Park HJ, Lee CM, Jung ID, Lee JS, Jeong YI, Chang JH, Chun SH, Kim MJ, Choi IW, Ahn SC, Shin YK, Yeom SR, Park YM. Quercetin regulates Th1/Th2 balance in a murine model of asthma. Int Immunopharmacol. 2009;9:261-7.

1390. Sharma S, Chopra K, Kulkarni SK, Agrewala JN. Resveratrol and curcumin suppress immune response through CD28/CTLA-4 and CD80 co-stimulatory pathway. Clin Exp Immunol. 2007;147:155-63.

1391. Shim JH, Choi HS, Pugliese A, Lee SY, Chae JI, Choi BY, Bode AM, Dong Z. (-)-Epigallocatechin gallate regulates CD3-mediated T cell receptor signaling in leukemia through the inhibition of ZAP-70 kinase. J Biol Chem. 2008;283:28370-9.

1392. Singh NP, Hegde VL, Hofseth LJ, Nagarkatti M, Nagarkatti P. Resveratrol (trans-3,5,4'-trihydroxystilbene) ameliorates experimental allergic encephalomyelitis, primarily via induction of apoptosis in T cells involving activation of aryl hydrocarbon receptor and estrogen receptor. Mol Pharmacol. 2007;72:1508-21.

1393. Song EK, Hur H, Han MK. Epigallocatechin gallate prevents autoimmune diabetes induced by multiple low doses of streptozotocin in mice. Arch Pharm Res. 2003;26:559-63.

1394. Devine A, Hodgson JM, Dick IM, Prince RL. Tea drinking is associated with benefits on bone density in older women. Am J Clin Nutr. 2007;86:1243-7.

1395. Chirumbolo S. Dietary assumption of plant polyphenols and prevention of allergy. Curr Pharm Des. 2014;20:811-39.

1396. Magrone T, Jirillo E. Influence of polyphenols on allergic immune reactions: mechanisms of action. Proc Nutr Soc. 2012;71:316-21.

1397. Merry TL, Ristow M. Mitohormesis in exercise training. Free Radic Biol Med. 2016;98:123-30.

1398. Dao MC, Meydani SN. Iron biology, immunology, aging, and obesity: four fields connected by the small peptide hormone hepcidin. Adv Nutr. 2013;4:602-17.

1399. Sazawal S, Black RE, Ramsan M, Chwaya HM, Stoltzfus RJ, Dutta A, Dhingra U, Kabole I, Deb S, Othman MK, Kabole FM. Effects of routine prophylactic supplementation with iron and folic acid on admission to hospital and mortality in preschool children in a high malaria transmission setting: community-based, randomised, placebo-controlled trial. Lancet. 2006;367:133-43.

1400. Doherty CP. Host-pathogen interactions: the role of iron. J Nutr. 2007;137:1341-4.

1401. Alfrey CP, Rice L, Udden MM, Driscoll TB. Neocytolysis: physiological down-regulator of red-cell mass. Lancet. 1997;349:1389-90.

1402. Johnson PC. The erythropoietic effects of weightlessness. In: Dunn CDR, editor. Current concepts in erythropoiesis. New York: John Wiley & Sons Ltd.; 1983. p. 279-300.

1403. Udden MM, Driscoll TB, Pickett MH, Leach-Huntoon CS, Alfrey CP. Decreased production of red blood cells in human subjects exposed to microgravity. J Lab Clin Med. 1995;125:442-9.

1404. Ganz T. Hepcidin--a peptide hormone at the interface of innate immunity and iron metabolism. Curr Top Microbiol Immunol. 2006;306:183-98.

1405. Ganz T. Hepcidin and iron regulation, 10 years later. Blood. 2011;117:4425-33.

1406. Lee P, Peng H, Gelbart T, Wang L, Beutler E. Regulation of hepcidin transcription by interleukin-1 and interleukin-6. Proc Natl Acad Sci USA. 2005;102:1906-10.

1407. Nemeth E, Rivera S, Gabayan V, Keller C, Taudorf S, Pedersen BK, Ganz T. IL-6 mediates hypoferremia of inflammation by inducing the synthesis of the iron regulatory hormone hepcidin. J Clin Invest. 2004;113:1271-6.

1408. Theriot CA, Zanello SB. Molecular effects of spaceflight in the mouse eye after space shuttle mission STS-135. Gravit Space Res. 2014;2:3-24.

1409. Theriot CA, Westby CM, Morgan JLL, Zwart SR, Zanello SB. High dietary iron increases oxidative stress and radiosensitivity in the rat retina and vasculature after exposure to fractionated gamma radiation. NPJ Microgravity. 2016;2:16014.

1410. Aubailly M, Santus R, Salmon S. Ferrous ion release from ferritin by ultraviolet-A radiations. Photochem Photobiol. 1991;54:769-73.

1411. Sannita WG, Acquaviva M, Ball SL, Belli F, Bisti S, Bidoli V, Carozzo S, Casolino M, Cucinotta F, De Pascale MP, Di Fino L, Di Marco S, Maccarone R, Martello C, Miller J, Narici L, Peachey NS, Picozza P, Rinaldi A, Ruggieri D, Saturno M, Schardt D, Vazquez M. Effects of heavy ions on visual function and electrophysiology of rodents: the ALTEA-MICE project. Adv Space Res. 2004;33:1347-51.

1412. Stevens RG, Morris JE, Anderson LE. Hemochromatosis heterozygotes may constitute a radiation-sensitive subpopulation. Radiat Res. 2000;153:844-7.

1413. Vanamala J, Glagolenko A, Yang P, Carroll RJ, Murphy ME, Newman RA, Ford JR, Braby LA, Chapkin RS, Turner ND, Lupton JR. Dietary fish oil and pectin enhance colonocyte apoptosis in part through suppression of PPARdelta/PGE2 and elevation of PGE3. Carcinogenesis. 2008;29:790-6.

1414. Kumar NG, Contaifer D, Madurantakam P, Carbone S, Price ET, Van Tassell B, Brophy DF, Wijesinghe DS. Dietary Bioactive Fatty Acids as Modulators of Immune Function: Implications on Human Health. Nutrients. 2019;11.

1415. Camandola S, Leonarduzzi G, Musso T, Varesio L, Carini R, Scavazza A, Chiarpotto E, Baeuerle PA, Poli G. Nuclear factor kB is activated by arachidonic acid but not by eicosapentaenoic acid. Biochem Biophys Res Commun. 1996;229:643-7.

1416. Kang JX, Weylandt KH. Modulation of inflammatory cytokines by omega-3 fatty acids. Subcell Biochem. 2008;49:133-43.

1417. Kim HH, Lee Y, Eun HC, Chung JH. Eicosapentaenoic acid inhibits TNF-alpha-induced matrix metalloproteinase-9 expression in human keratinocytes, HaCaT cells. Biochem Biophys Res Comm. 2008;368:343-9.

1418. Magee P, Pearson S, Allen J. The omega-3 fatty acid, eicosapentaenoic acid (EPA), prevents the damaging effects of tumour necrosis factor (TNF)-alpha during murine skeletal muscle cell differentiation. Lipids Health Dis. 2008;7:24.

Expedition 54 crewmember Mark Vande Hei rides the Canadarm2 Space Station Remote Manipulator System to a worksite during Extravehicular Activity 48. Photo Credit: NASA.

12 Oxidative Stress

Many natural processes produce ROS, including breathing, metabolism, and converting fats into fuels. Low levels of ROS are important for intracellular destruction of bacteria by phagocytes and redox signaling, and they are beneficial for maintaining homeostasis, in general (1419). The body has natural antioxidant defense systems that minimize damage from free radicals, if they are present in excessive amounts, then damage to proteins, lipids, and DNA can occur. Some sources of ROS and reactive nitrogen species during spaceflight include ionizing radiation exposure, EVA and EVA prebreathe protocols, exercise, and even diet (10, 746, 1420-1422)

Radiation Exposure

Long-duration exploration missions beyond low-Earth orbit will be accompanied by high-LET galactic cosmic rays consisting of high-energy protons and high-charge and high-energy nuclei (11). High-LET radiation deposits part of its energy in ion tracks known as cores and the remaining energy is dispersed randomly outside of the core by energetic electrons, whereas low-LET ionizing radiation, including x-rays or gamma rays, deposit energy uniformly in tissue (13). In addition to galactic cosmic rays, solar particle events comprised mainly of low- to medium-energy protons periodically bombard the solar system. The timing of these events depends on the phase of the 11-year solar cycle (14).

Galactic cosmic radiation exposures during exploration missions to Mars will be about 10 times higher than exposures on the ISS (15). These higher radiation doses will increase the astronauts' risk of both short- and long-term health effects. The maximum annual radiation exposure from galactic cosmic radiation during a Mars mission is predicted to be of the order of 300 to 450 mGy for the 365- to 900-day planetary mission with less than 50% of the dose from high atomic number (Z) and energy radiation (HZE) particles (1011).

Reactive Oxygen Species and Exercise

Exercise-induced fatigue and muscle atrophy are mediated in part by ROS. Electron spin resonance spectroscopy technology confirmed earlier findings from the 1950s suggesting that short-lived reactive intermediate molecules like ROS are present in skeletal muscle after exercise (1423). Since then, numerous studies have supported a role of ROS in skeletal muscle fatigue (1423-1425). Mitochondria are the major source of ROS in muscle cells, where a fine balance of ROS exists between maximizing force and minimizing fatigue (1420). Antioxidant-mediated depletion of ROS from unfatigued muscle yields decreased production of skeletal muscle force (1426). On the other hand, excess ROS can be detrimental in terms of fatigue. ROS can denature proteins directly associated with the sarcoplasmic reticulum Ca^{2+} release mechanism (1427), thus compromising tension development. Also, rat studies show that xanthine oxidase-induced ROS yields increased diaphragm fatigue, and that the elevated ROS during intense exercise is implicated in the onset of muscle fatigue (1428). Furthermore, decreased antioxidant status lowers exercise capacity and increases the onset of fatigue in human and animal studies (1423, 1425).

Astronauts perform prolonged upper-body exercise during EVA activity. One of the limiting factors in completing EVA tasks is forearm and hand muscle fatigue due to extensive tool operation. The fatigue often requires crewmembers to stop and rest, thereby prolonging the duration of EVA, and limits the number of tasks performed during each EVA. To date, there is little evidence showing that antioxidant supplementation has a benefit for improving muscle performance and inhibiting fatigue. Given the nature of the requirement for homeostasis of redox systems, there is a potential for antioxidant overload to decrease muscle force potential instead of having a protective effect.

Oxidative Damage Markers during Spaceflight and in Ground Analogs

Evidence for oxidative stress resulting from spaceflight exposure exists in multiple tissues, including ocular tissue (1117, 1429), urinary and blood biomarkers of damage to DNA, lipids, and protein (10, 111, 1300, 1430), and in gene expression (1431, 1432). Plasma malondialdehyde (MDA), 8-iso-prostaglandin $F_{2\alpha}$($PGF_{2\alpha}$), and urinary 8OHdG have been measured during and after flight as indicators of lipid peroxidation (MDA and $PGF_{2\alpha}$) and DNA damage (8OHdG) (110, 1300). A significant elevation of urinary 8OHdG has been noted after long-duration missions (Mir and ISS) (111). These data are supported by results from the ground-based analog NEEMO, in which crewmembers underwent 10- to 14-day saturation dives (753, 1433). In one study, urinary $PGF_{2\alpha}$ was significantly decreased during flight but elevated about 2.5-fold after flight (1300). Plasma MDA was increased both during and after flight (1300). In another ISS study with 13 astronauts, $PGF_{2\alpha}$ was approximately 65% higher during flight compared to preflight (863). In a Russian 120-day bed rest study, increased concentrations of markers of lipid peroxidation were found in subjects. This increase was mitigated with vitamin E (1434). In a study of mice launched to the ISS,

Figure 76. NASA astronaut Anne McClain works on the International Space Station's Port-4 truss structure during a six-hour, 39-minute spacewalk to upgrade the orbital complex's power storage capacity. Photo Credit: NASA.

oxidative stress impacted blood-brain barrier function (1435).

The apparent increases in oxidative damage observed during and after flight could be caused by a number of factors, including altered DNA repair mechanisms, decreased antioxidant defense systems, or simply increased oxidative stress. Microgravity does not affect the repair of double-strand chromosome breaks (1436, 1437); however, evidence exists that downregulation of antioxidant defense systems occurs during spaceflight (1438). Along with increases in markers of oxidative damage and decreases in antioxidant defense systems, a decrease in total antioxidant capacity also occurs.

Nutrients Associated with Antioxidant Protection and Oxidative Stress

Selenium

Selenium has been shown to play a role in the maintenance or induction of cytochrome P450, pancreatic function, DNA repair, enzyme activation, immune system function, and detoxification of heavy metals (1439). Selenium is also a cofactor for glutathione peroxidase, which plays a role in the reduction of organic peroxides and hydrogen peroxide. We previously reviewed the basics of selenium function (1). Postflight reductions in serum selenium of more than 10% have been observed after ISS flights (111). Whether this is related to intake or metabolism is not known.

Deficiency of selenium can lead to oxidation of biomolecules and cell injury. Excess selenium can lead to problems affecting gastrointestinal, neurological, cardiopulmonary, and renal systems (1439). Toxicity is not likely to occur except when selenium is consumed in large amounts in dietary supplements; however, care must be taken to avoid toxicity despite the relationship of selenium to cancer risk and antioxidant status.

Vitamin E

Oxidative stress can increase in microgravity and high-radiation environments (1021, 1300, 1440). The antioxidant properties of vitamin E may help to counteract the free-radical damage caused by high-LET radiation in space. Pretreatment with antioxidants may help decrease radiation damage during missions (1441), and it may be necessary to provide enough vitamin E for astronauts' blood levels of the vitamin to be higher during spaceflight than on Earth. However, knowledge gaps weaken the evidence for use of vitamin E as a countermeasure. Clinical trials have documented negative side effects of pharmacologic vitamin E supplementation alone or with other antioxidants; it can increase risks of cancer in humans and animals (1442-1445).

After ISS crewmembers had spent 4 to 6 months in space, their plasma γ-tocopherol was 50% less than preflight levels (111). No change in α-tocopherol occurred in these subjects.

Vitamin C

The term "vitamin C" actually refers to two different compounds—ascorbic acid and dehydroascorbic acid—both of which have activity against scurvy (1446, 1447). Vitamin C functions as an antioxidant because it acts as a reducing agent for most physiologically relevant ROS, reactive nitrogen species, singlet oxygen, and hypochlorite. It serves as a cofactor for enzymes involved in the biosynthesis of collagen, carnitine, and neurotransmitters (1446, 1447). Vitamin C also provides antioxidant protection by returning α-tocopherol to its biologically active state during lipid oxidation. The reducing agents glutathione and either reduced NADH or reduced NADPH regenerate the oxidation products of ascorbate (1446, 1447).

It has been suggested that vitamin C requirements should be greater for persons who are under excessive physical or emotional stress, given the role of ascorbate in the biosynthesis of steroid hormones and neurotransmitters. However, no substantial data show that vitamin C metabolism is altered in healthy subjects under mental or emotional stress (1374). As a cofactor in collagen synthesis, vitamin C has been investigated for potential effects on bone health (as described in Chapter 6).

Deficiency of vitamin C leads to fatigue, depressed immune function, scurvy (fatigue, muscle cramps, bruised and/or bleeding gums), and eventually even death. As noted in the introduction, scurvy resulted in more sailor deaths during the age of sail than all other causes of death combined (2). Toxicity of vitamin C leads to gastrointestinal distress, and has been reported in subjects consuming more than 1000 mg/d (637).

Vitamin C assessments of ISS crew-members have been conducted, with generally no changes after landing relative to before launch (Smith and Zwart, unpublished data). Recent long- and short-duration bed rest studies documented no statistically significant change in vitamin C; however, results showed a trend for an increase, which might be related to dietary intake during the study relative to the subjects' nominal intake (254, 262).

The stability of vitamin C in food supplies has been studied, and it is generally unstable at a neutral or alkaline pH and in high-oxygen environments (1448). Vitamin C is also unstable when exposed to light or heat (1448), and in irradiated foods (1449, 1450). Salem (1450) found that gamma irradiation of fresh onion bulbs significantly reduced their vitamin C content. This group also found that vitamin C content of onion bulbs had decreased about 50% after 6 months of storage. The destructive effects of gamma irradiation (10 kGy) on vitamin C were also evident in commercial spices such as basil, black pepper, cinnamon, nutmeg, oregano, parsley, rosemary, and sage (1451). Exposure of these spices to gamma rays for >3 months resulted in a marked increase in the concentration of quinone radicals. Radiation levels and sources used in these ground studies are generally higher and different than those that will be encountered in deep space. Limited data available from the ISS indicate that storage time impacts vitamin C concentration more than the level of radiation that the foods received (87); however, the stability of foods and vitamins should be validated in deep space, or using deep space relevant radiation sources (97), with a greater variety of foods.

Free-radical formation is increased in space because greater amounts of radiation are present than on Earth. Because of this and increases in other oxidative stressors, antioxidants such as vitamin C are in greater demand by the body to act as buffers and minimize the oxidative damage. Studies have shown that supplementation with vitamin C and other antioxidants can modify human tissue radiosensitivity and protect DNA against damage (1452, 1453). Just as important to consider, however, is the possibility that vitamin C could induce DNA damage. Cai and colleagues (1453) found that vitamin C can act as an antioxidant to prevent DNA damage caused by ionizing radiation. However, in the presence of copper, it can also act as a reducing agent to induce DNA damage. Because vitamin C can reduce redox-active metals such as iron and copper, this "antioxidant" can increase the pro-oxidant chemistry of these metals (1454). Thus, vitamin C can serve as both a pro-oxidant and an antioxidant, and the amount of it required by exploration crew-members needs to be carefully addressed (as does the amount of almost all nutrients).

Vitamin C has been shown to degrade over time with storage in the space food supply (84), as discussed in Chapter 3. Methods to improve stability are being investigated. Evaluation of the impact of vitamin C supplementation during exposure to oxygen or high-LET radiation should be investigated before recommendations can be made for supplement use during flight. This should be evaluated in a coordinated effort to find an antioxidant profile for space travelers. An evaluation of intake requirements needs to be made after data have been gathered about vitamin C status during and after flight, and preferably after data are available pertaining to the influence of spaceflight-induced stress on vitamin C.

Folate

Antioxidant properties of folate have been studied, and folate was found to have the ability to efficiently scavenge a diverse array of ROS (1455). Animal studies show that low folate status increases chromosome damage resulting from radiation exposure (1456-1459); however, it should be noted that excessive folate supplementation provided no additional benefit (1456). Similarly, cell models have shown that folate deficiency increases sensitivity to chromosome breakage from ionizing radiation (1458). Evidence exists that folate status decreases in subjects living in saturation diving conditions with increased partial pressure of oxygen for 10 to 14 days, which may be related to its antioxidant properties (758). In that environment, tissue iron stores increase, similar to how they are increased during spaceflight (753, 758, 1433). Folate status may be even more important during exploration missions than on the ISS because of known increases in iron storage during long-duration spaceflight (111) and exposure to ionizing radiation. Cell models show the ability of folate to reduce iron toxicity in cases of iron overload by oxidizing free or chelated iron (1455).

References for Chapter 12

1. Smith SM, Zwart SR, Kloeris V, Heer M. Nutritional biochemistry of space flight. New York: Nova Science Publishers; 2009.

2. Bown SR. Scurvy. New York: St. Martin's Press; 2003.

10. Zwart SR, Morgan JLL, Smith SM. Iron status and its relations with oxidative damage and bone loss during long-duration space flight on the International Space Station. Am J Clin Nutr. 2013;98:217-23.

11. Norbury JW, Slaba TC, Aghara S, Badavi FF, Blattnig SR, Clowdsley MS, Heilbronn LH, Lee K, Maung KM, Mertens CJ, Miller J, Norman RB, Sandridge CA, Singleterry R, Sobolevsky N, Spangler JL, Townsend LW, Werneth CM, Whitman K, Wilson JW, Xu SX, Zeitlin C. Advances in space radiation physics and transport at NASA. Life Sci Space Res (Amst). 2019;22:98-124.

13. Cekanaviciute E, Rosi S, Costes SV. Central nervous system responses to simulated galactic cosmic rays. Int J Mol Sci. 2018;19.

14. Kiffer F, Boerma M, Allen A. Behavioral effects of space radiation: A comprehensive review of animal studies. Life Sci Space Res (Amst). 2019;21:1-21.

15. Krukowski K, Feng X, Paladini MS, Chou A, Sacramento K, Grue K, Riparip LK, Jones T, Campbell-Beachler M, Nelson G, Rosi S. Temporary microglia-depletion after cosmic radiation modifies phagocytic activity and prevents cognitive deficits. Sci Rep. 2018;8:7857.

84. Cooper M, Perchonok M, Douglas GL. Initial assessment of the nutritional quality of the space food system over three years of ambient storage. NPJ Microgravity. 2017;3:17.

87. Zwart SR, Kloeris VL, Perchonok MH, Braby L, Smith SM. Assessment of nutrient stability in foods from the space food system after long-duration spaceflight on the ISS. J Food Sci. 2009;74:H209-17.

97. La Tessa C, Sivertz M, Chiang IH, Lowenstein D, Rusek A. Overview of the NASA space radiation laboratory. Life Sci Space Res (Amst). 2016;11:18-23.

110. Smith SM, Davis-Street JE, Rice BL, Nillen JL, Gillman PL, Block G. Nutritional status assessment in semiclosed environments: ground-based and space flight studies in humans. J Nutr. 2001;131:2053-61.

111. Smith SM, Zwart SR, Block G, Rice BL, Davis-Street JE. The nutritional status of astronauts is altered after long-term space flight aboard the International Space Station. J Nutr. 2005;135:437-43.

254. Zwart SR, Crawford GE, Gillman PL, Kala G, Rodgers AS, Rogers A, Inniss AM, Rice BL, Ericson K, Coburn S, Bourbeau Y, Hudson E, Mathew G, Dekerlegand DE, Sams CF, Heer MA, Paloski WH, Smith SM. Effects of 21 days of bed rest, with or without artificial gravity, on nutritional status of humans. J Appl Physiol (1985). 2009;107:54-62.

262. Morgan JLL, Zwart SR, Heer M, Ploutz-Snyder R, Ericson K, Smith SM. Bone metabolism and nutritional status during 30-day head-down-tilt bed rest. J Appl Physiol (1985). 2012;113:1519-29.

637. Thompson J. Vitamins, minerals and supplements: overview of vitamin C (5). Community Pract. 2007;80:35-6.

746. Tuomainen TP, Loft S, Nyyssonen K, Punnonen K, Salonen JT, Poulsen HE. Body iron is a contributor to oxidative damage of DNA. Free Radic Res. 2007;41:324-8.

753. Smith SM, Davis-Street JE, Fesperman JV, Smith MD, Rice BL, Zwart SR. Nutritional assessment during a 14-d saturation dive: the NASA Extreme Environment Mission Operations V Project. J Nutr. 2004;134:1765-71.

758. Zwart SR, Jessup JM, Ji J, Smith SM. Saturation diving alters folate status and biomarkers of DNA damage and repair. PLoS One. 2012;7:e31058.

863. Lee SMC, Ribeiro LC, Martin DS, Zwart SR, Feiveson AH, Laurie SS, Macias BR, Crucian BE, Krieger S, Weber D, Grune T, Platts SH, Smith SM, Stenger MB. Arterial structure and function during and after long-duration spaceflight. J Appl Physiol (1985). 2020;129:108-23.

1011. Patel Z, Huff J, Saha J, Wang M, Blattnig SR, Wu H. Evidence Report: Risk of cardiovascular disease and other degenerative tissue effects from radiation exposure. [online]. National Aeronautics and Space Administration. https://humanresearchroadmap.nasa.gov/Evidence/other/Degen.pdf. 2016.

1021. Stein TP. Space flight and oxidative stress. Nutrition. 2002;18:867-71.

1117. Jones JA, McCarten M, Manuel K, Djojonegoro B, Murray J, Feiversen A, Wear M. Cataract formation mechanisms and risk in aviation and space crews. Aviat Space Environ Med. 2007;78:A56-66.

1300. Stein TP, Leskiw MJ. Oxidant damage during and after spaceflight. Am J Physiol Endocrinol Metab. 2000;278:E375-82.

1374. Institute of Medicine. Dietary reference intakes for vitamin C, vitamin E, selenium, and carotenoids. Washington, DC: National Academy Press; 2000.

1419. Sharifi-Rad M, Anil Kumar NV, Zucca P, Varoni EM, Dini L, Panzarini E, Rajkovic J, Tsouh Fokou PV, Azzini E, Peluso I, Prakash Mishra A, Nigam M, El Rayess Y, Beyrouthy ME, Polito L, Iriti M, Martins N, Martorell M, Docea AO, Setzer WN, Calina D, Cho WC, Sharifi-Rad J. Lifestyle, oxidative stress, and antioxidants: Back and forth in the pathophysiology of chronic diseases. Front Physiol. 2020;11:694.

1420. Powers SK, Jackson MJ. Exercise-induced oxidative stress: cellular mechanisms and impact on muscle force production. Physiol Rev. 2008;88:1243-76.

1421. Azzam EI, Jay-Gerin JP, Pain D. Ionizing radiation-induced metabolic oxidative stress and prolonged cell injury. Cancer Lett. 2012;327:48-60.

1422. Li M, Gonon G, Buonanno M, Autsavapromporn N, de Toledo SM, Pain D, Azzam EI. Health risks of space exploration: targeted and nontargeted oxidative injury by high-charge and high-energy particles. Antioxid Redox Signal. 2014;20:1501-23.

1423. Reid MB. Muscle fatigue: mechanisms and regulation. In: Sen CK, Packer L, Hänninen O, editors. Handbook of oxidants and antioxidants in exercise. Amsterdam: Elsevier Science B.V.; 2000. p. 599-630.

1424. Upton AC. The biological effects of low-level ionizing radiation. Sci Am. 1982;246(2):41-9.

1425. O'Neill CA, Stebbins CL, Bonigut S, Halliwell B, Longhurst JC. Production of hydroxyl radicals in contracting skeletal muscle of cats. J Appl Physiol (1985). 1996;81:1197-206.

1426. Reid MB, Khawli FA, Moody MR. Reactive oxygen in skeletal muscle. III. Contractility of unfatigued muscle. J Appl Physiol (1985). 1993;75:1081-7.

1427. Essig DA, Nosek TM. Muscle fatigue and induction of stress protein genes: a dual function of reactive oxygen species? Can J Appl Physiol. 1997;22:409-28.

1428. Lawler JM, Cline CC, Hu Z, Coast JR. Effect of oxidant challenge on contractile function of the aging rat diaphragm. Am J Physiol. 1997;272:E201-7.

1429. Mao XW, Pecaut MJ, Stodieck LS, Ferguson VL, Bateman TA, Bouxsein M, Jones TA, Moldovan M, Cunningham CE, Chieu J, Gridley DS. Spaceflight environment induces mitochondrial oxidative damage in ocular tissue. Radiat Res. 2013;180:340-50.

1430. Rizzo AM, Corsetto PA, Montorfano G, Milani S, Zava S, Tavella S, Cancedda R, Berra B. Effects of long-term space flight on erythrocytes and oxidative stress of rodents. PLoS One. 2012;7:e32361.

1431. Baqai FP, Gridley DS, Slater JM, Luo-Owen X, Stodieck LS, Ferguson V, Chapes SK, Pecaut MJ. Effects of spaceflight on innate immune function and antioxidant gene expression. J Appl Physiol (1985). 2009;106:1935-42.

1432. Gridley DS, Slater JM, Luo-Owen X, Rizvi A, Chapes SK, Stodieck LS, Ferguson VL, Pecaut MJ. Spaceflight effects on T lymphocyte distribution, function and gene expression. J Appl Physiol (1985). 2009;106:194-202.

1433. Zwart SR, Kala G, Smith SM. Body iron stores and oxidative damage in humans increased during and after a 10- to 12-day undersea dive. J Nutr. 2009;139:90-5.

1434. Zezerov AE, Ivanova SM, Morukov BV, Ushakov AS. [Lipid peroxidation in the human blood during a 120-day period of anti-orthostatic hypokinesia]. Kosm Biol Aviakosm Med. 1989;23:28-33.

1435. Mao XW, Nishiyama NC, Byrum SD, Stanbouly S, Jones T, Holley J, Sridharan V, Boerma M, Tackett AJ, Willey JS, Pecaut MJ, Delp MD. Spaceflight induces oxidative damage to blood-brain barrier integrity in a mouse model. FASEB J. 2020;34:15516-30.

1436. Pross HD, Casares A, Kiefer J. Induction and repair of DNA double-strand breaks under irradiation and microgravity. Radiat Res. 2000;153:521-5.

1437. Kiefer J, Pross HD. Space radiation effects and microgravity. Mutat Res. 1999;430:299-305.

1438. Hollander J, Gore M, Fiebig R, Mazzeo R, Ohishi S, Ohno H, Ji LL. Spaceflight downregulates antioxidant defense systems in rat liver. Free Radic Biol Med. 1998;24:385-90.

1439. Terry EN, Diamond AM. Selenium. In: Erdman JW, Jr., MacDonald IA, Zeisel SH, editors. Present knowledge in nutrition. 9th ed. Washington, DC: International Life Sciences Institute Press; 2010. p. 568-85.

1440. Fang YZ, Yang S, Wu G. Free radicals, antioxidants, and nutrition. Nutrition. 2002;18:872-9.

1441. Pence BC, Yang TC. Antioxidants: radiation and stress. In: Lane HW, Schoeller DA, editors. Nutrition in spaceflight and weightlessness models. Boca Raton, FL: CRC Press; 2000. p. 233-52.

1442. Klein EA, Thompson IM, Jr, Tangen CM, Crowley JJ, Lucia MS, Goodman PJ, Minasian LM, Ford LG, Parnes HL, Gaziano JM, Karp DD, Lieber MM, Walther PJ, Klotz L, Parsons JK, Chin JL, Darke AK, Lippman SM, Goodman GE, Meyskens FL, Jr., Baker LH. Vitamin E and the risk of prostate cancer: the Selenium and Vitamin E Cancer Prevention Trial (SELECT). JAMA. 2011;306:1549-56.

1443. Sayin VI, Ibrahim MX, Larsson E, Nilsson JA, Lindahl P, Bergo MO. Antioxidants accelerate lung cancer progression in mice. Sci Transl Med. 2014;6:221ra15.

1444. Bjelakovic G, Nikolova D, Gluud C. Antioxidant supplements and mortality. Curr Opin Clin Nutr Metab Care. 2014;17:40-4.

1445. Bjelakovic G, Nikolova D, Gluud C. Meta-regression analyses, meta-analyses, and trial sequential analyses of the effects of supplementation with beta-carotene, vitamin A, and vitamin E singly or in different combinations on all-cause mortality: do we have evidence for lack of harm? PLoS One. 2013;8:e74558.

1446. Jacob RA. Vitamin C. In: Shils ME, Olson JA, Shike M, editors. Modern nutrition in health and disease. 8th ed. Malvern, PA: Lea & Febiger; 1994. p. 432-48.

1447. Johnston CS. Vitamin C. In: Erdman JW, Jr., MacDonald IA, Zeisel SH, editors. Present knowledge in nutrition. 9th ed. Washington, DC: International Life Sciences Institute Press; 2010. p. 248-60.

1448. Henshall JD. The effect of processing on the nutritive value of fruit and vegetable products. Proc Nutr Soc. 1973;32:17-22.

1449. Fan X, Thayer DW. gamma-Radiation influences browning, antioxidant activity, and malondialdehyde level of apple juice. J Agric Food Chem. 2002;50:710-5.

1450. Salem SA. Effect of gamma radiation on the storage of onions used in the dehydration industry. J Sci Food Agric. 1974;25:257-62.

1451. Calucci L, Pinzino C, Zandomeneghi M, Capocchi A, Ghiringhelli S, Saviozzi F, Tozzi S, Galleschi L. Effects of gamma-irradiation on the free radical and antioxidant contents in nine aromatic herbs and spices. J Agric Food Chem. 2003;51:927-34.

1452. Jagetia GC, Rajanikant GK, Baliga MS, Rao KV, Kumar P. Augmentation of wound healing by ascorbic acid treatment in mice exposed to gamma-radiation. Int J Radiat Biol. 2004;80:347-54.

1453. Cai L, Koropatnick J, Cherian MG. Roles of vitamin C in radiation-induced DNA damage in presence and absence of copper. Chem Biol Interact. 2001;137:75-88.

1454. Buettner GR, Jurkiewicz BA. Catalytic metals, ascorbate and free radicals: combinations to avoid. Radiat Res. 1996;145:532-41.

1455. Joshi R, Adhikari S, Patro BS, Chattopadhyay S, Mukherjee T. Free radical scavenging behavior of folic acid: evidence for possible antioxidant activity. Free Radic Biol Med. 2001;30:1390-9.

1456. Endoh K, Murakami M, Araki R, Maruyama C, Umegaki K. Low folate status increases chromosomal damage by X-ray irradiation. Int J Radiat Biol. 2006;82:223-30.

1457. Endoh K, Murakami M, Umegaki K. Vulnerability of folate in plasma and bone marrow to total body irradiation in mice. Int J Radiat Biol. 2007;83:65-71.

1458. Beetstra S, Thomas P, Salisbury C, Turner J, Fenech M. Folic acid deficiency increases chromosomal instability, chromosome 21 aneuploidy and sensitivity to radiation-induced micronuclei. Mutat Res. 2005;578:317-26.

1459. Courtemanche C, Huang AC, Elson-Schwab I, Kerry N, Ng BY, Ames BN. Folate deficiency and ionizing radiation cause DNA breaks in primary human lymphocytes: a comparison. FASEB J. 2004;18:209-11.

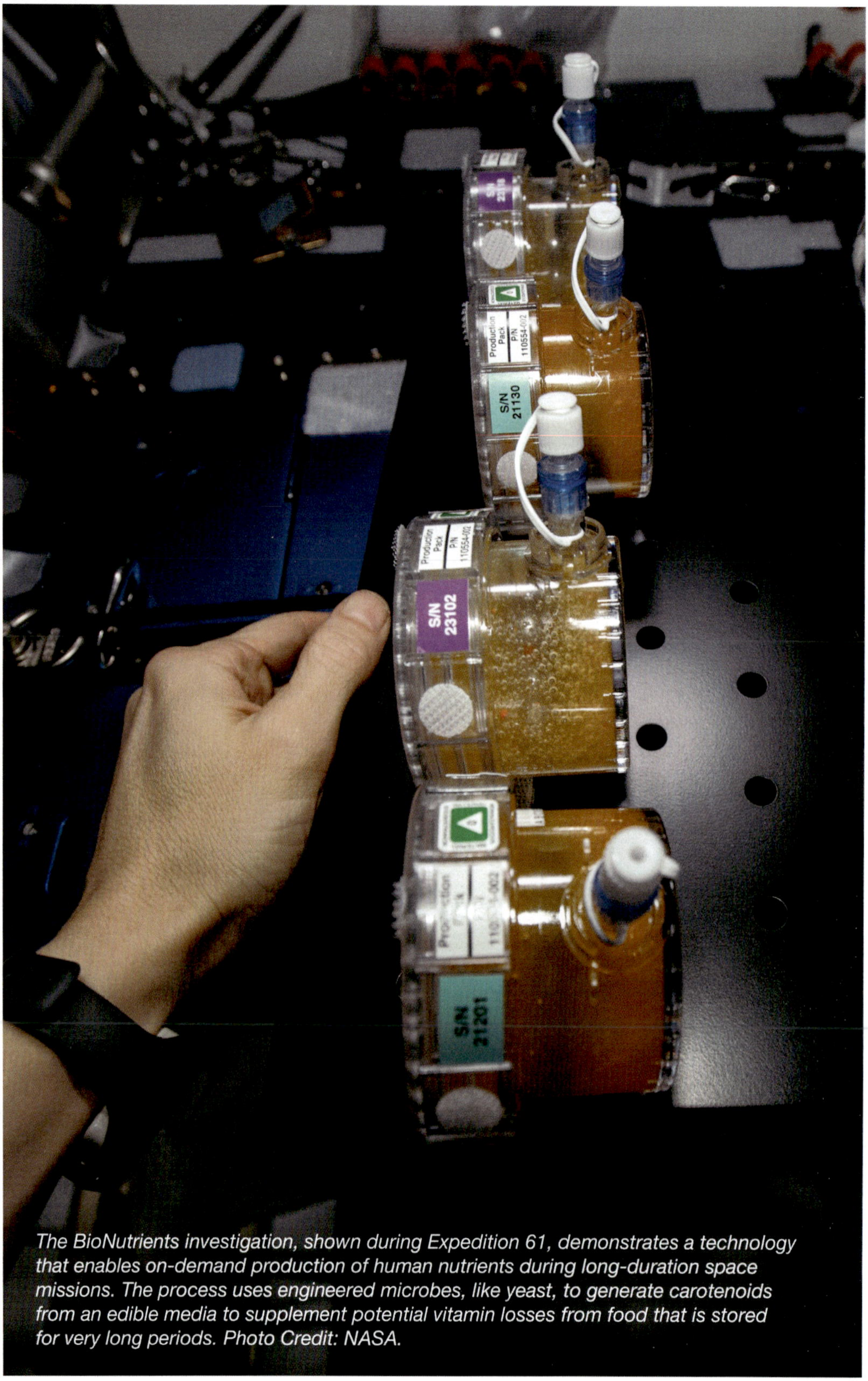

The BioNutrients investigation, shown during Expedition 61, demonstrates a technology that enables on-demand production of human nutrients during long-duration space missions. The process uses engineered microbes, like yeast, to generate carotenoids from an edible media to supplement potential vitamin losses from food that is stored for very long periods. Photo Credit: NASA.

The benefits of supplements are such that individual nutrients can be obtained when the diet cannot meet needs. Drawbacks to supplements include the potential for side effects, interactions with medications, and the fact that isolated nutrients may not provide the same protective effect as they would in the matrix of the whole food. For example, more than 100 phytochemicals in tomatoes likely contribute to the chemoprotective effect of tomato puree in addition to the lycopene known to protect against certain types of cancers. Tomato puree has much stronger dose-dependent, antimutagenic effects and lowers biomarkers of oxidative stress more than pure lycopene alone (1460, 1461). Similarly, omega-3 fatty acids have different effects on vasodilation, depending on whether they are supplied as a supplement or in a whole food (1462, 1463).

Besides the fact that supplements lack the synergistic effects of nutrients in whole foods, there are numerous examples of negative side effects associated with supplement use. Symptoms can range from gastrointestinal effects, dizziness, or decreased white blood cell count (from ipriflavone, which is synthesized from the soy isoflavone daidzein) to increased cancer risk (ß-carotene in the CARET study) or increased risk of stroke (1243, 1464-1466).

Provision of nutrients through supplements also ignores the fact that in some cases—for example, the omega 3:omega 6 ratio—the negative effects of other foods cannot be overcome simply by provision of supplements. Although this phenomenon is more difficult to document, it is likely the reason that epidemiological data continue to show benefits of dietary patterns over supplements.

The issue of supplement use often arises with discussion of nutrient requirements for space travelers and the use of nutrients as countermeasures to the negative effects of spaceflight, especially oxidative damage and radiation-induced cancer risk. It is generally agreed that nutrients should be provided to astronauts in standard foods instead of supplements (35-37, 128, 1467). The need for more detailed information about the "psychophysiology of hunger and eating" was noted decades ago during the early space programs (98), but this topic has yet to be studied in detail. It is clear from astronauts' experiences that when humans are in an isolated environment far from home, food becomes a psychological factor that can be a source of support or a source of frustration.

NASA currently does not recommend that astronauts take general nutritional supplements (beyond vitamin D) during flight for several reasons. Experience to date indicates that crewmembers do not consume the recommended amount of energy intake; accordingly, intake of many individual nutrients is therefore also inadequate. Unfortunately, the concept of a vitamin and mineral supplement to remedy this is unwarranted, as the primary problem—inadequate intake of food/energy—will not be resolved by a supplement. This situation may even be worsened if crewmembers believe that taking the supplement reduces the need for adequate food consumption, and thus eat even less. Furthermore, when many nutrients are provided as oral supplements, they are not metabolized by the body as they are when in foods (53). Changes in bioavailability and metabolism of nutrients can increase the risk of malnutrition.

Vitamin or mineral supplements should be used only when the nutrient content of the nominal food system does not meet the requirements for a given nutrient, or when data show that the efficacy of single (or multiple) nutrient supplementation is advantageous. To date, one supplement has met this standard: vitamin D. Vitamin D supplements have been provided to all U.S. crewmembers on the ISS. Early crews received 400 IU vitamin D3 per day (111). However, this was initially raised to 800 IU per day (37). This level allows maintenance of serum 25-hydroxyvitamin D around 75 nmol/L (124). More recently, 1000 IU vitamin D3 supplements have been provided for crews to take daily. The difference between 800 and 1000 is likely negligible, based on Antarctic dosing studies (603). A clear deficit of that nutrient in the space food system must be identified before a supplement is recommended, as was the case with vitamin D. Stability of nutrients in the form of supplements would also need to be addressed; shelf lives for exploration travel must be particularly long. Supplements, if they are recommended, would need to be tested in ground models for their efficacy in maintaining nutrient status, their stability over a long duration (3 to 5 y), and their potential interaction with pharmaceuticals.

Most importantly, supplements will need rigorous testing to demonstrate that the level used is not toxic to other body systems, and will need close monitoring during flight to ensure that their interactions with the spaceflight environment do not prevent them from being effective or safe. For example, ground-based studies have shown that high doses of antioxidants, when provided in situations where oxidant stressors are present (such as cigarette smoking), can actually have a detrimental effect (1468). Recent studies have also found that supplementation with certain antioxidants such as vitamin E and vitamin A can increase risks of cancer and all-cause mortality (1444, 1445).

An understanding of interactions between nutrients and drugs used in medical care is necessary to implement safe and effective medical care and clinical intervention operations for astronauts on long-duration missions. Long-term use of over-the-counter pharmaceuticals can induce subclinical and clinically relevant micronutrient deficiencies, thus it will be important to assess any chronic medications that are potentially taken on an exploration-class mission lasting several years. The most common studies of nutrient-drug interactions concern their effects on influencing food intake, nutrient's or drug's absorption, distribution, biotransformation, function, catabolism, and excretion (1469).

Generally, astronauts are healthy individuals. Those selected to be astronauts do not have chronic diseases. However, over the course of their career, they may develop hypertension as do 29% of adults (1470), or hypercholesterolemia as do 27% of adults in the general population (1471), as reported from the National Health Interview Survey. As a result, astronauts may need to take chronic medications, which can affect nutrient status (1469). Similarly, the aging process itself can lead to changes that require chronic medications, such as proton pump inhibitors for reducing gastric acid production.

Normally, drugs must undergo biotransformation to allow their activation or excretion. For the activity of a drug to be terminated by excretion, the compound must be made water-soluble by biotransformation. For most drugs, this process yields a water-soluble compound that is less active than the original compound. Biotransformation occurs in two phases. Phase I is an oxidation or hydrolysis reaction to expose, add, or cleave a functional group. Cytochrome P450 enzymes are involved in this process.

Humans have 12 families of cytochrome P450 enzymes; however, CYP1, CYP2, and CYP3 are the forms most commonly used in drug metabolism (1472). Cytochrome P450 enzymes are unique in their ability to use a wide range of substrates (1473). Phase II biotransformation involves the conjugation of the parent compound to a polar group (i.e., acetate, glucuronides, sulfates, amino acids, glutathione), which inactivates most drugs. Biotransformation of drugs is influenced by several factors that could be affected by spaceflight and the space food system. These factors include: dietary factors, nutrient metabolism, monoamine oxidase inhibitors, and antacids and proton pump inhibitors.

Dietary Factors

Dietary factors (either excess or deficiency) can influence both phases of drug biotransformation. In phase I, three factors are required: a sufficient energy source (because of the high energy demands of this system); a protein source for enzyme synthesis; and iron for cytochrome formation (1474). Phase II requires glucose, sulfur-containing amino acids, and glutathione (1474).

The effects of nutrients on drug metabolism have been well studied in animal models; however, relatively few dietary factors have been studied in humans (1474, 1475). Results from animal studies must be carefully weighed because of some differences between the cytochrome P450 enzymes of animals and humans. One of the most well documented food-drug interactions is between grapefruit juice and a number of medications (1476, 1477). Flavonoid compounds such as naringin, naringenin, limonin, and obacunone, which are present in grapefruit juice, act as substrates for particular intestinal cytochrome P450 enzymes (CYP3A4 and CYP1A2). Within hours of ingestion, grapefruit juice decreases CYP3A4 protein expression for up to 24 hours (1478, 1479). The decrease in CYP3A4 is associated with a decreased capability for drug metabolism and, therefore, increased drug bioavailability and exposure to a higher dose of the particular medication than intended.

Other foods, nutrients, or supplements known to affect phase I and II biotransformations and cytochrome P450 enzymes include protein, carbohydrates, lipids, certain vitamins, minerals, charbroiled foods, red wine, monosodium glutamate and aspartate, and herbs such as St. John's wort (1474, 1475, 1480-1483). Generally, high-protein diets increase drug metabolism, and low-protein diets decrease drug metabolism. For instance, antipyrine and theophylline are metabolized more rapidly when subjects are on a high-protein diet (1475). Other macronutrients, including carbohydrates, can affect phase I and phase II biotransformation reactions when intakes are very high or low. Theophylline (for asthma) is particularly sensitive to dietary protein:carbohydrate ratios; increasing the ratio can decrease effectiveness of the drug, and decreasing the ratio may lead to toxicity of the drug (1484). Fatty acids in the diet can also affect cytochrome P450 enzymes because they can be metabolized by these enzymes. Specifically, CYP2E1 is responsible for lipid peroxidation; activity of this enzyme is enhanced in the presence of highly polyunsaturated fatty acids such as fish oils.

Metabolism of Nutrients

Some nutrients are metabolized by cytochrome P450 enzymes; therefore, drugs or other nutrients that alter the activity of these enzymes can alter nutrient metabolism. Vitamin D and vitamin A are two examples of nutrients whose metabolism involves cytochrome P450 enzymes. Exposure of 7-dehydrocholesterol to sunlight converts this substrate to previtamin D_3. Previtamin D_3 undergoes an isomerization to form vitamin D_3, a biologically inactive compound. CYP27A is a mitochondrial mixed-function oxidase that is responsible for hydroxylating vitamin D_3 to form 25-hydroxyvitamin D_3 (1485). CYP3A4 has been found to be a 25-hydroxylase as well (1486). CYP27B converts 25-hydroxyvitamin D_3 to 1,25-dihydroxyvitamin D_3. CYP24 is a 24-hydroxylase that hydroxylates the vitamin D side chain and ultimately terminates hormonal activity of the vitamin. Inhibition of CYP24 has recently been targeted in the development of novel anti-cancer drugs. Because 1,25-dihydroxyvitamin D_3 exerts antiproliferative and differentiating effects on many cell types including cancer, preventing its inactivation by inhibiting CYP24 activity may prove to be beneficial in treating cancer (1487). Certain drugs are known to activate CYP24 activity, including rifampin, isoniazid, and phenobarbital (1488, 1489). Several studies show a relationship between the use of these drugs and osteomalacia (1490, 1491), which is caused by a deficiency of vitamin D. The discovery of the involvement of CYP3A4 in the metabolism of vitamin D may explain the effects on the vitamin D metabolism of numerous drugs, including inducers or inhibitors of this enzyme (e.g., grapefruit juice, erythromycin, omeprazole, carbamazepine, and dexamethasone), or implicate them in unexplained effects on vitamin D metabolism. Vitamin A metabolism involves the actions of CYP1A2 and CYP4A4 in the conversion of retinol to retinoic acid (1492, 1493). Inducers of CYP1A2 (e.g., cigarette smoke, cruciferous vegetables, broiled beef, rifampin) may affect vitamin A metabolism.

Monoamine Oxidase Inhibitors

First-generation monoamine oxidase inhibitors include agents such as antidepressants (phenelzine, tranylcypromine, pargyline, and selegiline), chemotherapeutic drugs (procarbazine), antiprotozoal drugs (furazolidone), and analgesics (meperidine). Monoamine oxidase is responsible for metabolizing dietary phenylethylamines, including tyramine, in the gastrointestinal tract and in the liver. Inhibitors of monoamine oxidase prevent the breakdown of these compounds; therefore, the compounds are taken up in the brain. Tyramine displaces norepinephrine from storage vesicles in the brain, which results in release of a flood of norepinephrine at synapses. Acute hypertension and the potential for stroke or myocardial infarction could result from this process (1474). Fermented foods and protein-rich foods that have begun to spoil are rich in phenylethylamines (1474).

Antacids and Proton Pump Inhibitors

By altering the pH of the stomach, chronic antacid or proton pump medications can negatively affect the bioavailability of several nutrients including phosphate, thiamin, folate, vitamin B_{12}, vitamin C, iron, and vitamin A that depend on low pH for the uptake into intestinal cells (1474, 1494, 1495). Antacids can precipitate folic acid at a pH greater than 4.0, thus rendering it insoluble and not available for absorption (1496). A high pH also affects thiamin bioavailability because the vitamin is not stable at high pH (1474). Similarly, at a neutral pH, the antioxidant action of vitamin C on dietary nitrites is hindered. Normally, dietary nitrite is quickly reduced to nitric oxide by ascorbic acid in the acidic gastric juice and it is then absorbed by the mucosa. However, at neutral pH, the nitrite does not react with ascorbic acid and instead accumulates in the stomach, which can increase the likelihood that potentially carcinogenic N-nitroso compounds will be formed (1495). These changes are observed mostly in subjects who are infected by Helicobacter pylori and are taking proton-pump inhibitors (1495).

Vitamin B_{12} and vitamin A are also malabsorbed at higher pH because an acidic environment is essential for their release from dietary proteins. Because large stores of vitamin B_{12} exist in the body, malabsorption of this vitamin is unlikely to lead to deficiency unless a subject has been taking proton pump inhibitors chronically for at least 2 years (1494). Results from population studies, however, are inconsistent (1494). Age is a contributing factor, as well as genetic polymorphisms that inhibit CYP450 (1469). This would be particularly harmful if vitamin B_{12} stores were low before initiation of therapy.

Anti-Hypertensives: Angiotensin-Converting Enzyme Inhibitors

There is some evidence that long-term treatment with Angiotensin-Converting Enzyme (ACE) inhibitors may increase the risk for zinc deficiency (1497). The mechanism may be due to chelation of zinc and may enhance its excretion (1498).

Oral Contraceptives

It is common for astronauts to continually suppress their menstrual cycles during ISS missions (1499). Women who take oral contraceptives may be at a higher risk for nutrient deficiencies (1469). One example is folate. Oral contraceptives may play a role in increasing metabolism and urinary excretion of folate (1500), as the use of these medications is associated with folate status (1501). Regarding vitamin B_6, results are not conclusive as to whether oral contraceptives affect status, and the answer seems to rely on the biomarker of vitamin B_6 status that is analyzed. When erythrocyte transaminase is used as a functional biomarker of vitamin B_6 status, half of women taking oral contraceptives were vitamin B_6 deficient compared to 18% of women not taking the medication (1502). In a dietary-controlled depletion-repletion study, vitamin B_6 requirements were not higher in women taking oral contraceptives based on numerous markers of vitamin B_6 status (1503, 1504). There is evidence that tryptophan metabolism may be altered with contraceptive use by some other means than through a vitamin B_6 deficiency (1505). Other nutrients that may be affected by oral contraceptive use include vitamin B_{12}, calcium, magnesium, and vitamins C and E (1469). It will be prudent to monitor crewmembers' status of these nutrients—in particular, leading up to their flights—among women who choose to take oral contraceptives during long-duration missions.

Pharmacology and Drug-Nutrient Interactions

Currently no data are available that pertain to specific drug-nutrient interactions during spaceflight. The main concerns for a long-duration mission lasting several years involve the use of pharmacological agents that are taken chronically. Side effects will be especially harmful if the status of all nutrients is not adequate at the beginning of a long-duration mission. Addressing these concerns of drug-nutrient interactions before a mission will be especially crucial for crewmembers who embark on exploration-class missions lasting several years.

References for Chapter 13

35. National Aeronautics and Space Administration Johnson Space Center. Nutritional requirements for Extended Duration Orbiter missions (30-90 d) and Space Station Freedom (30-120 d). Report No.: JSC-32283. Houston, TX: National Aeronautics and Space Administration Lyndon B. Johnson Space Center, 1993.

36. National Aeronautics and Space Administration Johnson Space Center. Nutritional requirements for International Space Station (ISS) missions up to 360 days. Report No.: JSC-28038. Houston, TX: National Aeronautics and Space Administration Lyndon B. Johnson Space Center, 1996.

37. National Aeronautics and Space Administration Johnson Space Center. Nutrition requirements, standards, and operating bands for exploration missions. Report No.: JSC-63555. Houston, TX: Lyndon B. Johnson Space Center; 2005.

53. American Dietetic Association. Position of the American Dietetic Association: fortification and nutritional supplements. J Am Diet Assoc. 2005;105:1300-11.

98. Smith MC, Berry CA. Dinner on the moon. Nutr Today. 1969;4:37-42.

111. Smith SM, Zwart SR, Block G, Rice BL, Davis-Street JE. The nutritional status of astronauts is altered after long-term space flight aboard the International Space Station. J Nutr. 2005;135:437-43.

124. Smith SM, Heer MA, Shackelford LC, Sibonga JD, Ploutz-Snyder L, Zwart SR. Benefits for bone from resistance exercise and nutrition in long-duration spaceflight: evidence from biochemistry and densitometry. J Bone Miner Res. 2012;27:1896-906.

128. Lane HW, Smith SM. Nutrition in space. In: Shils ME, Olson JA, Shike M, Ross AC, editors. Modern nutrition in health and disease. 9th ed. Baltimore, MD: Lippincott Williams & Wilkins; 1999. p. 783-8.

603. Smith SM, Gardner KK, Locke J, Zwart SR. Vitamin D supplementation during Antarctic winter. Am J Clin Nutr. 2009;89:1092-8.

1243. Omenn GS, Goodman GE, Thornquist MD, Balmes J, Cullen MR, Glass A, Keogh JP, Meyskens FL, Jr., Valanis B, Williams JH, Jr., Barnhart S, Cherniack MG, Brodkin CA, Hammar S. Risk factors for lung cancer and for intervention effects in CARET, the Beta-Carotene and Retinol Efficacy Trial. J Natl Cancer Inst. 1996;88:1550-9.

1444. Bjelakovic G, Nikolova D, Gluud C. Antioxidant supplements and mortality. Curr Opin Clin Nutr Metab Care. 2014;17:40-4.

1445. Bjelakovic G, Nikolova D, Gluud C. Meta-regression analyses, meta-analyses, and trial sequential analyses of the effects of supplementation with beta-carotene, vitamin A, and vitamin E singly or in different combinations on all-cause mortality: do we have evidence for lack of harm? PLoS One. 2013;8:e74558.

1460. Polivkova Z, Smerak P, Demova H, Houska M. Antimutagenic effects of lycopene and tomato puree. J Med Food. 2010;13:1443-50.

1461. Basu A, Imrhan V. Tomatoes versus lycopene in oxidative stress and carcinogenesis: conclusions from clinical trials. Eur J Clin Nutr. 2007;61:295-303.

1462. Hoshi T, Tian Y, Xu R, Heinemann SH, Hou S. Mechanism of the modulation of BK potassium channel complexes with different auxiliary subunit compositions by the omega-3 fatty acid DHA. Proc Natl Acad Sci USA. 2013;110:4822-7.

1463. Hoshi T, Wissuwa B, Tian Y, Tajima N, Xu R, Bauer M, Heinemann SH, Hou S. Omega-3 fatty acids lower blood pressure by directly activating large-conductance Ca2+-dependent K+ channels. Proc Natl Acad Sci USA. 2013;110:4816-21.

1464. Nicastro HL, Dunn BK. Selenium and prostate cancer prevention: insights from the Selenium and Vitamin E Cancer Prevention Trial (SELECT). Nutrients. 2013;5:1122-48.

1465. Dunn BK, Richmond ES, Minasian LM, Ryan AM, Ford LG. A nutrient approach to prostate cancer prevention: the Selenium and Vitamin E Cancer Prevention Trial (SELECT). Nutr Cancer. 2010;62:896-918.

1466. Sesso HD, Buring JE, Christen WG, Kurth T, Belanger C, MacFadyen J, Bubes V, Manson JE, Glynn RJ, Gaziano JM. Vitamins E and C in the prevention of cardiovascular disease in men: the Physicians' Health Study II randomized controlled trial. JAMA. 2008;300:2123-33.

1467. Smith SM, Davis-Street J, Rice BL, Lane HW. Nutrition in space. Nutr Today. 1997;32:6-12.

1468. Goodman GE, Thornquist MD, Balmes J, Cullen MR, Meyskens FL, Jr., Omenn GS, Valanis B, Williams JH, Jr. The Beta-Carotene and Retinol Efficacy Trial: incidence of lung cancer and cardiovascular disease mortality during 6-year follow-up after stopping beta-carotene and retinol supplements. J Natl Cancer Inst. 2004;96:1743-50.

1469. Mohn ES, Kern HJ, Saltzman E, Mitmesser SH, McKay DL. Evidence of drug-nutrient interactions with chronic use of commonly prescribed medications: An update. Pharmaceutics. 2018;10.

1470. National Center for Health Statistics (US). National Center for Health Statistics (US) Health, United States, 2015: with special feature on racial and ethnic health disparities. Hyattsville, MD. 2016.

1471. Weissman JF, Pratt LA, Miller EA, Parker JD. Serious psychological distress among adults: United States, 2009-2013. NCHS Data Brief. 2015:1-8.

1472. Hardman J, Limbird L. Goodman and Gilman's the pharmacological basis of therapeutics. New York: McGraw Hill; 1996.

1473. Guengerich FP, Miller GP, Hanna IH, Martin MV, Leger S, Black C, Chauret N, Silva JM, Trimble LA, Yergey JA, Nicoll-Griffith DA. Diversity in the oxidation of substrates by cytochrome P450 2D6: lack of an obligatory role of aspartate 301-substrate electrostatic bonding. Biochemistry (Mosc). 2002;41:11025-34.

1474. Utermohlen V. Diet, nutrition, and drug interactions. In: Shils ME, Olson JA, Shike M, Ross AC, editors. Modern nutrition in health and disease. 9th ed. Baltimore, MD: Lippincott Williams & Wilkins; 1998.

1475. Guengerich FP. Influence of nutrients and other dietary materials on cytochrome P-450 enzymes. Am J Clin Nutr. 1995;61:651S-8S.

1476. Bailey DG, Spence JD, Edgar B, Bayliff CD, Arnold JM. Ethanol enhances the hemodynamic effects of felodipine. Clin Invest Med. 1989;12:357-62.

1477. Kane GC, Lipsky JJ. Drug-grapefruit juice interactions. Mayo Clin Proc. 2000;75:933-42.

1478. Lown KS, Bailey DG, Fontana RJ, Janardan SK, Adair CH, Fortlage LA, Brown MB, Guo W, Watkins PB. Grapefruit juice increases felodipine oral availability in humans by decreasing intestinal CYP3A protein expression. J Clin Invest. 1997;99:2545-53.

1479. Lundahl J, Regardh CG, Edgar B, Johnsson G. Relationship between time of intake of grapefruit juice and its effect on pharmacokinetics and pharmacodynamics of felodipine in healthy subjects. Eur J Clin Pharmacol. 1995;49:61-7.

1480. Piver B, Berthou F, Dreano Y, Lucas D. Inhibition of CYP3A, CYP1A and CYP2E1 activities by resveratrol and other non volatile red wine components. Toxicol Lett. 2001;125:83-91.

1481. Chan WK, Nguyen LT, Miller VP, Harris RZ. Mechanism-based inactivation of human cytochrome P450 3A4 by grapefruit juice and red wine. Life Sci. 1998;62:PL135-42.

1482. Roby CA, Anderson GD, Kantor E, Dryer DA, Burstein AH. St John's Wort: effect on CYP3A4 activity. Clin Pharmacol Ther. 2000;67:451-7.

1483. Fujita K. Food-drug interactions via human cytochrome P450 3A (CYP3A). Drug Metabol Drug Interact. 2004;20:195-217.

1484. Fagan TC, Walle T, Oexmann MJ, Walle UK, Bai SA, Gaffney TE. Increased clearance of propranolol and theophylline by high-protein compared with high-carbohydrate diet. Clin Pharmacol Ther. 1987;41:402-6.

1485. Saarem K, Pedersen JI. Sex differences in the hydroxylation of cholecalciferol and of 5 beta-cholestane-3 alpha, 7 alpha, 12 alpha-triol in rat liver. Biochem J. 1987;247:73-8.

1486. Gupta RP, Hollis BW, Patel SB, Patrick KS, Bell NH. CYP3A4 is a human microsomal vitamin D 25-hydroxylase. J Bone Miner Res. 2004;19:680-8.

1487. Schuster I, Egger H, Reddy GS, Vorisek G. Combination of vitamin D metabolites with selective inhibitors of vitamin D metabolism. Recent Results Cancer Res. 2003;164:169-88.

1488. Pascussi JM, Robert A, Nguyen M, Walrant-Debray O, Garabedian M, Martin P, Pineau T, Saric J, Navarro F, Maurel P, Vilarem MJ. Possible involvement of pregnane X receptor-enhanced CYP24 expression in drug-induced osteomalacia. J Clin Invest. 2005;115:177-86.

1489. Self TH, Chrisman CR, Baciewicz AM, Bronze MS. Isoniazid drug and food interactions. Am J Med Sci. 1999;317:304-11.

1490. Shah SC, Sharma RK, Hemangini, Chitle AR. Rifampicin induced osteomalacia. Tubercle. 1981;62:207-9.

1491. Goraya JS, Gupta PN, Gupta RK, Bahadur R, Parmar VR. Anticonvulsant induced osteomalacia. Indian Pediatr. 2000;37:325-9.

1492. Chen H, Howald WN, Juchau MR. Biosynthesis of all-trans-retinoic acid from all-trans-retinol: catalysis of all-trans-retinol oxidation by human P-450 cytochromes. Drug Metab Dispos. 2000;28:315-22.

1493. Roberts ES, Vaz AD, Coon MJ. Role of isozymes of rabbit microsomal cytochrome P-450 in the metabolism of retinoic acid, retinol, and retinal. Mol Pharmacol. 1992;41:427-33.

1494. Force RW, Nahata MC. Effect of histamine H2-receptor antagonists on vitamin B_{12} absorption. Ann Pharmacother. 1992;26:1283-6.

1495. Mowat C, McColl KE. Alterations in intragastric nitrite and vitamin C levels during acid inhibitory therapy. Best Pract Res Clin Gastroenterol. 2001;15:523-37.

1496. Russell RM, Golner BB, Krasinski SD, Sadowski JA, Suter PM, Braun CL. Effect of antacid and H2 receptor antagonists on the intestinal absorption of folic acid. J Lab Clin Med. 1988;112:458-63.

1497. Suliburska J, Skrypnik K, Szulinska M, Kupsz J, Markuszewski L, Bogdanski P. Diuretics, Ca-antagonists, and angiotensin-converting enzyme inhibitors affect zinc status in hypertensive patients on monotherapy: a randomized trial. Nutrients. 2018;10.

1498. Samaras D, Samaras N, Lang PO, Genton L, Frangos E, Pichard C. Effects of widely used drugs on micronutrients: A story rarely told. Nutrition. 2013;29:605-10.

1499. Jain V, Wotring VE. Medically induced amenorrhea in female astronauts. NPJ Microgravity. 2016;2:16008.

1500. Shojania AM, Hornady GJ, Barnes PH. The effect of oral contraceptives on folate metabolism. Am J Obstet Gynecol. 1971;111:782-91.

1501. Shere M, Bapat P, Nickel C, Kapur B, Koren G. Association between use of oral contraceptives and folate status: A systematic review and meta-analysis. J Obstet Gynaecol Can. 2015;37:430-8.

1502. Salkeld RM, Knorr K, Korner WF. The effect of oral contraceptives on vitamin B_6 status. Clin Chim Acta. 1973;49:195-9.

1503. Brown RR, Rose DP, Leklem JE, Linkswiler HM. Effects of oral contraceptives on tryptophan metabolism and vitamin B_6 requirements in women. Acta Vitaminol Enzymol. 1975;29:151-7.

1504. Donald EA, Bosse TR. The vitamin B_6 requirement in oral contraceptive users. II. Assessment by tryptophan metabolites, vitamin B_6, and pyridoxic acid levels in urine. Am J Clin Nutr. 1979;32:1024-32.

1505. Leklem JE, Brown RR, Rose DP, Linkswiler HM. Vitamin B_6 requirements of women using oral contraceptives. Am J Clin Nutr. 1975;28:535-41.

14 Conducting Space Research

Although ground-based research offers the opportunity to study a greater number of subjects in a more-controlled environment, often using more-invasive protocols, nothing is quite as exciting and informative than the research conducted during actual spaceflight. These studies are constrained and challenged by many factors, including crew time, launch and return mass, sample storage, fluid handling in microgravity, and more. In this section, we describe some of these challenges, and how the ISS has allowed research to happen. We also provide an overview of some ground-based analogs that allow for research in a space-like environment.

Flight Research

Blood Collection

Blood collections have been occurring in space since the 1970s, and phlebotomy techniques are the same with or without gravity. The turning point for nutrition (and biochemistry) research on the ISS came in 2006, when the capability for collection, processing, and frozen storage of blood and urine samples was brought to orbit. Crewmembers are trained in procedures and the use of required equipment. Depending on the planned crew complement and schedules, many crewmembers are trained for auto-phlebotomy—i.e., drawing their own blood. In October 2006, early in the Expedition 14 mission, Michael Lopez-Alegria collected the first blood samples to be drawn on the ISS (Figure 77). After the samples are collected, they are allowed to clot, and are then centrifuged (Figure 78).

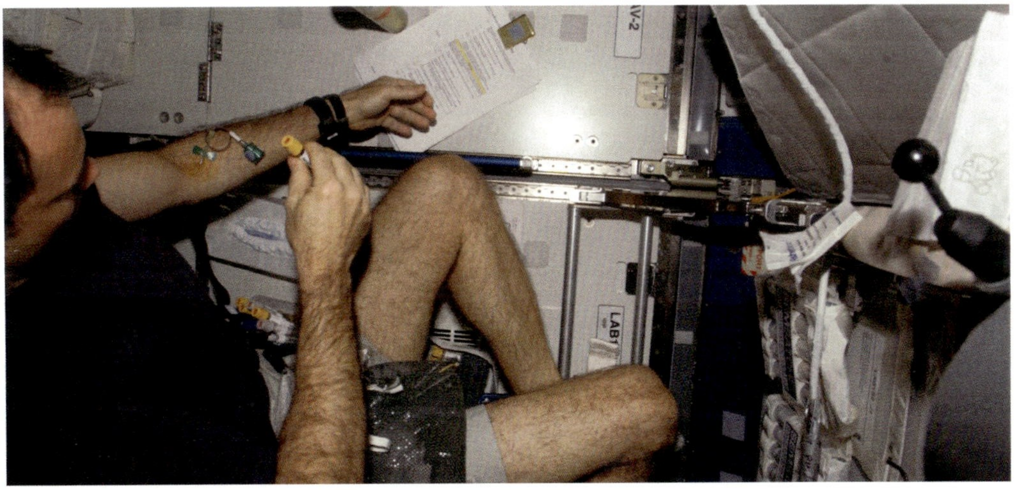

Figure 77. NASA astronaut Michael Lopez-Alegria collects the first blood sample on the ISS on October 5, 2006, having inserted the needle himself. The collection tubes can be seen (one in hand, the others in elastic bands on his belt assembly), along with a sharps container and detailed procedures (both Velcroed to the wall). Photo Credit: NASA.

Figure 78. ESA crewmember Samantha Cristoforetti centrifuging blood samples on the ISS. Photo Credit: NASA.

Urine Collection

The nominal toilet on the ISS (aka, the Waste Collection System) does not allow for the collection of samples to be returned to Earth. Thus, another technique is required for experimental purposes. Most often, urine is collected by using urine collection devices (UCDs) (Figure 79). A UCD is essentially a bag with a one-way valve on one end, allowing urine entry while voiding, and a port at the other end to withdraw syringe samples. Each void, typically over a 24-hour period, is collected in this manner. Two or three syringes are used per void to withdraw about 6 to 7 mL of urine. Before flight, a small amount of lithium chloride solution is added to the bags. After the void is complete, the UCD is kneaded to facilitate mixing of the lithium chloride with the void.

After the syringe(s) are collected, they are placed in the freezer (described below), and the UCD is placed in a ziplock bag to provide another layer of containment (Figure 80). The ziplock is then placed in a urine containment bag (UCB) (Figure 81). Typically, after the day's collections are

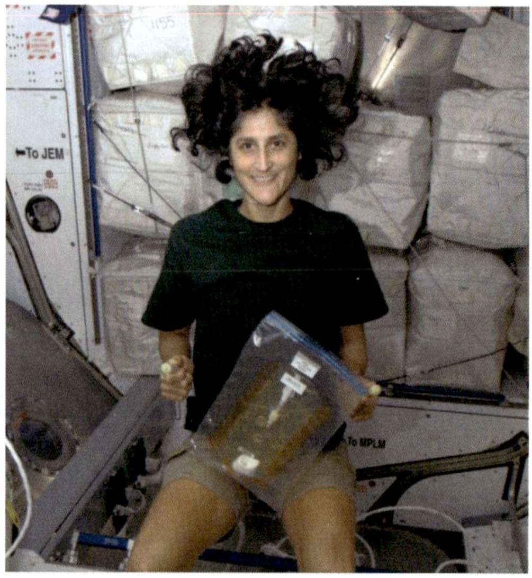

Figure 80. NASA astronaut Sunita Williams shown here with a UCD, placed in a ziplock bag to provide another layer of containment. Photo Credit: NASA.

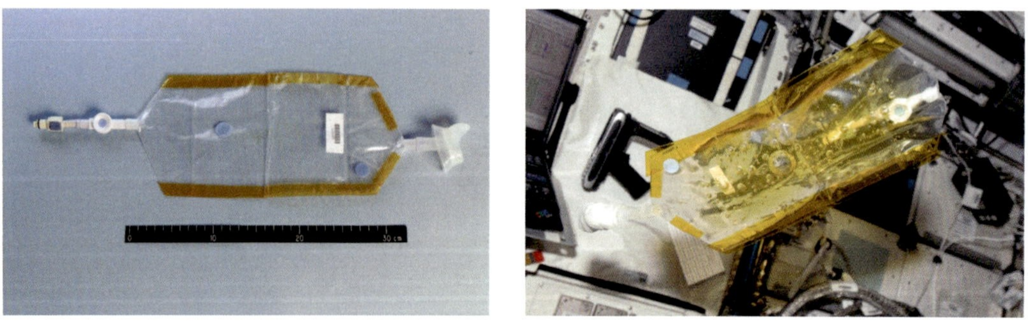

Figure 79. Left: UCD, shown here with a female adapter. Right: a UCD with a male adapter shown floating on the ISS. Photo Credits: NASA.

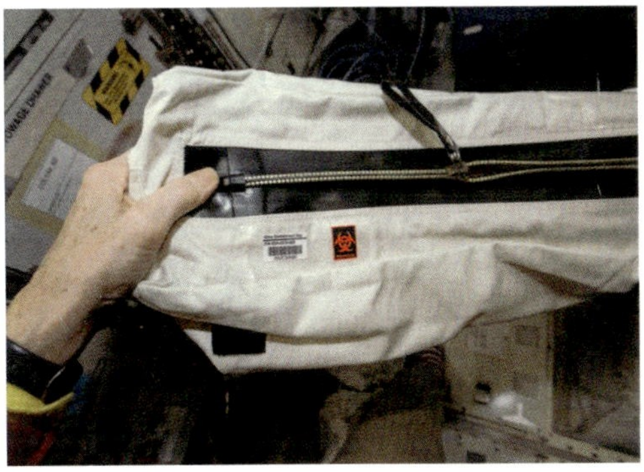

Figure 81. UCB, used for holding discarded UCDs until they can be disposed of along with other trash from the ISS. Photo Credit: NASA.

complete, the UCBs are stowed for eventual disposal with other ISS trash. Most trash is discarded in departing cargo vehicles that are not designed for reentry (i.e., they burn up coming back through the atmosphere). Before the Space Shuttle was retired in 2011, some trash was brought home on Space Shuttle vehicles.

After the samples are returned to Earth, the lithium concentration in the urine of each syringe is determined to allow back-calculation of the urine void volume so that 24-hour pools may be created from the individual voids.

Frozen Storage

The other key piece of hardware launched to the ISS in 2006 was the freezer, the minus eighty (degrees) laboratory freezer (MELFI) for the ISS (Figure 82). The three MELFIs located on the ISS allow increased stowage volume for intervals between returns to Earth. Each MELFI has four dewars (double-walled containers). On the outside of the MELFI, the dewars are covered. Each dewar has four trays, which are pulled out to store samples (Figure 83). The MELFIs are primarily designed for ultracold storage (temperatures below -80°C), and typically maintain temperatures close to -96°C. They are capable of refrigerated storage as well; typically, one of the four dewars will be at refrigerator temperature, while the others will be at -96°C.

Figure 82. NASA astronaut Mike Barratt puts samples in the MELFI, which is typically maintained at -96°C. Photo Credit: NASA.

Figure 83. NASA astronaut Nicole Stott stores samples from her first day of the Nutrition experiment in MELFI, located in the JAXA Experiment Module. Photo Credit: NASA.

Sample Return

Samples are returned to Earth whenever possible. The Space Shuttle was the only ride home for frozen blood and urine samples before its retirement in 2011. Since then, the SpaceX Dragon is the only space cargo vehicle that is able to return payloads from the ISS (Figure 85). Other cargo vehicles exist but are designed to bring supplies and equipment to the ISS—not to return them to Earth. Thus, these other vehicles will burn up in the atmosphere on return, by design. The SpaceX capsules splash down in the ocean, typically off the coast of California.

Frozen samples are transferred from the MELFI to either passive or active devices to maintain them in a frozen state until reaching ground personnel. "Double Cold Bags" (Figure 84) contain specially designed ice packs to maintain samples at a temperature lower than -30°C for up to 125 hours. A powered -96°C freezer is also flown on many flights to increase the volume of returning samples.

Figure 84. NASA astronauts Jeff Williams and Kate Rubins prepare to transfer samples from the MELFI to the Double Cold Bags for sample return to Earth. Photo Credit: NASA.

Figure 85. Picture from the Pacific Ocean showing the SpaceX Dragon capsule following its splashdown west of Baja California, Mexico, returning from a 5-day, 16-hour and 5-minute mission to the ISS. Photo Credit: NASA.

Dietary Intake Recording During Spaceflight

Methods of recording food intake have evolved over the course of human spaceflight. On Mercury, Gemini, and Apollo missions, meals were planned and provided for each crewmember. The crewmembers reported any foods they did not eat or completely consume (116, 117, 862).

Skylab missions in the mid-1970s included metabolic diets. Crews provided daily reports to the ground support team of any foods not eaten. Dietitians would then calculate any missing nutrient intake. The crew were directed to take protein and mineral supplements to maintain consistent intake of key nutrients: kcals, protein, calcium, nitrogen, and potassium (368, 369, 1506).

When required for specific research protocols, detailed dietary intake data has been obtained through written food intake logs or even with barcode scanning. Barcode scanning often seems an attractive alternative; however, it comes with its own set of issues when used during spaceflight.

Not all space foods have barcode labels. Or, for many commercially packaged items, the label is not in the database on the reader, thus the item information will not be displayed on the screen. Additionally, many of the space foods do not have flat surfaces on their packaging; wrinkles in the label can be difficult for the barcode reader to detect.

On Space Shuttle missions, crews were provided with foods from menus they had selected before the flight (with the assistance of a dietitian), and they ate ad libitum while on orbit. Only a handful of missions that included life sciences experiments required detailed monitoring of dietary intake. In most of those cases, monitoring was done either using a basic food log, or using barcode technology where the crew could scan the food package label to record intake. Because the Space Shuttle was a closed system, the remaining food inventory and even the trash were inspected to validate the intake data (101). This barcode technique was implemented on Mir missions for crews participating in experiments requiring data on dietary intake.

With the implementation of the nutritional assessment protocol on the ISS (initial testing was performed in ground-based studies and during flight with the last two U.S. astronauts on Mir), a food frequency questionnaire was developed and deployed on laptop computers (110, 111, 1507). The questionnaire provided a list of foods categorized by nutrient content. Crewmembers would report the number of items they consumed for each category in the past week. The data were analyzed, and six key nutrients—energy, fluid, calcium, protein, sodium, and iron—were reported weekly to flight surgeons. Later, potassium was also added to this list. The food frequency questionnaire was intended as a clinical tool to easily, and relatively quickly, estimate dietary intake as opposed to more-detailed, exact, and time-consuming diet records. Nonetheless, concerns were often raised about the astronauts' ability to recall dietary intake for this reporting. This was shown not to be a major concern, largely because the food choices were limited and repeated approximately every 8 days, the portion sizes were fixed, and the nutrient content of the foods was well defined.

Some astronauts on the ISS chose to keep detailed dietary records, typically with a simple spreadsheet. This approach was also adopted for episodic use in some experiments on the space station. When crews were asked whether this required much time, the response was that this took essentially no time. That, while eating, they could grab a laptop, type in what they were eating, and they were done. Subsequently, an iPad App was developed to record detailed dietary intake.

The ISS food intake tracker, or ISS FIT (Figure 86 and Figure 87), was developed using NASA's open innovation processes. TopCoder helped crowdsource the detailed development of the ISS FIT, from initial concept to final prototype. The development process included working with the Astronaut Office to ensure ease of use, and to develop an intuitive interface that can display real-time information to the user. Ground testing was conducted during chamber study missions (i.e., the Human Exploration Research Analog [HERA]) at the Johnson Space Center where subjects consumed space food. This testing yielded valuable updates to the software and user interface. Although we will not belabor the details here, most of the difficulty in deploying the iPad software application on the ISS involved interfacing the iPads with the server on the ISS to store and transfer the data to Earth. The initial application was uplinked in June 2016. Astronaut Kate Rubins deployed the application to iPads on the ISS on August 11, 2016.

Figure 86. ISS FIT, seen floating on the ISS. Photo Credit: NASA.

Figure 87. NASA astronaut Peggy Whitson uses the ISS FIT. Photo Credit: NASA.

In 2019, and again in 2020, updates to the software were deployed to the ISS, mostly to help the server interface and to fix a few bugs in the original application (e.g., the user could capture an image of a food item for data entry; however, the image files were corrupted somewhere between the application and the ground support team).

Through Expedition 63 in 2020, after more than 3500 days of use by 22 astronauts, we have detailed dietary data from more than 89% of those days.

The ISS FIT provides accurate data for the continuing weekly reports to flight surgeons, and provides invaluable data on dietary intake that can be evaluated in relation

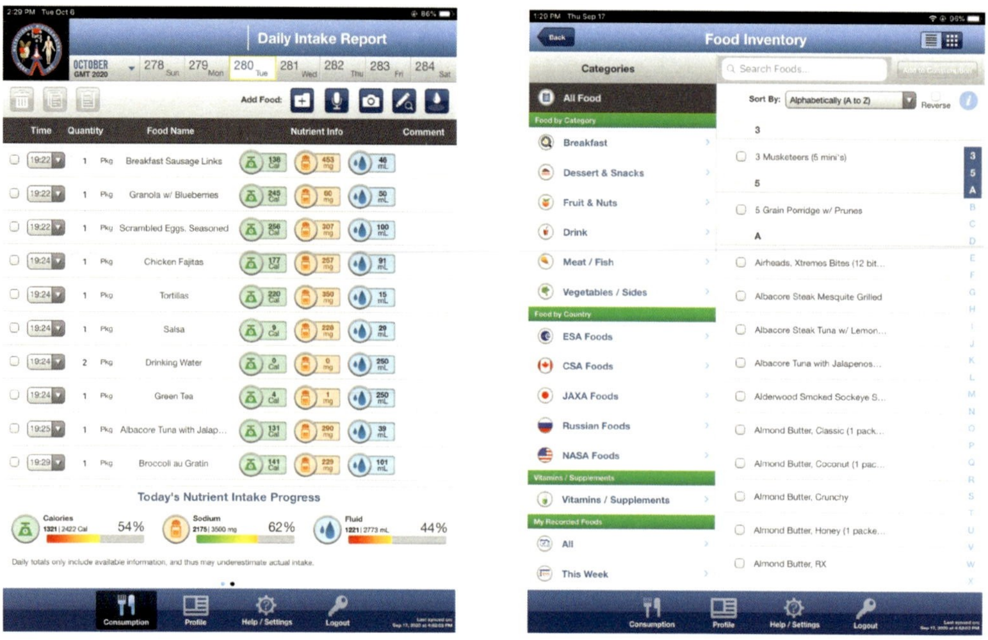

Figure 88. Screenshots from ISS FIT. Image Credits: NASA.

to other systems (e.g., musculoskeletal, cardiovascular health, immune). Throughout this book, we provide data on dietary intake that was collected from ISS FIT, along with the data from crewmembers who logged detailed intake using a spreadsheet.

Body Mass Measurement

Determining body mass is one of the most basic overall measures of health, as noted every time one visits a physician's office on Earth. Determination of "weight" in weightlessness, however, presents some unique challenges, as described (113, 153). There are two devices on the ISS: a Body Mass Measurement Device, which uses spring oscillation, and a Space Linear Acceleration Mass Measurement Device, which uses the physics of the equation: *force = mass x acceleration.* Figure 89 shows images of the two devices available on the ISS.

Ground-based Analogs

As described throughout this text, ground-based analogs of spaceflight are required to allow testing that either cannot feasibly be conducted during flight or needs to be conducted/validated before advancing to flight testing. Although bed rest and other models have been described in the text, we focus here on habitats that recreate elements of spacecraft or space missions.

Despite the central importance of food, the nutrition it provides, and the psychosocial roles it fills, there have been limited evaluations of the integrated interaction of food and nutrition with other human health risks in spaceflight. For example, although ground-based data indicate the importance of food and nutrition in cognitive performance (61), few reports may indicate the impact of food intake and nutritional status on cognitive performance over extended

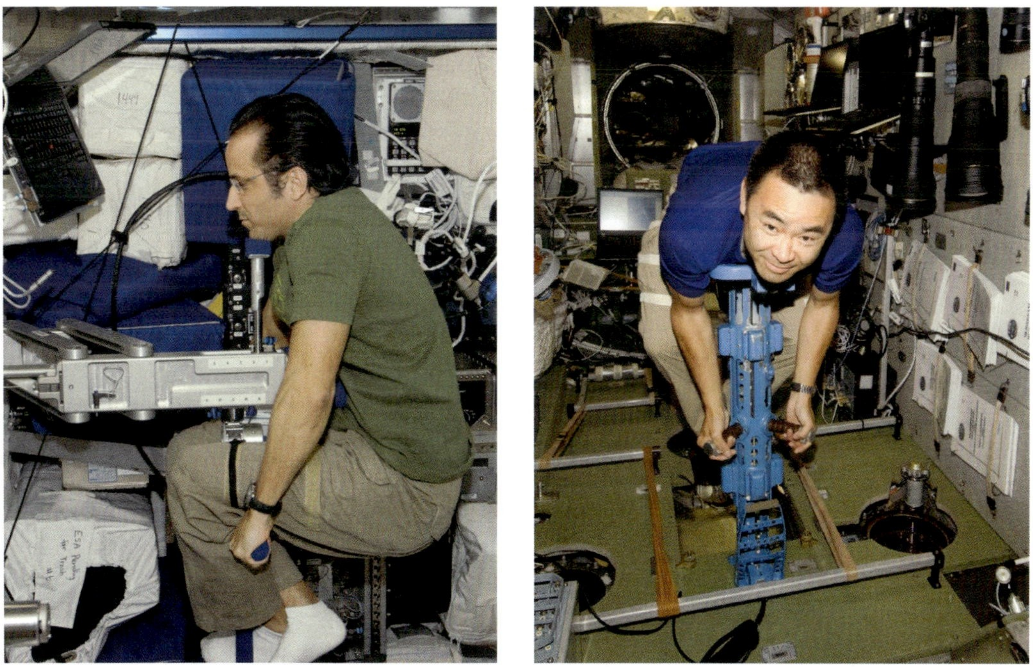

Figure 89. Left: NASA astronaut Joe Acaba works with the Space Linear Acceleration Mass Measurement Device in the Columbus laboratory of the ISS. Right: JAXA astronaut Aki Hoshide uses the Body Mass Measurement Device in the Zvezda Service Module of the ISS. Photo Credits: NASA.

isolation and confinement, with high-tempo mission-realistic workload and sleep deprivation. Crew time on the ISS to evaluate extensive integrated factors is limited, and, as described in Chapter 3, future exploration food systems may be much more restricted than the ISS food system. Although data obtained from the ISS contribute important health and performance data that include spaceflight-associated risk profiles (i.e., stress, microgravity, radiation), they do not accurately define the risks in relation to future exploration mission risk profiles (i.e., isolation and confinement for multiple years, extreme distance from Earth with no immediate return capability, greater radiation risk, no resupply, more-limited food system, and performance of regular high-energy tasks such as EVAs).

Ground-based spaceflight analog missions that include mission-realistic crew selection, procedures, protocols, and stressors provide an opportunity to begin establishing integrated health and performance outcomes in relation to realistic exploration food system design and nutritional intake. Although food studies in ground-based spaceflight analogs to date have been limited, the need for these studies is evident. For example, the food system was not evaluated in the Russian Mars 500 Program; however, the analog reports identified food as one of the greatest problems in isolation (82).

Changes in nutritional status were measured in several short-duration analogs, including the EXEMSI (80), thereby indicating the importance of understanding food intake within limited choice, closed food systems, and changes in nutritional requirements that may occur in extreme environments. Reduced caloric intake and behavioral impacts were associated with meal replacement in 30 days in the HERA (Figure 90), despite acceptable pre-mission sensory

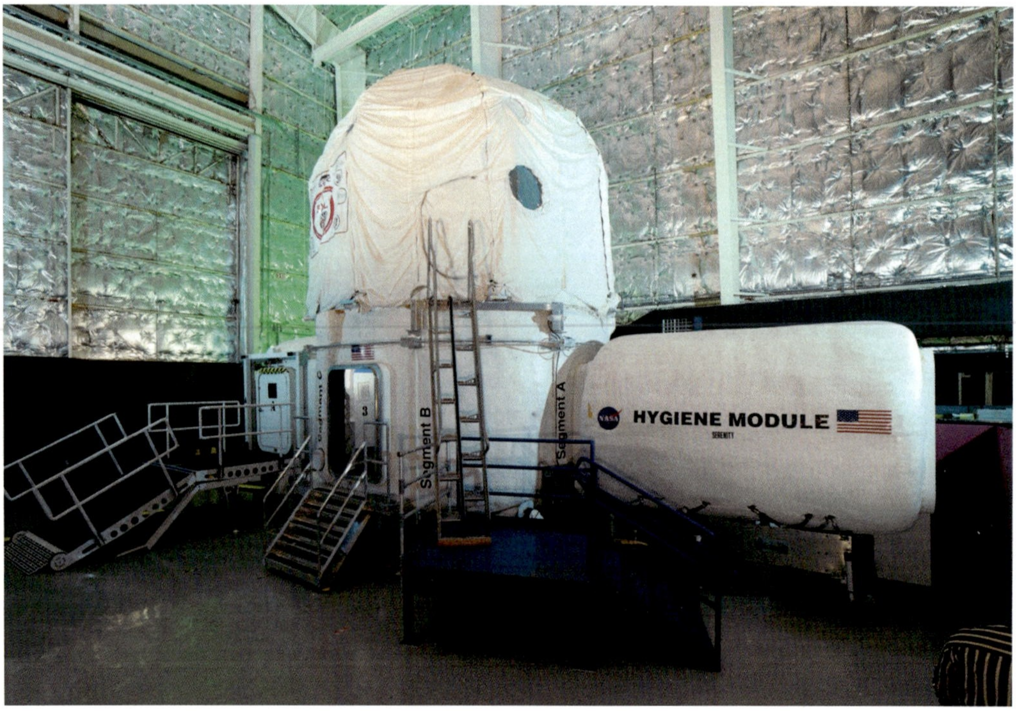

Figure 90. HERA at the Johnson Space Center. Photo Credit: NASA.

evaluations, further supporting the importance of understanding food system design impacts in closed systems (74).

Changes in nutritional status were measured in NEEMO V (753), an undersea habitat that provides a normoxic yet hyperbaric environment (1508). This has been used to simulate the effects of spaceflight on iron and folate metabolism, along with effects on oxidative stress (753, 758, 1433) and immune system function (1509).

Many analogs do not have spaceflight-realistic food systems (e.g., many have included full kitchens, cold storage, fresh foods, and cooking capabilities), thus limiting their use to single-nutrient studies. However, the data that have been obtained indicate their potential as a resource to fill data gaps. For example, the results of the evaluation of vitamin D status and supplementation and its impact on viral reactivation at McMurdo Station in Antarctica contributed to establishing adequate supplementation for spaceflight crews (603, 604). The Antarctic provides a valuable analog for many elements of spaceflight, most notably isolation and stress. However, during the Antarctic winter (March – October), when there is no sunlight, the lack of ultraviolet light exposure means the only source of vitamin D is through diet or supplement.

Some analogs evaluated the inclusion of bioregenerative foods. A crew of eight lived in Biosphere 2, a closed-system environment with finite natural resources and no resupply for 2 years. Subjects depended on food entirely produced within the mission. Average body mass losses of 17% were attributed to food production challenges, effectively demonstrating the risk of food scarcity with a production-dependent system, and the significant amount of crew time that had to be devoted to food production tasks (1510). Additionally, the food system in this study was deficient in vitamins B_{12} and D, as defined by government RDA standards, and therefore the crew had to be supplemented (1511, 1512). These deficiencies were largely due to the limited animal foods in the diet. Vitamin D status was not measured; however, methylmalonic acid was measured to assess vitamin B_{12} status, and one crewmember became vitamin B_{12} deficient (1513). One other issue that arose during Biosphere 2 was from high concentrations of atmospheric nitrous oxide in the habitat (1513). Nitrous oxide can irreversibly inactivate methionine synthase, a vitamin B_{12}-dependent enzyme, and essentially a vitamin B_{12} deficiency can develop (1514).

The 1990's Lunar Mars Life Support Test Project (LMLSTP) in a 20-foot chamber at the Johnson Space Center supported testing of space foods, crop growth, waste recycling, and more (110, 1515). LMLSTP crew also evaluated a fresh food menu and found crew time requirements to be excessive with the available technologies (1515). These types of missions identified important knowledge and technology gaps to advancing bioregenerative systems for exploration.

Analog opportunities with mission-realistic food system scenarios are needed that can evaluate the interaction between food system design, nutritional intake, and health and performance outcomes. This information will be critical to establish accurate risk profiles, and to inform risk/resources trades for different mission scenarios. However, these risk profiles and resource trades ultimately need to be validated with the full stress, altered gravity, and radiation impacts of spaceflight to ensure successful food and nutrition support for exploration missions.

References for Chapter 14

61. Lieberman HR. Nutrition, brain function and cognitive performance. Appetite. 2003;40:245-54.

74. Sirmons TA, Roma PG, Whitmire AM, Smith SM, Zwart SR, Young M, Douglas GL. Meal replacement in isolated and confined mission environments: Consumption, acceptability, and implications for physical and behavioral health. Physiol Behav. 2020;219:112829.

80. Milon H, Decarli B, Adine AM, Kihm E. Food intake and nutritional status during EXEMSI. Experimental Campaign for the European Manned Space Infrastructure. Adv Space Biol Med. 1996;5:79-91.

82. Poláčková Šolcová I, Šolcová I, Stuchlíková I, Mazehóová Y. The story of 520 days on a simulated flight to Mars. Acta Astronaut. 2016;126:178-89.

101. Lane HW, Gretebeck RJ, Schoeller DA, Davis-Street J, Socki RA, Gibson EK. Comparison of ground-based and space flight energy expenditure and water turnover in middle-aged healthy male US astronauts. Am J Clin Nutr. 1997;65:4-12.

110. Smith SM, Davis-Street JE, Rice BL, Nillen JL, Gillman PL, Block G. Nutritional status assessment in semiclosed environments: ground-based and space flight studies in humans. J Nutr. 2001;131:2053-61.

111. Smith SM, Zwart SR, Block G, Rice BL, Davis-Street JE. The nutritional status of astronauts is altered after long-term space flight aboard the International Space Station. J Nutr. 2005;135:437-43.

113. Heer M, Boerger A, Kamps N, Mika C, Korr C, Drummer C. Nutrient supply during recent European missions. Pflugers Arch. 2000;441:R8-14.

116. Rambaut PC, Smith MC, Jr, Wheeler HO. Nutritional studies. In: Johnston RS, Dietlein LF, Berry CA, editors. Biomedical results of Apollo (NASA SP-368). Washington, DC: National Aeronautics and Space Administration; 1975. p. 277-302.

117. Rambaut PC, Leach CS, Johnson PC. Calcium and phosphorus change of the Apollo 17 crew members. Nutr Metab. 1975;18:62-9.

153. Zwart SR, Launius RD, Coen GK, Morgan JLL, Charles JB, Smith SM. Body mass changes during long-duration spaceflight. Aviat Space Environ Med. 2014;85:897-904.

368. Whedon GD, Lutwak L, Reid J, Rambaut PC, Whittle MW, Smith MC, Leach CS. Mineral and nitrogen metabolic studies on Skylab orbital space flights. Trans Assoc Am Physicians. 1974;87:95-110.

369. Whedon GD, Lutwak L, Rambaut PC, Whittle MW, Reid J, Smith MC, Leach C, Stadler CR, Sanford DD. Mineral and nitrogen balance study observations: the second manned Skylab mission. Aviat Space Environ Med. 1976;47:391-6.

603. Smith SM, Gardner KK, Locke J, Zwart SR. Vitamin D supplementation during Antarctic winter. Am J Clin Nutr. 2009;89:1092-8.

604. Zwart SR, Mehta SK, Ploutz-Snyder R, Bourbeau Y, Locke JP, Pierson DL, Smith SM. Response to vitamin D supplementation during Antarctic winter is related to BMI, and supplementation can mitigate Epstein-Barr Virus Reactivation. J Nutr. 2011;141:692-7.

753. Smith SM, Davis-Street JE, Fesperman JV, Smith MD, Rice BL, Zwart SR. Nutritional assessment during a 14-d saturation dive: the NASA Extreme Environment Mission Operations V Project. J Nutr. 2004;134:1765-71.

758. Zwart SR, Jessup JM, Ji J, Smith SM. Saturation diving alters folate status and biomarkers of DNA damage and repair. PLoS One. 2012;7:e31058.

862. Leach CS, Rambaut PC, Johnson PC. Adrenocortical responses of the Apollo 17 crew members. Aerosp Med. 1974;45:529-34.

1433. Zwart SR, Kala G, Smith SM. Body iron stores and oxidative damage in humans increased during and after a 10- to 12-day undersea dive. J Nutr. 2009;139:90-5.

1506. Whedon GD, Lutwak L, Reid J, Rambaut P, Whittle M, Smith M, Leach C. Mineral and nitrogen balance study: results of metabolic observations on Skylab II 28-day orbital mission. Acta Astronaut. 1975;2:297-309.

1507. Soller BR, Cabrera M, Smith SM, Sutton JP. Smart medical systems with application to nutrition and fitness in space. Nutrition. 2002;18:930-6.

1508. Anglin KM, Kring JP. Lessons from a space analog on adaptation for long-duration exploration missions. Aerosp Med Hum Perform. 2016;87:406-10.

1509. Strewe C, Crucian BE, Sams CF, Feuerecker B, Stowe RP, Choukér A, Feuerecker M. Hyperbaric hyperoxia alters innate immune functional properties during NASA Extreme Environment Mission Operation (NEEMO). Brain Behav Immun. 2015;50:52-7.

1510. Walford RL, Mock D, Verdery R, MacCallum T. Calorie restriction in biosphere 2: alterations in physiologic, hematologic, hormonal, and biochemical parameters in humans restricted for a 2-year period. J Gerontol A Biol Sci Med Sci. 2002;57:B211-24.

1511. Silverstone SE. Food production and nutrition for the crew during the first 2-year closure of Biosphere 2. Life Support Biosph Sci. 1997;4:167-78.

1512. Silverstone SE, Nelson M. Food production and nutrition in Biosphere 2: results from the first mission September 1991 to September 1993. Adv Space Res. 1996;18:49-61.

1513. Marino BD, Mahato TR, Druitt JW, Leigh L, Lin G, Russell RM, Tubiello FN. The agricultural biome of Biosphere 2: Structure, composition and function. Ecol Eng. 1999;13:199-234.

1514. Koblin DD, Watson JE, Deady JE, Stokstad EL, Eger EI, 2nd. Inactivation of methionine synthetase by nitrous oxide in mice. Anesthesiology. 1981;54:318-24.

1515. Kloeris V, Vodovotz Y, Bye L, Stiller CQ, Lane E. Design and implementation of a vegetarian food system for a closed chamber test. Life Support Biosph Sci. 1998;5:231-42.

Artist's rendering of the proposed Gateway lunar orbital outpost. Built with commercial and international partners, the Gateway is critical to sustainable lunar exploration and will serve as a model for future missions to Mars. Image Credit: NASA.

15 Summary

As we write this section of the book in the fall of 2020, the Space Shuttle has been retired for almost a decade, the ISS is celebrating 20 years of continuous crewed operations, and commercial vehicles just started bringing crews to the ISS from American soil. The second 1-year stay on the ISS was recently completed.

Much effort and planning are underway for missions to return humans to the Moon. As vehicles are designed for these missions, the challenges for the food system will be similar to those met by all previous space food systems: mass and volume of the food system and its associated packaging will need to be limited; refrigerators and freezers will not be available. Additional challenges are being raised to water and calorie requirements, and consideration is even being given to increasing the fat content of the diet to reduce mass and volume; questions remain as to whether hot and cold water will be available to the crews on early lunar missions. As we look beyond the Moon to future Mars missions, acceptability of the food items will become even more important on these multi-year missions. New challenges will include a need for even longer shelf life stability (i.e., 5 years) potentially with reduced resource allocation and infrastructure compared to the ISS.

Long-term plans for exploration will include the establishment of settlements, which will need to be more Earth-independent and self-sustainable. This may require the growing of plants to aid in the recycling of air and water within the habitat (825). These crops could then also be available for use in the food system. The food system may further evolve as crew time becomes less of a resource constraint (with increased robotic capability, or transition from exploration to settlements). The presence of partial gravity will allow crops to be processed into ingredients (e.g., milling wheat into flour) and then used to prepare menu items for crew consumption (1516). The research to support these endeavors, especially the growing of crops (or possibly even other novel systems not discussed here) that will sustain a crew and not just supplement the meals made on Earth, still has some distance to go (96). These long-term missions will require careful planning of nutrition. Understanding nutrient requirements and utilizing the food system to fulfill them will allow mitigation of some of the negative effects of microgravity on human physiology. Even a marginal nutrient deficiency over a long enough period could be devastating. After the requirements are defined and we have a detailed understanding of absorption, metabolism, and excretion of each nutrient, provision of these nutrients and an understanding of their stability in the space environment (for the months to years before they are consumed) will be critical.

Nutrition is essential for health—on Earth and in space. Determining the nutritional requirements for travelers on short-, medium-, and long-duration exploration missions will be crucial for ensuring crewmembers' health and safety, during the mission and after their return. At this point, most of the requirements match terrestrial nutrient recommendations. This will help stave off nutrient deficiency but will not mitigate disease risk. Food and nutrition offer a multisystem countermeasure that requires no additional crew time than that already allotted for meals. We need research to define and develop an optimized food system to mitigate disease risks during spaceflight.

Some of this is underway. Care needs to be taken to avoid excess amounts of any nutrient; however, the risks of using food and nutritional countermeasures relative to those of using pharmacological countermeasures are negligible in comparison.

This document summarizes evidence demonstrating why inadequate food and nutrition is a risk during long-term space travel, and the implications of this risk. Just as for the sailors who left Europe in ships, it is not enough to have food; one must have the right food.

References for Chapter 15

96. Anderson MS, Barta D, Douglas G, Fritsche R, Massa GD, Wheeler R, Quincy C, Romeyn M, Motil B, Hanford A, editors. Key gaps for enabling plant growth in future missions. AIAA Space and Astronautics Forum and Exposition; 2017; Orlando, FL: AIAA.

1516. Lane HW, Kloeris V, Perchonok M, Zwart S, Smith SM. Food and nutrition for the moon base: what have we learned in 45 years of spaceflight. Nutr Today. 2007;42:102-10.

16 Appendices

Authors

Scott M. Smith is Nutritionist and Manager for Nutritional Biochemistry at the NASA Johnson Space Center in Houston, Texas. This group is charged with keeping crews healthy with respect to nutrition, including using nutrition as a means to optimize astronaut health and safety. To this end, they conduct ground-based and flight research to understand how nutrition can mitigate the negative effects of spaceflight on the human. He has conducted research on the Space Shuttle, the Russian space station Mir, and ongoing research on the International Space Station. He has led several ground-based research projects, including studies vitamin D in of crews wintering over in Antarctica, studies of crews living on the bottom of the ocean, and test subjects spending weeks-to-months in bed. Smith participated in the definition of the current nutritional requirements for extended-duration spaceflight. He is the Co-Chair of the Multilateral Medical Operations Panel - Nutrition Working Group.

Sara R. Zwart is a Senior Scientist and Deputy Manager of the Nutritional Biochemistry Laboratory at the NASA Johnson Space Center in Houston, Texas. She has been involved with research investigating relationships between nutrition and side effects of spaceflight, including bone loss, changes in iron metabolism, and oxidative damage. She has also worked with ground-based analogs of spaceflight, including cell culture models, NASA Extreme Environment Mission Operations (NEEMO) projects, extra-vehicular activity analogs at the Neutral Buoyancy Laboratory at the Johnson Space Center, and bed rest models.

Grace L. Douglas is the Lead Scientist for NASA's Advanced Food Technology research effort and the Manager of the Space Food Systems Laboratory at the NASA Johnson Space Center in Houston, Texas. Her research focuses on determining methods, technologies, and requirements for developing a safe, nutritious, and palatable food system that will promote astronaut health during long-duration space missions. She works with both ground-based analogs and spaceflight experiments to determine risk-resource trades that may factor into vehicle designs and mission concepts.

Martina Heer is Senior Nutritionist, Professor and Program Director of Nutritional Sciences at the IU International University of Applied Sciences, Erfurt, Germany, and Adjunct Professor at the University of Bonn, Institute of Food and Nutrition Sciences, Bonn, Germany. She also represents the European Space Agency (ESA) in the Multilateral Medical Operations Panel's Nutrition Working Group for the International Space Station (ISS) and is a member of the ESA Nutrition Expert Committee. Previously, she headed the Space Physiology Division, Institute of Aerospace Medicine, at the German Aerospace Center (DLR) for 6 years. Her main research interest is to understand the interaction of nutrition and nutrients with metabolism and other physiological systems such as the musculoskeletal and cardiovascular systems. Her spaceflight studies started with Space Shuttle missions and missions to the Russian space station Mir, and they continue with experiments on the ISS. The space studies are combined with extensive research in the form of space analog studies on the ground.

Acknowledgments

This book represents a review of many areas of research as seen from the perspective of a few space nutritionists and a food scientist; however, many people have contributed to this research and we would like to recognize as many as we can.

At the heart of all space life sciences research are the astronauts who bravely soar into space. Beyond their required duty of flying and maintaining the spacecraft that is their home and workplace and refuge from the space environment and all that that entails, they also volunteer to be operator and/or subject (aka guinea pig) for science experiments. Without their efforts and dedication to this process, none of the research on space physiology and medicine would be possible, and we are greatly in their debt.

Our Laboratory Teams have played a central role in much of the work reviewed herein. Although few original data are reported, the primary publications represent the efforts of many individuals. We recognize the NASA Nutritional Biochemistry Laboratory (NBL) team, a continually evolving group of dedicated individuals who work tirelessly to ensure that all samples, from flight- or ground-based studies, are collected, processed, and analyzed according to detailed plans and procedures. Sample and data management represent a somewhat tedious, but absolutely critical, element of this research, and the NBL team members handle this with unparalleled grace and tenacity.

We also recognize the NASA Space Food Systems Laboratory team for their efforts to produce and provision safe, acceptable, and nutritious foods that meet the challenging requirements of spaceflight, as well as theirs, and others, continued research and development efforts to improve upon this system in accordance with research findings.

Spaceflight research is literally unlike anything on Earth. The teams of review and support staff, from the engineers who develop flight hardware to trainers who work with the crews to accomplish on-orbit data and sample collection, to experiment support personnel who watch over every aspect of a study, all ensure that nothing escapes completion. Again, these teams represent evolving and ever-changing groups of names, but without their dedication, these studies would simply not be possible. Similarly, NASA management personnel across organizations and over the years have supported efforts to allow these research projects to happen. The NASA Human Research Program (HRP), established in 2006, set the stage for conduct of most of the studies from which we obtained the International Space Station data reported herein. The HRP includes the Human Health and Countermeasures Element, where the Nutrition Risk part of the human spaceflight research plan resides. Although many considered nutrition an afterthought on the list of potential countermeasures—or worse, thought nutrition to be simply what the food system provided—others continue to help fight the good fight.

We are indebted to many of the scientists at NASA who took time to review sections of the text. Specifically, Dr. Brian Crucian for Immune, Dr. Meghan Downs for the Energy and Muscle, Dr. Steve Laurie and Dr. Brandon Macias for Ocular Health, Dr. Stuart Lee for Cardiovascular, Sara Mason for Renal Stone, and Dr. Jean Sibonga for Bone. Their input was extremely helpful and valuable, and the authors take blame for any mistakes or oversights remaining.

If any of this is readable, you can thank the two outstanding technical editors—Kerry George and Susan Breeden. Kerry worked with us as we were writing, which one imagines is a bit like painting a car while it speeds down the highway. She did her best, but all flaws remain the fault of the authors.

We are grateful to Cynthia Bush, Senior Graphic Design Specialist/Illustrator at the Johnson Space Center in Houston. The products of her efforts to create the cover and several of the specialized figures herein are outstanding. She was subsequently also responsible for the content layout work. If what you hold in your hands (or see on a screen) looks good, it is thanks to Cindy.

As evidenced by the affiliations of Dr. Martina Heer, the collaboration between U.S. and German investigators over the past 20-plus years has promoted growth and expansion of knowledge, as any good collaboration does. European Space Agency (ESA) and German Aerospace Center (DLR) support of nutrition research has contributed greatly to this field of science as reviewed herein. Similar to those described above for NASA, a management structure and dedicated laboratory support team have enabled outstanding research.

We are indebted to many for the opportunities we have had to conduct research, to publish research, and to review research herein. We hope you find this volume useful for your own knowledge base.

SMS, SRZ, GLD, MH.

List of Figures

Abbreviations

8OHdG	8-hydroxy-2'-deoxyguanosine
ACE	Angiotensin-Converting Enzyme
ADP	adenosine diphosphate
AMP	adenosine monophosphate
ARED	Advanced Resistance Exercise Device
ATP	adenosine triphosphate
BH_2	dihydrobiopterin
BH_4	tetrahydrobiopterin
BMD	bone mineral density
BR	bed rest (day)
BSAP	bone-specific alkaline phosphatase
Ca	calcium
cal	calorie
CEVIS	Cycle Ergometer with Vibration Isolation System
CNS	central nervous system
CoA	coenzyme A
CO_2	carbon dioxide
COLBERT	Combined Operational Load Bearing External Resistance Treadmill
CSA	Canadian Space Agency
CSF	cerebrospinal fluid
CSM	Crew Specific Menu
d	day
DLR	German Aerospace Center
DNA	deoxyribonucleic acid
DRI	dietary reference intake
DXA	dual-energy x-ray absorptiometry
EBV	Epstein-Barr virus
EE	energy expenditure
eNOS	endothelial nitric oxide synthase
Eq	equivalent
ESA	European Space Agency
EVA	extravehicular activity (space walk)
FAD	flavin adenine dinucleotide
FADH2	flavin adenine dinucleotide (reduced)
FD	flight day
5-MTHF	5-methyltetrahydrofolate
g	gram
g	acceleration due to gravity (1g = Earth gravity)
GI	gastrointestinal
GLA	gamma-carboxyglutamic acid
Gy	Gray
Gz	gravitational force applied to the vertical axis of the body (i.e., from head to foot)
HERA	Human Exploration Research Analog
h, hr	hour

HRP	Human Research Program
Hz	hertz
HZE	High atomic number (Z) and energy radiation
IOM	Institute of Medicine (since renamed the National Academy of Medicine)
iRED	interim resistance exercise device
ISS	International Space Station
IU	international unit
J	joule
JAXA	Japan Aerospace Exploration Agency
JSC	Johnson Space Center
k	kilo
kcal	kilocalorie
KCit	potassium citrate
kg	kilogram
KHCO3	potassium bicarbonate
KMgCit	potassium magnesium citrate
L-x	x days before launch
L	liter
LBNP	lower-body negative pressure
LET	linear energy transfer
LMLSTP	Lunar Mars Life Support Test Project
µ	micro
m	meter, milli
M	molar
MDA	malondialdehyde
MELFI	minus eighty (-80°C) laboratory freezer for ISS
mg	milligram
ml	milliliter
mmol	millimole
MMP	matrix metalloproteinase
Mol	mole
mOsm	milliosmole
MRI	magnetic resonance imaging
MTRR	methionine synthase reductase
n	nano
n	number of subjects in a subsample
N	number of subjects in a sample of a population
NAD	nicotinamide adenine dinucleotide
NADH	reduced form of nicotinamide adenine dinucleotide
NADH2	nicotinamide-adenine dinucleotide
NADP	nicotinamide adenine dinucleotide phosphate
NADPH	reduced form of nicotinamide adenine dinucleotide phosphate
NASA	National Aeronautics and Space Administration
NBL	Nutritional Biochemistry Laboratory
NEAP	net endogenous acid production
NEEMO	NASA Extreme Environment Mission Operations

NF-κB	NF-kappa B
NK	natural killer
nmol	nanomole
NTX	n-telopeptide
O2	oxygen
P	probability, phosphate
PGF2α	8-iso-prostaglandin F2α
PL	pyridoxal
PLP	pyridoxal 5'-phosphate
PM	pyridoxamine
PMP	pyridoxamine 5'-phosphate
PN	pyridoxine
PNP	pyridoxine 5'-phosphate
Post	after flight or bed rest
PPAR	peroxisome proliferation activating receptor
Pre	before flight or bed rest
psi	pound(s) per square inch
psia	pound(s) per square inch absolute
PTH	parathyroid hormon
r	bivariate correlation coefficient
QCT	quantitative computerized tomography
R+x	x days after landing (recovery) or end of bed rest
RBC	red blood cell
RDA	recommended dietary allowance
RNA	ribonucleic acid
RNS	reactive nitrogen species
ROS	reactive oxygen species
SANS	Spaceflight Associated Neuro-ocular Syndrome
SD	standard deviation
SMO	Supplemental Medical Objective
STS	Space Transportation System
TEE	total energy expenditure
THF	tetrahydrofolate
U	unit
UCB	urine containment bag
UCD	urine collection device
ULLS	unilateral limb suspension
UPA	Urine Processor Assembly
U.S.	United States
USOS	United States Operating Segment (of ISS)
UTMB	University of Texas Medical Branch
VDR	vitamin D receptor
WHO	World Health Organization
WISE	Women International Space Simulation for Exploration
y	year

Index

Note: All terms are listed only at spelled-out version.
See Appendix for list of acronyms and abbreviations.

D

E

F

I

J

K

L

M

P

S

T

U

V

W

Z